The Collector's Guide to
OLD U.S. STOCKS AND BONDS

The Collector's Guide
to

OLD U.S. STOCKS AND BONDS

To

Andrew C. Hall, Sr.

Dick & Nancy
Good Luck
Uncle Andy
6-20-84

VANTAGE PRESS
New York / Washington / Atlanta
Los Angeles / Chicago

FIRST EDITION

Published by Vantage Press, Inc.
516 West 34th Street, New York, New York 10001

Manufactured in the United States of America
ISBN: 533-05793-0
Library of Congress Catalog Card No.: 83-90299

TABLE OF CONTENTS

PREFACE

Ever since the beginning of the Industrial Revolution, there have been persons banding together to form companies or corporations for industries, railroads, mines, etc.

To participate in the ownership of the organization, certificates were issued by the corporation at its formation and during the ensuing years. The certificates, be they shares, bonds, warrants, or temporary certificates, represent ownership.

To thwart counterfeiting, artists were employed to design very intricate borders and very pleasing pictures, generally placed at the top of the certificates. Many stock certificates and bonds have pictures of very old scenes, called "vignettes." These include pictures of wood-burning trains, old steamboats, horse-drawn streetcars, and rustic ramblings. Often, more than one vignette is shown.

The collecting of bonds and stock certificates is a fascinating hobby that started in Europe and has become very popular here in the United States. The author is a collector and is not involved in the business of selling. The prices shown reflect top quality as to condition (no stains, creases, tears, or smudges). This book should be used only as a guide. Supply, demand, the economy, plus the ever-growing number of collectors, will tend to cause fluctuation of the prices, shown in the following pages, along with these different factors:

(A) Condition of the item: if it is stained, wrinkled, etc.
(B) Attached transfer stamps are generally desirable.
(C) An issued certificate is generally more valuable and desirable than one that is unissued, of the same corporation.
(D) A certificate that has been issued and not cancelled is generally more valuable.
(E) There are some items that have never been issued.
(F) Asking prices in different geographic areas.
(G) A president's signature missing due to a "cut cancel."
(H) A "cut cancel" affecting the appearance of a quality vignette.

(I) The age of the date plus the scarceness of the item affect the price greatly, just like with other collectibles.
(J) Railroad items with beautiful old train vignettes will be more valuable than those without.
(K) A bond that still has coupons attached is more desirable.
(L) A famous person's signature on any item will enhance the value of that particular item. A word of advice: check all of the signatures. Some collectors are now searching for less well-known signatures.
(M) During the twenty months it took to edit and publish this book, prices stated were subject to fluctuation. The reader should take this time element into consideration when trying to establish value.

Now that you know all these factors about varying values, you might understand the pricing a little better. If you are just starting, you would do well to attend antique and paper collecting shows. There are many throughout the States.

The beginner does not have to invest large amounts of money, as there are many interesting low-cost certificates; but, bear in mind, if you go for railroad items, that's different. However, other beautiful vignettes are also desirable.

The reader-collector should be made aware that there are hundreds of thousands of corporations. It would be virtually impossible for all certificates to be listed. If you find one not listed, first look at the date, then see if it has been issued. Next, check to see if it has been cancelled. Now look at its condition along with the beauty of the vignette. Finally, look through the book for a similar industry, date, and vignette. Then, judge for yourself. You are not expected to be an expert, as collecting is not an exact science.

Now, to the many collectors and beginners who have looked for a book like this, just as I have done in countless bookstores, the following pages are dedicated to you.

LEGEND:

(U) - Unissued
(I) - Issued
(I-N) - Issued, not cancelled

ACKNOWLEDGMENTS

Writing this book about bonds and stock certificates would have been impossible had it not been for numerous persons and companies.

Other collectors like myself and various suppliers that have contributed to the contents of this book, either in material, and/or information are:

Irwin Brotman	Ray Anthony
David Beach	Don Offill
Hugh Holbert	Natalie D. Hall Sturm
Ken Praag	Button Wood Galleries
Jerry Rillahan	R. M. Smythe
Clinton Hollis	La Barre Galleries
Jack Curry	American Vignettes
C. & W. Anderson's	W & H Collectibles
John Sanderson	Stanley Gibbons
Fred Robinson	Keys
Joe Spira	Bank Note Reporter
Fred Herrigel	Todd Johnson
Bill Brandt	Robert Greenwalt
Walt Alcott	Greg Berglund

I am sure there are many others whom I have met at various shows, stores, and meetings who have had an influence on my collecting information and material.

Add to this list my wife, Roberta, who helped by cataloging and typing this whole manuscript.

The Collector's Guide to
OLD U.S. STOCKS AND BONDS

CAPITAL $2,500,000.

ADVENTURE CONSOLIDATED COPPER COMPANY

Number C 205

Shares 10

INCORPORATED UNDER THE LAWS OF THE STATE OF MICHIGAN.

This Certifies that Stackpole & Gay are the Proprietors of Ten Shares of the Capital Stock of the Adventure Consolidated Copper Company transferable only on the books of said Company by the holder hereof in person or by Attorney, on surrender of this Certificate.

JAN 3 1899 189

CANCELLED. AMERICAN LOAN & TRUST JAN 17 1899

OLD COLONY TRUST COMPANY JAN 16 1899

Secretary President

THIS CERTIFICATE IS NOT VALID UNTIL COUNTERSIGNED BY TRANSFER AGENT AND REGISTRAR.

ONE HUNDRED THOUSAND SHARES

TWENTY-FIVE DOLLARS EACH

INCORPORATED UNDER THE LAWS OF MONTANA

No. 69

SHARES

ALHAMBRA FLUME AND MERCANTILE COMPANY

Shares $1.00 Each. Capital Stock $100,000

CAPITAL STOCK $100,000

100,000 SHARES, $1.00 EACH

This is to Certify, That

is the owner of Shares

of the Capital Stock of the Alhambra Flume & Mercantile Company,

transferable on the books of the Company in person or by

Attorney upon the surrender of this Certificate.

Helena, M. T., this day of 188

Secy. Pres.

FULL-PAID AND NON-ASSESSABLE

JOURNAL PUBL. CO. PRINT, HELENA, MONT.

MINES

Abide Extension Mining (I), 1940s, Nevada, Eagle vignette 2.50
Abington Mining (I), 1880s, Maine, Working miners 48.00
Acacia Gold Mining (I), 1900s, Arizona 17.00
Acacia Gold Mining (I), 1900s, Colorado, Mines vignette 15.00
Acme Mining (I-N), 1930s, California, Company logo 6.00
Acme Mines & Mill (I-N), 1930s, Nevada 6.00
Acme Uranium Mines (I), 1950s, Allegorical figures 3.00
Acme Uranium Mines (I-N), 1950s, Two men and one woman vignette, with stamp 5.00
Adventure Consolidated Copper Company (I), 1890s, Michigan, Two elk vignette and state seal, revenue stamps 18.00
Adventure Consolidated Copper Company (I), 1900s, Michigan, Two elk vignette and state seal 9.00
Adventure Copper (I), 1860s, Michigan, State seal 30.00
Adventure Copper (I), 1900s, State seal 10.00
Ahmeek Mining (I), 1910s, Michigan, Two beavers at work 15.00
Ahmeek Mining (I), 1920s, Michigan, Two beavers at work 12.00
Ajax-Divide Mining (I), 1910s, Nevada, Mining vignettes, gold seal 10.00
Ajax-Nevada Gold Mining (U), 1900s, Nevada, Milling and mining vignette 10.00
Alabama Gold and Copper Mining (I), 1890s, Signed by Sheriff Garret (who shot Billy the Kid) 1,500.00
Aladdin Gold Mining (I), 1930s, Nevada, Aladdin vignette 5.00
Alaska Gold Mines (I), 1910s, Eagle vignette 18.00
Alaska Gold Fields Lt. (I), 1890s 28.00
Alaska-Mexican Gold Mining (I), 1900s, California, Working miners vignette 40.00
Alaska Mildred (I), 1900s, Oregon, Mountain and bay vignette 40.00
Alaska-Natazhat Consolidated Mines (I), 1910s, Figures and seal 20.00
Alaska Treadwell Gold Mining (I), 1890s, Mining and mountain vignette 30.00
Alaska Treadwell Gold Mining (I), 1930s, Snow capped mountains and miners vignette 15.00
Alaska-United Gold Mining (I), 1890s, California, Goddess and miners vignette 40.00
Albemarle Dixie Equipment Mining (U), 1900s, Territory of Arizona 7.00
Alden Coal Mining (I), 1910s, Mining and mountain scene vignette 15.00
Algoma Consolidated Corporation (I), 1930s, Figures and logo vignette 15.00
Algomah Mining (I), 1910s, Michigan, Miners using drills vignette 20.00
Alhambra Flume and Mercantile (U), 1880s, Montana Territory 12.00
Alleghany Mining Company (I), 1880s, Colorado, Large vignette of mountain town 30.00
Alma Lincoln Mining (I), 1930s, Eagle vignette 8.00
Alpewa Mining (I-N), 1900s, Washington, Three mining vignettes 16.00
Alta-Idaho-Gold and Copper Mining (I), 1900s, Three mining vignettes 20.00
Alvarado Mining and Milling (I), 1910s, Mining scene vignette 30.00
Amador Coalition Mines, (I-N), 1920s, Nevada, Eagle 4.00
Ambassador Mines (I), 1930s, Washington, With stamps 3.00
American Alkal (I), 1900s, Mountain scene and eagle 12.00
American and Mexican Silver Mining (I), 1860s, Bond, Mining vignette and portrait of Washington, stamp 325.00
American Coal Company of Alleghany County (I), 1860s, Maryland, Train and ship vignette 90.00
American Coal Company of Alleghany County (I), 1970s, Maryland, Train and ship vignette 85.00
American-Mexican Mining and Smelting (I-N), 1920s, Arizona, Smelting scene 18.00
American Mining (I), 1850s, Indian maiden, hunter and eagle vignette 155.00
American Mining-Norwich Mine (I), 1850s, Allegorical figures in three vignettes 56.00

◀ ***Adventure Consolidated Copper Company (I), 1890s, Michigan**, Two elk vignette and state seal, revenue stamps* ***18.00***
◀ ***Alhambra Flume & Mercantile (U) 1880's Montana Territory*** ***12.00***

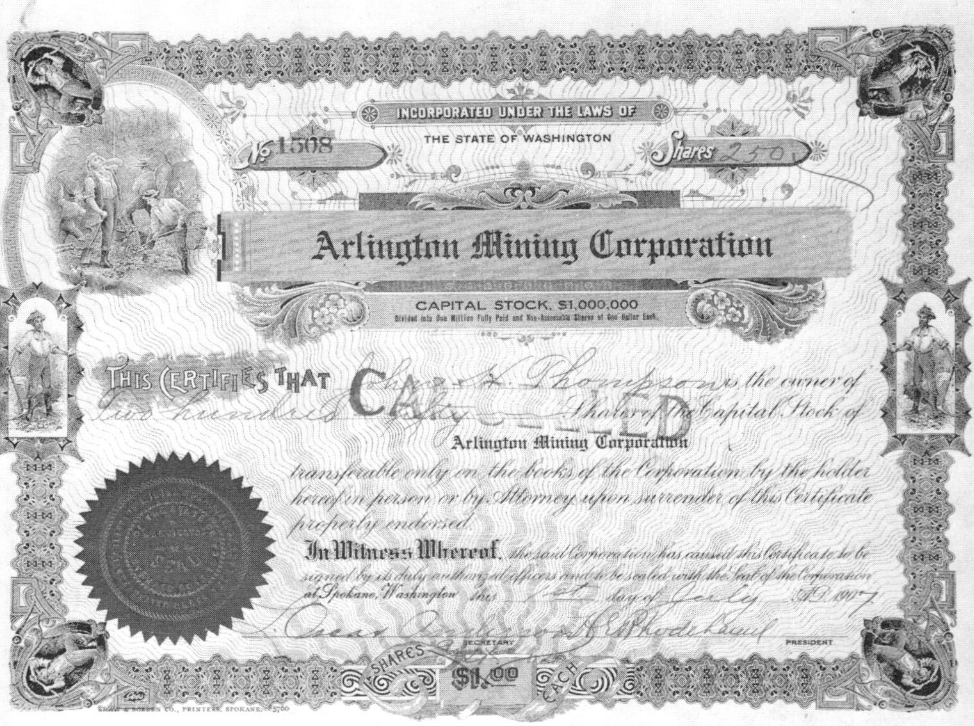
INCORPORATED UNDER THE LAWS OF
THE STATE OF WASHINGTON
No 1508
Shares 250
Arlington Mining Corporation
CAPITAL STOCK, $1,000,000
Divided into One Million Fully Paid and Non-Assessable Shares of One Dollar Each.
THIS CERTIFIES THAT
is the owner of
Shares of the Capital Stock of
Arlington Mining Corporation
transferable only on the books of the Corporation by the holder hereof in person or by Attorney upon surrender of this Certificate properly endorsed.
In Witness Whereof, the said Corporation has caused this Certificate to be signed by its duly authorized officers and to be sealed with the Seal of the Corporation at Spokane, Washington this day of A.D. 1907
SECRETARY
PRESIDENT
SHARES $1.00 EACH

INCORPORATED UNDER THE LAWS OF THE STATE OF COLORADO.
NUMBER
1891
SHARES
-1000-
The Anchor Gold Mining and Milling Company.
CAPITAL STOCK, $1,250,000.
This Certifies that
is the owner of
-ONE THOUSAND-
Shares of the Capital Stock of
The Anchor Gold Mining & Milling Company, full paid and non-assessable
transferable only on the books of the Corporation by the holder hereof in person or by Attorney upon surrender of this Certificate properly endorsed.
In Witness Whereof the said Corporation has caused this Certificate to be signed by its duly authorized officers and to be sealed with the Seal of the Corporation
at Colorado Springs, Colo. day of A.D. 190
President
SHARES $1.00 EACH.

American Reclamation Company (U), 1910s, Arizona, Eagle, capitol building and Indian vignette	12.00
American Smokeless Coal (I), 1900s, Gold bond, bold seal	35.00
American River Water and Mining (I-N), 1860s, California, Bond	230.00
Amygdaloid Mining (I,) 1970s, Michigan, Lady vignette, with stamp	40.00
Anaconda (I), 1960s, Company vignette	5.00
Anaconda Gold Mining (I), 1890s, Colorado, Gold seal	28.00
Anchor Gold Mining and Milling (I-N), 1900s, Gold mining vignette	15.00
Anglo-Californian Gold Mining (I), 1850s	40.00
Anglo-Californian Gold Mining (I-N), 1850s, California	95.00
Annie C. Gold Mining (I-N), 1890s, Mining vignette	35.00
Apex Gold Mining and Milling (I), 1900s, Colorado Territory, Miners loading ore cars vignette	15.00
Arcadian Consolidated Mining (I), 1920s, Working miners vignette	20.00
Argentine Cobalt (I), Maine, Train and ship vignette	20.00
Arizona Commercial Mining (I), 1920s, Mining vignette	8.00
Arizona Commercial Mining Company (I), 1920s, Miners working and jackhammer equipment vignette	10.00
Arizona Extension Silver Mines (I), 1920s, Nevada, No vignette	5.00
Arizona Patagonic Silver Mining (I), 1920s, Lady vignette	7.00
Arlington Mining (I), 1900s, Washington, Seven mining vignettes	12.00
Arlington Mining (I), 1900s, Washington, Man with lion vignette	8.00
Arlington Mining (I), 1910s, Seven working miners vignettes	8.00
Arlington Mining (I), 1920s, Seven working miners vignettes	6.00
Arno Gold Mining (I-N), 1890s, Embossed seal	6.00
Arrow Gold Mining (I-N), 1900s, Colorado, Embossed seal, company logo	6.00
Arrowhead Development (I-N), 1920s, Three mine vignettes	10.00
Atlanta Mines (I), 1900s, Arizona Territory, Eagle vignette	10.00
Atlantic and Pacific Mining and Tunnel Company (I-N), 1880s, Lady and moneybag vignette	80.00
Atlas Wonder Mining Company (U), 1910s, California, State seal	8.00
Arato Mining and Development Company (I), 1880s, World globe vignette	45.00
Atrato Mining (I), 1880s, Gold dredger, two state seals vignettes	50.00
Auburn and Rock Creek Gold Mining (I-N), 1880s, California	45.00
Aurora Mining (I), 1900s, Arizona Territory, Allegorical figures vignette	50.00
Ave-Maria Gold Quartz Mine (I-N), 1850s, California	95.00
Ave-Maria Gold Quartz Mine (I), 1880s, Certificate of proprietorship	85.00
Azteca Copper Mining (I), 1920s, Seal	8.00
Bagdad Copper (I), 1920s, Woman and generator vignette	8.00
Bagdad Copper (I), 1930s, Woman and generator vignette	7.00
Baker Hansen Prospecting, Mining and Development (I), 1910s, Arizona	8.00
Balbach-Hoornbeck Mines Syndicate (I-N), 1910s, Bond, Eagle on shield vignette, green seal	15.00
Bald Butte Gold Mines (I), 1930s, Montana	12.00
Bald Mountain Mining Coonpany (I), 1880s, New York, Mining scene vignette	68.00
Baldy Sour Mining (I-N), 1870s, Nevada, Flag and eagle vignette, gold seal	56.00
Baltimore–Nova Scotia Mining Company (I), 1900s, West Virginia, Bond, with stamps	10.00
Banker Mining and Milling (I), 1900s, Colorado, Gold seal, mining vignette plus six miners in certificate border, also stamp	18.00
Banner State Gold, Silver and Copper Mining (U), 1900s, Colorado, State seal, two vignettes of goddess and eagle	8.00

◀***Arlington Mining Corporation (I), 1900s, Washington,*** *Seven mining vignettes* ***12.00***

◀***Anchor Gold Mining and Milling Company (I-N), 1900s,*** *Gold mining vignette* ***15.00***

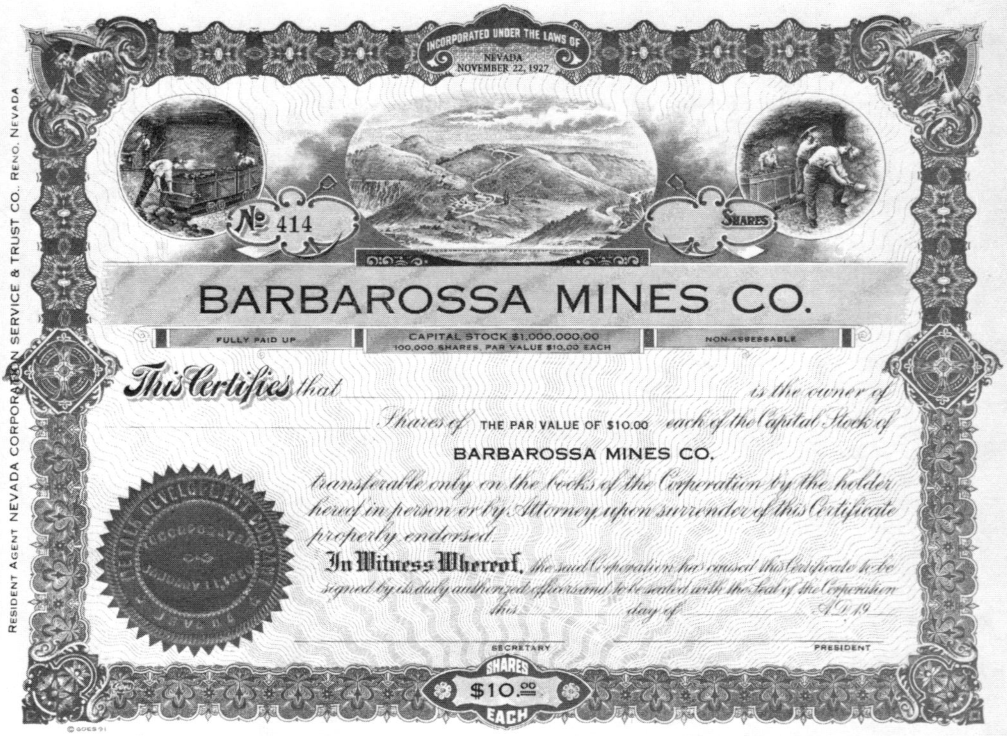
INCORPORATED UNDER THE LAWS OF
NEVADA
NOVEMBER 22, 1927
№ 414
SHARES
BARBAROSSA MINES CO.
FULLY PAID UP
CAPITAL STOCK $1,000,000.00
100,000 SHARES, PAR VALUE $10.00 EACH
NON-ASSESSABLE
This Certifies that is the owner of
Shares of THE PAR VALUE OF $10.00 each of the Capital Stock of
BARBAROSSA MINES CO.
transferable only on the books of the Corporation by the holder hereof in person or by Attorney upon surrender of this Certificate properly endorsed.
In Witness Whereof, the said Corporation has caused this Certificate to be signed by its duly authorized officers and to be sealed with the Seal of the Corporation this day of A.D. 19
SECRETARY
PRESIDENT
SHARES
$10.00
EACH
RESIDENT AGENT NEVADA CORPORATION SERVICE & TRUST CO., RENO, NEVADA
© GOES 91

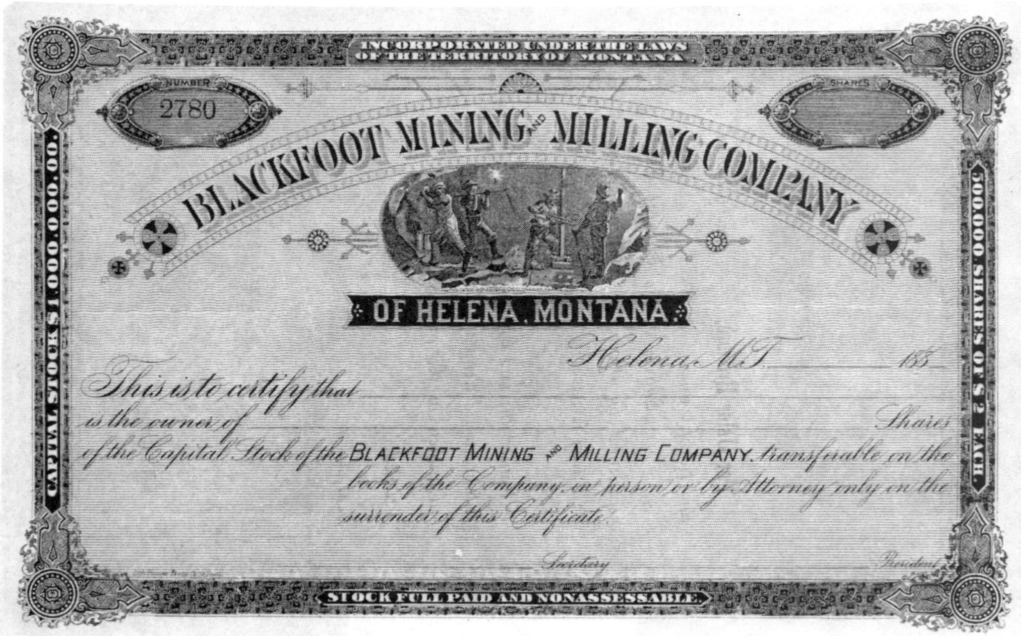
INCORPORATED UNDER THE LAWS OF THE TERRITORY OF MONTANA.
NUMBER
2780
SHARES
BLACKFOOT MINING AND MILLING COMPANY
OF HELENA, MONTANA.
CAPITAL STOCK $1,000,000.00
100,000 SHARES OF $ 2 EACH
Helena, M.T. 188
This is to certify that
is the owner of Shares
of the Capital Stock of the BLACKFOOT MINING AND MILLING COMPANY, transferable on the books of the Company, in person or by Attorney only on the surrender of this Certificate.
Secretary
President
STOCK FULL PAID AND NONASSESSABLE.

Bannock Ditch and Mining (U), 1870s, Farmer vignette	38.00
Barbarossa Mines (U), Two ore car mining vignettes and mountain scene, gold seal	3.00
Barry-Hollinger Gold Mines (I-N), 1920s, No vignette	2.00
Basic Resources (I), 1960s, Utah, Smaller certificate	1.00
Basic Resources (I), 1960s, Utah, Eagle vignette	1.00
Basin Gold and Copper (I-N), 1890s, Two mining vignettes	20.00
Basin Gold and Silver Mining (I-N), 1890s, Mining vignettes	23.00
Basin Gold and Silver Mining (I-N), 1910s, Miners in mine vignette	15.00
Basin Mine and Concentrate (U), 1890s, Montana, Large eagle with flag vignette	8.00
Basin Montana Tunnel (I), 1950s, Eagle vignette	4.00
Batchelor-Khedive Mines (U), 1900s, Colorado	5.00
Baundary Red Mountain Mining (I-N), 1922, Washington, Elk vignette	8.00
Bear Creek Development (I-N), 1920s, Two mining vignettes plus large mountain and smelting scene, gold seal	9.00
Beaver Head Hydraulics Mining (I), 1880s, Strip mining vignette	50.00
Beaver Head Hydraulics Mining (I), 1880s, Hydraulic mining scene	95.00
Belcher Extension Consolidated Mines (I-N), 1920s, Nevada	7.00
Bigbull Consolidated Mining (I), 1890s, Colorado, Working miners vignette	15.00
Bigbull Consolidated Mining (I), 1900s, Colorado, Working miners vignette	12.00
Big Canon Copper Mining (I), 1860s, Mountain and river scene vignette	215.00
Big Five Mining (I), 1910s, Wyoming, "5" Logo	5.00
Big Ledge Copper (I), 1920s, Arizona, Working miners vignette	12.00
Big Smoke Uranium (I-N), 1950s, Washington, Large eagle, harbors, and ships scene	2.00
Big Vein Pocahontas Coal (U), 1900s	5.00
Bingham Mary Copper (I-N), 1900s, Utah	32.00
Black Bear Consolidated (I), 1930s, Nevada, Company logo	2.00
Blackfoot Mining and Milling (U), 1880s, Territory of Montana, Large mining scene, old ore train and mining scene on reverse	25.00
Blacklick and Conemaugh Petroleum and Mining (U), 1860s, Three vignettes	22.00
Black Mountain Copper Company (I), 1900s, Arizona Territory, Workers in mine vignette	27.00
Blue Jacket Copper (I), 1910s, Idaho, Mining scenes, gold seal	17.00
Bodie Tunnel and Mining (I), 1870s	40.00
Boise Basin Mines Merger Company (U), 1910s, Washington, Mining camp with railroad tracks vignette	10.00
Bolivia Gold Exploration Company (I), 1910s, California, Three mining vignettes (panning and sluicing), gold seal	10.00
Bonanza Chief Mining (I), 1880s, Montana Territory, Miners and Indian maiden vignettes	50.00
Bonanza Gold Mines (I), 1930s, Utah, Figures vignette	6.00
Boston and Ely Consolidated Mining (I), 1910s, No vignette	3.00
Boston Gold-Copper Smelting (I), 1900s, Maine, Red seal	12.00
Boston Montana Mining (I), 1920s	7.00
Boston Occidental Mining (I), 1900s, Colorado	20.00
Boston and Sonora Mining (U), 1900s, Eagle vignette at bottom	6.00
Boulder Smelting (U), 1890s, Montana, Large company logo	6.00
Boundary Camp Mining and Milling (I), 1900s, South Dakota, Mining vignette	23.00
British Guiana Gold Concessions (I-N), 1900s, Maine, Lion vignette	22.00
Braceville Coal (U), 1800s, Illinois	4.00
Branch Mountain Mining and Milling (I), 1900s, South Dakota	5.00
Branch Mint Mining and Milling (I), 1900s	8.00

Barbarossa Mines (U), *Two ore car mining vignettes and mountain scene, gold seal* ***3.00***

Blackfoot Mining and Milling Company (U), 1880s, Territory of Montana, *Large mining scene, old ore train and mining scene on reverse* ***25.00***

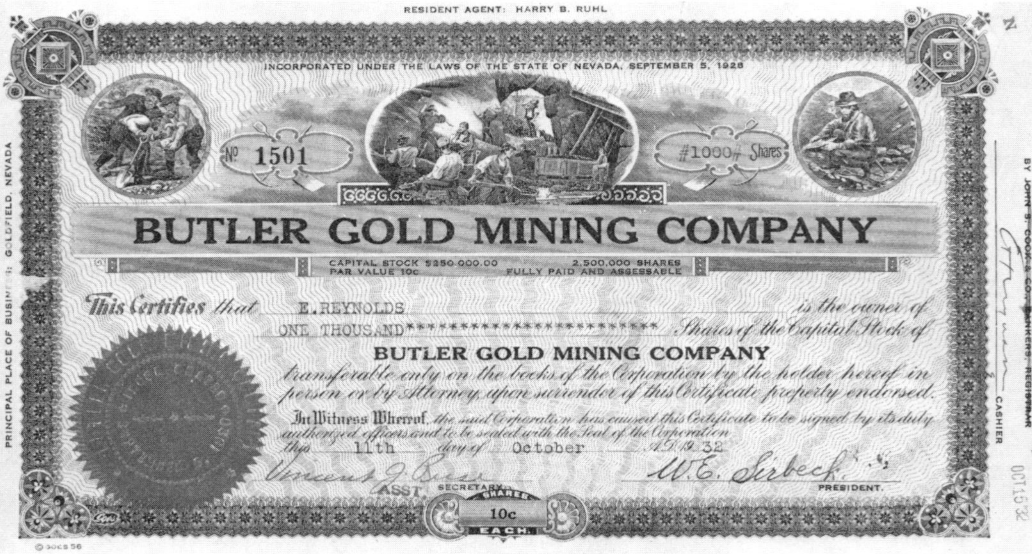
RESIDENT AGENT: HARRY B. RUHL

INCORPORATED UNDER THE LAWS OF THE STATE OF NEVADA, SEPTEMBER 5, 1928

No 1501

#1000 Shares

BUTLER GOLD MINING COMPANY

CAPITAL STOCK $250,000.00 PAR VALUE 10c

2,500,000 SHARES FULLY PAID AND ASSESSABLE

This Certifies that E. REYNOLDS is the owner of ONE THOUSAND*********************** Shares of the Capital Stock of

BUTLER GOLD MINING COMPANY

transferable only on the books of the Corporation by the holder hereof in person or by Attorney upon surrender of this Certificate properly endorsed.

In Witness Whereof, the said Corporation has caused this Certificate to be signed by its duly authorized officers and to be sealed with the Seal of the Corporation this 11th day of October A.D. 1932

ASST. SECRETARY

PRESIDENT.

SHARES 10c EACH

PRINCIPAL PLACE OF BUSINESS: GOLDFIELD, NEVADA

REGISTERED AT GOLDFIELD, NEVADA BY JOHN S. COOK & CO. BANKERS, REGISTRAR

CASHIER

OCT 15 32

INCORPORATED UNDER THE LAWS OF THE STATE OF MONTANA

No 71

Shares

Butte-Corbin Mining Company

CAPITAL STOCK $300,000.00

FULL PAID NON-ASSESSABLE

This Certifies that is the owner of Shares of the Capital Stock of

BUTTE-CORBIN MINING COMPANY

full paid and non-assessable transferable only on the books of the Corporation on surrender of this Certificate properly endorsed.

In Witness Whereof, the said Corporation has caused this Certificate to be signed by its duly authorized officers and to be sealed with the seal of the Corporation

Helena, Montana, this day of A.D. 19

SECRETARY

PRESIDENT.

SHARES 10 CENTS EACH

Brandenburg Coal Mining (I), 1910s, Gold bond, large mining vignette	70.00
British Guiana Gold Concessions (I-N), 1900s, Maine, Lion, unicorn vignette with seal	23.00
Brittenstene Silver Mining (I-N), 1880s, Colorado, Five working miners vignette	65.00
Brokers' Gold Mining Company (U), 1890s, Colorado, Miners in tunnel vignette	12.00
Buck Mountain Coal Company (I), 1860s, Miners and elk vignette	75.00
Buffalo and Susquehana Coal and Coke Company (I), 1900s, Bond signed by C. W. Goodyear	34.00
Buffalo Mines (I), 1910s	15.00
Buffalo Placer Mining and Milling (I), 1910s, Colorado, Gold bond	12.00
Bullfrog Pioneer Extension Mines (I), 1910s, Arizona, Mining vignette	22.00
Bullion Gold and Silver Mining (I), 1930s, California	4.00
Bull Valley Gold Mining (I), 1910s, Utah, Miners at work vignette, also six miner vignettes on border	12.00
Bunker Hill Consolidated Mining Company (I), 1920s, California, Gold seal, eagle on rock vignette	9.00
Bunker Hill Consolidated Mining Company (I), 1920s, California, Gold seal, eagle on rock vignette	8.00
Butler Gold Mining (I-N), 1930s, Gold seal, three mining vignettes	8.00
Butte and London Copper Development Company (I-N), 1900s, Montana, Gold seal, seven vignettes of miners	16.00
Butte and Yerington Copper (I), 1900s, Montana, Eagle vignette	8.00
Butte and Yerington Copper (I), 1910s, Montana, Eagle vignette	7.00
Butte Copper Consolidated Mines (I-N), 1920s, South Dakota, Ornate border	4.00
Butte Copper Mining and Smelting (I), 1900s, Vignette of elk	6.00
Butte Copper Mining and Smelting (I-N), 1900s, Vignette of elk	8.00
Butte-Corbin Mining (U), 1900s, Montana, Large mining scene, gold seal, four mining vignettes in border	6.00
Butte Ramsdell Copper (I), 1910s, Montana, Mining vignette	7.00
Butte Ramsdell Copper (I), 1920s, Montana, Mining vignette	5.00
Butterfly-Terrible Gold Mining (I), 1870s, State seal	15.00

Cabin Creek Kanawha Company (I), 1870s, State seal	43.00
Cabin Creek and Kanawha Coal Company (I), 1880s, West Virginia, Bond	130.00
Cactus Mining (I), 1880s, Utah, Eagle vignette	110.00
Cadillac Consolidated Mining (I), 1880s, Mining vignette	35.00
Caladonia Mining (I-N), 1920s, Idaho, Working miners vignette	7.00
Calaveras Water and Mining Company (I), 1880s, California	25.00
Calaveras Water and Mining Company (I-N), 1880s, California	35.00
California Consolidated Mining and Milling (I), 1900s, Arizona Territory, Mining vignette	30.00
California-Divide Mining (I-N), 1910s, Nevada, Miners sluicing for gold vignette, gold seal	13.00
California Liberty Gold Mines (U), 1900s, Arizona, Mine vignette	15.00
Calumet and Arizona Mining (I), 1910s, Arizona Territory, Mining vignette	11.00
Calumet and Arizona Mining (I), 1920s, Arizona Territory, Mining vignette	8.00
Calumet and Copper Creek Mining (I), 1900s, Nevada, Bond, Mining scene vignette	38.00
Cambria County Coal (I), 1910s, Pennsylvania, Miners and coal cars vignettes	18.00
Cambria County Coal Company (U), 1910s, Two mining vignettes	11.00
Cameron Gold and Silver Mining (I-N), 1880s, Colorado, Gold seal	46.00
Cannon Ball Gold Mining (I), 1900s, Colorado, Cannon vignette and gold seal	17.00
Capuzaya Mining (I-N), 1900s, Mining vignette	30.00
Carsons Creek Consolidated Mining (I), 1850s, California, Allegorical figure in chariot	60.00
Cascade Mining, 1870s, Indian and sailor at harbor vignette	35.00

◀ ***Butler Gold Mining Company (I-N), 1930s,*** *Gold seal, three mining vignettes* ***8.00***

◀ ***Butte-Corbin Mining (U), 1900s, Montana,*** *Large mining scene, gold seal, four mining vignettes in border* ***6.00***

No. D 1237 INCORPORATED UNDER THE LAWS OF NEVADA 100 Shares

CASH BOY CONSOLIDATED MINING COMPANY

CAPITAL STOCK 2,000,000 SHARES PAR $1.00 EACH

ASSESSABLE.

PRINCIPAL OFFICE, RENO, NEVADA.
RESIDENT AGENT, F. H. NORCROSS

This Certifies, That Hamilton B. Wills is the owner of One Hundred Shares of the Capital Stock of the

CASH BOY CONSOLIDATED MINING COMPANY, ASSESSABLE.

transferable only on the Books of the Corporation by the holder hereof in person or by Attorney, upon surrender of this Certificate properly endorsed.

In Witness Whereof, this Corporation has caused this certificate to be signed by its authorized officers and sealed with the Seal of the Corporation, at Carson, Nevada, this 20th day of Aug A.D. 1920

SECRETARY PRESIDENT

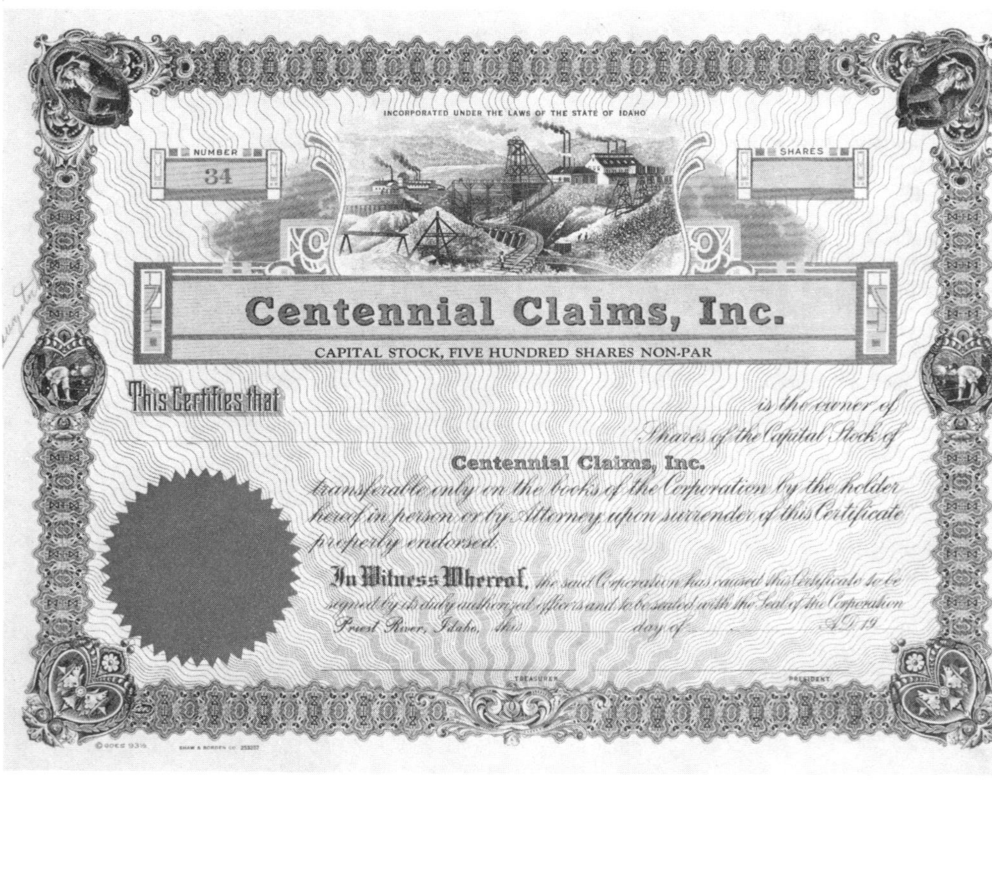

INCORPORATED UNDER THE LAWS OF THE STATE OF IDAHO

NUMBER 34 SHARES

Centennial Claims, Inc.

CAPITAL STOCK, FIVE HUNDRED SHARES NON-PAR

This Certifies that is the owner of Shares of the Capital Stock of

Centennial Claims, Inc.

transferable only on the books of the Corporation by the holder hereof in person or by Attorney upon surrender of this Certificate properly endorsed.

In Witness Whereof, the said Corporation has caused this Certificate to be signed by its duly authorized officers and to be sealed with the Seal of the Corporation Priest River, Idaho, this day of A.D. 19

TREASURER PRESIDENT

Cascade Mining Company (U), **1880s, Colorado**, Indian, sailor, ship, teepee and state seal vignettes	25.00
Cash Boy Consolidated Mining (I), 1910s, Nevada	6.00
Cash Boy Consolidated Mining (I-N), 1920s	6.00
Cash Entry Mining (I), 1910s, Company logo	4.00
Castle Dome Mining and Smelting (I), 1880s, Castle turret vignette	60.00
Castle Rock Milling and Mines (U), 1910s, Colorado, Working miners vignette	10.00
Catherine Mining and Exploration (I), 1900s, Nice mining vignette	22.00
Catalpa Mining (I), 1880s, Working miners vignette	60.00
Catalpa Mining (I), 1900s, Working miners vignette	50.00
Cedar Hollow Lime Company (I), 1830s, Mountain scene vignette	95.00
Centennial Claims (U), Idaho, Gold seal	3.00
Centennial Claims (U), 1930s, Washington	8.00
Centennial Mines (I), 1930s, Idaho, With stamps and attached accounting sheet, large milling and smelting operation in mountain vignette, also four mining vignettes in border, gold seal	7.00
Chain O'Mines (I), Nevada, Voting trust certificate	4.00
Chain O'Mines (I), 1930s, Nevada, Gold bond	7.00
Chance Silver Mining (U), 1870s, Two vignettes	20.00
Chaparral Hill Gold Mining (I)	4.00
Charleston Mining, Manufacturing and Improvement Company (U), **1890s**, Red seal	12.00
Chicamonstone Copper Mining (U), 1890s	15.00
Chico Gold and Silver Mining (U), 1860s, Nevada mining scene	39.00
Clara-Swansea Mining (I), 1920s, Nevada, Working miners with ore car vignette	9.00
Clara-Swansea Mining (U), 1920s, Nevada, Working miners with ore care vignette	2.00
Claremont Peak Grovel Gold Mine (I), 1810s, California	28.00
Clear Creek Mining and Development (U), 1870s, Colorado	17.00
Clememcau Mining (I,) 1940s, Arizona, Portrait vignette	10.00
Clinton Iron Company (I), 1870s, Seated woman vignette	44.00
Clove Spring Iron Works (U), 1870s, Allegorical figures	40.00
Cobalt Central Mines (I), 1900s, Two miners vignette	10.00
C-O-D Gold Mining (U), Colorado	8.00
Colonial Silver Mines (I-N), 1900s, Three figures vignette	12.00
Colorado Blue Bell Mining (I), 1900s, Eagle vignette	13.00
Colorado City and Manitau Mining (I), 1900s, Working miners vignette	15.00
Colorado Cripple Creek Gold Mining (I), 1890s Colorado, Miners at work vignette	62.00
Colorado Tungsten Mines (U), 1900s, Eagle vignette, gold seal	6.00
Columbia Development Comapny (I-N), Arizona Territory, Working miners with ore cars vignette	18.00
Comet Mining (I-N), 1880s, Utah Territory, Large vignette of miners and ore cars	95.00
Commercial Coal (I) 1900s, Pennsylvania, Loaded coal car vignette	18.00
Commercial Coal (I), 1910s and 1920s, Pennsylvania, Loaded coal car vignette	15.00
Comstock and Keystone Mining (I), 1940s, Large eagle vignette, with stamps	4.00
Comstock Limited (I), 1930s, Nevada	5.00
Comstock Tunnel Company (I), 1880s, Nevada, Gold Bond with coupons and eagle vignette	37.00
Comstock Tunnel Company (I), 1880s, New York, Eagle vignette	40.00
Concordia Virginia Mining Co. (I), 1920s, Three mining vignettes with stamps	8.00
Consolidated Arizona Smelting Company (I), 1910s, Large smelting works vignette	35.00
Consolidated Chollar-Gould, Savage Mines (I), 1950s, California	1.00
Consolidated Coal Company (U), Ore cars with donkey engine in mine (specimen)	25.00
Consolidated Esperanza Mining Co. (I), 1870s, Miners vignette	135.00
Consolidated Gold Corporation (I), 1920s, Embossed seal	6.00
Consolidated Mines and Smelting (I), 1930s, Miners vignette	16.00

◀ ***Cash Boy Consolidated Mining Company (I-N), 1920s*** — ***6.00***

◀ ***Centennial Claims, Inc.*** *(U), Working miners vignette* — ***3.00***

Incorporated under the Laws of the State of Nevada, July 21, 1921
No 1845
400 Shares
Concordia Virginia Mining Co.
CAPITAL STOCK $150,000.00 1,500,000 SHARES
FULLY PAID ASSESSABLE
This Certifies that HARRY R. MITCHELL is the owner of
FOUR HUNDRED Shares of the Capital Stock of
CONCORDIA VIRGINIA MINING CO.
transferable only on the books of the Corporation by the holder hereof in person or by Attorney upon surrender of this Certificate properly endorsed.
In Witness Whereof, the said Corporation has caused this Certificate to be signed by its duly authorized officers and to be sealed with the Seal of the Corporation
OCT 26 1928
SECRETARY
PRESIDENT
SHARES 10c. EACH
J. J. QUINLAN, RESIDENT AGENT, VIRGINIA CITY, NEV.

CERTIFICATE FOR LESS THAN ONE HUNDRED SHARES
CAPITAL $10,000,000.
SHARES $25. EACH.
Number 26027
Shares 10
COPPER RANGE COMPANY
INCORPORATED UNDER THE LAWS OF THE STATE OF MICHIGAN
This Certifies That Mrs. Minnie Huber
is the owner of Ten Shares
Full Paid and Non-Assessable of the Capital Stock of the Copper Range Company transferable on the books of the Company by the holder hereof in person or by attorney on the surrender of this certificate properly endorsed.
This certificate is not valid until countersigned by the Transfer Agent and registered by the Registrar.
Witness the seal of the Company and the signatures of its duly authorized officers at the City of Boston, Mass.
APR 26 1919
SHARES $25 EACH
STATE STREET TRUST COMPANY, REGISTRAR.
ASSISTANT SECRETARY.
VICE PRESIDENT.

Consolidated Nevada-Utah Mining (I), 1910s, Miners working by lantern vignette	17.00
Consolidated Republican Mountain Mining Company (U), 1870s, Colorado, Indian princess and state seal vignette	24.00
Consolidated Republican Mountain Mining Company (U), 1880s, Colorado, Indian princess and state seal vignette	17.00
Consolidated South Spring Hill Mining (I), 1890s	32.00
Consolidated Virginia and Andes Corporation (I), 1830s, Nevada, Gold seal, three vignettes of working miners at camp	9.00
Consolidated Virginia Mining (I), 1930s, Nevada, Company logo with stamps (10)	15.00
Contact Gold Mining and Tunnel Company, 1890s, Colorado, Lady with star vignette	28.00
Contact Gold Mining and Tunnel Company, 1900s, Colorado, Lady with star vignette	24.00
Continental Mining Company (I-N), 1880s, Three mining vignettes	50.00
Cook Gold Mining of Colorado (I,) 1860s	180.00
Copper Knob Mining (I), 1880s, Cherub and mine vignettes	49.00
Copper Metals Company (I), 1910s, Territory of Arizona, Gold bond	30.00
Copper Range Company (I), 1910s, Michigan, Mining vignette	5.00
Copper Range Company (I), 1950s and 1960s, Michigan,Three bare-chested miners vignette	3.00
Copperfield Mining (I), 1920s, Working miners vignette, seal	6.00
Corbin Copper Company (I), 1910s, Michigan, Ore cars at mine entrance vignette	25.00
Cory Mine Limited (I-N), 1930s, Erupting volcano with flowing lava scene	4.00
Coulterville Virginia Mining (I-N), 1880s, Fine pink certificate	75.00
Cracker Jack Mining (I), 1900s, Arizona, Two mining vignettes and smelting plant	35.00
Creede Contact Mining (I), 1910s, Colorado, State seal	6.00
Crescant Mining (I), 1900s, Large mining vignette	36.00
Cresson Consolidated Gold Mining and Milling (I), Colorado	9.00
Cripple Creek Gold Rock Mining (I-N), 1890s, Colorado, Mining vignette	30.00
Cromwell Mining and Development (I), 1890s, Miners vignette	14.00
Crown Mining (I), 1880s, Nice mountain mining vignette, embossed seal	95.00
Cullman Coal and Coke (I), 1900s, Alabama, Mining vignette	27.00
Cumberland Consolidated Gold Mining (I-N), 1900s, Iowa, Red seal	6.00
Curtis Minerals (I-N), 1960s, Utah, Large eagle vignette	1.00
Cusa-Mexicana Mining (I-N), Miners vignette	12.00
Cuyuna-Sultana Iron Company (I), 1910s, Miners panning for gold vignette	24.00
Cyclone Mining (U), 1900s, South Dakota, Two mining vignettes and smelting plant	12.00
Dahl Mining (I-N), 1950s, Washington, Large eagle vignette	1.00
Dahlgren Mining (I), 1880s, Mining vignette	35.00
Dahlonega Gold Mining (I), 1880s, Eagle and flag vignette	50.00
Daly Mining (I), 1930s, Utah, Three mining vignettes, gold seal	3.00
Davenport Consolidated Gold Mining (U), 1910s, Nevada, Mining scene plus six miners in border	6.00
Davidson Copper Mining (I), 1860s, Embossed seal, milling plant vignette	110.00
Death Valley Arcalvada Consolidated Mines (I), 1900s, Gold bond, large smelting scenes	40.00
Death Valley Big Bell Mining (U), 1900s, Arizona, Three mining vignettes	22.00
Death Valley Consolidated Mining (I), Nevada	30.00
Decatur Silver Mining Company (I), 1880s, Colorado, Mining vignette	50.00
Deep River Copper Company (I), 1860s, Seminude woman vignette	90.00
Deep Tunnel Mining (I-N), 1930s, Three mining vignettes	13.00
Defender Gold Mining (I), 1890s, Colorado	36.00
Defense Metals (U), Idaho, Open pit mining and mill vignette	4.00
Del Norte Comstock Company (I), 1960s, Seated lady vignette	230.00

◀ ***Concordia Virginia Mining Co. (I), 1920s,*** *Three mining vignettes with stamps* ***8.00***

◀ ***Copper Range Company (I), 1910s, Michigan,*** *Mining vignette* ***5.00***

No. 3788 — -78- Shares

DALY MINING COMPANY

Capital Stock $4,000,000 | Incorporated Nov. 22, 1884, under the Laws of the State of Utah | 200,000 Shares

This Certifies that ------ GEORGE S. LAMBOURNE ------ is the owner of EXACTLY SEVENTY EIGHT SHARES EXACTLY Shares of the Capital Stock of

DALY MINING COMPANY

transferable only on the books of the Corporation by the holder hereof in person or by Attorney upon surrender of this Certificate properly endorsed.

In Witness Whereof, the said Corporation has caused this Certificate to be signed by its duly authorized officers and to be sealed with the Seal of the Corporation at Salt Lake City, Utah, this 10 day of November A.D. 1953

SECRETARY — PRESIDENT

SHARES $20 EACH

© GOES 5619

No. 897 — Shares

CAPITAL STOCK $500,000

LOCATION OF WORKS: CALAVERAS CO., CAL.

500,000 Shares — $1.00 Each

Oakland, Cal. 189

This Certifies that

is entitled to Shares

of the Capital Stock of the

Edna Gold Mining Company,

Transferable on the Books of the Company by endorsement hereon and surrender of this Certificate.

Secretary — Incorporated April 13, 1896 — President

Delaware Mining (I), 1860s, Michigan, Vignettes of hunters, farmers, and pioneers, with stamp	75.00
Delaware Mining (I), 1860s, Michigan, State Seal, embossed seal	75.00
Denbigh Mining (I), 1920s, Two mining vignettes, plus woman with banner	28.00
Des Moines Gold Mining (I-N), 1890s, Colorado, Miners and mountains vignette	25.00
Desert Gold Mines (I-N), 1910s, Arizona, Miners vignette	22.00
Dexter Mining Company (I), 1900s, Wyoming, Bond, two miners pushing ore car vignette	15.00
Diamond Black Butte Consolidated Mining (I), 1900s, Mining vignettes	22.00
Dinero Consolidated Mining and Tunnel (I), 1900s, Colorado, Working miners and mountain scene	12.00
Divide City Mining (I-N), 1920s, Three mining vignettes, gold seal	9.00
Divide Extension Consolidated (I), 1930s, Nevada, Company logo with stamp	4.00
Dixie Extension Consolidated Mine (I), 1930s, Nevada, Company logo with stamp	4.00
Donna Louisa Mining (I), 1900s, Two mining vignettes, gold seal	22.00
Douglas Mining and Leasing (I-N), 1920s, Vignette of elk	5.00
Eames Petroleum Gold and Silver Smelting (I-N), 1880s	40.00
Eames Petroleum Iron (I-N), 1880s	38.00
Early Silver Mining Company (U), 1880s, Colorado, Working miners vignette	25.00
Eastern Montana Mining and Smelting (I), 1870s, Mining vignette	95.00
Eastern Montana Mining and Smelting (U), 1870s, Mining vignette	25.00
Eastern Oregon Gold Mining (I), 1890s, Bond	28.00
Eastern Oregon Gold Mining (I-N), 1880s	35.00
Edna Gold Mining Company (U), 1890s, California, Mining vignette	10.00
El Paso Extension Gold Mines (U), 1910s, Colorado	4.00
El Salvador Silver Mines (I), 1910s, Eagle vignette	15.00
Elkhorn Coal Corporation (I), 1910s, Coal train vignette	9.00
Ellensburgh Mining, Milling and Smelting (I), 1870s, Horse and man before smelting plant vignette	160.00
Ely Consolidated Copper (I), 1920s, Nevada, Eagle vignette	8.00
Ely-Witch Copper (I), 1900s, Odd head and wing vignette, embossed seal	13.00
Ely-Witch Copper (I-N), 1900s, Odd Head and wing vignette, embossed seal	16.00
Empire Gold and Silver Mining (I), 1860s, Bond, two mining vignettes plus seminude woman with shield	360.00
Empire Lee Mining (I), Colorado, Grey seal	5.00
Empire Lee Mining (I-N), 1920s, Company logo, grey seal	7.00
Empire State Silver Mining (I), 1860s, Nice scenic vignette	140.00
Ethel Consolidated Mines (I-N), 1900s, Washington, Trees and buildings vignette	30.00
Etowah Gold Mining (U), 1900s, Three mining vignettes	10.00
Eureka Climax Mining (U), 1910s, Nevada, Large mining vignette	4.00
Excelsior Coal (I), 1870s, Mining vignette	30.00
Excelsior Coal (U), 1870s, Mining vignette	13.00
Excelsior Drift Gold Mining (U), 1890s, train and factory vignette	12.00
Exchequer Gold and Silver Mining (I), 1900s, Ten paid assessments, elegant printing	10.00
Exchequer Mining (I), 1900s, Nevada, Company logo and miners vignette	11.00
Fagan Consolidated Silver Mines (I-N), 1920s, Nevada, Eagle with flag vignette	15.00
Fairbanks Gold and Silver Mining (I), 1880s, Colorado, Bond, mining vignette, state seal, gold seal	185.00
Fairview Gold Mining (I), 1880s, Colorado, Mining vignette	67.00
Fairview Golden Boulder Mining (U), 1900s, Golden boulder vignette	9.00
Farmer Jones Gold Mining (U), 1900s, Large mining scene with mining vignette at bottom	4.00
Farmsville Coal and Iron (U), 1890s, Mining scene with two factory vignettes	17.00

◀***Daly Mining (I), 1930s, Utah,*** *Three mining vignettes, gold seal* ***3.00***

◀***Edna Gold Mining Company (U), 1890s, California,*** *Mining vignette* ***10.00***

P. A. Simon, Resident Agent

Principal Place of Business, Mina, Nevada

Incorporated Under the Laws of the State of Nevada, November, 1919

№ 1363

SHARES 1000

Fagan Consolidated Silver Mines Company

CAPITAL STOCK $300,000.00
DIVIDED INTO 3,000,000 SHARES OF THE PAR VALUE OF 10c PER SHARE
FULLY PAID AND NON-ASSESSABLE

This Certifies that Epstein & Gartland is the owner of EXACTLY ONE THOUSAND Shares of the Capital Stock of

Fagan Consolidated Silver Mines Company

transferable only on the Books of the Corporation in person or by Attorney on surrender of this Certificate properly endorsed.

In Witness Whereof, the duly authorized officers of this Corporation have hereunto subscribed their names and caused the corporate Seal to be hereto affixed.

this 26 day of Nov A.D. 192

B F Baxby, Asst SECRETARY — P. A. Simon, PRESIDENT

NUMBER 1715

SHARES 50

ORGANIZED UNDER THE LAWS OF THE STATE OF NEVADA JANUARY 16TH, 1931

GENII CONSOLIDATED MINES COMPANY, LTD.

CAPITAL STOCK, $2,500,000
DIVIDED INTO 2,500,000 SHARES, PAR VALUE $1.00 EACH
FULLY PAID AND NON-ASSESSABLE

PRINCIPAL PLACE OF BUSINESS: 308 CLAY PETERS BLDG., RENO, NEVADA
WM. P. SEEDS, RESIDENT AGENT.

This Certifies That M. GROTYOHN. is the owner of FIFTY ONLY Shares of the Capital Stock of

Genii Consolidated Mines Company, Ltd.

transferable only on the Books of the Corporation in person or by Attorney on surrender of this Certificate properly endorsed.

In Witness Whereof, the duly authorized officers of this Corporation have hereunto subscribed their names and caused the corporate Seal to be hereto affixed

this day of NOV 23 1931 A. D. 19

M Grotyohn, ASST. SECRETARY — PRESIDENT

NOT VALID UNLESS COUNTERSIGNED BY REGISTRAR
COUNTERSIGNED AND REGISTERED
REGISTRATION SURETY COMPANY
SAN FRANCISCO, CALIFORNIA
ASST. SECRETARY
NOV 23 1931

Farwell Consolidated Mining (I), 1880s	43.00
Favorite Gold Mining (I), 1890s, Colorado, Mountains vignette, embossed seal	14.00
Favorite Gold Mining (I), 1900s, Colorado, Mountains vignette, embossed seal	10.00
Federal Hill Mining (U), 1900s, Two mining vignettes, seal	6.00
Findley Gold Mining Company (I), 1900s, Colorado, Rust seal	12.00
First National Mining (U), 1900s, Nevada, Loaded ore cars with miners and two burros at mining scene	12.00
Flagstaff Gold Mining Company (U), 1920s, Oregon, Three vignettes of mining scene, mountains and valleys	8.00
Flora Bell Mining (I), 1910s, Bond	12.00
Flusey Lead Company (I), 1900s, Washington, Miners vignette	12.00
Fredericksburg Mining (U), 1860s, One Indian and one naked man vignettes	70.00
Free Coinage Gold Mining (I), 1890s, Colorado, train, ship, and eagle vignette	20.00
Furnace Creek Copper (I), 1900s, California	11.00
Furnace Valley Copper Company (I), 1900s, California, Miners and horses working in tunnel vignette, seal	26.00
G. V. B. Mining (I), 1890s, Working miners vignette	40.00
Game Ridge Consolidiated Mines (I), 1900s, Train and smelter vignette	37.00
Game Ridge Consolidated Mining Company (I), Trustee certificate	40.00
Game Ridge Consolidated Mining Company (I-N), 1880s, Miners drilling in mine vignette	48.00
Garfield Consolidated Mining (I), 1890s, Wyoming	33.00
Garner Creek Gold Mining (I), 1900s, Colorado, Large mining vignette	20.00
Garner Creek Gold Mining (I), 1920s, Colorado, Large mining vignette	6.00
Genii Consolidated Mines Company, Ltd. (I-N), 1930s, Nevada, Large miners vignette	10.00
Geronimos Limited (I)	25.00
Gibraltar Silver Hill Mining (I-N), 1920s, Nevada, Mining vignette	10.00
Gila Copper Sulphate Company (I), 1910s, Arizona, Three vignettes	19.00
Gila River Mining of New Orleans (U), 1800s, New Mexico, Eagle and statue vignette	20.00
Gilbert Gold Pan Mining (U), 1900s, Nevada, Mining vignette	6.00
Gilpin-Eureka Mines Company (I), 1910s, Vignette of figures	8.00
Gilpin-Hurricane Gold Mining Co., the (I-N), 1910s, Mining vignette, gold seal	17.50
Glen Alden Coal Company (I), 1930s, Bond	8.00
Glen Alden Coal Company (I), 1930s, Miners working vignette	8.00
Glen Alden Coal Company (I), 1930s, Scrip certificate	1.00
Globe Dominion Copper Mine (I-N), 1910s, State seal	10.00
Gold and Silver Mining (U), 1860s, Mining scene, horses, and wagon vignette	15.00
Gold Center Mining and Development (I-N), 1900s, Arizona Territory, Mountain vignette	20.00
Gold Cliff Mining and Reduction of Arizona (I-N), 1890s, Eagle vignette	38.00
Gold Collar Mining and Milling, 1900s, Arizona, Embossed seal	8.00
Gold Eagle Mining and Milling (I), 1900s, Eagle vignette	15.00
Gold Exploration Company (I), 1890s, Colorado, Mining vignette	17.00
Gold Field and Bull Frog Coop Prospecting Mining (I), 1900s, Arizona, Portrait of Lincoln vignette	32.00
Gold Hill and Lee Mountain Mining (U), 1880s, Montana Territory, Mountain and mining scenes	25.00
Gold Hill Mining (U), California, Large smelting plant in Grass Valley vignette	18.00
Gold King Consolidated Mines (I), 1900s, Mine smelter with train vignette	25.00
Gold Mountain Company (I-N), 1880s, Nevada, 1,000 shares to Mark Twain	30.00
Gold Point Consolidated Mines, Incorporated (I), 1910s, Miners vignette	10.00
Gold Reef Consolidated Mining (I), 1900s, Nevada, Company logo	10.00
Gold Reef Consolidated Gold and Silver Mining (U), 1900s, Company logo	7.00

◀ ***Fagan Consolidated Silver Mines (I-N), 1920s, Nevada***, *Eagle with flag vignette*	*15.00*
◀ ***Genii Consolidated Mines Company, Ltd. (I-N), 1930s, Nevada***, *Large miners vignette*	*10.00*

INCORPORATED UNDER THE LAWS OF
ARIZONA
No 1076
Shares 500
The Gilpin Hurricane Gold Mining Co.
CAPITAL STOCK $3,000,000
This Certifies that John B. Nelson is the owner of
Five Hundred Shares of ONE DOLLAR each of the Capital Stock of
The Gilpin Hurricane Gold Mining Co., fully paid and non-assessable,
transferable only on the books of the Corporation by the holder hereof in person or by Attorney upon surrender of this Certificate properly endorsed.
In Witness Whereof, the said Corporation has caused this Certificate to be signed by its duly authorized officers and to be sealed with the Seal of the Corporation
this 7th day of July A.D. 1910
THE GILPIN HURRICANE GOLD MINING CO.
CORPORATE SEAL
ARIZONA
SECRETARY
PRESIDENT
SHARES $1.00 EACH

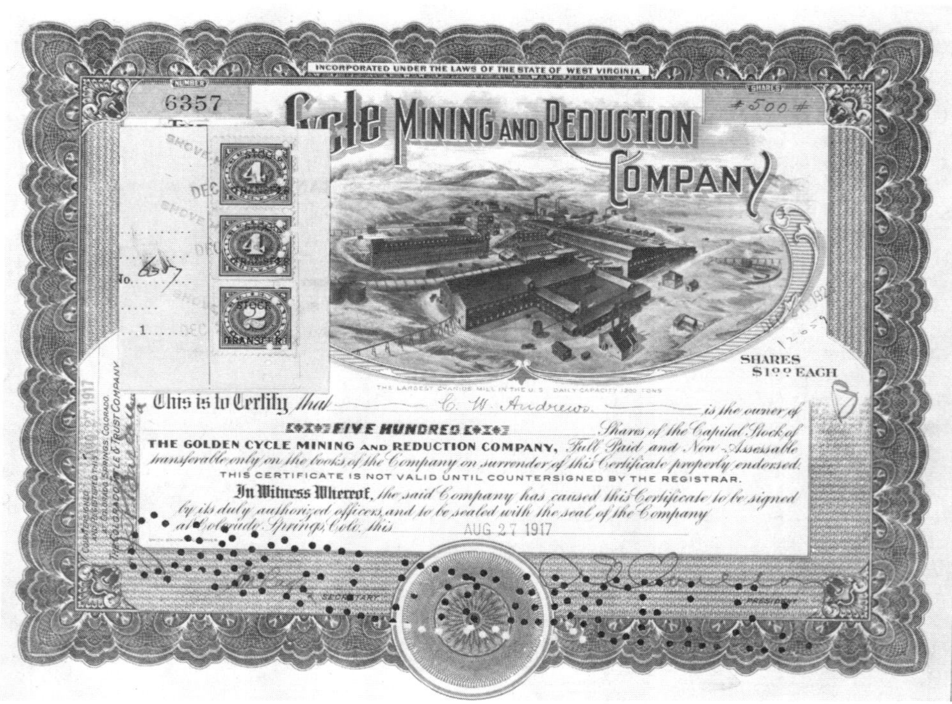
INCORPORATED UNDER THE LAWS OF THE STATE OF WEST VIRGINIA
NUMBER
6357
SHARES
#500#
Cycle Mining and Reduction Company
THE LARGEST CYANIDE MILL IN THE U.S. DAILY CAPACITY 1200 TONS
SHARES $1.00 EACH
This is to Certify that C. W. Andrews. is the owner of
FIVE HUNDRED Shares of the Capital Stock of
THE GOLDEN CYCLE MINING AND REDUCTION COMPANY, Full Paid and Non-Assessable
transferable only on the books of the Company on surrender of this Certificate properly endorsed.
THIS CERTIFICATE IS NOT VALID UNTIL COUNTERSIGNED BY THE REGISTRAR.
In Witness Whereof, the said Company has caused this Certificate to be signed by its duly authorized officers, and to be sealed with the seal of the Company
at Colorado Springs, Colo. this AUG 27 1917
COUNTERSIGNED AND REGISTERED THIS AUG 27 1917 AT COLORADO SPRINGS, COLORADO.
THE COLORADO TITLE & TRUST COMPANY
SECRETARY
PRESIDENT
STOCK TRANSFER
4½
STOCK TRANSFER
2

Gold Shield Mining Company (I), 1900s, Illinois, Mining vignette	17.00
Gold Tunnel Mining (I-N), 1900s, Arizona Territory, Working miners vignette	60.00
Gold Valley Main Tunnel and Mining (U), 1860s, California	20.00
Golden Age Number Two Mining and Milling Company (I), 1900s, Colorado	23.00
Golden Anchor Mining (I-N), 1900s, Arizona, Woman with wreath	23.00
Golden Cycle Mining and Reduction Company (I), 1910s, Large mining plant vignette	15.00
Golden Cycle Mining and Reduction Company (I), 1920s, Large mining plant vignette	6.00
Golden Cycle Mining and Reduction Company (I), 1930s, Large mining plant vignette	5.00
Golden Cycle Mining Company (I), 1910s, Temporary certificate with stamps	5.00
Golden Cycle Mining Company (I), 1920s, Colorado, Cripple Creek mines vignette, embossed seal	10.00
Golden Cycle Mining Company (I), 1950s, Milling plant vignette	4.00
Golden Cycle Mining Company (U), Temporary certificate	3.00
Golden Stairs Mining and Leasing (I), 1890s, Working miners vignette, embossed seal	16.00
Golden Treasure Company (I), 1900s, Arizona, Embossed seal	15.00
Goldfield Blue Bell Mining (I), 1900, Arizona, Mining vignette	17.00
Goldfield Combination Fraction Mining (I-N), 1910, Nevada, Working miners vignette, with stamps	17.50
Goldfield Deep Mines (I), 1950, Nevada	4.00
Goldfield Deep Mines (I-N), 1950, Nevada	6.00
Goldfield Ruby Hill Mining (I-N), 1900s, Arizona, Grey seal	9.00
Goldfield Treasure Mining (I), 1900s, Arizona Territory, Two mining vignettes	22.00
Good Morning Gold Mining Investment (I), 1900s, Arizona Territory, Miners with ore car at mine entrance, two miners on border vignettes	30.00
Gould and Curry Mining (I), 1920s	6.00
Gould and Curry Mining (I), 1930s, With stamps	8.00
Governor Low Gold and Silver Mining (U), 1860s, Nevada Territory, Eagle vignette	55.00
Granville Gold Company (I), 1880s, Working miners vignette	110.00
Grapevine Mining (I-N), 1900s, Nevada, Three mining vignettes	11.00
Great Caribo Gold Company (I), 1900s, South Dakota, Nine mining vignettes plus vials of gold nuggets	240.00
Great Northern Iron Ore (I), 1930s, Mining scene vignette	7.00
Great Northern Iron Ore (I), 1970s, Mining scene vignette	5.00
Great Northern Iron Ore Properties (I), 1970s, Western miners at mine shaft vignette, trustee's certificate	10.00
Great Republic Gold and Silver Mining (I), 1860s, Queen Victoria and Lincoln vignettes	170.00
Great Republic Gold and Silver Mining (I), 1860s, Miners at mine head and old railroad engine vignettes	65.00
Great Republic Gold and Silver Mining of Virginia (I), 1860s, Bond, fifty sterling, portrait of Queen Victoria and Lincoln, vignette of woman with winged eagle	365.00
Great Western Gold Mining and Milling (U), Mining vignette	10.00
Greater American Mining Company (I), Allegorical figures	20.00
Green Cananea Copper Company (I), 1930s, Mining vignette	5.00
Green Gold-Silver Company (I-N), 1900s, Mining vignette	18.00
Greene Gold-Silver Company (I), 1900s, Working miners vignette	21.00
Grey Eagle Consolidated Mining (I), 1880s, Colorado, Working miners, eagle vignettes, seal	60.00
Grimes Divide Mining (I-N), 1910s, Nevada, Eagle and distant ships vignette	8.00
Gruss Mining Company (I), 1920s, California, Large eagle vignette	5.00
Grutt-Davis Mines (U), 1900s, Nevada, Gold mining vignette along river	10.00
Guanajuato Consolidated Mining and Milling (I), 1890s	27.00
Guanajuato Consolidated Mining and Milling (I), 1900s, Two vignettes with eagles	25.00

◀ ***Gilpin-Hurricane Gold Mining Co., The (I-N), 1910s,*** *Mining vignette, gold seal* ***17.50***

◀ ***Golden Cycle Mining and Reduction Company (I), 1910s,*** *Large mining plant vignette* ***15.00***

INCORPORATED UNDER THE LAWS OF
Nevada, October 14th, 1916

NUMBER 255

SHARES ----500-----

Gold Point Consolidated Mines, Incorporated

Capital Stock $2,000,000 2,000,000 Shares

FULLY PAID UP AND FOREVER NON-ASSESSABLE

Principal Office
221 Odd Fellows Building
Reno, Nevada

Resident Agent
Mack and Green
221 Odd Fellows Building
Reno, Nevada

THIS CERTIFIES that ------A. N. Campbell------ is the owner of ***FIVE HUNDRED*** Shares of the Capital Stock of

Gold Point Consolidated Mines, Incorporated

Transferable only on the Books of the Corporation in person or by Attorney on surrender of this Certificate.

In Witness Whereof, the duly authorized officers of this Corporation have hereunto subscribed their names and caused the corporate Seal to be hereto affixed this ----------28th---------- day of -----December------ A.D. 1918.

Assistant Secretary

President

CANCELLED

SHARES $1.00 EACH

Guanajuato Consolidated Mining Company (I), 1920s, Virginia, American eagle and seal vignette 10.00
Guanajuato Consolidated Mining Company (I), 1930s, Virginia, American eagle and seal vignette 7.00
Guy Silver Mining (I), 1880s, Idaho Territory, Mining vignette 110.00

Hagan Coal Company (U), Working miners vignette, plus six men in border 6.00
Hailey-Ola Coal (U), 1900s, Oklahoma Territory, Flying eagle vignette 46.00
Hale and Norcross Mining Company (I), 1900s, Comstock lode, miner vignette 25.00
Hale and Norcross Mining Company (I), 1910s, Comstock lode, miner vignette 13.00
Hale and Norcross Mining Company (U), 1900s, Miner vignette 6.00
Hancock Reorganized Gold and Silver Mining (I), 1860s, Mining vignette, Quaker 42.00
Happy Jack Gold and Silver Mining (I), 1890s, Colorado, Working miners and ore cars vignette 45.00
Hartford Zinc (I), 1890s, Eagle vignette 22.00
Hartford Zinc (U), 1890s, Eagle vignette 6.00
Helca Mining and Milling (I), 1880s, Colorado, State seal 50.00
Helga Gold and Copper Mining (I-N), 1890s, Washington, Smelting plant vignette, gold seal, with stamps 20.00
Henwood Mines (U), 1860s, Old railroad scene 20.00
Herbertsville Quartz and Mining (I-N), 1850s, California 200.00
Hercules Wonder Mining Company (U), 1900s, Nevada, Eagle vignette 10.00
High Ore Gold Mining (I), 1900s, Nevada, Miners panning for gold, gold seal vignette 24.00
Highlander Mill and Mining (I-N), 1900s, Miners at mine entrance 40.00
Hinds Consolidated Mining (I), 1900s, Miner vignette 26.00
Hinsdale Horse Company (U), 1900s, Two mining vignettes 10.00
Hite Gold Quartz Company (I), 1880s, Mountain scenery vignette 75.00
Home Stake Mining (I), 1980s, California, Indians watching train vignette 15.00
Honest Gold and Silver Mining Company (U), 1860s, California, Mining vignette 33.00
Hortense Mining and Milling Company (U), 1900s, Colorado, Mining vignette 12.00
Hudson Bay Mining and Smelting (I), 1940s, Dogsled, airplane, and mine vignette 15.00
Hull Copper Company (I), 1900s, Arizona, Miners at work vignette 15.00
Humboldt River Gold and Silver Mining (I-N, 1860s), Working miners 115.00
Hunnapah Mining and Smelting (I), 1900s 12.00
Huron Copper Mining (I), 1890s, Michigan, Miners at work vignette, state seal 45.00
Huron Gold Ores Company (I), 1910s, Colorado, Mining vignette 12.00
Hurricane Mining (I-N), 1900s, Arizona Territory, Ship vignette 60.00

Idaho Mining and Milling (U), Eagle vignette 3.00
Idaho-Nevada Consolidated Gold Mines (I), 1920s, 7.5 percent gold bond, burning torch vignette. (Gold mine bonds are not plentiful.) 6.00
Imperial Consolidated Mining (I), 1910s, Arizona, Eagle vignette, seal 12.00
Indiana Mining Company (I), 1910s, Indians vignette 40.00
Indiana Mining Company (I), 1920s, Michigan, Indian chief vignette 36.00
Indian Queen Mining and Milling (I), 1880s, Indian maiden with bow and spear vignette 52.00
Industry Gold and Silver Mining (U), 1870s, Nevada, Large vignette of miner and ore car 32.00
Inferno Mining, Milling, and Power (I), 1920s, Colorado, Gold seal 8.00
Inter-Mountain Mining and Industrial Association (I), 1900s, Arizona, Embossed seal 10.00
International Minerals and Chemicals (I), 1970s, Mining vignette 3.00
International Mines Development Company (I), 1910s, Mining vignettes 10.00
International Syndicate of Mines (I-N), 1910s, Railroad coal cars vignette 12.00
Interstate Gold Beach and Bar Mining (I), 1900s, Colorado, Train and buildings vignette 12.00

◀ ***Gold Point Consolidated Mines, Incorporated (I), 1910s,*** *Miners vignette* ***10.00***

Number
C5650
Shares
50
COMMON STOCK $22,000,000. PREFERRED STOCK $3,000,000.
GREENE GOLD-SILVER COMPANY
INCORPORATED UNDER THE LAWS OF THE STATE OF WEST VIRGINIA
2,500,000 SHARES
SHARES $10 EACH
This is to Certify that
is the owner of
FIFTY
shares of the
Common Stock of the Greene Gold-Silver Company transferable only on the books of the company in person or by attorney on the surrender of this certificate properly endorsed.
COMMON
MAR 11 1907
SECRETARY.
PRESIDENT.
CAPITAL STOCK $25,000,000.
FULL PAID AND UNASSESSABLE

VIRGINIA MINING DIST. NEV.
CAPITAL
$112,000.
HALE & NORCROSS
MINING
Company
Nº 10258
-100-
SHARES
112,000 SHARES
$1.00 EACH
SAN FRANCISCO
1914
THIS CERTIFIES that
is entitled
to
Shares of the Capital Stock
OF THE HALE & NORCROSS MINING CO.
Transferable on the books of the Company by endorsement thereon and surrender of this Certificate.
SECRETARY.
PRESIDENT.

Interstate Mining Company (U), **1890s**, **Montana**, Miss Liberty, farmer, train, riverboat and blacksmith vignette **35.00**
Invincible Gold and Silver Mining and Milling (I), **1890s, Colorado**, Lake in mountains scene **16.00**
Invincible Gold and Silver Mining and Milling (I), **1900s, Colorado**, Lake in mountains scene **12.00**
Invincible Gold Mining (I), **1860s, Colorado**, With stamp **110.00**
Iowa Gulch Mining of Leadville (I), **1880s, Colorado**, Three different mining vignettes, plus seals **110.00**
Irwin Coal Company (I), **1850s**, Woman with eagle and four corner vignettes **235.00**
Isabella Gold Mining (I), **1890s**, Large eagle on flag, train, buffalo, and Indian vignette **15.00**
Isabella Gold Mining (I), **1900s**, Large eagle on flag, train, buffalo, and Indian vignette **8.00**
Island Creek Coal Company (I), **1920s**, Large mining vignette **12.00**
Island Creek Coal Company (I), **1930s**, Large mining vignette **10.00**
I-X-L Mining and Milling (I), **1880s**, Gold seal **75.00**

January Jones Leasing and Developing (I), **1900s, Nevada**, Miners at work and miners in border, seven vignettes **32.00**
Jay Gould Mining Company (U), **1880s, Montana Territory**, Working miners vignette **50.00**
Jefferson and Teton Mining (U), **1900s (but signed by president), Montana**, Eagle with flag vignette **5.00**
Jefferson Coal Company (I), **1890s**, Eagle vignette **15.00**
Jefferson Coal Company (U), **1890s**, Eagle vignette **4.00**
Jefferson Mines (I-N), **1920s, Montana**, Working miners vignette and mine and mountain vignette **10.00**
J-I-B Mining (I), **1920s**, Eagle vignette **8.00**
Jumbo Extension Mining (I), **1910s, Arizona**, Gold seal **15.00**
Jumbo Extension Mining (I-N), **1920s, Arizona**, Gold seal **15.00**
Jumbo Mining and Development (U), **1800s**, Large eagle, ship, Capitol dome vignette **9.00**
Juniata Mining and Manufacturing Company (U), **1800s**, Eagle, factories, and ship vignette, miners vignette, old train vignette, and portrait vignette **25.00**

Kent Mining (I), **1880s**, Embossed seal **28.00**
Kentucky Block Cannel Coal Company (I), **1900s**, Gold bond **27.00**
Keweenau Copper (I-N), **1900s, Michigan**, Elk and eagle vignette **20.00**
King Edward Silver Mines (I), **1900s**, King Edward vignette **15.00**
Kirkland Iron (I), **1880s**, Beehive vignette **43.00**
Klamath Placer Mining (I), **1900s**, Gold bond, Indian on horse vignette, plus mountain mining scene vignette **130.00**

Lacalifornia Mining and Milling (I), **1900s, Arizona Territory**, Mining vignette **20.00**
"La Fe" Mining (U), **1900s, Texas**, Three mining vignettes **7.00**
Lake Caswell Mines (I-N), **1930s** **2.00**
Lake Copper Company (I), **1910s, Michigan**, Miss Liberty and workers vignette **10.00**
Lake Copper Company (I), **1920s, Michigan**, Miss Liberty and workers vignette **9.00**
Lake Erie, Alliance and Wheeling Coal Company (U), **1900s**, Miners with ore car, train, ship, blacksmith, and farmer vignette **25.00**
Langdon-Henzey Coal Mining (I-N), **1890s**, Bond, miners vignette **43.00**
La Reforma Mining (I-N), **1900s**, Scarce, only two known, three surface mining vignettes, gold seal **20.00**
La Rose Mines (I), **1920s**, Working miners vignette **6.00**
L C O, Inc. Nevada Mines **1.00**
Lehigh and Wilkes-Barre Corporation, 1920s, Specimen bond **95.00**
Lehigh Coal and Navigation Company (I), **1860s**, Building vignette, revenue stamp **55.00**

◀ ***Greene Gold-Silver Company (I), 1900s,*** *Working miners vignette* ***21.00***
◀ ***Hale and Norcross Mining Company (I), 1910s,*** *Comstock lode, miner vignette* ***13.00***

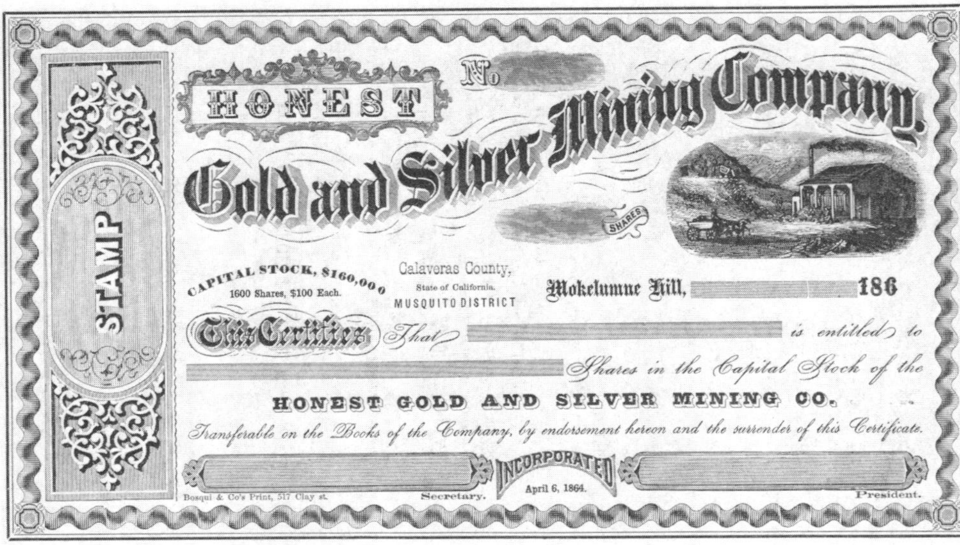

No

HONEST

Gold and Silver Mining Company.

SHARES

CAPITAL STOCK, $160,000

1600 Shares, $100 Each.

Calaveras County,

State of California.

MUSQUITO DISTRICT

Mokelumne Hill, 186

STAMP

This Certifies That is entitled to Shares in the Capital Stock of the

HONEST GOLD AND SILVER MINING CO.

Transferable on the Books of the Company, by endorsement hereon and the surrender of this Certificate.

INCORPORATED

April 6, 1864.

Bosqui & Co's Print, 517 Clay st.

Secretary.

President.

INCORPORATED UNDER THE LAWS OF THE STATE OF

Montana.

NUMBER

737

SHARES

CAPITAL STOCK. $500 000.00.

Inter-State Mining Company,

SHARES $1.00 EACH. OF HELENA, MONTANA. ASSESSABLE.

This certifies that is the owner of Shares of the Capital Stock of

Inter-State Mining Company,

transferable only on the Books of the Corporation in person or by Attorney on surrender of this Certificate.

In Witness Whereof the duly authorized officers of this Corporation have hereunto subscribed their names and caused the corporate Seal to be hereto affixed at this day of A.D. 189

Secretary.

President.

Shares $1.00 Each.

Lehigh Coal and Navigation Company (I), 1860s, Mining village in mountains vignette	**90.00**
Lehigh Coal and Navigation Company (I), 1920s, Two photos and horses with eagle	**15.00**
Lehigh Coal and Navigation Company (I), 1930s, Portrait of Two founders vignette	**5.00**
Lehigh Coal and Navigation Company (I), 1940s, Vignette of two founders	**4.00**
Lehigh Coal and Navigation Company (I), 1950s and 1960s, vignette of two founders	**3.00**
Le-Nouveau Mondo Mining (I-N), 1850s	**95.00**
Lewis Mountain Mining and Milling, 1910s, Colorado, Eagle vignette, seal	**10.00**
Lewis Mountain Mining and Milling, 1920s, Colorado, Eagle vignette, seal	**8.00**
Liberty Mining (I) 1850s,	**88.00**
Lincoln Bessemer Company (I), 1880s, Gold seal, mining vignette	**78.00**
Lisbon Valley Uranium (I), 1950s, Eagle vignette	**4.00**
Little Bell Consolidated Mining Company (I), 1910s, Utah, Working miners by candles vignette	**20.00**
Little Bell Gold Mining (I), 1900s, Colorado, Two mining vignettes	**22.00**
Little Butte Extension Mining (I-N), 1890s, Working miners vignette, gold seal	**22.00**
Little Chief Mining (I), 1880s, Colorado, Large mining vignette	**95.00**
Logan County Mining and Manufacturing (I), 1850s, Two ore trains and tunnels vignettes, red seal	**360.00**
London Mining (I), 1880s, Gold bond	**45.00**
London Mining (I), 1880s, Colorado	**30.00**
Louise Mining Company (I), 1910s, Utah, Three small mining vignettes	**10.00**
Lubec Lead and Zinc Company (I) 1900s, Miners vignette	**10.00**
Lucky Mc-Uranium Corporation (I), 1950s, Nevada, Large vignette of mining camp	**7.00**
Lump Gulch Silver Mines Company (U), 1900s, Montana, One signature, eagle with flag vignette, gold seal	**10.00**
Luning Consolidated Silver Mines (I), 1920s, Unique mining vignette	**12.00**
Lykens Valley Coal Mine (I), 1830s, Working blacksmith, embossed seal	**250.00**
Lykens Valley Coal Mine (I), 1840s	**125.00**
Lykens Valley Coal Mines (I), 1850s	**75.00**
Lynch–Pine Creek Mining (U), Idaho, Two mining vignettes, one mountain vignette	**9.00**
McLeod River Mining (I-N), 1930s, Grey seal, company logo	**4.00**
McMillan Gold Mines (I-N), 1930s	**4.00**
Macnamara Mining and Milling (I-N), 1920s, Nevada, Small certificate	**12.00**
Macnamara Mining and Milling (I), 1910s, Nevada	**7.00**
Madeleine Mining Company (I-N), Utah, Two mining vignettes	**15.00**
Maginnis Mining Company (U), 1890s, Montana	**10.00**
Magma Copper (I), 1910s, Large smelting plant in mountains vignette	**4.00**
Magma Copper (I), 1920s, Large smelting plant in mountains vignette	**3.00**
Magma Copper (I), 1930s, 1940s, 1950s and 1960s, Large smelting plant in mountains vignette	**2.00**
Magma Silver Lead Mines (U), 1900s, Washington, Eagle and ships vignette, gold seal	**5.00**
Maid of Orleans Oil, Chemical, Mining and Developing, 1900s	**7.00**
Maine and New Hampshire Granite (I), 1890s, Train and mountains vignette	**28.00**
Malachite Mining (I), 1870s, Mine scene, Indian maidens vignettes	**78.00**
Mammoth Gold Mining (I-N), 1900s, Mining scene in mountains, with stamp	**35.00**
Manhattan Gold Mines (I-N), Two stamps	**10.00**
Manhattan Silver Mining of Nevada (U), 1860s, Mining vignette	**48.00**
Maricopa Mica Mining Company (U), 1890s, Arizona Territory, Two mining vignettes, plus a female vignette	**10.00**

◀ ***Honest Gold and Silver Mining Company (U), 1960s, California,*** *Mining vignette* — ***33.00***

◀ ***Interstate Mining Company (U), 1890s, Montana,*** *Miss Liberty, farmer, train, riverboat, and blacksmith vignette* — ***35.00***

INCORPORATED UNDER THE LAWS
OF THE TERRITORY OF MONTANA
JAY GOULD
CAPITAL
$2,000,000.
MINING
COMPANY
SHARES
$ 5 EACH.
ASSESSABLE
No 470
HELENA, M.T.
Shares.
This is to Certify that
is entitled to
Shares of Five Dollars Each
of the Capital Stock of the JAY GOULD MINING COMPANY.
Transferable only on the Books of the Company in person or by Attorney on
the surrender of this Certificate.
Witness. The Seal of the Company and the signatures of the President and
Secretary at Helena, M.T. this day of 18
Secretary
President.

SHARES $ 50 EACH.
NUMBER
SHARES
JUNIATA MINING AND MANUFACTURING COMPANY
TYRONE, BLAIR CO. PA.
STATE OF
PENNSYLVANIA
This is to Certify that
entitled to
Shares in the Capital Stock of
the JUNIATA MINING & MANUFACTURING CO. Transferable only in person
or by attorney on the books of the said Company on surrender of this Certificate
Witness the Signatures of the President and
Treasurer and the Corporate Seal of the said Company
at Tyrone, Penna. 18
President.
Treasurer.

Mariposa Land and Mining (I), 1870s, California, Unique grizzly bear scene 53.00
Mariposa Land and Mining (I), 1880s, California, Unique grizzly bear scene 47.00
Marquette Iron (I), 1920s, Mining vignette 15.00
Maryland and New York Iron and Coal Company (I), 1840s, Bond 300.00
Maryland Gold Mining (I-N), 1860s, Mining scenes 150.00
Maryland Smokeless Company (I), 1900s, West Virginia, Gold bond with stamps, miners 75.00
Mascot Mining (I-N), 1900s, Three mining vignettes, gold seal 15.00
Massachusetts and New Mexico Consolidated Mining Company (I), 1880s, Bonds with coupons, eagle vignette 65.00
Massachusetts and New Mexico Consolidated Mining Company (I), 1880s, Miners at mine shaft vignette 43.00
Mattie-Bullfrog Mining and Milling (I), 1900s, Territory of Arizona, Large mining scene, gold seal 22.00
Merced Gold Mining (I), 1890s, Montana, Mining vignette 32.00
Mercer Mining and Manufacturing Company, 1860s, Train vignette, revenue stamp 115.00
Merrimac Consolidated Mines (I), 1900s, Colorado, Mining vignette, gold seal 12.00
Mexican Gold and Silver Mining (I), 1920s 6.00
Mexican Premier Mines (I), 1920s, Idaho 4.00
Mexico Consolidated Mining and Smelting (I), 1910s, Maine 16.00
Middlefork Mining Company (U), 1880s, Montana Territory 15.00
Middle States Coal and Iron Mines (I), 1900s, Large mining vignette flanked by two women 38.00
Midway Gold Mining (I), 1900s 9.00
Midway Gold Mining (I-N), 1900s, Colorado, Gold seal 5.00
Mildred Gold Mining (I), 1910s, Arizona, Working miners vignettes, embossed seal 22.00
Mills Post and White Consolidated Silver Mining (UI), 1860s, Nevada Territory, Mining vignette 28.00
Milwaukee Mines (U), 1900s, Idaho, Seal 4.00
Milwaukee Mines (I-N), 1930s 4.00
Milwaukee Mines 1940s 1.00
Milwaukee Mining and Milling Company (I), 1910s, New Mexico, Two mining vignettes 16.00
Milwaukee Mining and Milling Company (U), 1910s, New Mexico, Large eagle with shield vignette, gold seal 6.00
Mineral Spring Mining (I), 1860s, Miner at work vignette 155.00
Miners's Hope Gold and Silver Mining Company (U), 1870s, Nevada, Miners with packs and shovels vignette 35.00
Miners' Hope Tunnel Gold and Silver Mining (U), 1800s, Several miners vignette, one signature 37.00
Mines Company of America (I-N), 1910s, Maine,Miners equipment vignette 18.00
Mines Developing and Operating (U), 1900s, New Jersey, Allegorical figures with state seal 4.00
Mining Development Corporation (I), Three mining vignettes 8.00
Mining Development Corporation (U), Montana, Founders participation certificate, mine works exterior vignette 5.00
Mission Development (I), 1950s, Facsimile signature of J. Paul Getty 5.00
Mitchell Mining Company (I), 1900s 18.00
Mitchell Mining Company (I-N), 1900s, Arizona, Large mining scene, with stamps 15.00
Mogul Drainage and Transportation Tunnel and Mining (I), 1900s, Seal 15.00
Mohawk Mining (I), 1910s, Indian chief vignette 28.00
Mohawk Mining (I), 1920s, Indian chief vignette 26.00

Jay Gould Mining Company (U), 1880s, Montana Territory, *Working miners vignette* ***50.00***

Juniata Mining and Manufacturing Company (U), 1800s, *Eagle, factories, and ship vignette, miners vignette, old train vignette, and portrait vignette* ***25.00***

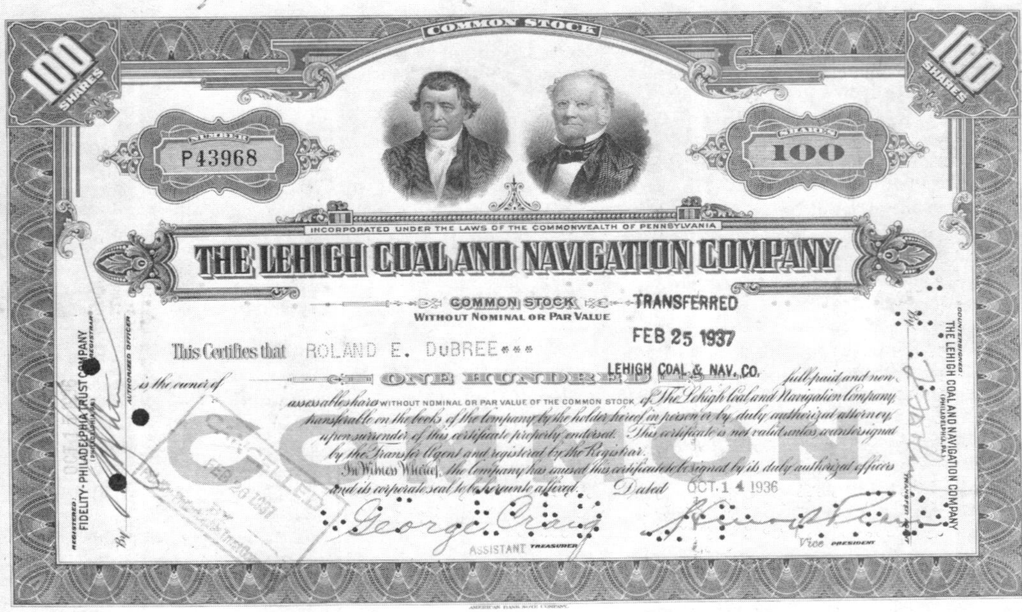

COMMON STOCK

100 SHARES

NUMBER P43968

SHARES 100

INCORPORATED UNDER THE LAWS OF THE COMMONWEALTH OF PENNSYLVANIA

THE LEHIGH COAL AND NAVIGATION COMPANY

COMMON STOCK
WITHOUT NOMINAL OR PAR VALUE

TRANSFERRED
FEB 25 1937
LEHIGH COAL & NAV. CO.

This Certifies that ROLAND E. DuBREE***
is the owner of ONE HUNDRED full paid and non-assessable shares WITHOUT NOMINAL OR PAR VALUE OF THE COMMON STOCK of The Lehigh Coal and Navigation Company transferable on the books of the Company by the holder hereof in person or by duly authorized attorney upon surrender of this certificate properly endorsed. This certificate is not valid unless countersigned by the Transfer Agent and registered by the Registrar.

In Witness Whereof, the company has caused this certificate to be signed by its duly authorized officers and its corporate seal to be hereunto affixed. Dated OCT. 1 4 1936

ASSISTANT TREASURER

VICE PRESIDENT

REGISTERED: FIDELITY-PHILADELPHIA TRUST COMPANY (PHILADELPHIA) REGISTRAR

AUTHORIZED OFFICER

COUNTERSIGNED: THE LEHIGH COAL AND NAVIGATION COMPANY (PHILADELPHIA, PA.) TRANSFER AGENT

CANCELLED FEB 26 1937

AMERICAN BANK NOTE COMPANY

No. 230

SHARES

INCORPORATED UNDER THE LAWS OF MONTANA

LUMP GULCH SILVER MINES COMPANY

CAPITAL STOCK $1,000,000

FULLY PAID NON-ASSESSABLE

This Certifies that ________ is the owner of ________ Shares of the Capital Stock of

Lump Gulch Silver Mines Company

transferable only on the Books of the Corporation in person or by Attorney on surrender of this Certificate properly endorsed.

In Witness Whereof, the duly authorized officers of this Corporation have hereunto subscribed their names, and caused the corporate Seal to be hereto affixed at Helena, this ____ day of ____ A.D. 19__

Secretary President

SHARES $1.00 EACH

Mojave Consolidated Gold and Silver Mining (I), 1870s, Arizona		135.00
Mollie Gibson Consolidated Mining and Milling (I), 1890s, Mining scene		55.00
Mollie Gibson Mining (I), 1910s		20.00
Molybdenum Mining Company (I), 1900s, Colorado, Smelting plant in mountains vignette		16.00
Montana Clinton Copper (U), 1900s, Montana,		3.00
Montana Coal and Coke (I), 1900s, Bond, ore train, ovens, and workers vignette		24.00
Montana Gold and Gem Mining Company (U), 1890s, Montana, Miners and ore cars vignette		40.00
Montana Mining (I), 1890s, California		20.00
Montevideo Mining and Milling (I), 1890s, Colorado, Large mining vignette, gold seal		25.00
Montezuma Mining Company (I-N), 1900, The beehive vignette		10.00
Monument Uranium (I), 1970s, Utah, Mining vignette, gold seal		5.00
Moraine Mining (UI), 1900s, Illinois, Eagle vignette		3.00
Morington Mining (I-N), 1920s, Nevada		8.00
Morris and Essex Mutual Coal Company (I), 1860s, Large vignette of Indian, ship, train, and seven figures, revenue stamp		95.00
Mother Lode Coalition Mines (I), 1920s, Working miners vignette		11.00
Mother Lode Coalition Mines (I), 1940s, Working miners vignette		9.00
Mother Lode Gold Mining (I), 1900s, Washington, Liberty and flag, gold seal		18.00
Mounier Metallurgical Company (I), 1860s, Colorado, State seal plus stamp		42.00
Mountain Queen Mining (I), 1880s, Colorado, Two mining vignettes plus large smelting works, silver seal		90.00
Mount Hayden Mining and Milling (I), 1910s, Colorado, Mining vignette, gold seal		16.00
Mount Pleasant Coal Company (I), 1870s, Bond, old train in mountains vignette		245.00
Mount Tritle Copper (I), 1900s Arizona, Nice mining vignette		16.00
Mowry Silver Mining (I), 1880s, Miner vignette		35.00
Myrtle Gold Mining (I), 1900s, Arizona Territory, Allegorical figure		50.00
Nacimiento Copper Company (I-N), 1880s, Territory of New Mexico, Gold bond, with all coupons, large mining vignette		130.00
Nancy Donaldson Mining Company (I-N), 1900s, Wyoming, Mines in Nevada		9.00
National Anthracite Coal Company (I), 1850s, Pennsylvania, Train, eagle and so on, eight vignettes		373.00
National Tunnel and Mines (I), 1940s, Working miners vignette		5.00
National Nickel Company (I-N), 1890s, Mining vignette		25.00
Natomas Company (I), California, Large gold-dredging vignette		11.00
Nevada Belmont Copper Mines (U), 1900s, Arizona, Train, miner and mules vignettes		7.00
Nevada Boy Goldfield Mining (I-N), 1900s, South Dakota, Lady vignette, gold seal		20.00
Nevada Eagle Gold Mine and Milling (U), 1900s, Eagle vignette		15.00
Nevada-Goldfield Lease Company (I), 1900s, Embossed seal		15.00
Nevada Hills Florence Mining, 1890s		10.00
Nevada-Ramona Mining and Milling Company (I), 1900s, Nevada, Scenic vignette with Indian and harbor		18.00
Nevada Silver Horn Mining (I), 1920s		10.00
New Almaden Quicksilver Mines (I), California		6.00
New Bedford Silver Mining Company of Utah (I), 1880s, Utah Territory, Winged eagle vignette		95.00
New Cornelia Copper Company (I), 1920s, Machinery loading ore cars vignette		8.00
New Dominion Copper (I), Arizona, Mining vignette		8.00
New Dominion Copper (U), Arizona, Mining vignette		3.00
New Emma Silver Mining (I), 1880s, Mining vignette, embossed seal		30.00
New England Mining of Colorado (I), 1860s, Colorado, With revenue stamps		130.00

◀ ***Lehigh Coal and Navigation Company (I), 1930s,*** *Portrait of two founders vignette* ***5.00***

◀ ***Lump Gulch Silver Mines Company (U), 1900s, Montana,*** *One signature, eagle with flag vignette, gold seal* ***10.00***

INCORPORATED UNDER THE LAWS OF THE STATE OF
ILLINOIS
Mines in Arizona

NUMBER 245

SHARES

MARICOPA MICA MINING COMPANY

Capital Stock $1,000,000.

This Certifies that ______ is the owner of ______ Shares of Ten Dollars each of the Capital Stock of MARICOPA MICA MINING COMPANY. Full paid and non-assessable transferable only on the Books of the Corporation in person or by Attorney on surrender of this Certificate.

In Witness Whereof the duly authorized officers of this Corporation have hereunto subscribed their names and caused the corporate Seal to be hereto affixed.
this ______ day of ______ A.D. 189

Secretary President

SHARES $10 EACH

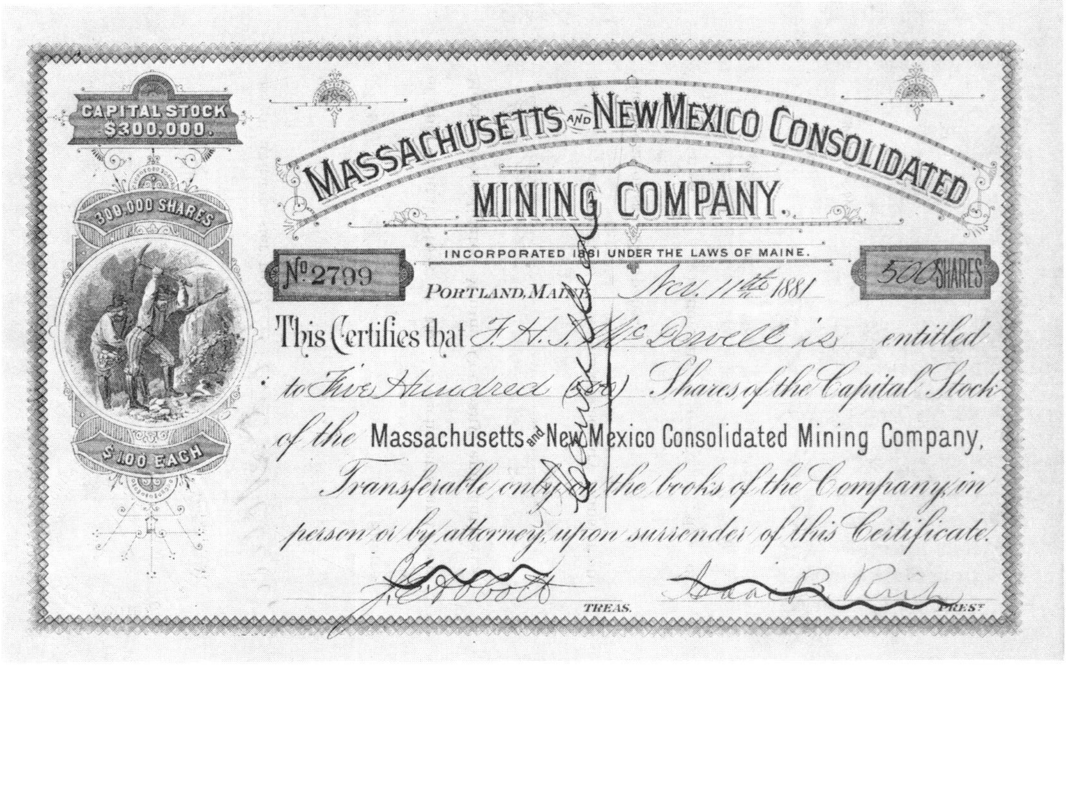

CAPITAL STOCK $300,000.

300,000 SHARES

$100 EACH

MASSACHUSETTS AND NEW MEXICO CONSOLIDATED MINING COMPANY.

INCORPORATED 1881 UNDER THE LAWS OF MAINE.

No. 2799

500 SHARES

PORTLAND, MAINE, Nov. 11th 1881

This Certifies that F. H. T. McDowell is entitled to Five Hundred (500) Shares of the Capital Stock of the Massachusetts and New Mexico Consolidated Mining Company, Transferable only on the books of the Company in person or by attorney, upon surrender of this Certificate.

J. E. Abbott TREAS.

PREST.

New Idria Mining and Chemical (I), 1960s, Nevada, Eagle vignette	**3.00**
New Idria Mining and Chemical (I-N), 1960s, Nevada	**4.00**
New Idria Mining and Chemical (I), 1970s, Nevada, Eagle vignette	**2.00**
New Jersey Consolidated Mines (I-N), Idaho, Woman with flag and eagle vignette	**6.00**
New Mexico Minerals (I), 1960s, Large eagle vignette	**2.00**
New Mexico Mining (I), 1860s, Hole from mining stamp	**55.00**
New Mexico Mining Company (I), 1850s, New Mexico, Small mining town with church in mountains vignette	**130.00**
New Quincy Mining (I), 1920s, Utah, Working miners vignette	**7.00**
New Tonopah Dividend Mining Company (I), 1920s, Two mining vignettes	**10.00**
New Tonopah Dividend Mining Company (I-N), 1930s, Lady vignette, gold seal	**11.00**
New York and Calaveras County Gold Mining (I), 1880s, Scenic view vignette	**60.00**
New York and Montana Mining and Discovery (I), 1860s, Miners vignette, with revenue stamp	**195.00**
New York and Silver Mining (I), 1860s, Mining vignette	**125.00**
New York and Ohio Coal (I), 1870s, Bond, miners at work vignette	**245.00**
New York and Ohio Coal (I), 1890s, Bond, gold seal, woman vignette	**160.00**
New York and Providence Mining, Milling and Smelting (I-N), 1880s, Three mining vignettes	**65.00**
New York and Utah Prospecting and Mining Company (I-N), 1860s, New York, Mining vignette	**145.00**
New York Central Gold Mining (I), 1890s, Large mining vignette	**30.00**
New York Central Gold Mining Company of Colorado (I), 1860s, Bond with stamp	**175.00**
Newark Mining and Milling Company (I-N), 1910s, Maine, Gold bond, working miners vignette	**15.00**
Newark Mining and Milling Company (I), 1910s, Working miners vignette	**45.00**
Newfoundland Gold Mining Company (U), 1880s, Colorado, Working miners in mine with ore car vignette	**18.00**
Newmont Mining (I), 1950s, Eagle between two men vignette	**2.00**
Newmont Mining (I), 1960s and 1970s, Eagle between two men vignette	**1.00**
Nixon Nevada Mining (I-N), 1910s	**10.00**
Nome Exploration Company (U), 1900s, Alaska, Large mining vignette	**22.00**
Non Pareil Mining and Smelting (I-N), 1880s	**45.00**
North American Dredging Company of Nevada (I-N), 1900s, Gold bond with coupons, gold mining vignette	**20.00**
North American Mining (I), 1920s, Eagle vignette	**6.00**
North American Mines (U), 1900s, Eagle with shield vignette, president's signature	**3.00**
North American Mining (U), Colorado, Eagle vignette	**4.00**
North Butte Mining (I), 1900s, Mining scene vignette	**4.00**
North Butte Mining (I), 1910s, Mining vignette	**4.00**
North Butte Mining (I), 1920s, Mining vignette	**3.00**
North Butte Mining (I), 1930s, Mining vignette	**3.00**
North Lake Mining (I), 1920s, Michigan, Working miners vignette	**25.00**
North Mexican Mining and Milling (I), 1880s	**30.00**
North Span Uranium Mines (I-N), 1950s, Warrant	**1.00**
North Standard Gold and Silver (I), 1870s, California	**35.00**
North Standard Gold and Silver (I), 1880s, California	**30.00**
North Utah Mining (I), 1900s, Large mining vignette	**25.00**
Northern Mining and Smelting (U), 1890s	**17.00**
Norwegian Consolidated Mining (I), 1900s, California, Working miners vignettes, gold seal	**25.00**
Norwegian Consolidated Mining (U), 1900s, Arizona Territory	**6.00**

◀ ***Maricopa Mica Mining Company (U), 1890s, Arizona Territory,*** *Two mining vignettes, plus a female vignette* ***10.00***

◀ ***Massachusetts and New Mexico Consolidated Mining Company (I), 1880s,*** *Miners at mine shaft vignette* ***43.00***

INCORPORATED UNDER THE LAWS OF ARIZONA.

CAPITAL STOCK, $8.000.000.00.

100

Mitchell Mining Company

Prescott, Ariz. Mar 12 1907

-100-
SHARES

№ 11460

800,000 SHARES.

PAR VALUE $10.00 EACH

This certifies that W. C. Douglas is the owner of One hundred shares of the capital stock of the MITCHELL MINING COMPANY. Fully paid and non-assessable. Transferable only on the Books of the Company in person or by Attorney on surrender of this Certificate.

IN WITNESS WHEREOF the duly authorized officers of this Corporation have hereunto subscribed their names and caused the corporate Seal to be hereunto affixed this day and year aforesaid.

COUNTERSIGNED & REGISTERED this 13 day of MAR 1907
KNICKERBOCKER TRUST COMPANY, REGISTRAR.
by
SECRETARY.

Philip S. Dyer
VICE President.

Asst. Secretary.

FULL PAID.

Incorporated under the laws of
MAINE.

NON-ASSESSABLE.

NUMBER
81

SHARES
=3000=

The Montezuma Mining Company.

CAPITAL, $750,000.

PREFERRED STOCK, $250,000.
SHARES, $10.00 EACH.

COMMON STOCK, $500,000.
SHARES, $5.00 EACH.

This Certifies, *that* Katharine Fricke *is the owner of* Three thousand *Shares of the Preferred Stock of* **THE MONTEZUMA MINING COMPANY,** *par value Ten Dollars per share, transferable only on the books of the Company, in person or by Attorney, on the surrender of this Certificate.*

The Preferred Stock is entitled to receive dividends (cumulative) at the rate of seven per cent. per annum out of net earnings available for dividends in any calendar year before any dividend whatever shall be declared on the Common Stock in such year; then the surplus of said net earnings if any, is to be applied to dividends on Common Stock in said calendar year. That in the event of liquidation or dissolution of the corporation Preferred Stock shall first be paid in full at par. The Company reserve the right to retire any or all of the Preferred Stock on and after January 1, 1905, at $11.00 and dividends

PREFERRED

In Witness Whereof, *the duly authorized officers of this Corporation have hereunto subscribed their names and caused the corporate Seal to be hereto affixed this* twenty sixth *day of* April *A. D. 190*5.

Richard Briggs
PRESIDENT.

F. H. Fricke
TREASURER.

Oakland-Goldfield Mining (I-N), 1900s, Nevada	15.00
Oatman Combination Mining (I), 1910s, Large eagle with shield vignette	6.00
Ohio Central Coal (I), 1880s, Bond, miners in mine with ore cars vignette	185.00
Ohio Copper Company of Utah (I), 1920s, Miners working in tunnel vignette	17.00
Ojibway Mining (I), 1910s, Michigan, Indian chief vignette	50.00
Old Gold Mines (I), 1900s Wyoming	8.00
Old Gold Mining (I-N), 1920s, Company logo	9.00
Olympic Mining (I), 1900s, Washington, Mountains, mine, and stream vignette, gold seal	15.00
Omega Mining (I), 1900s, Arizona Territory, Mining vignette	15.00
Onandago Copper (I), 1930s, Michigan	4.00
Ontario Silver Mining Company 1910s, Utah, Beehive vignette	12.00
Operator Consolidated Mines (I-N), 1930s, Three mining vignettes, gold seal	10.00
Ophir Gold Mines (I), 1950s, Lady vignette and Colorado seal	2.00
Ora Tahoma Mining (U), Three mining vignettes, gold seal	3.00
Oregon Gold Prospecting and Promoting (I), 1900s, Bond, eagle vignette	25.00
Oriental Gold Mining (I), 1880s, Miner and standing woman vignette	55.00
Original Bullfrog Mines (U), 1900s, Arizona, Bullfrog imprint	35.00
Original Hidden Treasure Mining Company (U), 1860s, Nevada, Eagle vignette	25.00
Original Hidden Treasure Mining Company (U), 1870s, Eagle vignette	21.00
Oro Amigo Plating Mining (I-N), 1920s, Nice mining vignette	12.00
Orphan Bell Mining and Milling Company (I), 1890s, Colorado, Working miners vignette	30.00
Orphan Bell Mining and Milling Company (U), 1900s, Colorado, Working miners vignette	12.00
Orphan Gold Mining (I), 1900s, Railroad plus workers vignette	15.00
Overland gold (I) 1890s,	11.00
Owensburg Coal (I-N), 1920s, Deer in mountains vignette	12.00
Pacific Coal and Transportation (I), 1900s, Gold bond, miners working with ore cars in mine vignette	85.00
Pacific Copper (I-N), 1900s, Scarce (only two known), with stamp	18.00
Pacific Copper Mining Company (I), 1910s, Arizona, Two mining vignettes	16.00
Pacific Smelting and Mining (I), 1910s, Eagle vignette	18.00
Palouse Coal (U), 1900s, Mining camp vignette	15.00
Pan-American Mining and Developing (I), 1940s, Mining vignette	17.00
Panther Creek Mining (I), 1900s,	20.00
Park Tunnel and Mining and Milling (I), 1910s, Working miners vignette, seal	9.00
Parrot Silver and Copper (I), 1890s, Montana	12.00
Patino Mines and Enterprises (I), 1950s, Delaware, Miners and equipment vignette	5.00
Patricia Mining (I), 1920s, Idaho, Attached accounting sheet with stamp, four mining vignettes	8.00
Patterson Mines, Inc. (I-N), 1930s, Washington, Gold seal, two mining vignettes, large mountain scene	7.00
Patti-Rosa Gold Mining (U), 1890s, Mining vignette	14.00
Pay Divide Mining (I), 1920s, Nevada, Three $1,000 paid assessments, with stamp	6.00
Paymaster Gold Mining and Milling (U), 1900s, Gold seal	15.00
Peerless Gold Mine Development Company (U), 1890s, California	9.00
Pelican and Dives Mining (I), 1880s, Working miners scene	55.00
Pemberton Hydraulic Gold Mining (I), 1870s, California, Mine scene	80.00
Pemberton Hydraulic Gold Mining (I), 1880s, California, Mine scene	70.00
Penn Valley Coal (I), 1920s, Bond	4.00
Pennsylvania Consolidated Mining (I), 1890s, California	18.00
Penn-Yan Mining Company (U), 1880s, Montana, Vignette of gold and silver coins in color	78.00
Peruvian Mining, Smelting and Refining (I), 1900s, Eagle, justice and llama vignette	7.00

◀ ***Mitchell Mining Company (I-N), 1900s, Arizona,*** *Large mining scene, with stamps* ***15.00***

◀ ***Montezuma Mining Company, The (I-N), 1900s,*** *Beehive vignette* ***10.00***

CERTIFICATE FOR LESS THAN ONE HUNDRED SHARES

NUMBER 19497

SHARES -25-

NEW CORNELIA COPPER COMPANY

INCORPORATED UNDER THE LAWS OF THE STATE OF DELAWARE.

This Certifies that PAINE, WEBBER & CO. -----
is the owner of ----- TWENTY FIVE ----- fully paid and non-assessable Shares of the Capital Stock of New Cornelia Copper Company of the par value of Five (5) dollars each, transferable in person or by attorney upon surrender of this certificate properly endorsed.
This Certificate is not valid until countersigned by the Transfer Agent and registered by the Registrar.
Witness the seal of New Cornelia Copper Company and the signatures of its duly authorized officers this DEC 8-1928

CAPITAL STOCK

CANCELLED JAN 22 1929

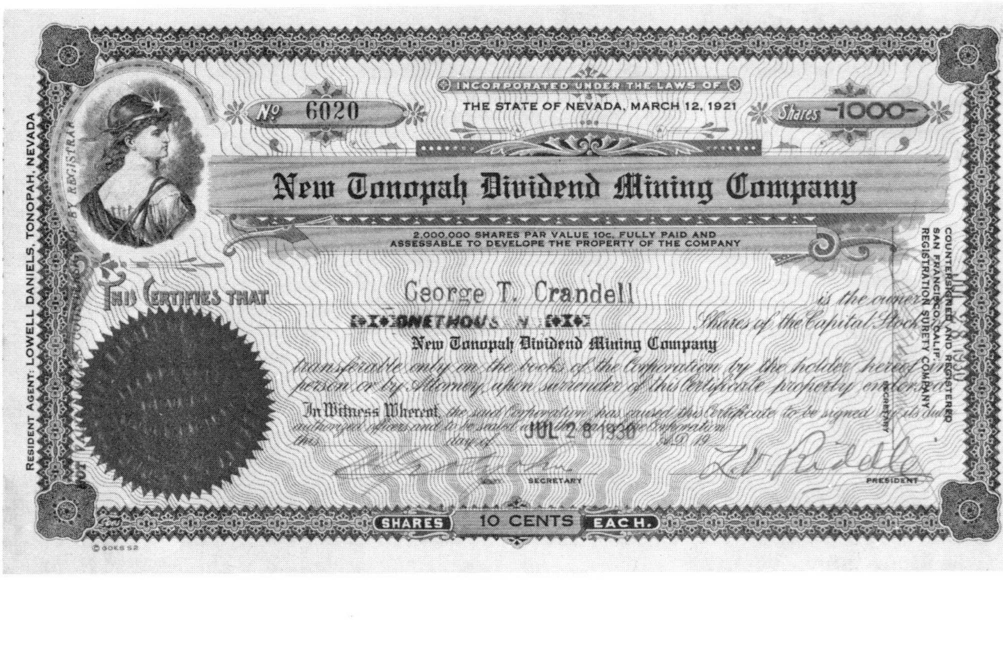
INCORPORATED UNDER THE LAWS OF THE STATE OF NEVADA, MARCH 12, 1921

No 6020

Shares -1000-

New Tonopah Dividend Mining Company

2,000,000 SHARES PAR VALUE 10c, FULLY PAID AND ASSESSABLE TO DEVELOPE THE PROPERTY OF THE COMPANY

This Certifies that George T. Crandell is the owner of ONETHOUSAND Shares of the Capital Stock of New Tonopah Dividend Mining Company transferable only on the books of the Corporation by the holder hereof in person or by Attorney upon surrender of this Certificate properly endorsed.

In Witness Whereof, the said Corporation has caused this Certificate to be signed by its duly authorized officers and to be sealed with the Seal of the Corporation this JUL 28 1930 day of A.D. 19

SECRETARY PRESIDENT

SHARES 10 CENTS EACH.

RESIDENT AGENT: LOWELL DANIELS, TONOPAH, NEVADA

TRANSFER OFFICE: 333 KEARNY ST., SAN FRANCISCO, CALIF.

COUNTERSIGNED AND REGISTERED SAN FRANCISCO, CALIF. REGISTRATION SURETY COMPANY

Pharmacist Gold Mining Company (I), 1910s, Wyoming 8.00
Phelps Dodge Corporation (I), 1920s and 1940s, Working miner vignette 6.00
Phelps Dodge Corporation (I), 1950s, New York, Seated figure before large open pit mine vignette 3.00
Phelps Dodge Corporation (I), 1950s and 1960s, Working miner vignette 4.00
Phenix Mining and Manufacturing (I-N), 1850s, Three vignettes 250.00
Philadelphia-Nevada Mining (I), 1900s, Arizona, Mining scene plus six individual miners in border vignettes 22.00
Phipps Quicksilver Mining (U), 1910s, Arizona, Mining town, miner, and burro (three vignettes) 5.00
Phoenix Copper (I), 1880s, Michigan, Winged eagle vignette 35.00
Phoenix Gold Mining (I), 1890s, Arizona, Mining and eagle vignettes 23.00
Phoenix Mining (I-N), 1900s, Idaho, Three mining vignettes and goddess 15.00
Piedmont Mining and Milling (U), 1900s, Waterfall vignette 10.00
Pigeon River Land and Mining La(I), 1900s, Minnesota, Larged winged eagle with train and ships vignette plus mining scene 55.00
Pioneer Coal (U), 1900s, Eagle vignette, rare 15.00
Pittsburg Johnnie Mining (U), Nevada 6.00
Plymouth Rock Mining Company (I), 1870s, Territory of New Mexico, Large mining vignette 45.00
Plymouth Rock Mining Company (U), 1870s, Territory of New Mexico, Large mining vignette 25.00
Plymouth Rock Mining Company (I), 1880s, Territory of New Mexico, Large mining vignette 40.00
Poney Meadows Mining (I), 1960s, Three vignettes and gold seal 5.00
Ponupo Mining and Transportation (U), 1890s, Mining vignette 15.00
Porcupine Northern Mining (I), 1910s 15.00
Portland Gold Mining (I), 1930s, Wyoming, Hard rock mining scene 7.00
Portland Mining (I), 1880s 25.00
Poto Gold Dredging Company (I-N), 1900s, Gold dredging vignette 18.00
Princeton Mining (I), 1900s, Colorado, Working miners and seal vignette 18.00
Progress Gold Mining (I), 1900s, Colorado, Gold seal 30.00
Prosperity Gold Mine (I), 1900s, Arizona Territory, Mining scene and six miners in border vignettes 22.00
Providence Tuolumne Gold Mines (I), 1940s, California, seal and mining vignette 7.00
Provident Coke and Mining (I), 1900s, Bond, coke ovens 14.00
Pulaski Anthracite Coal (I), 1900s, Bond 40.00

Quick Silver Mining (I), 1910s, Workers pouring molten ore vignette 35.00
Quincy Mining Company (I), 1850s, Michigan, Ships, trains, ladies and state seal vignettes 50.00
Quincy Mining Company (I), 1860s, Michigan, Ships, trains, ladies and state seal vignettes 40.00
Quincy Mining Company (I), 1890s, Scrip certificate 8.00
Quincy Mining Company (I), 1900s, Two moose with antlers vignette (state seal) 25.00
Quincy Mining Company (I), 1910s, Michigan, Two moose with antlers vignette (state seal) 20.00
Quincy Mining Company (I), 1920s, Michigan, Two moose with antlers vignette (state seal) 15.00
Quinterro Mining (I-N), 1860s, Miner vignette, state seal 120.00
Quito Gold Mining and Milling (I) 1900s, Colorado, Scenic mountain vignette 18.00

Ramsey-Nevada Mining (I-N) 1900s, Arizona Territory, Miners mountain scene vignettes 46.00
Rawhide Mining (I-N), 1910s, Nevada, Mining vignettes 17.00

◀ ***New Cornelia Copper Company (I), 1920s,*** *Machinery loading ore cars vignette* ***8.00***
◀ ***New Tonopah Dividend Mining Company (I-N), 1930s,*** *Lady vignette, gold seal* ***11.00***

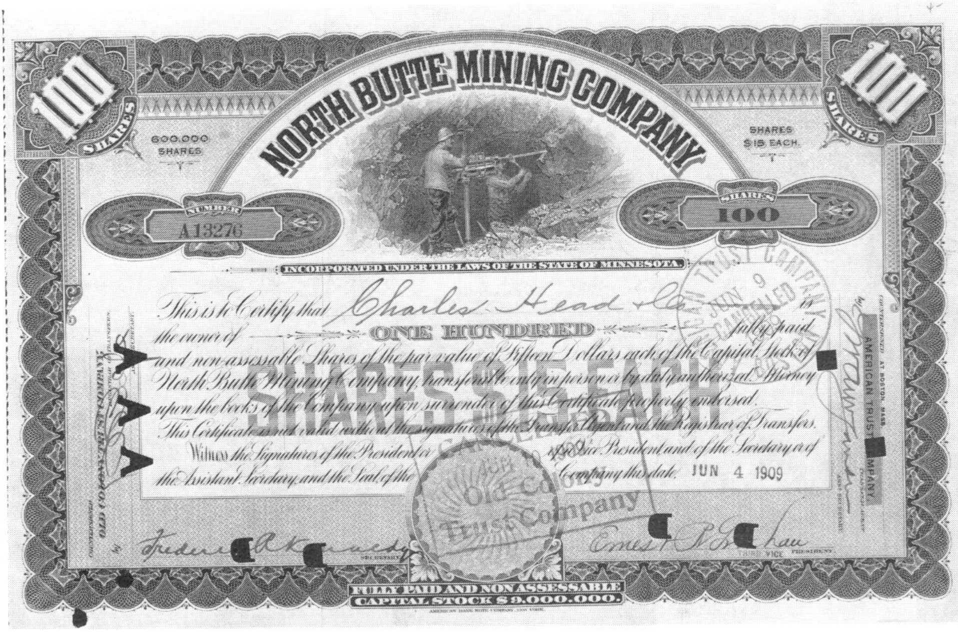
NORTH BUTTE MINING COMPANY
100 SHARES
600,000 SHARES
SHARES $15 EACH.
NUMBER A13276
SHARES 100
INCORPORATED UNDER THE LAWS OF THE STATE OF MINNESOTA.
This is to Certify that Charles Head & Co. is the owner of ONE HUNDRED fully paid and non-assessable Shares of the par value of Fifteen Dollars each of the Capital Stock of North Butte Mining Company, transferable only in person or by duly authorized Attorney upon the books of the Company upon surrender of this Certificate properly endorsed.
This Certificate is not valid without the signatures of the Transfer Agent and the Registrar of Transfers.
Witness the Signatures of the President or Vice President and of the Secretary or of the Assistant Secretary, and the Seal of the Company this date. JUN 4 1909
SHARES $15 EACH
AMERICAN TRUST COMPANY
Old Colony Trust Company
SECRETARY
VICE PRESIDENT
FULLY PAID AND NON ASSESSABLE
CAPITAL STOCK $9,000,000.

Incorporated under the laws of the State of Nevada, January 5, 1924
No 5997
1000 Shares
OPERATOR CONSOLIDATED MINES COMPANY
PAR VALUE 10 CENTS
CAPITAL STOCK, $300,000.00 :: 3,000,000 SHARES
ASSESSABLE
THIS CERTIFICATE IS NOT VALID UNTIL REGISTERED BY THE REGISTRAR
This Certifies that F. BOLLSCHWEILER is the owner of
ONE THOUSAND Shares of the Capital Stock of
OPERATOR CONSOLIDATED MINES COMPANY
transferable only on the books of the Corporation by the holder hereof in person or by Attorney, upon surrender of this Certificate properly endorsed.
In Witness Whereof, the said Corporation has caused this Certificate to be signed by its duly authorized officers and to be sealed with the Seal of the Corporation
this day of
ASSISTANT SECRETARY
VICE PRESIDENT
SHARES 10c PAR VALUE EACH
PRINCIPAL OFFICE, RENO, NEVADA. RESIDENT AGENT, NEVADA CORPORATION AGENCY CO.
COUNTERSIGNED NEVADA CORPORATION AGENCY CO. RENO, NEVADA TRANSFER AGENT
Countersigned and Registered: SECURITY REGISTRAR & TRANSFER CO. San Francisco Registrar
JUL 22 1936
Authorized Officer

Rattler Gold Mining (I), 1900s, Colorado	**17.00**
Ray Consolidated Gold Dredging (U), 1910s, Torch vignette	**5.00**
Ray Hercules Mines (I-N), 1920s	**6.00**
Raymond-Illinois Mining Company (I-N), Utah, Three mining vignettes	**14.00**
Red Hill Florence Mining (I-N), 1920s, Nevada	**10.00**
Reorganized Cracker Jack Mining Company (I-N), 1920s, Nevada	**12.00**
Reorganized Victory Divide Mining (I-N), 1920s, Eight assessments paid, gold seal, two mining vignettes	**14.00**
Republic Coal Company (U), 1900s, Montana, Mining vignette	**5.00**
Republic Iron Mask Gold Mining (U), Seven mining vignettes	**10.00**
Republic Mines (I), 1900s, Bond, eagle with flag vignette	**35.00**
Revenue Leasing and Mining (I), 1900s, Miners with wheelbarrow vignette	**18.00**
Revert Mining (I-N), 1920s, Nevada, Three assessments paid, gold seal	**10.00**
Revine Gold Mining (U), 1900s, Mountains vignette	**8.00**
Rex Mining (U), Nevada, Eagle vignette	**3.00**
Reynolds-Alaska Development (I-N), 1900s, Train, ship and figures vignette	**36.00**
Richland Mining Company (UI), 1900s, California, Three mining vignettes, gold seal	**13.00**
Richmond Coal and Mining and Manufacturing (I), 1890s, Gold bond, eagle and ore train loading vignette	**130.00**
Richmond Coal and Mining and Manufacturing (I), 1890s, Working miners vignette	**50.00**
Richmond Coal Mining (I), 1890s, Bond	**55.00**
Riddlesburg Coal and Iron (I-N), 1860s, Miners, and blacksmith vignettes, with stamp	**50.00**
Ridge Copper Company (I), 1880s, Michigan	**25.00**
Rio Delores Copper Company (I), 1900s Arizona, Working miners vignette	**14.00**
Rio Delores Copper Company (I), 1910s, Arizona, Working miners vignette	**10.00**
Rio Grande Copper Company (I), 1880s, Two mining vignettes plus two miners divided by state seal	**135.00**
Rio Plata (I-N), 1900s, Arizona, Miners and eagles vignette	**20.00**
Riverside Iron and Company (U), 1800s, Miners, boats, and train vignette	**27.00**
Riverside Iron and Coal Company of Scranton (U), 1800s, Miners, trains and riverboats vignette	**72.00**
Robb-Montbay Mines (I), 1930s	**10.00**
Roberta Gold (I-N), 1930s	**5.00**
Roberts Buena-Vista Mines, Consolidated, Inc, 1900s, Large smelting plant scene, flatcars, prospector with two burros vignettes	**5.00**
Robinson-Victory Mines (I), 1890s, Colorado, Huge mining operation vignette	**54.00**
Roosevelt Gold Mining (U), 1900s, Miners vignette, gold seal	**8.00**
Rosario Silver Mining (I-N), 1860s, Arizona, Working miners,	**77.00**
Rose-Lee Mining and Milling (I-N), 1890s, Many working miners, gold seal vignette	**29.00**
Rouchleau-Ray Iron Land Company (U), 1890s	**18.00**
Rouchleau-Ray Iron Land Company (I), 1890s, Two forest vignettes plus eagle in flight	**55.00**
Round Mountain Mining Company (I), 1900s, Nevada, Three mining vignettes, gold seal	**28.00**
Round Mountain Mining Company (I), 1910s, Boy's head vignette	**18.00**
Round Mountain Mining Company (I), 1910s, Nevada, Three mining vignettes, gold seal	**18.00**
Royal Tiger Mines (I), 1920s, Colorado, Allegorical figures	**20.00**
Ruby Hill Tunnel and Mining (I), 1880s, Nevada, Seated goddess	**50.00**
Sacramento Gold and Silver Mining (I), 1860s, California	**160.00**
Saint Croix and Lake Superior Mining (I), 1840s, Signed by Congressmen Rufus Choate, Caleb Cushing, and Robert Rontoul, Jr.	**325.00**
Saint Helena Gold Mine (I), 1880s, Bond	**46.00**

◀ ***North Butte Mining (I), 1900s,*** *Mining scene vignette* — ***4.00***

◀ ***Operator Consolidated Mines Company (I-N), 1930s,*** *Three mining vignettes, gold seal* — ***10.00***

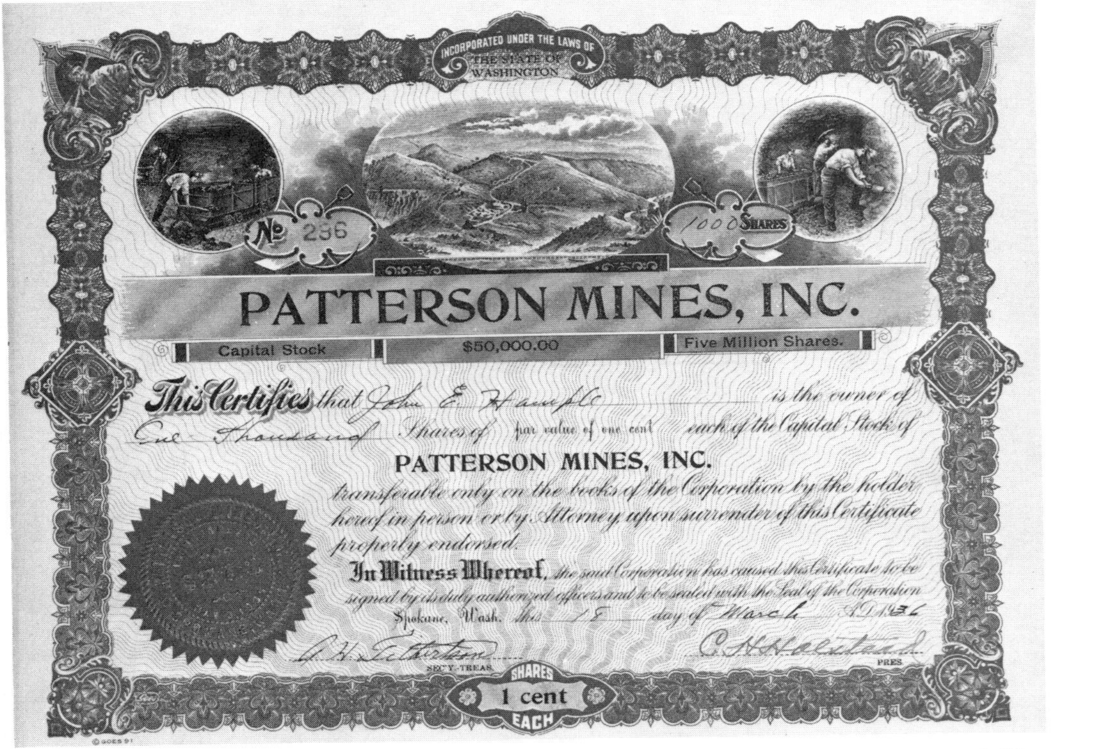
INCORPORATED UNDER THE LAWS OF THE STATE OF WASHINGTON
No 286
1000 SHARES
PATTERSON MINES, INC.
Capital Stock
$50,000.00
Five Million Shares.
This Certifies that is the owner of
One Thousand Shares of par value of one cent each of the Capital Stock of
PATTERSON MINES, INC.
transferable only on the books of the Corporation by the holder hereof in person or by Attorney upon surrender of this Certificate properly endorsed.
In Witness Whereof, the said Corporation has caused this Certificate to be signed by its duly authorized officers and to be sealed with the Seal of the Corporation
Spokane, Wash. this day of March A.D.
SEC'Y-TREAS.
PRES.
SHARES
1 cent
EACH

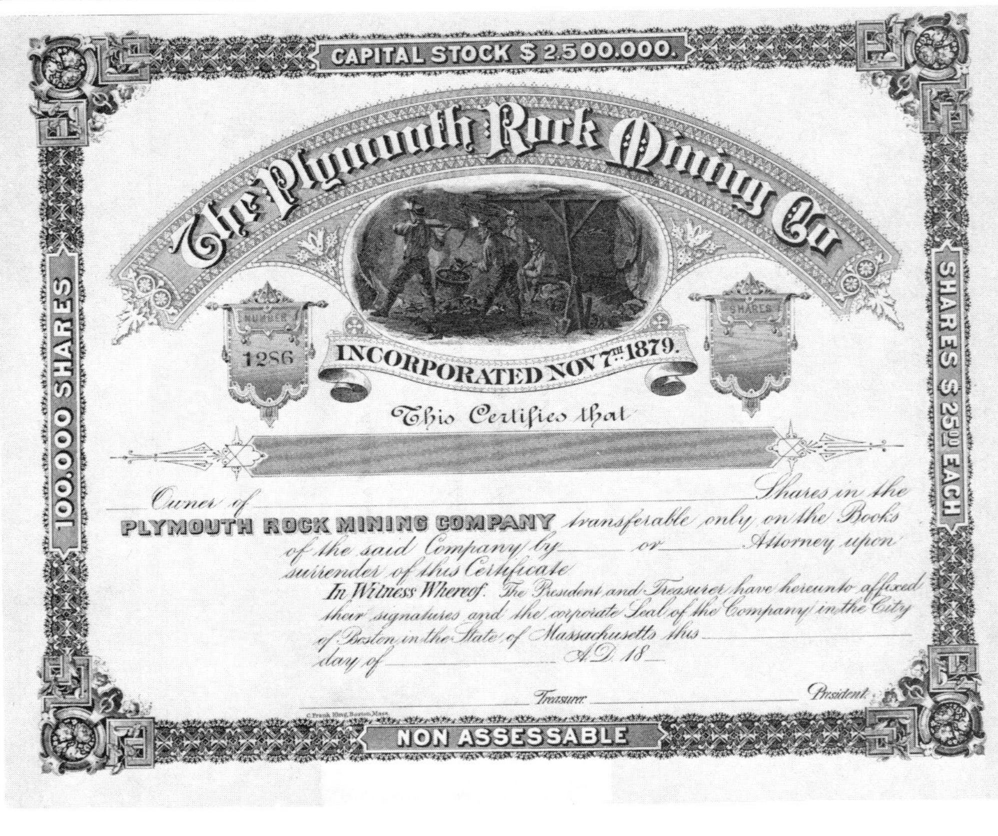
CAPITAL STOCK $ 2.500.000.
The Plymouth Rock Mining Co
NUMBER
1286
SHARES
INCORPORATED NOV 7TH 1879.
100,000 SHARES
SHARES $ 25.00 EACH
This Certifies that
Owner of Shares in the
PLYMOUTH ROCK MINING COMPANY transferable only on the Books of the said Company by or Attorney upon surrender of this Certificate
In Witness Whereof. The President and Treasurer have hereunto affixed their signatures and the corporate Seal of the Company in the City of Boston in the State of Massachusetts this day of A.D. 18
Treasurer.
President.
NON ASSESSABLE

Saint Joseph Lead Company (I), 1950s, Large mining vignette, grey seal	**4.00**
Saint Joseph Lead Company (I), 1960s, Mining scene	**3.00**
Saint Joseph Minerals (I), 1970s	**2.00**
Salero Mining (UI), 1800s, Stagecoach portrait vignettes	**25.00**
Sampo Mining and Development Company (I-N), 1900s, Three mining vignettes	**12.00**
San Juan and New Jersey Discovery and Mining (I), 1880s, Colorado, Embossed seal	**38.00**
San Juan Smelting and Refining(I), 1900s, Colorado, Gold seal	**10.00**
San Poil Mining and Water Power Company (I), 1900s, Washington, Miners vignette	**17.00**
Santa Fe Gold and Copper Mining (I), 1920s, New Mexico	**20.00**
Santa Paula Mining and Reduction (I), 1900s, California	**25.00**
Santa Rita Copper and Iron (I), 1890s, New Mexico, Miners working in mine vignette	**55.00**
Santa Rita Copper Mining (I), 1910s, Arizona, Three mining vignettes	**12.00**
Savage Gold and Silver Mining (I), 1920s, Nevada	**8.00**
Savage Gold and Silver Mining (I), 1920s, California	**10.00**
Savage Gold and Silver Mining (U), 1900s, Nevada	**8.00**
Schiller Mining of Trenton (I-N), 1890s, New Jersey, Working miners vignette	**40.00**
Schuyler Gold and Silver Mining (I), 1880s, Colorado, Mining vignette	**62.00**
Seal of Nevada Mining (U), 1880s	**20.00**
Selerno Mining and Manufacturing Company (U), 1870s, Arizona Territory, Large stagecoach vignette	**60.00**
Seneca Copper Corporation (I-N), 1920s, Bond, mining vignette	**15.00**
Seneca Mining (I), 1870s, Michigan, Mining vignette and woman with horn of plenty vignette	**120.00**
Seneca Mining (I), 1900s, Michigan, Double mining vignette, large state seal	**35.00**
Seneca Mining (I), 1910s, Michigan, Two unique mining vignettes	**25.00**
Sequatchie Coal and Iron (I), 1890s, Tennessee, Mining vignette	**35.00**
Sequatchie Coal and Iron (I), 1910s, Tennessee, Mining vignette	**25.00**
Sequatchie Coal and Iron (U),1890s, Tennessee, Mining vignette	**15.00**
Seven Stars Gold Mining (I-N), 1890s, Miners vignette	**55.00**
Shannon Copper Company (I), 1930s, Working miners and ore cars vignette	**20.00**
Shasta May Blossom Copper (I), 1920s, Arizona, Mining vignette	**12.00**
Sheridan Hill Mining and Smelting of Utah (I), 1870s, Smelting plant vignette	**66.00**
Sheriff Gold Mining (I), 1890s, Spread eagle vignette	**20.00**
Shoshone Chief Silver Mining (I), 1860s, Bond, gold sluicing, plus open pit mining vignettes, two vignettes of seated women, plus winged eagle between two ladies vignettes	**365.00**
Silver Bell Mines (I), 1950s, Colorado, Large eagle vignette, gold seal	**3.00**
Silver Bell Mines (U), Colorado, Woman with lion vignette	**2.00**
Silver Bell Mining (I), 1950s, Colorado, Lion and lady vignette	**5.00**
Silver Cliff Mining and Tunnel (I-N), 1880s, Montana Territory	**45.00**
Silver Crown Mining (I-N), 1880s, Colorado, Embossed seal	**38.00**
Silver Divide Mines (I-N), 1960s, Large smelting vignette, gold seal	**7.00**
Silver Hills Nevada Mines (I), 1920s, Three mining vignettes, gold seal	**8.00**
Silver Jacket Mining Company (U), 1870s, Nevada	**25.00**
Silver King of Arizona Mining (I-N), 1910s, Smelting plant vignette, embossed seal	**13.00**
Silver Rock Mining (I), 1880s, Colorado, Miners in tunnels vignettes	**60.00**
Silver Shield Mining and Milling company (I-N), 1920s, Mining scene vignette	**12.00**
Silvert Consolidated Mining (I), 1900s, Embossed seal	**8.00**
Simon South Silver Mines (I-N), 1910s, Nevada, Three mining vignettes, gold seal	**10.00**
Sioux Divide Mining Company (I-N), 1910s, Nevada, Eagle vignette	**10.00**

◀ ***Patterson Mines, Inc. (I-N), 1930s, Washington,*** *Gold seal, two mining vignettes, large mountain scene* ***7.00***

◀ ***Plymouth Rock Mining Company, The (U), 1870s, Territory of New Mexico,*** *Large mining vignette* ***25.00***

QUINCY MINING COMPANY

No. 23979

15 Shares

INCORPORATED UNDER THE LAWS OF THE STATE OF MICHIGAN.

CERTIFICATE FOR LESS THAN ONE HUNDRED SHARES

This Certifies that Grace H. Dodge, W. C. Osborn, C. H. Dodge, Trustees for Anna D. McCullough under will of Sarah H. Dodge

is the Proprietor of Fifteen Shares of the Capital Stock of the Quincy Mining Company, transferable only on the books of said Company by the holder hereof in person or by Attorney on surrender of this Certificate.

SHARES $25. EACH

Boston, 190

Secretary

President

THIS CERTIFICATE IS NOT VALID UNTIL COUNTERSIGNED BY TRANSFER AGENT AND REGISTRAR

OLD COLONY TRUST COMPANY, TRANSFER AGENT

AMERICAN TRUST COMPANY, REGISTRAR

NOT OVER ... SHARES

SHARES $25. EACH

AMERICAN BANK NOTE COMPANY, NEW YORK.

INCORPORATED UNDER THE LAWS OF THE STATE OF NEVADA, MAY 26, 1921

MINES IN TONOPAH DIVIDE MINING DISTRICT, ESMERALDA COUNTY, NEVADA

NUMBER 1300

SHARES 1000

Re-organized Victory Divide Mining Company

CAPITAL STOCK, $200,000 — FULLY PAID AND ASSESSABLE

2,000,000 SHARES — PAR VALUE 10c

This Certifies that R. C. Laub is the owner of ONE THOUSAND Shares of the Capital Stock of

RE-ORGANIZED VICTORY DIVIDE MINING COMPANY

transferable only on the books of the Corporation by the holder hereof in person or by Attorney upon surrender of this Certificate properly endorsed.

In Witness Whereof, the said Corporation has caused this Certificate to be signed by its duly authorized officers and to be sealed with the Seal of the Corporation this SEP 2 1921 day of A.D. 19

Asst. SECRETARY

PRESIDENT

SHARES 10c EACH

PRINCIPAL OFFICE: GOLDFIELD, NEVADA

RESIDENT AGENT: HARRY B. RUHL, GOLDFIELD, NEVADA

Registered at Goldfield, Nevada, SEP 2 1921. John S. Cook & Co., Bankers, Registrar. Cashier

Smuggler Divide Mining (I), 1920s, Nevada, Seven vignettes of miners, gold seal, with stamps 10.00
Smuggler Mining Company (I), 1930s, Nevada, Eagle vignette, with stamps 6.00
Smuggler Mining Company (I), 1940s, Nevada, Eagle vignette 4.00
Smuggler Union Mining (I), 1920s, Colorado, State seal 15.00
Sonora Central Mines (I), Arizona, Three mining vignettes 20.00
South Eastern Gold Mining Very large certificate with share coupons, orchid color 6.00
South Idaho Consolidated Mining and Milling (I), 1890s, California 20.00
South Park Mining and Developing (I), 1900s, Seven mining vignettes 10.00
South Park Mining and Development Company (I), 1910s, Seven mining vignettes 9.00
South Park Mining and Realty (U), 1910s, Montana, Mountain scene vignette 5.00
South Side Milling and Mining (I-N), 1880s, Large mountain scene and working miners vignettes 80.00
South Utah Mines and Smelters (I), 1910s 28.00
South Utah Mines and Smelters (I), 1920s 26.00
Southern Mining (U), 1890s, Ohio, Ship and church vignettes 10.00
Sovereign Gold Mines (I-N), 1900s, Bond 10.00
Spearhead Mining (I), 1920s, Surface entry vignette 15.00
Specie Basis Mining (I), 1860s, Arizona Territory, Large mining scene with stamp 160.00
Specie Basis Mining (I), 1860s, Bond, lake in mountains vignette 260.00
Spokane National (I), 1960s, Eagle on glove vignette, gold seal 2.00
Spokane National (I), 1960s, Nevada, Eagle, Indians, train vignette 3.00
Spokane Tin Mines (U), 1900s, Washington, Hill scene vignette 8.00
Stafford Meadow Coal and Iron (I), 1850s, Numerous vignettes 80.00
Stafford Meadow Coal and Iron Improvement Company (I), 1850s, Pennsylvania 48.00
Star of Nevada Silver Mining (I), 1870s, 30.00
Starmont Mining of Utah (I-N), train, cherubs, and Liberty seated dollar vignette 80.00
State Line Gold Mining (I), 1880s Nevada, Large scene of workers at mine head vignette 70.00
Stem-Winder Mining and Leasing (I), 1900s, Colorado, Embossed seal 9.00
Suffold Gold, Silver and Copper Mining (U), 1860s, Miners and ore car vignette 22.00
Sullivan Mining (I-N), 1880s, Working miners vignette 60.00
Sun-Hope Mining (U), Colorado, Three mining vignettes 3.00
Sunlight Copper Mining (I), 1900s, Wyoming, Winged eagle between two semi-nude women with train and ship in background vignette 43.00
Sunnyside Lead-Silver Mining (U), 1920s, Nevada, Eagle in shield vignette 3.00
Sunrise Silver Mine (U), 1900s, Idaho, Lighted torch vignette 4.00
Sunset Eclipse Gold Mining (I-N), 1900s, Black seal 10.00
Sunset Mines (I-N), 1950s, Idaho 3.00
Superior and Boston Copper Company (I-N), 1910s, Arizona, miners working vignette 25.00
Superior and Boston Copper Company (I-N), 1920s, Arizona, Three mining vignettes 20.00
Superior and Globe Copper Company (I-N), 1900s, Arizona 15.00
Superstition Consolidated Mining (I), 1910s, Arizona 35.00
Swastika Mining and Developing Company (I-N), 1910s, Utah, Three mining vignettes, three swastikas on certificate 30.00
Syndicate Mines (U), 1900s, Large mining vignette 6.00
Syndicate Mines, Inc. (U), 1920s, Working miners vignette 4.00

Tallapoosa Land, Mining and Manufacturing (I-N), 1910s, Territory of Arizona, Gold seal, three mining vignettes 25.00
Teziutlan Copper Mining and Smelting (I), 1920s, New Jersey, Ladies vignette 35.00

◀ ***Quincy Mining Company (I), 1900s,*** *Two moose with antlers vignette (state seal)* ***25.00***
◀ ***Re-organized Victory Divide Mining (I-N), 1920s,*** *Eight assessments paid, gold seal, two mining vignettes* ***14.00***

United States of America
INCORPORATED UNDER THE LAWS OF NEVADA, MARCH 28, 1906
PRINCIPAL PLACE OF BUSINESS GOLDFIELD, NEVADA.
NUMBER
6190
SHARES
10,000
ROUND MOUNTAIN MINING COMPANY
FULLY PAID AND NON-ASSESSABLE
CAPITAL STOCK $1,500,000.00
1,500,000 SHARES.
CANCELLED
This Certifies that is the owner of
Ten Thousand
Shares of the Capital Stock of Round Mountain Mining Company transferable only on the books of the Corporation by the holder hereof in person or by Attorney upon surrender of this Certificate properly endorsed.
In Witness Whereof, the said Corporation has caused this Certificate to be signed by its duly authorized officers, and to be sealed with the Seal of the Corporation at Goldfield, Nevada, this 14" day of January A.D. 1912
REGISTERED AND COUNTERSIGNED
American National Bank
REGISTRAR
PRESIDENT
SECRETARY
SHARES $1.00 EACH

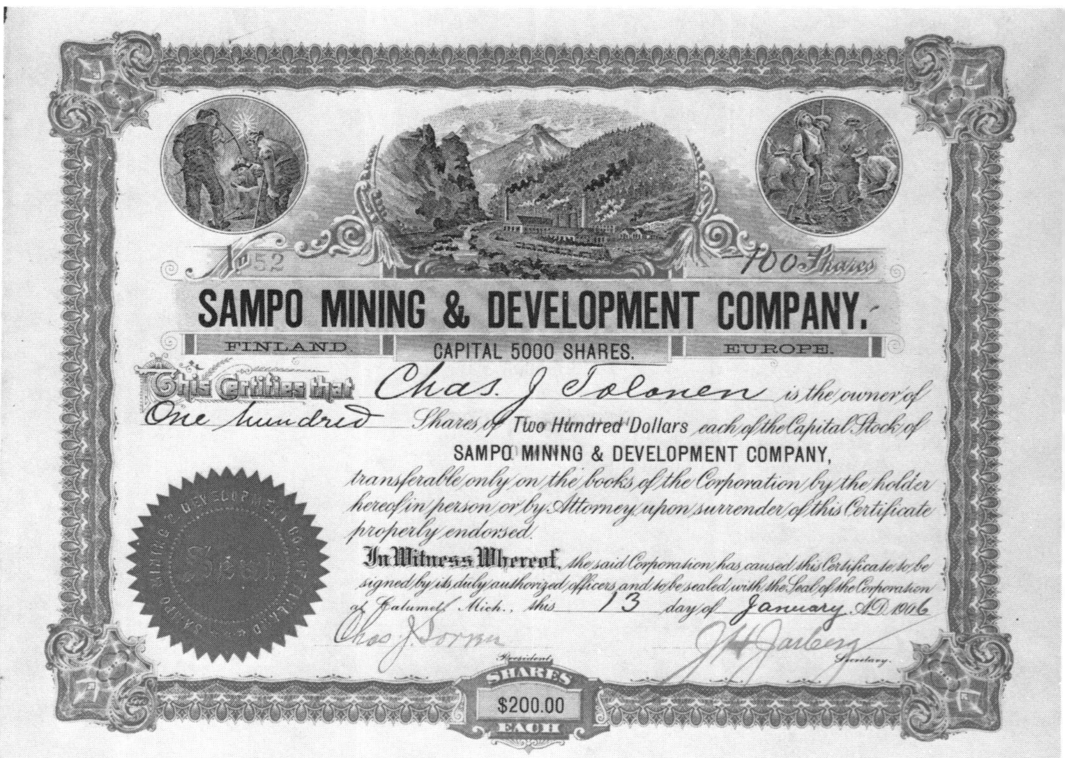
No 52
100 Shares
SAMPO MINING & DEVELOPMENT COMPANY.
FINLAND.
CAPITAL 5000 SHARES.
EUROPE.
This Certifies that Chas. J Tolonen is the owner of
One hundred Shares of Two Hundred Dollars each of the Capital Stock of
SAMPO MINING & DEVELOPMENT COMPANY,
transferable only on the books of the Corporation by the holder hereof in person or by Attorney upon surrender of this Certificate properly endorsed.
In Witness Whereof, the said Corporation has caused this Certificate to be signed by its duly authorized officers and to be sealed with the Seal of the Corporation at Calumet, Mich., this 13 day of January A.D. 1906
President.
Secretary.
SHARES
$200.00
EACH

Thomas Laughlin (I-N), 1900s, State seal 6.00
Timberlake Development and Mining (I-N), 1900s, Eagle, train and ship 9.00
Tom Reed Gold Mining Company (I), 1910s, Large, unique mining vignette 12.00
Tom Reed Gold Mines (I), 1920s, Three mining vignettes 9.00
Tomas Divide Mining (I), 1910s, Nevada, Two mining vignettes, with stamp, gold seal 9.00
Tombstone Consolidated Mines (U), 1900s, Arizona Territory, Two miners and mining camp vignettes 25.00
Tonapah Divide Mining (I), 1910s, Mine entry vignette 20.00
Tonapah Divide Mining (I), 1920s, Mine entry vignette 15.00
Tonapah Gold Mountain Mining Company (I), 1910s, Arizona Territory, Goddess vignette, signed by George Wingfield 30.00
Tonapah North Star Tunnel and Development (I), 1910s, Nevada, Miners vignette 10.00
Tonapah North Star Tunnel and Development (I), 1940s, Nevada, Eagle vignette 4.00
Tonapah North Star Tunnel and Development (I), 1950s, Nevada, Eagle vignette 2.00
Tonapah Oriental Mining (U), 1910s, Nevada, Mining vignette 5.00
Total Wreck Mining and Milling (I-N), 1880s, Miners and mountains scene 40.00
Trade Dollar Consolidated Mining (I-N), 1900s, Kentucky, Three miners vignette 30.00
Trail Mines (I), 1950s, Colorado, 2.00
Tribune Gold Mining and Milling (I), 1900s, Arizona, Bond, miner at work in mine vignette, gold bond 95.00
Trinity Copper Corporation (I), 1920s, Virginia, Company logo 20.00
Trinity Dredging (I), 1910s, Large gold dredge vignette 17.00
Trinity Dredging (U), 1910s, Large gold dredge vignette 6.00
Triunfo Gold and Silver Mining (I), 1860s, California, Mountain mining camp scene vignette 210.00
Triunfo Gold and Silver Mining (I), 1860s, Two winged eagles, mountain scene vignettes (smaller certificate) 200.00
Troy-Manhattan Copper (I), 1900s, Vignette of Manhattan 45.00
Trust Mining Company (I), 1890s, Washington, Miss Liberty, flag, eagle, and state seal vignette 25.00
Trust Mining Company (U), 1800s, Washington, Miss Liberty, flag, eagle and state seal vignette 6.00
Tuolumne Copper Mining (I), 1910s and 1920s, Arizona, Mining vignette 10.00
Tuolumne County Water (I), 1850s, Sluice mining vignette 160.00
Tuolumne County Water (I), 1860s, Huge vignette of methods to mine gold 100.00
Twentieth Century Mining (I), 1900s, Ship, train, and eagle vignettes 25.00

Uncle Ned Gold Mining (I), 1890s, Mining vignette plus six miners in border, gold seal 25.00
Uncle Ned Gold Mining (U), Mining vignette plus six miners in border, gold seal 9.00
Unidilla Mining (I), 1880s 42.00
Union Consolidated Mining (I), 1880s, Embossed seal 32.00
Union Hill Mines (I), 1910s, California, Eagle vignette 11.00
Unita Tunnel and Mining (I), 1910s, Wyoming, spread eagle vignette 29.00
United Gold Mining and Milling 5.00
United Gold Mining Company (I), 1900s, Colorado, Mining vignette, with stamps 30.00
United Mines of Arizona (I), 1910s, Miners in mine vignette 25.00
United States Reduction and Refining (I), 1910s, Eagle on shield vignette 25.00
United States Smelting (I), 1900s, Bond, smelters vignette, seal 32.00
United Water and Power Company of California (I), 1910s, Three mining vignettes 6.00
Unity Mining (U), 1880s, Maine, Mining scene vignette 16.00
Universal Mining (I-N), 1950s, Washington, Two mining vignettes plus large mountain scene, gold seal 5.00

◀ ***Round Mountain Mining Company (I), 1910s,*** *Boy's head vignette* ***18.00***
◀ ***Sampo Mining and Development Company (I-N), 1900s,*** *Three mining vignettes* ***12.00***

INCORPORATED UNDER THE LAWS OF
UTAH
NUMBER
A 4022
SHARES
-400-
Silver Shield Mining & Milling Co.
2,000,000 SHARES—PAR VALUE 15c EACH
PROPERTY IN TINTIC MINING DISTRICT, UTAH AND OTHER MINING DISTRICTS
This is to Certify that BELLE HILL is the owner of
----FOUR HUNDRED---- Shares of the Capital Stock of
SILVER SHIELD MINING & MILLING CO.
transferable only on the Books of the Corporation on surrender of this Certificate properly endorsed
In Witness Whereof the said Corporation has caused this Certificate to be signed by its duly authorized officers and its Corporate Seal to be hereunto affixed at Salt Lake City, Utah
this First day of November A.D. 1927
F. Searle
Ass't. SECRETARY
PRESIDENT
NON-ASSESSABLE

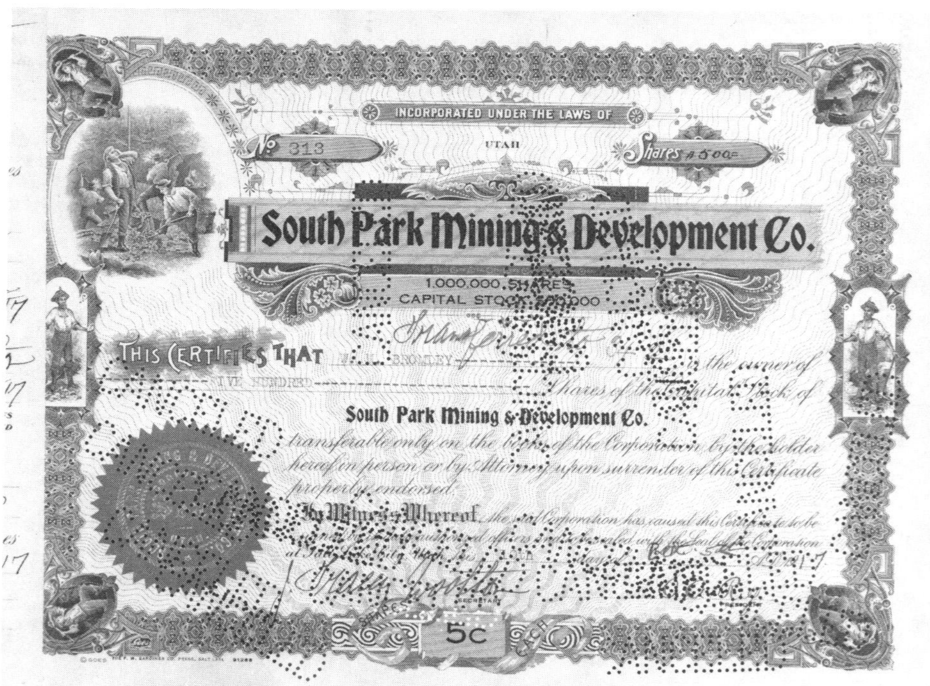
INCORPORATED UNDER THE LAWS OF
UTAH
No 313
Shares 500
South Park Mining & Development Co.
1,000,000 SHARES
CAPITAL STOCK
THIS CERTIFIES THAT BROMLEY is the owner of
FIVE HUNDRED Shares of the Capital Stock of
South Park Mining & Development Co.
transferable only on the books of the Corporation by the holder hereof in person or by Attorney upon surrender of this Certificate properly endorsed.
In Witness Whereof, the said Corporation has caused this Certificate to be signed by its duly authorized officers and to be sealed with the Seal of the Corporation
SECRETARY
PRESIDENT
5c

Utah-Apex Mining Company (I), 1900s, With stamps 12.00
Utah-Apex Mining Company (I), 1910s, 1920s, 1930s, Eagle atop beehive vignette 6.00
Utah-Bingham Mining (I), 1900s, Colorado, Mining vignette 14.00
Utah Consolidated Mining (I), 1900s, Drifting rigs vignette 17.00
Utah Metal and Tunnel Company (I), 1910s, Mountain mining town vignette 23.00
Utah Metal and Tunnel Company (I), 1940s, Mountain mining scene vignette 8.00
Utah Metal and Tunnel Company (I-N), 1930s, Mountain mining town vignette 12.00

V.A.M. Consolidated Mining (I-N), 1900s, Large eagle vignette, embossed seal 7.00
V-I Mining (I-N), 1920s, Large eagle vignette, gold seal 5.00
Van Anda Copper and Gold Company (I), 1890s 23.00
Van Anda Gold Mining (U), Two mining vignettes 15.00
Van Mining Company (U), 1890s, California, Large vignette of mine entrance and miner pushing mine car 14.00
Verde Combination Copper Company (I), 1910s Arizona, Miners working in mine vignette, embossed seal 8.00
Victor Gold Mining (I), 1890s, Colorado, Mining vignette 25.00
Victor Mining (I-N), 1880s, Colorado, Two mining vignettes 75.00
Victoria Chief Copper Mining and Smelting (I), 1900s, Indian chief vignette, embossed seal 13.00
Victoria Consolidated Mines (I), 1910s, Utah, Goddess and shield vignette 4.00
Victoria Consolidated Mining (I), 1910s, Utah, Woman with gold shield vignette, gold seal 4.00
Virginia Coal and Iron (I), 1860s, Train, arm with sledge vignette, with stamp 80.00
Virginia Gold Mining (I), 1880s 18.00
Virginia M. Consolidated Mining Company, The (I-N), 1900s, Colorado, Eagle vignette 15.00
Viznaga Gold Mining (I), 1900s, Arizona Territory, Mining camp in mountains vignette 54.00
Volcano Gold Mining (I), 1910s, Colorado 12.00
Vulcan Mining (I), 1840s, Blacksmith and semi-nudes vignette 135.00

War Eagle Mining (I), 1900s, Arizona, Working miners vignette, embossed seal 15.00
Waldorf Metals Company (I), 1910s, Arizona Territory 12.00
Wanderland Mining (I-N), 1900s, Wyoming 8.00
Warrior Copper Company, 1900s(I), Mining vignette 30.00
Washington Gold Mining (I), 1860s, Miners hauling ore with horses to mill and smelting plant vignette 100.00
Washington Mining (I), 1880s, Embossed seal 18.00
Wayne Coal (I), 1910s, Loaded ore train emerging from mine entry vignette 26.00
Wellington Mines (I), 1910s, Arizona 12.00
Wennerstein Mining (U), 1920s, Mining vignette with six miners in border 7.00
West End Consolidated Mining (I-N), Nevada 9.00
West Mariposa Gold Quartz Mine (I), 1850s 125.00
West Tonopah Consolidated Mining (I), 1900s, California 13.00
Western Nevada Copper Company (I), 1900s, Arizona, Mining vignette 30.00
Western States Coal (U), 1900s, Montana,State seal 4.00
Wheat Mining (I), 1880s, Michigan, River and mine scenes with seal of Michigan 65.00
Wheel of Fortune Gold Mining (I), 1890s, Colorado, Large mining scene 30.00
Whipple Gold Mining (I), 1860s, With stamp 77.00
White Caps Mining (I-N), 1920s, One paid assessment stamp 6.00
White Knob Mining (I), 1900s, Mining vignette 13.00

◀***Silver Shield Mining and Milling Company (I-N), 1920s,*** *Mining scene vignette* ***12.00***

◀***South Park Mining and Development Company (I), 1910s,*** *Seven mining vignettes* ***9.00***

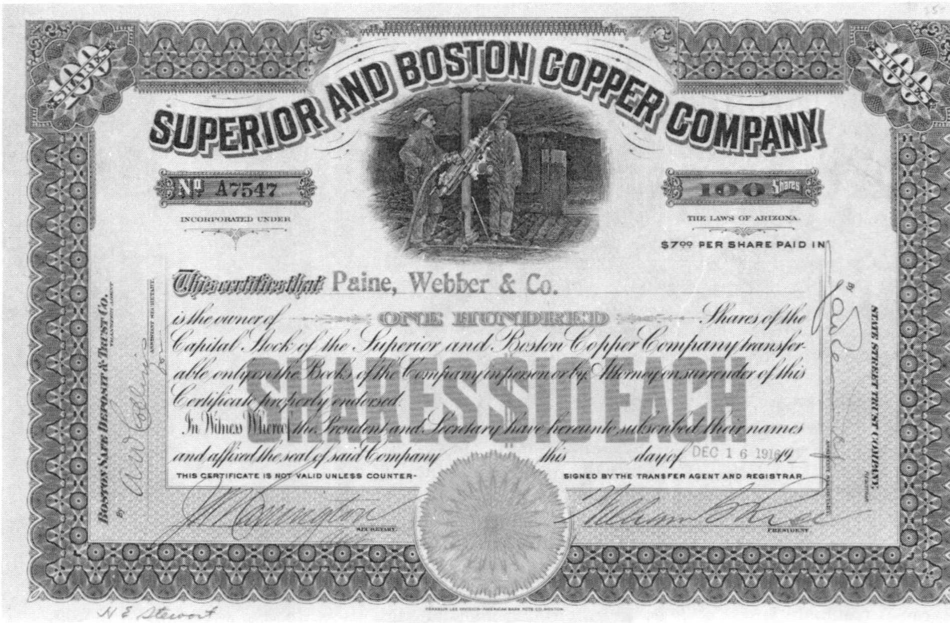

100 SHARES

SUPERIOR AND BOSTON COPPER COMPANY

No. A7547

100 Shares

INCORPORATED UNDER THE LAWS OF ARIZONA.

$7.00 PER SHARE PAID IN

This certifies that Paine, Webber & Co. is the owner of ONE HUNDRED Shares of the Capital Stock of the Superior and Boston Copper Company transferable only on the Books of the Company in person or by Attorney on surrender of this Certificate properly endorsed.

SHARES $10 EACH

In Witness Whereof the President and Secretary have hereunto subscribed their names and affixed the seal of said Company this day of DEC 16 1919

THIS CERTIFICATE IS NOT VALID UNLESS COUNTER-SIGNED BY THE TRANSFER AGENT AND REGISTRAR

BOSTON SAFE DEPOSIT & TRUST CO.

STATE STREET TRUST COMPANY

SECRETARY

PRESIDENT

N. E. Stewart

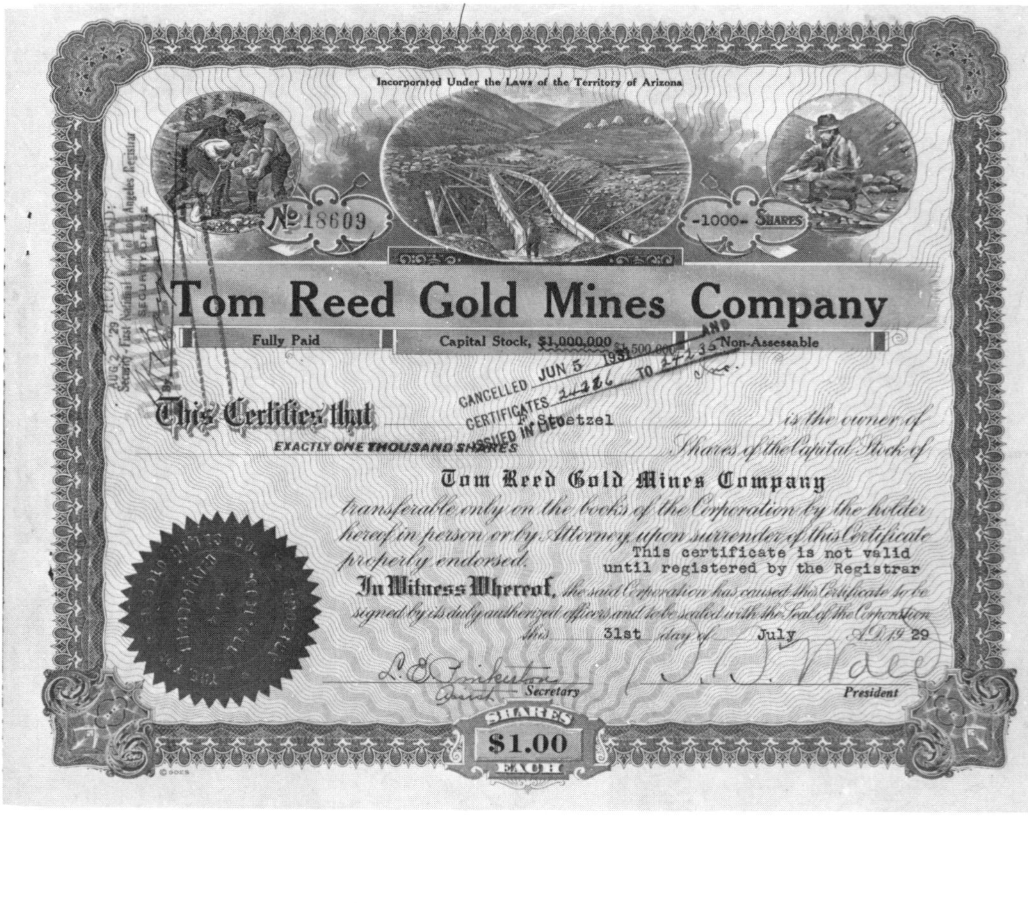

Incorporated Under the Laws of the Territory of Arizona

No. 18609

-1000- SHARES

Tom Reed Gold Mines Company

Fully Paid | Capital Stock, ~~$1,000,000~~ $1,500,000 | Non-Assessable

CANCELLED JUN 5 1931 CERTIFICATES 24126 TO 24135 AND ISSUED IN LIEU

This Certifies that F. Stoetzel is the owner of EXACTLY ONE THOUSAND SHARES Shares of the Capital Stock of

Tom Reed Gold Mines Company

transferable only on the books of the Corporation by the holder hereof in person or by Attorney upon surrender of this Certificate properly endorsed.

This certificate is not valid until registered by the Registrar

In Witness Whereof, the said Corporation has caused this Certificate to be signed by its duly authorized officers and to be sealed with the Seal of the Corporation this 31st day of July A.D. 1929

L. E. Pinkerton, Asst. Secretary

President

AUG 2 '29 REGISTERED: Security-First National Bank of Los Angeles, Registrar

SHARES $1.00 EACH

White Pine Mill and Mining of Nevada (I), 1860s, Miners hauling ore with horses to mill and smelting plant vignette **145.00**
White Star Mining (I), 1880s, Bond, large white star company logo **25.00**
Whitlatch Union Mining and Milling (U), 1880s, Mining scene **20.00**
Wilkes-Barre Coal Company (I), 1910s, Gold bond, mining scene of mine and jackhammer **40.00**
Williams Coal Company of Kanawha (I), 1870s, State seal of West Virginia **44.00**
Williams Coal Company of Kanawha (I), 1880s, Bond **125.00**
Willow Creek Gold Mining (I-N), Nevada, 1910s, Vignette of ore train, old prospector with two burros vignette **15.00**
Wisdom Silver Mining (I), 1920s, Mining vignette **10.00**
Wiswell Electric Mining Machinery Company (I), 1880s, Maine, State seal **48.00**
Wolverine Copper Mining (I), 1910s, Michigan, Miners vignette **15.00**
Wolverine Copper Mining (I), 1920s, Michigan, Miners vignette **11.00**
Wolverine Mining (I), 1900s, Utah, Two mining vignettes **20.00**
Wolverine Mining (I), 1910s, Michigan, Miners and equipment vignette **17.00**
Wonderland Mining (I-N), 1900s, Wyoming, Embossed seal **7.00**
World Exploration Company (I-N), 1920s, Large milling and smelting buildings in mountains scene vignette **8.00**

Yaeger Canon Copper Company (I-N), 1900s, Arizona Territory, Gold bond **35.00**
Yankee Girl Gold Mining Company of Bullfrog (I-N), 1900s, Three mining vignettes **28.00**
Yellow Metal Mining and Milling (I), 1900s, Wyoming, Large mining vignette **16.00**
Yerlington Mounton Copper Company (I-N), 1910s, Nevada, Working miners vignette **23.00**
Yguana Smelting and Mining (U), 1800s, Mining vignette **12.00**
Young Helca Mining and Smelting (I), 1880s, Working miners with ore car vignette, seal **45.00**
Yuba Consolidated Gold Fields (I), 1940s, Cancelled by Wells Fargo Bank **6.00**
Yuma Consolidated Mines and Mill (I), 1900s, Arizona Territory, Seated lady with winged eagle vignette **27.00**

Zapata Producing and Refining **18.00**
Zephyr Mining Company (I), 1880s, Colorado, Working miners vignette **160.00**
Zephyr Mining Company (U), 1880s, Colorado, Working miners vignette **30.00**

◀ ***Superior and Boston Copper Company (I-N), 1910s, Arizona,*** *Miners working vignette* ***25.00***
◀ ***Tom Reed Gold Mines (I), 1920s,*** *Three mining vignettes* ***9.00***

INCORPORATED UNDER THE LAWS OF THE
STATE OF WASHINGTON
AND
REGISTERED IN BRITISH COLUMBIA

No 60 Shares 209

TRUST MINING COMPANY

The Capital Stock, $50,000.

CANCELLED May 24 189_
FOLLOWING NO.
ISSUED INSTEAD.

Fully Paid. Non-assessable.

THIS CERTIFIES THAT E. E. Knowles is the owner of Two Hundred & Nine Shares of the Capital Stock of

Trust Mining Company

transferable only on the Books of the Corporation in person or by Attorney on surrender of this Certificate.

In Witness Whereof, *the duly authorized officers of this Corporation have hereunto subscribed their names and caused the corporate Seal to be hereto affixed at* SPOKANE, WASH. *this* 22 *day of* July *A.D. 189*7

Secretary. *President.*

SHARES $1.00 EACH

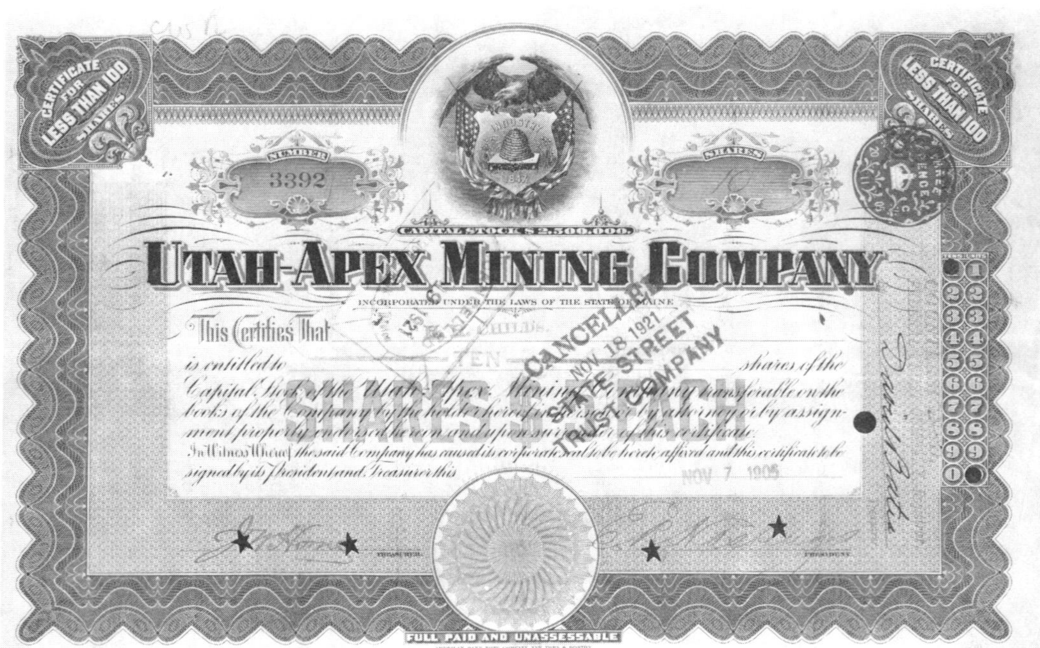
CERTIFICATE FOR LESS THAN 100 SHARES

NUMBER 3392 SHARES 10

CAPITAL STOCK $ 2,500,000.

UTAH-APEX MINING COMPANY

INCORPORATED UNDER THE LAWS OF THE STATE OF MAINE

This Certifies That E. E. CHILDS.

is entitled to TEN *shares of the Capital Stock of the Utah-Apex Mining Company transferable on the books of the Company by the holder hereof in person or by attorney or by assignment properly endorsed hereon and upon surrender of this certificate.*

In Witness Whereof the said Company has caused its corporate seal to be hereto affixed and this certificate to be signed by its President and Treasurer this NOV 7 1905

SHARES $5 EACH

CANCELLED NOV 18 1921 STATE STREET TRUST COMPANY

TREASURER. PRESIDENT.

FULL PAID AND UNASSESSABLE

RAILROADS

Stocks

Addison Railroad (I), 1870s, Old train and ship vignette	90.00
Akron, Canton and Youngstown Railroad (I), 1950s	8.00
Alabama and Vicksburg Railroad (I),1800s, Old train vignette	70.00
Alabama and Vicksburg Railroad (I), 1890s, Old train vignette	60.00
Alabama and Vicksburg Railroad (U), 1800s	20.00
Alabama and Vicksburg Railroad (U), 1900s, Train vignette	12.00
Albany Railroad (I), 1870s, Horse streetcar vignette	110.00
Albany Railroad (U), 1800s, Streetcar vignette	39.00
Allegany City Company (U), 1800s, Old train vignette	75.00
Amadore Railroad (U), 1890s, California	40.00
American Central Railroad (U)	17.00
American Express (I), 1860s, Dock scene vignette	675.00
American Express (I), 1860s, Train vignette, signed by Wells-Fargo	1600.00
American Express (I-N), 1860s, Dock scene vignette	790.00
American Safety Steel Rail Company (I-N), 1910s, Train vignette	17.00
Ann Arbor Railroad Company, The (I), 1900s, Old train vignette	44.00
Ann Arbor Railroad Company (I), 1920s, Old train vignette	22.00
Arlington and Lehigh Valley Traction (U), 1800s, Streetcar and semi-nude female vignette	18.00
Atchinson and Pikes Peak Railroad (U), 1860s, Old train vignette	80.00
Atlanta and Charlotte Airline Railway (I), 1890s, Old train vignette	45.00
Atlantic and Saint Lawrence Railroad (I), 1930s, Train vignette	39.00
Atlantic and Suburban Railroad (U), 1900s, Indian with spear on horse	30.00
Atlantic City and Shore Railroad (I), 1900s, Streetcar and bathers vignette	72.00
Atlantic Coast Line Railroad (I), 1950s, Train vignette	16.00
Attica and Allegany Valley Railroad (I), 1850s, Old train vignette	85.00
Attica and Buffalo Railroad (U), 1840s, Old steam train vignette	30.00
Aurora, Elgin and Chicago Railway (I), 1900s, Electric train vignette, with stamp	27.00
Bay City and East Saginaw Railroad (U), 1860s, Old steam train vignette	42.00
Bay City and Saginaw Railroad (U), 1860s, Train vignette	39.00
Baltimore and Cumberland Railway Company, The (U), 1890s, Train vignette	17.00
Baltimore and Ohio Railroad (I), 1850s, Old train vignette	190.00
Baltimore and Ohio Railroad (I), 1880s, Old train vignette	35.00
Baltimore and Ohio Railroad (I), 1890s, Miss America 1899 vignette	49.00
Baltimore and Ohio Railroad (I), 1890s, Tom Thumb train vignette	30.00
Baltimore and Ohio Railroad (I), 1900s and 1910s, Tom Thumb vignette	15.00
Baltimore and Ohio Railroad (I), 1920s, Tom Thumb train vignette	10.00
Baltimore and Ohio, Southwestern (I), 1890s, Old train at station, horse and buggy vignette	40.00
Baltimore and Ohio Southwestern (I), 1890s, Scrip certificate	10.00
Baltimore and Ohio, Southwestern (U), 1890s, Old train at station, horse and buggy vignette	15.00
Baltimore and Susquehanna Railroad (I-N), 1830s, Six percent note, early train at river vignette	80.00
Baltimore and Susquehanna Railroad (U), 1800s, Old train vignette	45.00
Baltimore and Yorktown Turnpike Railroad (I), 1880s, Horse trolley and covered wagon vignette	75.00
Baltimore Consolidated (I), 1890s, Streetcar vignette	29.00

◀ ***Trust Mining Company (I), 1890s, Washington,*** *Miss Liberty, flag, eagle, and state seal vignette* ***25.00***

◀ ***Utah-Apex Mining Company (I), 1900s,*** *With stamps* ***12.00***

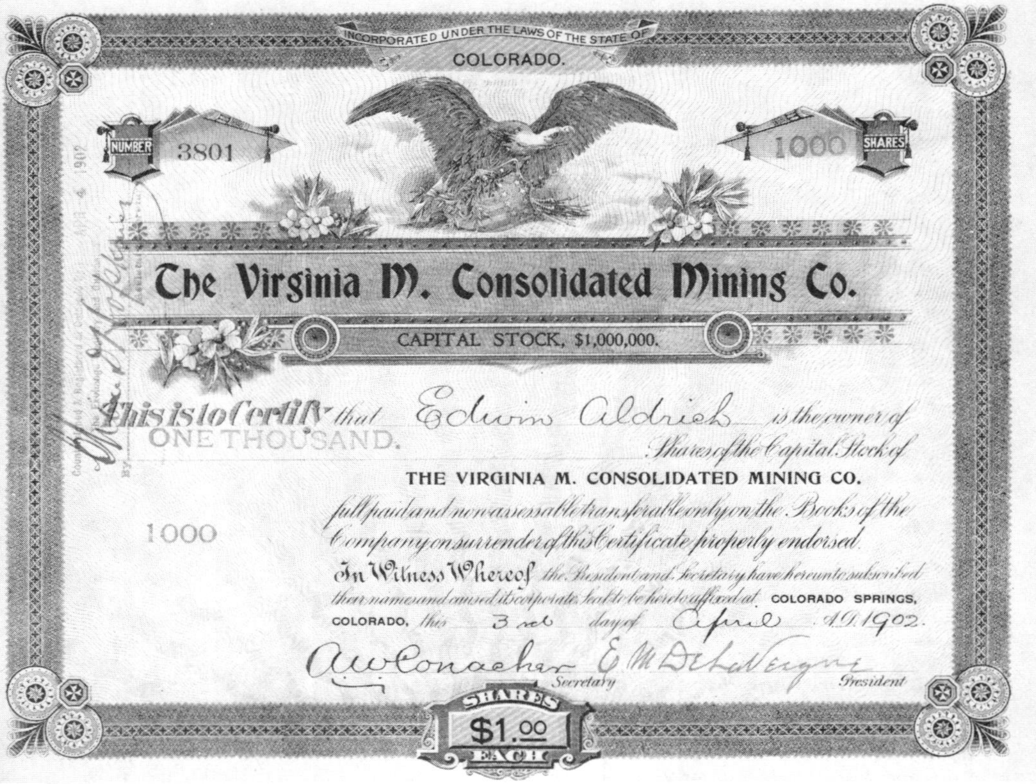

INCORPORATED UNDER THE LAWS OF THE STATE OF

COLORADO.

NUMBER 3801

1000 SHARES

The Virginia M. Consolidated Mining Co.

CAPITAL STOCK, $1,000,000.

This is to Certify that Edwin Aldrich is the owner of ONE THOUSAND. Shares of the Capital Stock of THE VIRGINIA M. CONSOLIDATED MINING CO. full paid and non assessable transferable only on the Books of the Company on surrender of this Certificate properly endorsed.

1000

In Witness Whereof the President and Secretary have hereunto subscribed their names and caused its corporate Seal to be hereto affixed at COLORADO SPRINGS, COLORADO, this 3rd day of April A.D. 1902.

A. W. Conacher, Secretary

E. M. De La Vergne, President

SHARES $1.00 EACH

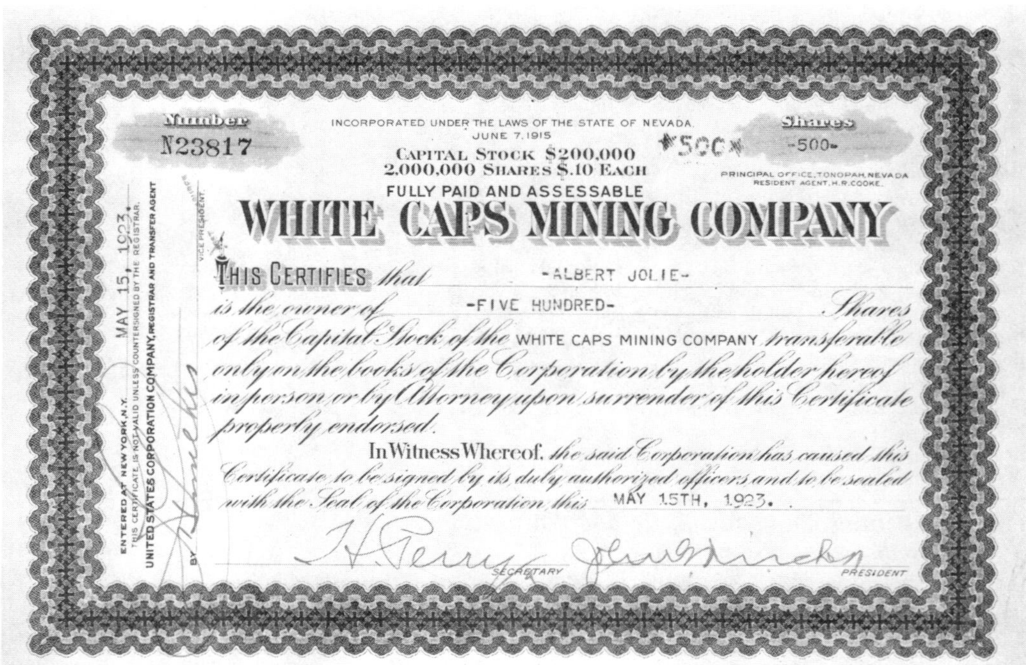

Number N23817

INCORPORATED UNDER THE LAWS OF THE STATE OF NEVADA. JUNE 7, 1915

CAPITAL STOCK $200,000

2,000,000 SHARES $.10 EACH

Shares *500* -500-

PRINCIPAL OFFICE, TONOPAH, NEVADA

RESIDENT AGENT, H. R. COOKE.

FULLY PAID AND ASSESSABLE

WHITE CAPS MINING COMPANY

THIS CERTIFIES that -ALBERT JOLIE- is the owner of -FIVE HUNDRED- Shares of the Capital Stock of the WHITE CAPS MINING COMPANY transferable only on the books of the Corporation by the holder hereof in person, or by Attorney upon surrender of this Certificate properly endorsed.

In Witness Whereof, the said Corporation has caused this Certificate to be signed by its duly authorized officers and to be sealed with the Seal of the Corporation this MAY 15TH, 1923.

SECRETARY

PRESIDENT

ENTERED AT NEW YORK, N.Y. MAY 15, 1923.

THIS CERTIFICATE IS NOT VALID UNLESS COUNTERSIGNED BY THE REGISTRAR.

UNITED STATES CORPORATION COMPANY, REGISTRAR AND TRANSFER AGENT

BY VICE PRESIDENT.

Baltimore Consolidated (U), 1890s, Streetcar vignette, scrip certificate	7.00
Bay Minette and Fort Morgan Railroad (I), 1930s, Eagle, gold seal	35.00
Beech Creek Railroad (U), 1800s, Old train vignette	35.00
Beech Creek, Clearfield and Southwestern Railroad (U), 1800s, Train vignette signed by Cornelius Vanderbilt	195.00
Belfast and Moosehead Lake Railroad (I), 1880s, Train vignette	55.00
Belgium National Railroad New York (I), 1950s, Temporary certificate	3.00
Bellingham and Northern Railroad (U), Eagle vignette	4.00
Bellingham Terminals and Railways (U), Eagle vignette	5.00
Belt Railroad and Stock Yard Company (U), 1880s, Train vignette	15.00
Belt Railroad and Stock Yard Railroad, The (I), Railroad scene vignette, signed by William Burford	65.00
Belt Railroad and Stock Yard Company, The (I), 1900s, Train vignette	15.00
Belt Railroad and Stock Yard Company, The (I), 1930s, Train station vignette	10.00
Belt Railroad and Stock Yard Company, The (I), 1940s, Train vignette	7.00
Belt Railroad and Stock Yard Company, The (I), 1950s,	4.00
Belt Railroad and Stock Yard Company, The (I-N), 1890s, Train vignette	30.00
Belt Railroad and Stock Yard Company, The (I-N), 1930s, Train vignette	20.00
Big Blackfoot Railroad (U), 1900s, Train vignette	20.00
Black River and Utica Railroad (I), 1850s, Old train vignette	95.00
Bleeker Street and Fulton Ferry Railroad (I), 1910s, Depot vignette	38.00
Bleeker Street and Fulton Ferry Railroad (I), 1920s,	34.00
Blue Ridge Railroad (I), 1860s, Old train vignette, four state seals, Henry Clews's signature	160.00
Boston and Main Railroad (I), Temporary certificate	5.00
Boston and Providence Railroad (I), 1830s, Train and ship vignette	295.00
Boston and Providence Railroad (I), 1840s, Train and ship vignette	265.00
Boston and Providence Railroad (I), 1850s, Train vignette	80.00
Boston and Providence Railroad (I), 1860s, Two trains vignette	75.00
Boston and Providence Railroad, 1870s	65.00
Boston and Providence Railroad, 1880s	60.00
Boston and Providence Railroad, 1890s	55.00
Boston and Worcester Railroad (I), 1850s, Train vignette	115.00
Boston and Worcester Railroad (I), 1860s, Train vignette	110.00
Boston and Worcester Street Railway (I), 1920s, Temporary certificate	12.00
Boston, Clinton and Fitchburg Railroad, 1860s, Train and ship vignette, with stamps	65.00
Boston, Clinton and Fitchburg Railroad, 1880s, State seal	37.00
Boston, Clinton and Fitchburg Railroad (I), 1870s, State seal	50.00
Boston, Clinton and Fitchburg Railroad (U), 1800s	17.00
Boston, Clinton, Fitchburg and New Bedford Railroad (I), 1870s, Train and ships vignette	45.00
Boston Consolidated Street Railway, 1880s, Ships vignette	65.00
Boston Consolidated Street Railway (I), 1910s, Electric train vignette	12.00
Boston Elevated Railway Company (I), 1900s, Elevated train vignette	13.00
Boston Elevated Railway Company (I), 1910s, Elevated train vignette	12.00
Boston Elevated Railway Company (I), 1920s, Elevated train vignette	10.00
Boston Elevated Railway Company (I), 1930s, Elevated train	9.00
Boston Railroad Holding Company (I), 1940s, Three figures vignette	25.00
Boston Terminal Company (I), 1890s	35.00
Boston Terminal Company (I), 1900s	13.00
Bozeman Street Railway (U)	8.00
Brandywine Railway (U), 1900s, Large elk vignette	12.00
Brazil Railroad Company (I), 1900s, Old train vignette	23.00
Broadway and Seventh Avenue Railroad (I), 1890s, Figures vignette	60.00

◀ ***Virginia M. Consolidated Mining Company, the (I-N), 1900s,*** ***Colorado,*** *Eagle vignette*	***15.00***
◀ ***White Caps Mining (I-N), 1920s,*** *One paid assessment stamp*	***6.00***

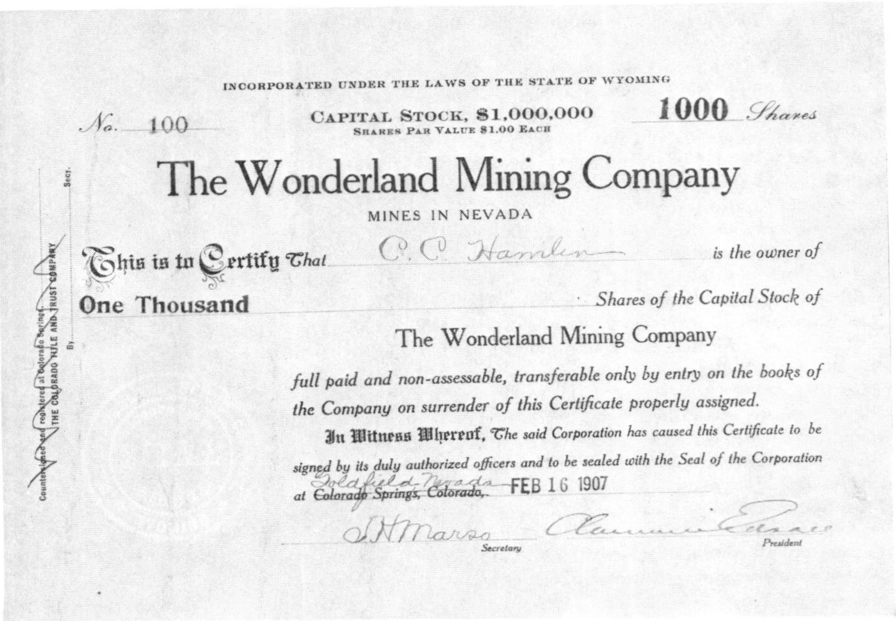

INCORPORATED UNDER THE LAWS OF THE STATE OF WYOMING

No. 100 — CAPITAL STOCK, $1,000,000 — SHARES PAR VALUE $1.00 EACH — 1000 Shares

The Wonderland Mining Company

MINES IN NEVADA

This is to Certify That C. C. Hamlin is the owner of

One Thousand Shares of the Capital Stock of

The Wonderland Mining Company

full paid and non-assessable, transferable only by entry on the books of the Company on surrender of this Certificate properly assigned.

In Witness Whereof, *The said Corporation has caused this Certificate to be signed by its duly authorized officers and to be sealed with the Seal of the Corporation at* ~~Colorado Springs, Colorado,~~ Goldfield Nevada FEB 16 1907

S. H. Marso, Secretary — President

Countersigned and registered at Colorado Springs, THE COLORADO TITLE AND TRUST COMPANY By ______ Secy.

Capital Stock $3,000,000 — 3,000,000 Shares $1.00 Each

Number N18151 — Shares *100*

YERINGTON MOUNTAIN COPPER COMPANY

This Certifies that L. J. Kleczka is the owner of ONE HUNDRED full paid Shares of the Capital Stock of the Yerington Mountain Copper Company, transferable only on the books of the Company, in person or by Attorney on surrender of this Certificate duly endorsed.

SHARES $1.00 EACH

Witness the Seal of the Company and the signatures of its duly authorized officers this APR 9 - 1919

Secretary — President

INCORPORATED UNDER THE LAWS OF THE STATE OF NEVADA

COUNTERSIGNED AT NEW YORK N.Y. UNITED STATES CORPORATION COMPANY, REGISTRAR AND TRANSFER AGENT

PRINCIPAL OFFICE TONOPAH, NEVADA — RESIDENT AGENT, P.S. BOOTH

Broadway and Seventh Avenue Railroad (I), 1890s, With hole cancel	**30.00**
Broadway and Seventh Avenue Railroad (I), 1900s	**50.00**
Broadway and Seventh Avenue Railroad (I), 1910s, Broadway scene vignette	**40.00**
Broadway and Seventh Avenue Railroad (I), 1930s	**12.00**
Brooklyn and Queens Transit (I), 1920s	**25.00**
Brooklyn and Queens Transit (I), 1940s	**20.00**
Brooklyn, Flatbush and Coney Island (I), 1870s, Old train vignette	**130.00**
Brooklyn, Manhattan Transit (I), 1930s	**21.00**
Brooklyn, Manhattan Transit (I), 1940s, Man and woman vignette	**18.00**
Brooklyn Rapid Transit (I), 1910s, Early streetcar vignette	**100.00**
Brooklyn Union Elevated Railroad (I), 1890s, Famous Brooklyn Bridge vignette	**120.00**
Buffalo and Erie Railroad (U), 1860s, Old train vignetted	**50.00**
Buffalo and Williamsville Railroad (I), 1880s, Old train vignette	**70.00**
Buffalo, New York and Erie Railroad (I), 1860s, Old train vignette	**82.00**
Buffalo, Thousand Islands and Portland Railway (U), 1890s, Old train vignette	**45.00**
Burlington and Missouri River Railroad (I), 1870s, Two trains vignette	**53.00**
Burlington, Cedar Rapids	**35.00**
Burlington, Cedar Rapids and Minneapolis Railroad (I), 1870s, Old train vignette	**365.00**
Burlington, Cedar Rapids and Minnesota Railway Company (U), 1800s, Old train vignette	**20.00**
Burlington, Cedar Rapids and Northern Railway Company (I), 1900s, Eagle vignette	**15.00**
Burrow's Train Control (I), 1920s, Large locomotive vignette	**30.00**
Bush Terminal Railroad (I), 1920s, Train vignette with young lady vignette	**9.00**
Bush Terminal Railroad (I), 1920s, Women vignette	**6.00**
Bush Terminal Railroad (I), 1930s, Ship and train vignette	**8.00**

Cairo and Saint Louis Railroad (I), 1880s, Two trains vignette	**80.00**
California Improvement Company (U), 1900s, Old train	**15.00**
California Railway (I), 1890s, Rare, old train, snow-capped mountain, and boat vignette	**155.00**
California Street Cable Railroad Company (I), 1920s, Cable car vignette	**65.00**
California Street Cable Railroad Company (U), Cable car vignette	**35.00**
Canajoharie and Catskill Railroad (U), 1830s	**40.00**
Canarsie Railroad (U), 1900s	**15.00**
Canon City, Florence and Royal Gorge Interurban Railway (U), Interurban vignette	**35.00**
Cape Fear and Cincinnati Railway 1890s (I)	**20.00**
Cayadutta Electric Railroad (I), 1890s	**17.00**
Cedar Falls and Minneapolis Railroad (I), 1890s, Old train vignette	**68.00**
Cedar Rapids and Missouri River (I), 1870s, Train vignette	**45.00**
Cedar Rapids and Northwestern (U), 1870s	**25.00**
Cedar Rapids and Saint Paul Railway (U), 1800s	**20.00**
Cedar Rapids, Iowa City and Southern Construction Company, Railroad Construction Company (I), 1910s and 1920s	**7.00**
Central Crosstown Railroad, 1890s	**42.00**
Central Crosstown Railroad, 1900s	**40.00**
Central Dock and Terminal Railroad (U), 1890s	**5.00**
Central of Georgia Railway (I), 1920s, Train vignette	**38.00**
Central of Georgia Railway (I), 1950s, Man with sledge vignette	**9.00**
Central of Georgia Railway (U), 1910s, Cotton pickers vignette	**17.00**
Central of Georgia Railway (U), 1910s, Train vignette	**22.00**
Central Ohio Railroad Company (I), 1860s, With many stamps, old train vignette	**100.00**
Central Ohio Railroad Company (I), 1870s, With many stamps, old train vignette	**95.00**
Central Pacific Railroad (I), 1940s, Train vignette	**23.00**

◀ ***Wonderland Mining (I-N), 1900s, Wyoming,*** *Embossed seal* ***7.00***

◀ ***Yerlington Mountain Copper Company (I-N), 1910s, Nevada,*** *Working miners vignette* ***23.00***

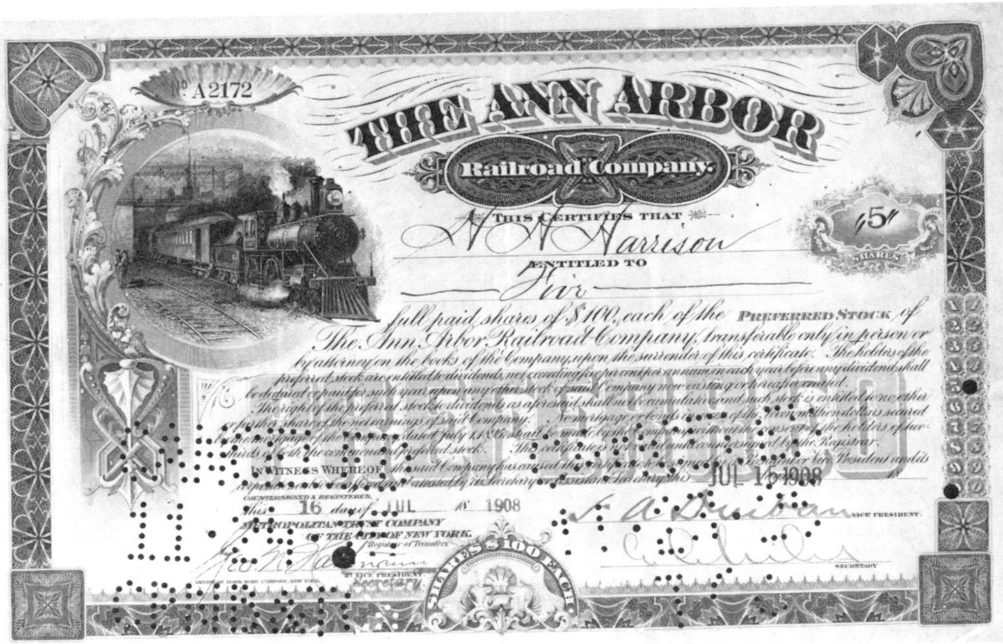
No. A2172
THE ANN ARBOR
Railroad Company.
THIS CERTIFIES THAT
ENTITLED TO
full paid shares of $100, each of the PREFERRED STOCK of
The Ann Arbor Railroad Company, transferable only in person or
by attorney on the books of the Company, upon the surrender of this certificate.
COUNTERSIGNED & REGISTERED,
METROPOLITAN TRUST COMPANY
OF THE CITY OF NEW YORK.
VICE PRESIDENT.
SECRETARY.
SHARES $100 EACH.
SHARES

INCORPORATED UNDER THE LAWS OF THE STATE OF MARYLAND
NUMBER
309
SHARES
THE
BALTIMORE & CUMBERLAND RAILWAY COMPANY
AUTHORIZED CAPITAL
$10,000,000.
SHARES
$50 EACH.
This is to Certify, that
the owner of
Shares of the Capital Stock of
THE BALTIMORE & CUMBERLAND RAILWAY COMPANY.
Transferable only on the Books of said Company in person or by Attorney
on surrender of this Certificate.
In Witness whereof, the President and Secretary and Treasurer
have hereunto set their hands, and affixed the Seal of the Company,
this
day of
A.D. 18
Secy. & Treas.
President.

Central Passenger Railway Company (I), 1900s, Streetcar vignette	**60.00**
Central Transportation Company (I), 1870s, Train vignette	**65.00**
Central Transportation Company (I), 1880s, No vignette	**35.00**
Central Transportation Company (I), 1880s, Old train vignette	**60.00**
Central Union Depot and Railway of Cincinnati (U), 1900s, Old train vignette	**27.00**
Central Vermont Railway (I), 1900s, Train vignette	**28.00**
Charles River Branch Railroad (I), 1850s, Seal	**55.00**
Charles River Street Railway (I), 1850s	**165.00**
Charles River Street Railway (I), 1880s, Horse trolley vignette	**65.00**
Charleston City Railway (I), 1860s	**60.00**
Charleston City Railway (I), 1890s, Streetcar vignette	**48.00**
Chattanooga, Rome and Southern Railroad (I), 1890s, With stamp	**75.00**
Chester, Darby and Philadelphia Railway (U), 1800s, Streetcar vignette	**25.00**
Chestnut Hill Railroad (I), 1940s, No vignette	**10.00**
Chestnut Hill Railroad (U), 1940s, No vignette	**4.00**
Chicago and Alton Railroad (I), 1860s, Train vignette, signed by S. Tilden	**50.00**
Chicago and Alton (I), 1890s, Four trains vignette	**37.00**
Chicago and Alton Equipment Association (I), 1900s, Semi-nude goddess vignette	**8.00**
Chicago and Alton Equipment Association (U), 1900s	**4.00**
Chicago and Alton Equipment Association Railroad (I), 1910s, Old train vignette	**35.00**
Chicago and Eastern Illinois Railroad Company (I), 1880s, Old train vignette	**55.00**
Chicago and Eastern Illinois Railroad Company (I), 1890s, Two trains vignette	**35.00**
Chicago and Eastern Illinois Railroad Company (I), 1890s, Two trains vignette, preferred	**45.00**
Chicago and Eastern Illinois Railroad Company (I), 1900s, Two trains vignettes	**24.00**
Chicago and Eastern Illinois Railroad Company (U), Two trains vignette	**18.00**
Chicago and Eastern Illinois Railroad Company (U), 1890s, Two trains vignette	**24.00**
Chicago and Eastern Illinois Railroad Company (U), 1920s, Train vignette	**12.00**
Chicago and Eastern Illinois Railroad Company (U), 1930s, Scrip certificate	**5.00**
Chicago and Eastern Illinois Railroad Company (U), 1930s, Train vignette	**8.00**
Chicago and Eastern Railroad (U), 1930s, Train vignette	**8.00**
Chicago and Rock Island Railroad (I), 1851–1853, Old train vignette	**125.00**
Chicago and Rock Island Railroad (I), 1854	**95.00**
Chicago and Rock Island Railroad (I), 1857, Train vignette	**85.00**
Chicago and Rock Island Railroad (U), 1851–1853, Old train vignette	**30.00**
Chicago and Rock Island Railroad (U), 1850s	**25.00**
Chicago and Southwestern Railway (U), 1870s, Old steam train vignette	**65.00**
Chicago, Burlington and Quincy Railroad (I), 1870s, Train vignette	**63.00**
Chicago, Burlington and Quincy Railroad Company (I), 1880s, Train vignette	**26.00**
Chicago, Burlington and Quincy Railroad Company (I), 1890s, Old train vignette, with stamps	**19.00**
Chicago, Burlington and Quincy Railroad Company (I), 1890s, Train vignette	**17.00**
Chicago, Great Western Railroad (I), 1930s, Two trains vignette	**20.00**
Chicago, Great Western Railroad (I), 1940s, Two trains vignette	**15.00**
Chicago, Great Western Railroad (I), 1950s, Two trains vignette	**12.00**
Chicago, Havana and Western Railroad (I), 1920s	**17.00**
Chicago, Indianapolis and Louisville Railroad (I), 1930s and 1940s, Conductor and brakeman vignette	**22.00**
Chicago, Indianapolis and Louisville Railroad (I), 1940s, Temporary certificate	**7.00**
Chicago, Indianapolis and Southern Railroad, (U), 1900s, Eagle on globe	**14.00**
Chicago, Kansas and Nebraska Railway (I), 1880s	**30.00**

◀ ***Ann Arbor Railroad Company, The (I),*** *Old train vignette*	***44.00***
◀ ***Baltimore and Cumberland Railway Company, The (U), 1890s,*** *Train vignette*	***17.00***

STATE OF INDIANA
The Belt Rail Road And Stock Yards Company
№ 6913
--50--
SHARES
COMMON STOCK
TRANSFERRED TO NEW CERTIFICATE # 94416
This is to Certify that LOUISE JANET GIASSER
is entitled to FIFTY (50) Shares of FIFTY DOLLARS each of the Common Capital Stock of THE BELT RAIL ROAD AND STOCK YARDS COMPANY, transferable only on the books of this Company in person or by Attorney on the surrender of this Certificate.
In Witness Whereof, The President and Secretary of said Company have hereunto set their hands and affixed the Seal of the Company at Indianapolis, this 20th day of July 1944.
--FIFTY--
SHARES
-50-
$50
Secretary
President

NUMBER
4750
SHARES
2
NOT OVER TWO SHARES *2*
INCORPORATED UNDER THE LAWS OF THE
COMMONWEALTH OF MASSACHUSETTS
BOSTON ELEVATED RAILWAY COMPANY
This Certifies that MRS. EDITH BRAMHALL CULLIS*****
*****TWO*****
In Witness Whereof
BOSTON ELEVATED RAILWAY COMPANY
JUN 20 1922
OLD COLONY TRUST COMPANY
AMERICAN TRUST COMPANY

Chicago, Kansas and Nebraska Railway (U), 1880s 12.00
Chicago, Lake Geneva and Pacific Railway (U), 1800s, Engine, boats vignette, state seal **20.00**
Chicago, Milwaukee and Gary Railway (I), 1900s, Train vignette **16.00**
Chicago, Milwaukee and Gary Railway (U), 1900s, Train and old auto vignette **14.00**
Chicago, Milwaukee and Puget Sound Railroad (U), 1900s **35.00**
Chicago, Milwaukee and Saint Paul Railway (I), 1870s, Old train vignette **65.00**
Chicago, Milwaukee and Saint Paul Railroad (U), 1900s, Electric train vignette **35.00**
Chicago, Milwaukee and Saint Paul Railroad (U), 1900s, Eagle vignette **25.00**
Chicago, Milwaukee and Saint Paul Railroad (U), 1920s and 1930s, Train vignette **8.00**
Chicago, Milwaukee, Saint Paul and Pacific Railroad (I), 1930s, Electric train vignette **10.00**
Chicago, New York Electric Airline Railroad (I), 1900s **15.00**
Chicago, Northern Pacific Railroad (I), 1890s, Train vignette **55.00**
Chicago, Northwestern Railway (I), 1880s, Six vignettes **95.00**
Chicago, Northwestern Railway (I), 1930s, Old trains, five vignettes **25.00**
Chicago, Northwestern Railway (I), 1940s, Two angels vignette **7.00**
Chicago, Northwestern Railway (I), 1950s **6.00**
Chicago Rapid Transit (I), 1930s, Eagle on shield **32.00**
Chicago, Rock Island and Pacific Railroad (I), 1870s, Scrip certificate **30.00**
Chicago, Rock Island and Pacific Railroad (I), 1880s, Train vignette **65.00**
Chicago, Rock Island and Pacific Railroad (I), 1890s, Old train vignette, common **50.00**
Chicago, Rock Island and Pacific Railroad (I), 1890s, Scrip certificate **40.00**
Chicago, Rock Island and Pacific Railroad (I), 1900s, Old train vignette **45.00**
Chicago, Rock Island and Pacific Railroad (I), 1910s, Preferred, old train vignette **35.00**
Chicago, Rock Island and Pacific Railroad (I), 1910s, Train vignette **25.00**
Chicago, Rock Island and Pacific Railroad 1940s, Train vignette **20.00**
Chicago, Rock Island and Pacific Railroad (I), 1940s, Two trains and shapely woman vignette **20.00**
Chicago, Rock Island and Pacific Railroad (I), 1950s, Two trains and shapely woman vignette **20.00**
Chicago, Rock Island and Pacific Railroad (I), 1960s and 1970s **5.00**
Chicago, Saint Paul, Minneapolis and Omaha Railway (I), Old train vignette **35.00**
Chicago, South Shore and South Bend Railroad (I), 1950s **8.00**
Chicago Southern Express (U), 1900s, Indian maiden vignette and state seal **10.00**
Chicago Southern Railway (I), 1900s **9.00**
Chicago Terminal Transfer Railroad Company (I), 1900s, Two trains vignette **25.00**
Chicago Terminal Transfer Railroad (U), 1900s, **8.00**
Chicago, Terre Haute and Western (I), 1910s **17.00**
Choctaw, Oklahoma and Gulf Railroad (I), 1890s, With stamps, Oklahoma ore train vignette **45.00**
Choctaw, Oklahoma and Gulf Railroad (I), 1900s, Train at station vignette **30.00**
Christopher and Tenth Street Railroad (I), 1910s, Horse-streetcars vignette **33.00**
Christopher and Tenth Street Railroad (I), 1920s and 1930s, Five streetcars vignette **28.00**
Cincinnati and Indiana Railroad (U), 1800s, Train vignette **28.00**
Cincinnati, Hamilton and Dayton Railroad (U), 1860s, Scrip certificate **12.00**
Cincinnati, Indianapolis, Saint Louis and Chicago Railroad (U), 1890s **37.00**
Cincinnati, Lafayette and Chicago Railroad (U), 1870s, Old train vignette **35.00**
Cincinnati, New Orleans and Texas Pacific Railway Company, The (I), 1870s, Train vignette **40.00**
Cincinnati, New Orleans and Texas Pacific Railway Company, The (I), 1880s, Old train vignette **40.00**
Cincinnati, New Orleans and Texas Pacific Railway Company, The (I), 1890s, Old train vignette **33.00**
Cincinnati, New Orleans and Texas Pacific Railway Company, The (I), 1900s, Old train vignette **24.00**
Cincinnati, New Orleans and Texas Pacific Railway Company, The (I), 1910s, Old train vignette **20.00**

◀***Belt Railroad and Stockyard Company, The (I), 1940s***, *Train vignette* ***7.00***
◀***Boston Elevated Railway Company (I), 1920s***, *Elevated train vignette* ***10.00***

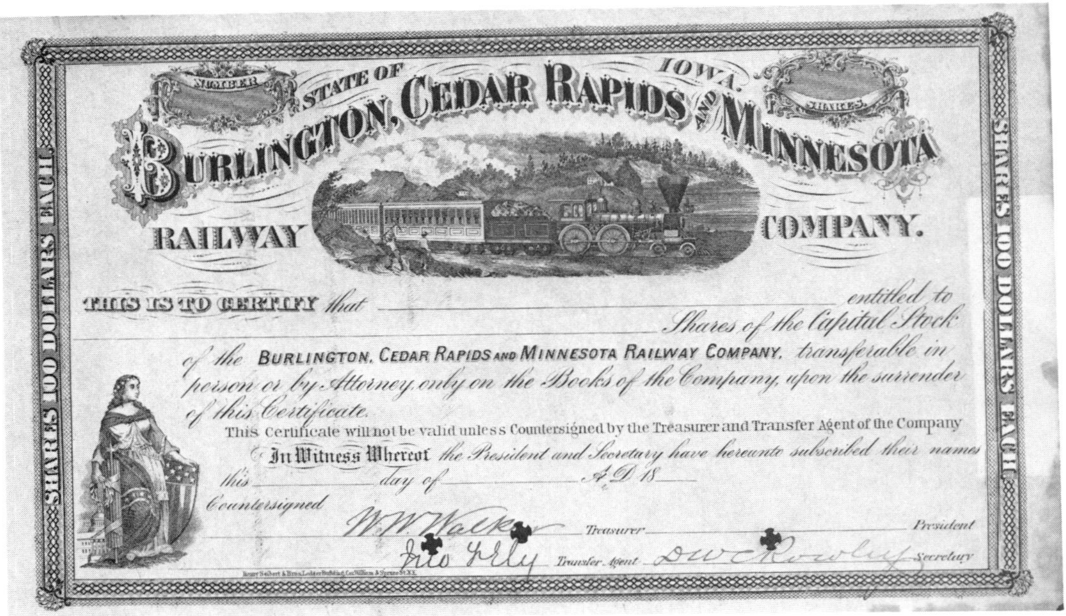

NUMBER

STATE OF IOWA.

SHARES

BURLINGTON, CEDAR RAPIDS AND MINNESOTA RAILWAY COMPANY.

SHARES 100 DOLLARS EACH

THIS IS TO CERTIFY that ______________________________ entitled to ______________________________ Shares of the Capital Stock of the BURLINGTON, CEDAR RAPIDS AND MINNESOTA RAILWAY COMPANY, transferable in person or by Attorney, only on the Books of the Company, upon the surrender of this Certificate.

This Certificate will not be valid unless Countersigned by the Treasurer and Transfer Agent of the Company

In Witness Whereof the President and Secretary have hereunto subscribed their names this __________ day of __________ A.D. 18____

Countersigned

W. W. Walker Treasurer ______________________________ President

Jno Ely Transfer Agent D W C Rowley Secretary

Number 190

"CENTRAL OHIO RAIL ROAD COMPANY" AS REORGANIZED

STATE OF OHIO

SHARES $50 EACH

This Certifies, that Elizabeth W. Duval is the owner of Fourteen Shares of the Preferred Capital Stock of the Central Ohio Rail Road Company as Reorganized, transferable only on the Books of the Company in person or by Attorney on the surrender of this Certificate.

In Witness whereof the President and Secretary have affixed their signatures, at the City of Zanesville, January 23 1879

Shares 14

Wm Wing Sec.y H Blandy Pres.t

Know all men by these presents that I, Elizabeth W. Duval do hereby appoint ______ Attorney for me to sell and transfer to Mary Rebecca Duval the whole of the above named shares, with power one or more Attornies under ______ to appoint.

Witness my hand ______ day of December 189_

In presence of John R______

Elizabeth W. Duval

Cincinnati, New Orleans and Texas Pacific Railway Company, The (I), 1920s, Old train vignette 16.00
Cincinnati, New Orleans and Texas Pacific Railway Company, The (I), 1930s, Old train vignette 12.00
Cincinnati, New Orleans and Texas Pacific Railway Company, The (U), 1870s, Train vignette 20.00
Cincinnati, New Orleans and Texas Pacific Railway Company, The (U), 1880s, Old train vignette, ships and horses vignette 20.00
Cincinnati Northern and Texas Pacific Railroad (I), 1900s, Old train vignette 30.00
Cincinnati Northern Railroad (I), 1930s, State seal 20.00
Cincinnati Northern Railroad (U), 1800s 22.00
Cincinnati Northern Railroad (U), 1900s, Old train vignette 20.00
Cincinnati Railway Tunnel Company (I), 1870s, Seal and signature of John C. Fremont 300.00
Cincinnati, Sandusky and Cleveland Railroad (U), 1800s, Old train vignette 35.00
Cincinnati, Wabash and Michigan Railroad (U), 1800s, Old train vignette 34.00
Cincinnati, Washington and Baltimore Railroad (I), 1880s, Trains vignette 35.00
Cincinnati, Washington and Baltimore Railroad (I), 1890s, Train vignette 30.00
Citizen's Passenger Railway (I), 1860s, State seal 50.00
Citizen's Passenger Railway Company (I), 1900s, State seal, two women vignette 10.00
Citizen's Passenger Railway Company and Tenth and Eleventh Streets (I), 1860s 45.00
City Railway Company (I), 1890s, Seminude goddess with light vignette 40.00
City Railway Company (I), 1900s, Seminude goddess with light vignette 37.00
City Railway Company (I), 1910s, Seminude goddess with light vignette 30.00
City Railway Company (I), 1920s, Seminude goddess with light vignette 24.00
City Railway Company (I), 1930s, Seminude goddess with light vignette 20.00
City Railway Company (I), 1940s, Seminude goddess with light vignette 10.00
Claremont University and Ferries Street Railroad (U), 1880s, Horse trolley vignette 35.00
Cleveland and Pittsburgh Railroad (U), 1800s, Train vignette 30.00
Cleveland and Pittsburgh Railroad (U), 1850s, Old train vignette 40.00
Cleveland and Toledo Railroad (I), 1850s, Train vignette 85.00
Cleveland and Toledo Railroad (I), 1860s, Receipt for certificate 10.00
Cleveland and Toledo Railroad (U), 1850s, Old train vignette 50.00
Cleveland and Toledo Railroad (U), 1860s, Old train vignette 40.00
Cleveland, Columbus, Cincinnati and Indianapolis Railroad (I), 1860s, Train vignette 85.00
Cleveland, Columbus, Cincinnati and Indianapolis Railroad (I), 1870s, Train and ship vignettes, portrait, with stamp 60.00
Cleveland, Columbus, Cincinnati and Indianapolis Railroad (I), 1880s, Train and ship vignettes 50.00
Cleveland, Columbus, Cincinnati and Indianapolis Railroad (U), 1880s, Train and ship vignettes 30.00
Cleveland, Painesville and Ashtabula Railroad (I), Train vignette, scrip certificate 20.00
Cleveland, Painesville and Ashtabula Railroad (I), 1850s, Train vignette 55.00
Cleveland, Painesville and Ashtabula Railroad (I), 1850s, Green seal, scrip 65.00
Cleveland, Painesville and Ashtabula Railroad (U), 1800s, Old train vignette 50.00
Cleveland, Painesville and Ashtabula Railroad (U), 1860s, Train vignette 40.00
Clinton Line Railroad (I), 1850s, Old train vignette 80.00
Colorado Northern Railway (I), 1880s, Train and boat vignette 110.00
Columbia and Puget Sound Railroad (I), Old train vignette 195.00
Columbia and Puget Sound Railroad (I), 1880s, Old train vignette 295.00
Columbia and Puget Sound Railroad (U), Old train vignette 25.00
Columbia and Puget Sound Railroad (U), 1880s, Old train vignette 40.00

◀ ***Burlington, Cedar Rapids and Minnesota Railway Company (U), 1800s,*** *Old train vignette* ***20.00***

◀ ***Central Ohio Railroad Company (I), 1870s,*** *With many stamps, old train vignette* ***95.00***

COMMON STOCK.
NUMBER A1771
-65-
SHARES
CHICAGO AND EASTERN ILLINOIS
Railroad Company.
$100
This is to certify that Mrs Emily C. Ladd
entitled to Sixty five shares of One Hundred Dollars each
of the COMMON Capital Stock of the Chicago and Eastern Illinois Railroad Company
transferable only on the books of the Company in person or by attorney upon the surrender of this certificate.
COMMON
In Witness whereof, the said Company has caused this certificate to be signed by its President and Treasurer this 8 day of MAY 1900
MAY 8 1900
Metropolitan Trust Company of the City of New York
CANCELLED
A2128 FOR 5933

UNITED STATES OF AMERICA
Chicago, Burlington and Quincy
STATE OF ILLINOIS
RAILROAD COMPANY
B3432
SHARES $100 EACH
6
This Certifies that HOMANS & CO are the holder of Six Shares in the Capital Stock of the Chicago Burlington and Quincy Railroad Company, transferable only on the Books of the Company in person or by Attorney at their Agency in New York upon the surrender of this Certificate.
12 day of Nov 1890.
CANCELLED NOV 15 1890
UNION TRUST CO.
Countersigned by
Transfer Clerk.
Cashier
American Bank Note Co. New-York & Boston.
UNDER 10 20 30 40 50 60 70 80 90 100 OVER 100 1000

Columbus and Maysville Railway (I), 1870s, Train and boat vignette	175.00
Columbus, Hocking Valley and Toledo Railway (I), 1880s, Old train vignette	65.00
Columbus, Hope and Greensburg Railroad (U), 1880s, Old train vignette	28.00
Columbus, Springfield and Cincinnati Railroad (U), 1800s, Old train vignette	35.00
Commonwealth Avenue Street Railway (I), 1890s	22.00
Commonwealth Avenue Street Railway (I), 1900s	20.00
Commonwealth Avenue Street Railway (U), 1890s	9.00
Commonwealth Avenue Street Railway (U), 1900s	7.00
Concord and Claremont Railroad (I), 1840s	135.00
Coney Island and Brooklyn Railroad (U), 1800s, Streetcar vignette	60.00
Coney Island and Brooklyn Railroad (U), 1900s, Streetcar vignette	30.00
Consolidated Railway Company, The (I), 1920s, Eagle vignette	25.00
Continental Express Company (U), 1900s	6.00
Continental Passenger Railway (I), 1870s, Eagle vignette	45.00
Continental Passenger Railway (I), 1880s, Eagle vignette	40.00
Covington Short Route Transfer Railway (I), 1890s	80.00
Cuba Consolidated Railroad (I), 1940s, Train, workers, and oxen vignette	10.00
Cuba Railroad (I), 1950s, New Jersey, Train vignette	20.00
Danville Belt Railroad (U), 1900s, State seal, Indian maiden vignette	10.00
Davenport, Clinton and Eastern Railroad (U), 1890s	17.00
Davenport, Clinton and Eastern Railroad (U), 1900s	8.00
Dayton Coal and Iron Railway (I), 1900s	28.00
Delaware and Lackawanna and Western (I), 1950s, Train vignette	15.00
Delaware and Lackawanna and Western, Specimen (I), Three vignettes	50.00
Delaware and Otsego Railroad (U), 1800s, Old train at station, train at bottom	40.00
Deming, Sierra Madre and Pacific Railroad (U), 1880s, Eagle vignette	95.00
Demoine Navigation and Railroad Company (I), 1850s, Old train and sidewheeler boats vignettes	135.00
Demoine Navigation and Railroad company (U) , Old train vignette	25.00
Denver and Rio Grande (I), 1880s, Miners vignette	80.00
Denver and Rio Grande (I), 1900s	40.00
Denver and Southwestern Railway (I), 1900s, Train at roundhouse vignette	30.00
Des Moines Northern and Western Railroad (U), 1890s, Eagle vignette	10.00
Detroit and Bay City Railroad (I), 1870s, Train at station vignette, signed by president	250.00
Detroit Citizens Street Railway (U), 1890s	12.00
Detroit, Fort Wayne and Bell Isle (U), 1800s	10.00
Detroit, Grand Rapids and Western Railroad (I), 1890s, Two trains at station vignette	75.00
Detroit Harbor Terminals (I), 1930s	12.00
Detroit, Hillsdale and Southwestern (I), 1890s, Train and seal vignette	30.00
Detroit, Hillsdale and Southwestern (I), 1950s, Train vignette	15.00
Detroit, Mackinac and Marquette Railroad (U), 1880s, Train vignette	40.00
Detroit, Monroe and Toledo Railroad (U), 1850s, Train and Indian vignette	45.00
Detroit, Rochester, Romeo, Lake Orion Railway (U), Old streetcar vignette	10.00
Detroit United Railway (U), 1900s, Old trolley car vignette	11.00
Dorchester and Milton Branch Railroad (I), 1840s, Indian and seal vignette	95.00
Dorchester and Milton Branch Railroad (I), 1850s, Red seal	85.00
Dorchester and Milton Branch Railroad (U), 1850s	50.00
Dublin and Southwestern (I), 1900s, Gold seal, eagle vignette	28.00
Dublin and Southwestern (U), 1900s, Eagle vignette	10.00

◀ ***Chicago and Eastern Illinois Railroad Company (I), 1900s,*** *Two train vignettes* ***24.00***

◀ ***Chicago, Burlington and Quincy Railroad Company (I), 1890s,*** *Train vignette* ***17.00***

-145-

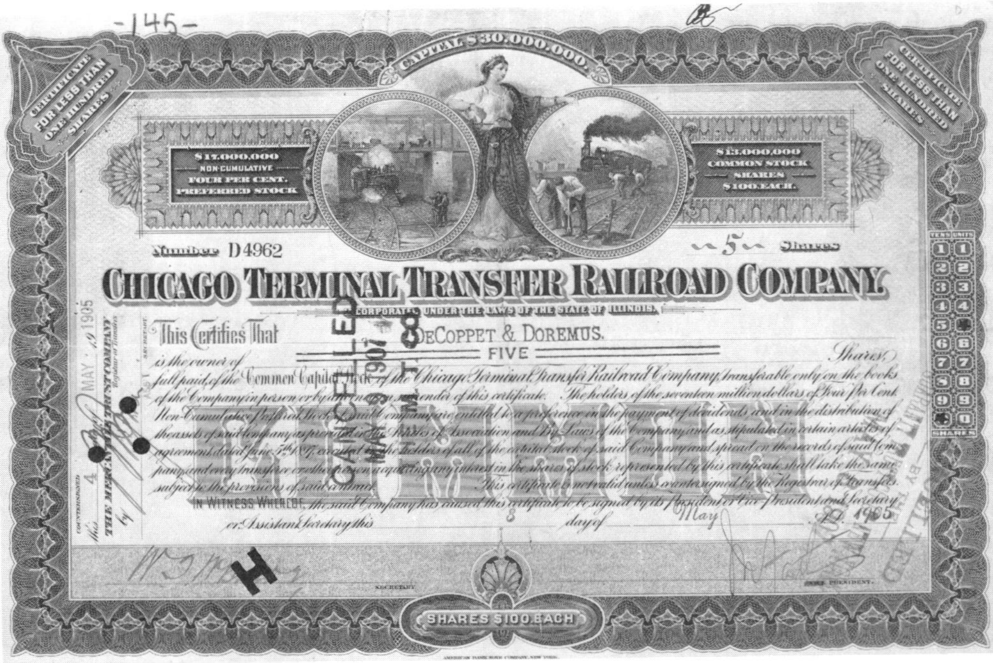

CAPITAL $30,000,000.

CERTIFICATE FOR LESS THAN ONE HUNDRED SHARES

$17,000,000 NON-CUMULATIVE FOUR PER CENT. PREFERRED STOCK

$13,000,000 COMMON STOCK SHARES $100.EACH.

Number D4962 — 5 — Shares

CHICAGO TERMINAL TRANSFER RAILROAD COMPANY.

INCORPORATED UNDER THE LAWS OF THE STATE OF ILLINOIS.

This Certifies That DeCOPPET & DOREMUS. is the owner of FIVE Shares, full paid, of the Common Capital Stock of the Chicago Terminal Transfer Railroad Company, transferable only on the books of the Company in person or by attorney on surrender of this certificate. The holders of the seventeen million dollars of Four Per Cent Non-Cumulative Preferred Stock of said company are entitled to a preference in the payment of dividends and in the distribution of the assets of said company as provided in the Articles of Association and By-Laws of the Company, and as stipulated in certain articles of agreement dated June 5th 1897, executed by the holders of all of the capital stock of said Company and spread on the records of said Company, and every transferee or other person acquiring any interest in the shares of stock represented by this certificate shall take the same subject to the provisions of said contract. This certificate is not valid unless countersigned by the Registrar of Transfers.

IN WITNESS WHEREOF, the said Company has caused this certificate to be signed by its President or Vice President and Secretary or Assistant Secretary this 8 day of May A.D. 1905.

Countersigned this 4 day of MAY 1905 THE MERCANTILE TRUST COMPANY, Registrar of Transfers, by

CANCELLED MAY 9 1907

SECRETARY

VICE PRESIDENT.

SHARES $100. EACH

1348 Cty 42

No. 1019

INCORPORATED UNDER THE LAWS OF THE STATE OF OHIO 1881

SHARES — 5 —

The Cincinnati, New Orleans and Texas Pacific RAILWAY COMPANY.

CAPITAL STOCK, $3,000,000.

SHARES, $100 EACH.

This is to Certify that E. B. Wilby is entitled to Five (5) Shares of ONE HUNDRED DOLLARS each of the Capital Stock of THE CINCINNATI, NEW ORLEANS & TEXAS PACIFIC RAILWAY COMPANY, transferable only on the books of the Company in person or by Attorney on the surrender of this Certificate.

Witness the Seal of the Company and the Signatures of the President and Secretary at Cincinnati this 8th day of October AD 1888

This Certificate is not Valid unless Countersigned by the Fidelity Safe Deposit and Trust Co. Cincinnati, Ohio, Registrar and Transfer Agent.

Sec'y

Pres't

Dubuque and Pacific (I), 1850s	**200.00**
Dubuque and Pacific (U), 1850s	**27.00**
Dubuque and Sioux City Railroad Corporation (I), 1870s	**58.00**
Dubuque and Sioux City Railroad Corporation (I), 1880s	**48.00**
Duluth, Saint Cloud, Glencoe and Western Railroad (U), 1900s, Old steam train vignette	**20.00**
Duluth Street Railway (U), 1900s, Streetcar vignette	**18.00**
Duluth Street Railway (U), 1920s, Streetcar vignette	**11.00**
Dunkirk, Allegheny, and Pittsburgh Railroad (U), 1870s	**40.00**
Dunkirk, Warren and Pittsburgh (U), 1880s, Old train vignette	**40.00**
East Harrisburg Passenger Railway (I), 1880s, Horse trolley vignette	**25.00**
East Pennsylvania Railroad (I), 1880s, Two trains vignette	**55.00**
East Pennsylvania Railroad (I), 1890s, Train and mule vignette	**45.00**
East Pennsylvania Railroad (I), 1940s, Train vignette	**20.00**
East Pennsylvania Railroad (U), 1900s, Train and mule vignette	**20.00**
East Shore and Suburban Railroad (I), 1900s, Interurban train vignette	**75.00**
East Shore and Suburban Railway (U), 1900s, California, Electric train vignette	**25.00**
East Tennessee, Virginia and Georgia Railway (I), 1880s, Train vignette	**60.00**
Easton Branch Railroad (U), 1850s	**22.00**
Electric Traction Company of Philadelphia (U), 1890s	**14.00**
Electric Traction Company of Philadelphia 1890s, Streetcar vignette	**37.00**
Elizabeth and Trenton Railroad (I), 1910s, Old open streetcar	**15.00**
Elizabethtown and Paducah Railroad (I), 1870s, One train and two buildings vignettes	**200.00**
Elkhart and Western Railroad (U), 1890s, Old train vignette	**30.00**
Ellenville and Kingston Railroad (I), 1900s, Old train emerging from a tunnel vignette	**55.00**
Elmira, Jefferson and Canandaigua Railroad (I), 1850s, Train vignette	**175.00**
Elmira, Jefferson and Canandaigua Railroad (I), 1860s, Train vignette	**90.00**
Elmira, Jefferson and Canandaigua Railroad (U), 1850s	**50.00**
Elmira, Jefferson, Canandaigua Railroad (I), 1870s	**70.00**
Empire Passenger Railroad (I), 1870s, Eagle and horse cars vignette	**60.00**
Erie and Cleveland (in Pennsylvania section) (I), 1850s, Train and ship vignette	**255.00**
Erie and North East Railroad, 1800s(I), Two ladies, Washington, and Franklin vignettes	**65.00**
Erie and Ohio Railroad (U), 1800s, Train, ship, and ladies vignettes	**53.00**
Erie Railroad (I), 1940s, Figures vignette	**8.00**
Erie Railroad Specimen,	**10.00**
Evansville and Crawfordsville Railroad (I), Train vignette	**60.00**
Evansville and Terre Haute (I), 1870s, Old train vignette	**60.00**
Evansville and Terre Haute (I), 1880s, Old train vignette	**55.00**
Fair Oaks Transit (U), 1910s, Eagle vignette	**6.00**
Fairmount Park and Haddington Passenger Railway (I), 1890s, Streetcar vignette	**55.00**
Fairmount Park Transportation (I), 1900s	**17.00**
Fairmount Park Transportation (I), 1910s	**15.00**
Fall River (U), 1850s, Train vignette	**40.00**
Flint and Pere Marquette Railway Company, The (I), 1870s, Old train vignette	**50.00**
Flint and Pere Marquette Railway Company, The (I), 1880s, Train vignette	**40.00**
Flint and Pere Marquette Railway Company, The (I-N), 1870s, Old train vignette, embossed seal	**70.00**
Flint and Pere Marquette (U), 1880s, Train vignette	**17.00**
Florida Railway (I), 1900s, Train vignette	**95.00**

◀ ***Chicago Terminal Transfer Railroad Company (I), 1900s,*** *Two trains vignette* ***25.00***

◀ ***Cincinnati, New Orleans and Texas Pacific Railway Company, The (I), 1880s,*** *Old train vignette* ***40.00***

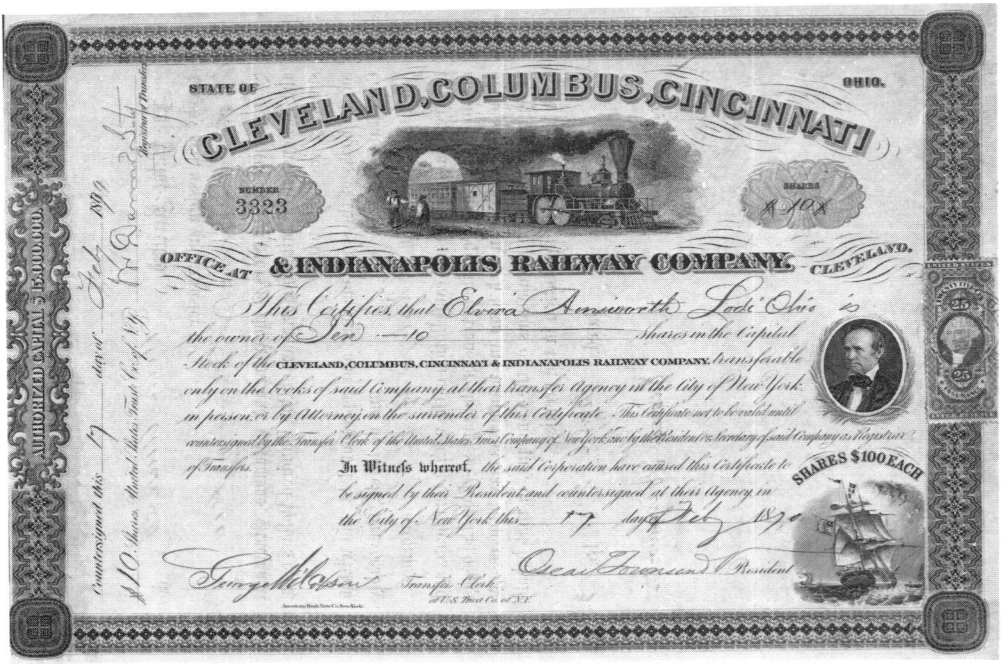

STATE OF OHIO.

CLEVELAND, COLUMBUS, CINCINNATI & INDIANAPOLIS RAILWAY COMPANY.

OFFICE AT CLEVELAND.

NUMBER 3323

SHARES 10

AUTHORIZED CAPITAL $15,000,000.

This Certifies, that Elvira Ainsworth Lodi Ohio is the owner of Ten 10 Shares in the Capital Stock of the CLEVELAND, COLUMBUS, CINCINNATI & INDIANAPOLIS RAILWAY COMPANY, transferable only on the books of said Company at their transfer Agency in the City of New York, in person, or by Attorney, on the surrender of this Certificate. This Certificate not to be valid until countersigned by the Transfer Clerk of the United States Trust Company of New York and by the President or Secretary of said Company as Registrar of Transfers.

In Witness whereof, the said Corporation have caused this Certificate to be signed by their President, and countersigned at their Agency in the City of New York this 17 day of Feb 1870

Transfer Clerk of U.S. Trust Co. of N.Y.

President

SHARES $100 EACH

Countersigned this 17 day of Feb 1870

American Bank Note Co. New York.

PENNSYLVANIA PENNSYLVANIA

The Continental Passenger Railway Company

OF PHILADELPHIA

190 NUMBER

15 SHARES

E PLURIBUS UNUM

This Certifies that Isaac Kemble entitled to Fifteen Shares in the Capital Stock of THE CONTINENTAL PASSENGER RAILWAY COMPANY OF PHILADELPHIA transferable only on the Books of the said Company in person or by attorney upon the surrender of this Certificate.

Witness the Corporate seal of the said Company at Philadelphia Feby 6 1877

Treas.

Presi.

CAPITAL $600.000.

SHARES $50 EACH

AMERICAN BANK NOTE CO PHILADELPHIA

Fonda, Johnstown and Gloversville Railroad (I), 1900s, Train vignette	30.00
Fonda, Johnstown and Gloversville Railroad (U), 1900s, Train vignette	7.00
Forest City Railroad (I), 1800s, Old train vignette	50.00
Fort Dodge, Desmoines and Southern Railroad 1900s to 1930s	18.00
Fort Pitt Traction Company (I), 1890s, Streetcar vignette	45.00
Fort Wayne and Jackson Railroad (I), 1940s, Old train vignette	22.00
Fort Wayne and Jackson Railroad (I), 1950s, Old train vignette	15.00
Fort Wayne, Cincinnati and Louisville Railroad (I), 1880s, Train vignette	55.00
Fort Wayne, Cincinnati and Louisville Railroad (U), 1800s, Train vignette	30.00
Framingham and Lowell Railroad (U), 1800s	25.00
Frankfort, Southwark and Philadelphia City Passenger Railroad (I), 1870s, Streetcar vignette	65.00
Frankfort, Southwark and Philadelphia City Passenger Railroad (I), 1880s, Horse trolley vignette	60.00
Frankfort, Southwark and Philadelphia City Passenger Railroad (I), 1890s, Trolley vignette	40.00
Frankfort, Southwark and Philadelphia City Passenger Railroad (I), 1900s	35.00
Frankfort, Southwark and Philadelphia City Passenger Railroad (I), 1910s, Winged vignette	25.00
Frankfort, Southwark and Philadelphia City Passenger Railroad (I), 1920s, Winged vignette	20.00
Frankfort, Southwark and Philadelphia City Passenger Railroad (I), 1930s, Winged vignette	10.00
Frankfort, Southwark and Philadelphia City Passenger Railroad (I), 1940s	6.00
Fulton County Narrow Gauge Railroad (U), 1800s, Old train vignette	50.00
Gallatin Valley Electric Railway (I), 1900s	35.00
Gallatin Valley Electric Railway (U), 1900s	10.00
Gary and Interurban Railroad (I), 1900s, Interurban car vignette	18.00
Gary and Interurban Railroad (I), 1910s, Interurban vignette	10.00
Gauley and Meadow River Railroad (I), 1910s, Train vignette	25.00
Geneva, Corning and Southern Railroad Company (I), 1910s, Train vignette	25.00
Geneva, Corning and Southern Railroad Company (U), 1800s, Train vignette	25.00
Geneva, Corning and Southern Railroad Company (U), 1900s, Train vignette	20.00
Georgia and Florida Railroad 1930s	20.00
Georgia Railroad and Banking Company (I), 1840s, Old steam train vignette	135.00
Georgia Railroad and Banking Company (I), 1850s, Portrait and train vignettes	125.00
Germantown and Northern (I), 1940s	13.00
Germantown Passenger Railway Company (I), 1860s, Eagle vignette, girl, woman, with horses, workmen vignettes, with stamps	60.00
Germantown Passenger Railway Company (I), 1880s, Three vignettes	50.00
Germantown Passenger Railway Company (I), 1890s, Eagle vignette	55.00
Germantown Passenger Railway Company (I), 1900s, Eagle and horses vignettes	40.00
Germantown Passenger Railway Company (I), 1920s, Eagle and horses vignettes	29.00
Gilpin Tramway Company (I), 1890s, Train vignette	85.00
Gordon Heights Railway (U), 1890s, State seal	18.00
Grand Junction Railroad and Depot Company (I), 1850s	150.00
Grand River Valley Railroad (U), 1800s, Train and lady vignette	35.00
Great Falls Terminal Railroad (U), 1900s	10.00
Great Northern Railroad 1970s, Equipment trust	12.00
Great Northern Railway (I), Photo vignette	12.00
Great Plains Railway (U), Eagle, train and ship vignette	3.00
Green and Coats Street Philadelphia Passenger Railway (I), 1860s, Horse trolley vignette	50.00
Green Cove Springs and Melrose (I), 1880s, Train vignette	75.00
Greenbay and Minnesota Railroad (U), 1870s, Two old trains and long bridge vignette	35.00
Greenbay and Western Railroad (I), 1900s, Train vignette	23.00

◀ ***Cleveland, Columbus, Cincinnati and Indianapolis Railroad (I), 1870s,*** *Train and ship vignettes, portrait, with stamp* ***60.00***

◀ ***Continental Passenger Railway (I), 1870s,*** *Eagle vignette* ***45.00***

No. 441 — 50 SHARES

Demoine Navigation & Rail Road Company

Endowed with the Lands and Franchises accruing from grants made by the Governments of the United States and of the State of Iowa

For the Improvement of the Valley of the Demoine from the junction of Illinois, Missouri and Iowa, through Iowa, into Minnesota

MISSOURI, IOWA AND MINNESOTA

CAPITAL STOCK $3,000,000

INCORPORATED 1854.

THIS IS TO CERTIFY that Gideon W. Burbank is entitled to Fifty Shares of One hundred Dollars each in the Capital Stock of the DEMOINE NAVIGATION & RAIL ROAD COMPANY. The said Stock is transferable only on the books of said Company at the Office of their Treasurer in the City of New York or at any transfer agency at the pleasure of the holder by the said G. W. Burbank in person or by his Attorney on the surrender of this Certificate.

IN WITNESS WHEREOF the said Company have caused this Certificate to be signed by the President and Treasurer. Dated at NEW YORK, this 21st day of Sept. 1855

Treasurer — President

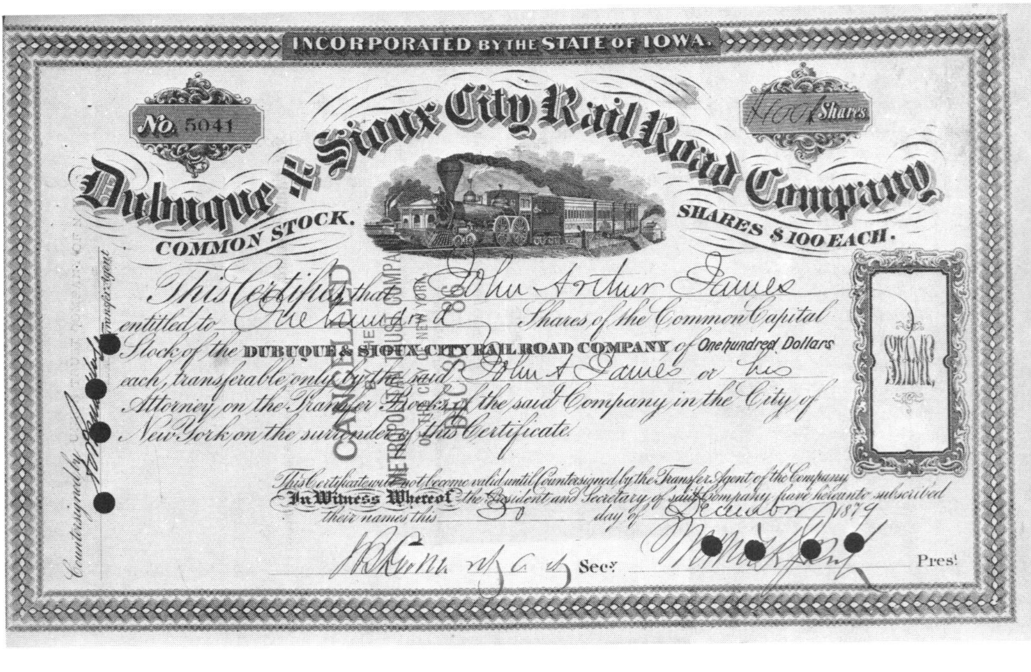

INCORPORATED BY THE STATE OF IOWA.

No. 5041 — Shares

Dubuque & Sioux City Rail Road Company

COMMON STOCK. SHARES $100 EACH.

This Certifies that John Arthur James is entitled to One hundred Shares of the Common Capital Stock of the DUBUQUE & SIOUX CITY RAIL ROAD COMPANY of One hundred Dollars each, transferable only by the said John A. James or his Attorney on the Transfer Books of the said Company in the City of New York on the surrender of this Certificate.

This Certificate will not become valid until Countersigned by the Transfer Agent of the Company.

In Witness Whereof the President and Secretary of said Company have hereunto subscribed their names this 30 day of December 1879

Sec.y — Pres.t

Countersigned by — Transfer Agent

CANCELLED

STAMP

Greenbay and Western Railroad (I), 1910s, Train vignette	23.00
Greenbay and Western Railroad (I), 1920s, Train vignette	20.00
Greenbay and Western Railroad (I), 1930s, Train vignette	15.00
Greenbay and Western Railroad (I), 1950s, Train vignette	10.00
Greenbrier and New River Railroad (I), 1880s, Eagle vignette	75.00
Greenville and Columbia Railroad Company, The (I), **1850s**, Old train and portraits vignettes	100.00
Greenville and Columbia Railroad Company, The (U), **1800s**, Train vignette	36.00
Gulf and Sabine River Railroad (I), 1910s	14.00
Gulf, Florida and Alabama Railway 1910s, Train and ships vignettes	30.00
Gulf, Mobile and Northern Railroad (I), 1930s, Train vignette	10.00
Gulf, Mobile and Northern Railroad (I), 1940s, Train vignette	4.00
Gulf, Mobile and Northern Railroad (I), 1950s, Train vignette	6.00
Gulf, Mobile and Ohio (I), 1940s, Train vignette	5.00
Gulf, Mobile and Ohio (I), 1950s, Train vignette	5.00
Gulf, Mobile and Ohio (I), 1960s, Train vignette	4.00
Gutheil Park Railroad (U), Gold seal and eagle vignette	8.00
Hancock and Pennsylvania Railroad (I), 1800s, Old train vignette	45.00
Hannibal and Saint Joseph Railroad (U), 1800s, Old train and seal vignette	43.00
Harlem River and Port Chester Railroad Company (I), 1860s, State seal vignette	75.00
Harrisburg Railroad (I), 1910s,	10.00
Harrisburg Railroad (I), 1920s	7.00
Harrisburg Railroad (I), 1930s	4.00
Harrisburg Railroad (I), 1940s	3.00
Harrisburg Traction Company (I), 1890s, Old streetcar, gold seal with trolley	35.00
Harrison Branch Company (U), 1800s	20.00
Hartford and Connecticut Valley Railroad (I), 1880s, Train and ships vignettes	60.00
Hartford and Connecticut Western Railroad (I), 1890s, Train vignette	35.00
Hartford and Connecticut Western Railroad (I), 1920s, Train vignette	25.00
Hartford and Connecticut Western Railroad (I), 1940s, Train vignette	18.00
Hartford and New Haven Railroad (I), 1860s, With stamp	65.00
Hartford and Springfield Railway (I), 1900s, Streetcar vignette	35.00
Hartford and Springfield Railway (I), 1910s, Streetcar vignette	30.00
Helena, Hot Springs and Smelter Railroad (U), 1880s, Montana Territory, Unique engine vignette	65.00
Helena, Red Mountain Railroad (U), **1880s**, Old steam train vignette	65.00
Hestonville, Mantua and Fairmont Railroad (I), Streetcar vignette	40.00
Hinsdale Company (U), **1800s**, Old train vignette	75.00
Holman Locomotive Speeding Truck Company (I), 1890s, Train vignette	28.00
Horn Pond Branch Railroad (U), 1800s	25.00
Houston and Great Northern Railroad (I), 1870s, Train vignette, signed by Galasha Grow	235.00
Houston and Great Northern Railroad (U), 1870s, Seal of Texas	85.00
Houstonic Railroad (U), 1850s	20.00
Hudson and Manhattan (I), 1940s, Train under harbor vignette	22.00
Hudson and Manhattan (U), 1900s, Train vignette	20.00
Huntingdon and Broad Top Mountain Railroad Coal Company, The (I), 1860s, Old steam train vignette, with stamps	110.00
Huston and Manhattan Railroad (U), **1910s**, Interurban vignette	12.00
Idaho and Washington Northern Railroad (I), 1900s, Eagle vignette	28.00
Idaho and Washington Northern Railroad (I), 1910s, Eagle vignette	25.00

◀ ***Demoine Navigation and Rail Road Company (I), 1850s,*** *Old train and sidewheeler boats vignettes* ***135.00***

◀ ***Dubuque and Sioux City Rail Road Corporation (I), 1870s*** ***58.00***

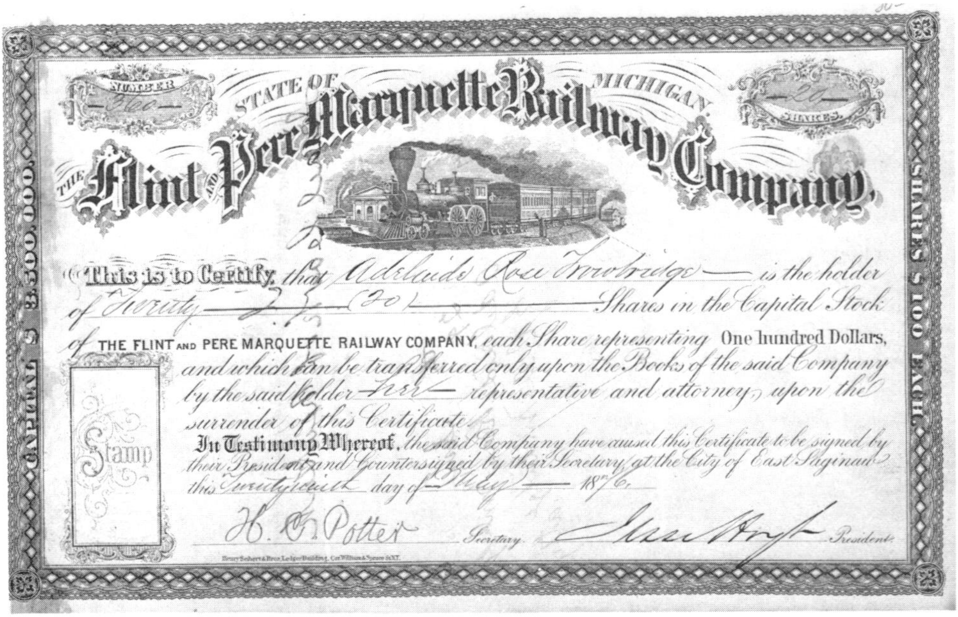

NUMBER 360

20 SHARES

STATE OF MICHIGAN

THE Flint AND Pere Marquette Railway Company

CAPITAL $ 3,500,000.

SHARES $ 100 EACH.

This is to Certify, that Adelaide Rose Trowbridge is the holder of Twenty (20) Shares in the Capital Stock of THE FLINT AND PERE MARQUETTE RAILWAY COMPANY, each Share representing One hundred Dollars, and which can be transferred only upon the Books of the said Company by the said holder her representative and attorney, upon the surrender of this Certificate.

Stamp

In Testimony Whereof, the said Company have caused this Certificate to be signed by their President and Countersigned by their Secretary, at the City of East Saginaw this Twenty sixth day of May 1876.

H. C. Potter Secretary. President.

Henry Seibert & Bros. Ledger Building, Cor. William & Spruce St. N.Y.

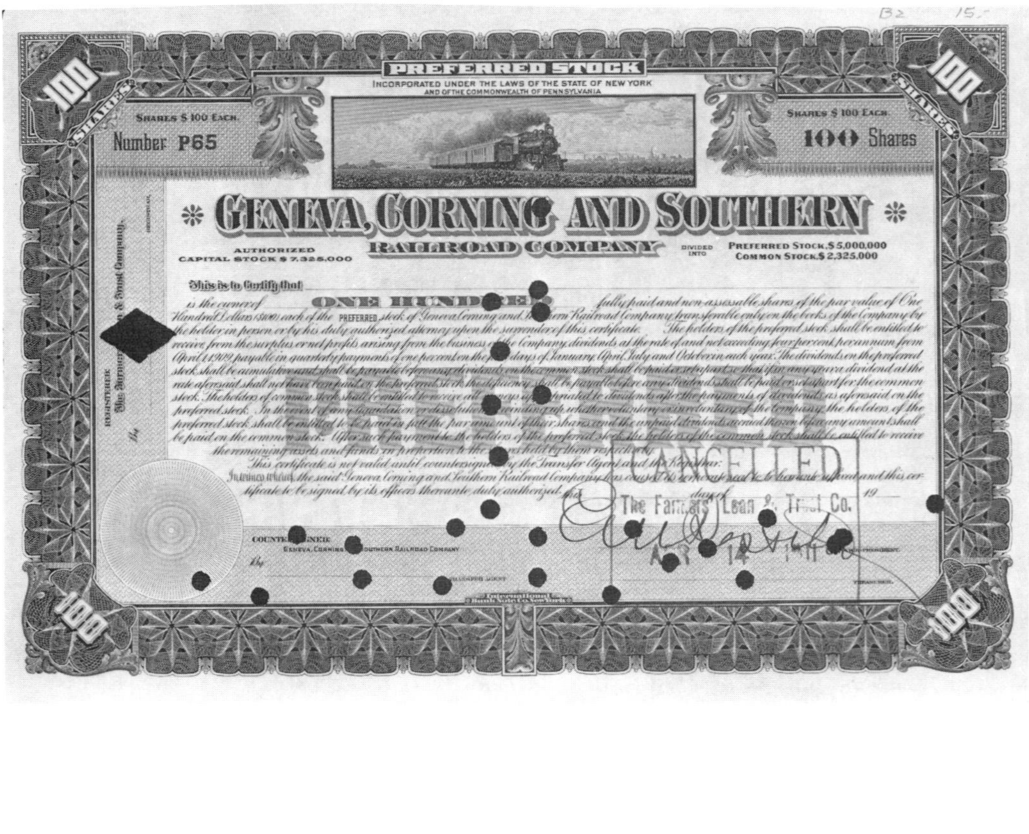

PREFERRED STOCK

INCORPORATED UNDER THE LAWS OF THE STATE OF NEW YORK AND OF THE COMMONWEALTH OF PENNSYLVANIA

100 SHARES

SHARES $ 100 EACH.

Number P65

SHARES $ 100 EACH.

100 Shares

GENEVA, CORNING AND SOUTHERN RAILROAD COMPANY

AUTHORIZED CAPITAL STOCK $ 7,325,000

DIVIDED INTO PREFERRED STOCK, $ 5,000,000 COMMON STOCK, $ 2,325,000

This is to Certify that

is the owner of ONE HUNDRED fully paid and non-assessable shares of the par value of One Hundred Dollars ($100) each of the PREFERRED stock of Geneva, Corning and Southern Railroad Company transferable only on the books of the Company by the holder in person or by his duly authorized attorney upon the surrender of this certificate. The holders of the preferred stock shall be entitled to receive, from the surplus or net profits arising from the business of the Company, dividends at the rate of and not exceeding four percent per annum from April 1, 1909, payable in quarterly payments of one percent on the first days of January, April, July and October in each year. The dividends on the preferred stock shall be cumulative and shall be payable before any dividends on the common stock shall be paid or set apart, so that if in any year a dividend at the rate aforesaid shall not have been paid on the preferred stock the deficiency shall be payable before any dividend shall be paid or set apart for the common stock. The holders of common stock shall be entitled to receive all moneys appropriated to dividends after the payments of dividends as aforesaid on the preferred stock. In the event of any liquidation or dissolution or winding up, whether voluntary or involuntary, of the Company, the holders of the preferred stock shall be entitled to be paid in full the par amount of their shares and the unpaid dividends accrued thereon before any amount shall be paid on the common stock. After such payment to the holders of the preferred stock the holders of the common stock shall be entitled to receive the remaining assets and funds in proportion to the shares held by them respectively.

This certificate is not valid until countersigned by the Transfer Agent and the Registrar.

In witness whereof, the said Geneva, Corning and Southern Railroad Company has caused its corporate seal to be hereunto affixed and this certificate to be signed by its officers thereunto duly authorized, this dated 19

CANCELLED

The Farmers' Loan & Trust Co.

APR 14 1911

COUNTERSIGNED GENEVA, CORNING AND SOUTHERN RAILROAD COMPANY

By TRANSFER AGENT

PRESIDENT.

TREASURER.

REGISTERED The Farmers' Loan & Trust Company.

By

International Bank Note Co. New York

Idaho and Western Railway (U), **1900s**, Gold seal	12.00
Illinois Central Railroad (I), **1860s**	30.00
Illinois Central Railroad (I), **1880s**, Scrip certificate, signed by Stuyvesent Fish	30.00
Illinois Central Railroad (I), **1880s**, With route map	35.00
Illinois Central Railroad (I), **1920s**, Eagle vignette	5.00
Illinois Central Railroad (I), **1920s**, Equipment gold note, large eagle vignette	11.00
Illinois Central Railroad (I), **1920s**, With map of tracks	20.00
Illinois Central Railroad (I), **1940s and 1950s**, With railroad route map vignette	15.00
Illinois Central Railroad (I), **1960s**, Diesel and steam trains vignette	4.00
Indiana, Alabama and Texas Railroad (I-N), **1880s**	80.00
Indianapolis and Cincinnati Railroad (U), **1800s**, Old train with four signatures vignette	40.00
Indianapolis Belt Railroad and Stockyard (I)	5.00
Indianapolis, Cincinnati and Lafayette Railroad (U), **1860s**	30.00
Interborough Consolidated Corporation (IRT) (I), **1910s**, Subway vignette	32.00
Interborough Consolidated Corporation (IRT) (I), **1920s**, Winged figure vignette	15.00
International and Great Northern Railroad (I), **1870s**, Cowboys vignette	85.00
International and Great Northern Railroad (U), **1870s**, Cowboys vignette	37.00
International Grand Trunk Railroad (U), **1880s**, New Mexico Territory vignette	80.00
International Railroad (U), **1870s**, Cattle roundup and old train vignette	95.00
International Railroad of Central America (I), **1940s**, Train and ox carts vignette	12.00
Iowa Falls and Sioux City Railroad (U), **1880s**, Early train vignette	17.00
Iowa Falls and Sioux City Railroad (I), **1870s**, Train vignette	50.00
Ironton Railroad (I), **1860s**, Train and portraits vignette	65.00
Ironton Railroad (I), **1860s**, Blacksmiths vignette	60.00
Jackson Coal Railroad (U), **1880s**, Old train vignette	19.00
Jackson, Lansing and Saginaw Railroad (U), **1900s**, Three vignettes	25.00
Jamaica and Brooklyn (U), **1890s**	15.00
Jamaica and Brooklyn (I), **1890s**	20.00
Jamestown and Franklin Railroad (U), Signed, old-train vignette	40.00
Jamestown, Westfield and Northwestern Railroad (U), **1900s**, Trolley car vignette	10.00
Jenkintown Electric Railway Company (U), **1890s**	7.00
Jersey Shore, Pine Creek and Buffalo Railway (U), **1800s**, State seal	24.00
Jersev Shore, Pine Creek and Buffalo Railway (U), **1800s**, Large vignette	35.00
Johnson Street Passenger Railway (U), **1890s**	15.00
Johnstown, Gloversville and Kingsboro Horse Railroad (U), **1890s**, Streetcar vignette	10.00
Joliet and Chicago Railroad (I), **1890s**, Old steam train vignette	60.00
Joliet and Chicago Railroad (I), **1920s**, Old steam train vignette	40.00
Joliet and Chicago Railroad (I), **1930s**, Train vignette	15.00
Joliet and Chicago Railroad (I), **1940s**, Old funnel train vignette	12.00
Junction Railroad (I), **1850s**, Old train vignette	80.00
Junction Railroad (U), **1870s**, New York	25.00
Kaaterskill Railroad (U), **1800s**, Old steam train vignette	30.00
Kalamazoo and South Haven Railroad (U), **1800s**, State seal	30.00
Kalamazoo and White Pigeon Railroad (U), **1800s**, Train vignette	30.00
Kanawha and Michigan Railroad (I), **1910s**, Train vignette	50.00
Kanawha and Michigan Railway (U), **1890s**, Old train vignette	30.00
Kanawha and Michigan Railway (U), **1900s**	20.00
Kanawha and West Virginia Railroad (U), **1900s**, Old train and factory and books vignette	28.00
Kankakee and Urbana Traction Company (I), **1910s**, Eagle	45.00
Kansas City, Clay County and Saint Joe Railway (I), **1920s**, Interurban vignette	30.00

◀ ***Flint and Pere Marquette Railway Company, The (I-N), 1870s,*** *Old train vignette, embossed seal* ***70.00***

◀ ***Geneva, Corning and Southern Railroad Company (U), 1900s,*** *Train vignette* ***20.00***

SHARES $50 EACH.
STATE OF PENNSYLVANIA.
GERMANTOWN PASSENGER RAIL WAY COMPANY.
CAPITAL,
This Certifies that C.W. Kunkel is
entitled to Two hundred Shares in the Capital Stock of the
Germantown Passenger Rail Way Company, transferable only on the Books
of the said Company in Person or by Attorney, upon surrender of this
Certificate. Witness the Corporate Seal of the Company at Philadelphia,
October 9th 1868
Adam Wartman Pres.
American Bank Note Company.

THE GREENVILLE & COLUMBIA RAIL ROAD Co.
CAPITAL STOCK $2,000,000.
No
Shares
SHARES $20.00 EACH.
This Certifies, that J. H. Ostendorf is
the proprietor of Five Shares in the Capital
Stock of the above named Company. Transferable only on
the books of said Company, on the surrender of this Certificate.
In Witness whereof, the Corporate Seal of said
Company is hereunto affixed at Columbia, S.C.
this day of May 185
Auditor Treasurer President.

Kansas City, Fort Scott and Memphis (U), **1900s**, Train vignette	20.00
Kansas City, Mexico and Orient Railway (I), **1910s**, Train vignette	37.00
Kansas City, Saint Louis and Chicago Railroad (I), **1940s**, Old funnel train vignette	30.00
Kansas City Viaduct and Terminal Railways (I), **1900s**, Riverboats vignette	45.00
Kennebec and Portland Railroad (U), **1800s**, Three trains vignette	18.00
Kentucky and South Atlantic Railroad (I), **1880s**, Eagle vignette	45.00
Kentucky Central Railroad (I), **1890s**, Train vignette	45.00
Keokuk and Des Moines Railway Company, The (I), **1870s**, Surveying scene vignette	80.00
Keokuk and Des Moines Railway Company, The (I), **1870s**, City scene vignette	85.00
Keokuk and Des Moines Railway Company, The (I), **1880s**, Indians and train vignette	60.00
Keokuk and Des Moines Railway (I), **1890s**, Two train vignette and Indians and surveyors	60.00
Keokuk and Des Moines Railway (I), **1900s**, Surveyor scene vignette	40.00
Keokuk and Des Moines Railway Company, The (U), **1900s**, Eagle vignette	10.00
Kings County Elevated Railroad (I), **1870s**, Surveying scene	75.00
Kings County Elevated Railroad (U), **1900s**, Vignette of hall	25.00
Lackawanna and Wyoming Valley Rapid Transit Railroad (U), **1900s**, Two horses and eagle vignette	25.00
Lake Erie, Alliance, and Wheeling Railroad (U), **1900s**	15.00
Lake Erie, Youngstown, and Southern Railroad (U), **1900s**, Old train	30.00
Lake Huron and North Ontario 1900s, Train, ship, and world globe vignette	25.00
Lake Shore Railway (U), **1800s**, Old funnel train vignette	50.00
Lake Superior and Southern Railroad (U), **1880s**	14.00
Lake Superior and Southwestern (U), **1880s**	15.00
Lawrenceburg and Indianapolis Railroad (U), **1800s**, Old train vignette	500.00
Lehigh and Mahanon Railroad (I), **1860s**, Train vignette	45.00
Lehigh and New York Railroad (I), **1890s**, Old train vignette	20.00
Lehigh and New York Railroad (U), **1890s**, Old train and man polishing train vignette	16.00
Lehigh and New York Railroad (U), **1890s**, Old train and man stoking furnace vignette	15.00
Lehigh Avenue Railway (U), **1890s**	18.00
Lehigh Car Manufacturing Company (I), **1870s**, Old train vignette	110.00
Lehigh, Schuylkill Valley (I), **1880s**, Three old trains vignette	60.00
Lehigh Valley Railroad, 1930s, Reclining maiden and locomotive vignette	10.00
Lehigh Valley Railroad, 1940s, Kneeling maiden vignette	7.00
Lehigh Valley Railroad (I), **1890s**, Old steam train and portrait vignette	50.00
Lehigh Valley Railroad (I), **1900s**, Old steam train vignette	35.00
Lehigh Valley Railroad (I), **1950s**	5.00
Lehigh Valley Railroad (I), **1950s**, Streamliner with angel and old car vignette	6.00
Lehigh Valley Transit (I), **1910s**, State seal, horses vignette	9.00
Lexington and Eastern Railway (I), Eagle vignette	8.00
Lexington Union Station (I), Eagle vignette	8.00
Lexington Union Station (I), **1900s**	6.00
Lexington Union Station (I), **1910s**	5.00
Lexington Union Station (I), **1920s and 1930s**	4.00
Linville River Railway (I), **1900s**, Logging train vignette	20.00
Linville River Railway (U), **1900s**, Logging train vignette	8.00
Little Falls and Dolgeville Railroad (U), **1900s**, Company logo, two small dragons	18.00
Little Falls and Herkimer Street Railway (U) **1900s**, Lady with flag and eagle	22.00
Little Miami Railroad Company, Inc. (U), **1800s, Ohio**, Tom Thumb engine and passenger car train vignette	15.00
Loop and Lookout Railroad (I), **1920s**, Train vignette	30.00

◀ ***Germantown Passenger Rail Way Company (I), 1860s,*** *Eagle vignette, girl, woman, with horses, workmen vignettes, with stamp*	***60.00***
◀ ***Greenville and Columbia Railroad Company, The (I), 1850s,*** *Old train and portraits vignettes*	***100.00***

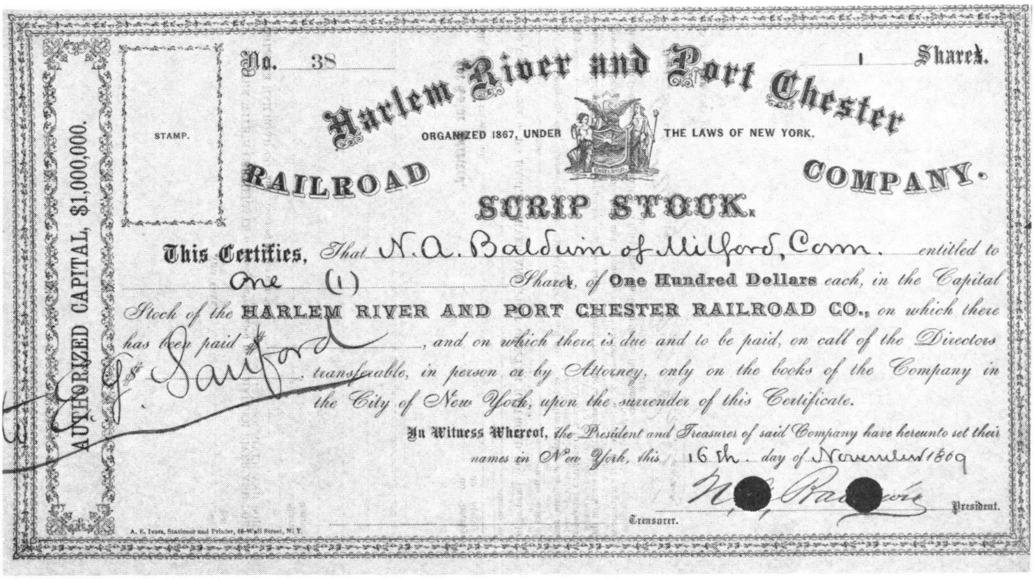

AUTHORIZED CAPITAL, $1,000,000.

STAMP.

No. 38 1 Shares.

Harlem River and Port Chester

ORGANIZED 1867, UNDER THE LAWS OF NEW YORK.

RAILROAD COMPANY.

SCRIP STOCK.

This Certifies, That N. A. Baldwin of Milford, Conn. entitled to One (1) Shares, of One Hundred Dollars each, in the Capital Stock of the HARLEM RIVER AND PORT CHESTER RAILROAD CO., on which there has been paid $, and on which there is due and to be paid, on call of the Directors ; transferable, in person or by Attorney, only on the books of the Company in the City of New York, upon the surrender of this Certificate.

In Witness Whereof, the President and Treasurer of said Company have hereunto set their names in New York, this 16th day of November 1869

Treasurer. President.

A. E. Ivers, Stationer and Printer, 44 Wall Street, N. Y.

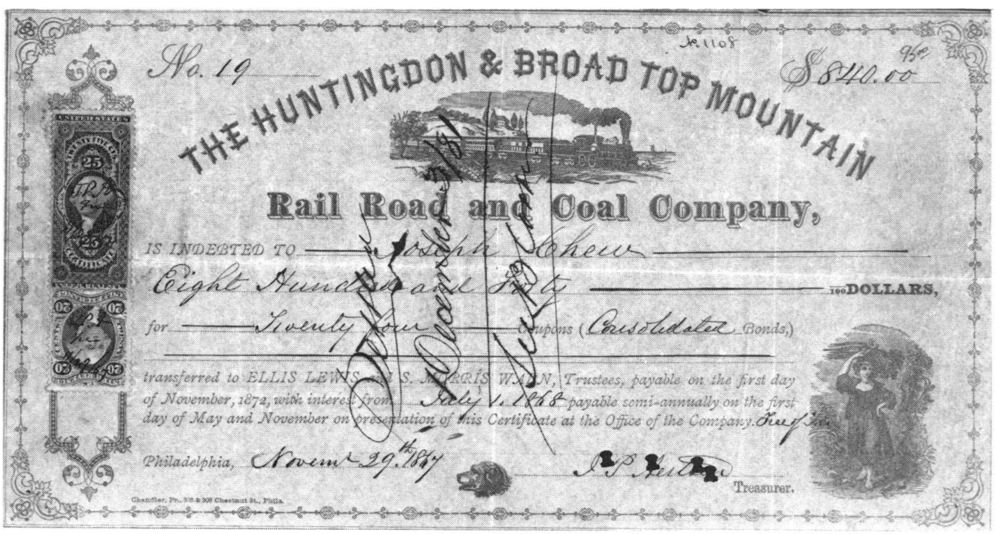

No. 19 $840.00

THE HUNTINGDON & BROAD TOP MOUNTAIN

Rail Road and Coal Company,

IS INDEBTED TO Joseph Shew

Eight Hundred and Forty DOLLARS,

for Twenty four Coupons (Consolidated Bonds,)

transferred to ELLIS LEWIS and S. MORRIS WALN, Trustees, payable on the first day of November, 1872, with interest from July 1, 1868 payable semi-annually on the first day of May and November on presentation of this Certificate at the Office of the Company.

Philadelphia, Novem 29th 1867

Treasurer.

Chandler, Pr. 306 & 308 Chestnut St., Phila.

Louisiana and Missouri River Railroad (U), Hole, cancelled, old train vignette	**25.00**
Louisiana and Missouri River Railroad (U), 1880s, President's signature	**50.00**
Louisville and National Railroad (U), 1910s, Train vignette	**10.00**
Louisville Railroad Company (I), 1890s, Streetcar and lady vignette	**45.00**
Louisville Railroad Company (I), 1900s, Trolley vignette	**15.00**
Louisville Railroad Company (U), 1890s, Trolley vignette	**12.00**
Louisville Railroad Company (U), 1900s, Trolley vignette	**8.00**
Lowell and Framingham Railroad (I), 1880s	**50.00**
Lowell and Framingham Railroad (U), 1800s	**25.00**
Lykens Valley Railroad and Coal Company (I), 1850s, Horses vignette	**110.00**
Lykens Valley Railroad and Coal Company (I), 1860s, Horses vignette, stamp	**95.00**
McKeesport and Belle Vernon Railroad (U), 1880s, Old train vignette	**30.00**
Mack Elevated Railway Supply (I-N), 1890s,	**33.00**
Mahoning and Shenango Railway Light Company (I), 1910s, Seminude woman with light and streetcar vignette	**20.00**
Mahoning Coal Railroad (U), 1800s, Coal miner vignette	**35.00**
Mahoning Coal Railroad (U), 1800s, Train, ship and two men vignettes	**25.00**
Mahopac Falls Railroad (U), 1880s, Fancy old steam engine vignette	**25.00**
Malden and Melrose Railroad (I), 1850s, State seal, horse streetcar vignette	**55.00**
Manhattan Railway (I), 1920s, Seal	**22.00**
Manhattan Transit (I), 1910s, Lady vignette	**37.00**
Manufacturers Railroad (U), 1860s	**15.00**
Marietta and North Georgia Railway (I), 1890s	**30.00**
Market Street Railway (I), 1920s, Eagle vignette	**25.00**
Market Street Railway (I), 1930s, Eagle vignette	**20.00**
Market Street Railway (I), 1940s and 1950s, Eagle vignette	**15.00**
Marquette, Houghton and Ontonagon Railroad (U), 1870s, Old train vignette	**30.00**
Marquette, Houghton and Ontonagon Railroad (U), 1880s	**25.00**
Maysville and Big Shandy Railroad (I), 1890s, Old train vignette	**50.00**
Maysville and Lexington Railroad (I), 1880s, Train and blacksmith vignette	**50.00**
Maysville and Lexington Railroad (U), 1870s, Old steam train vignette	**30.00**
Merchants Union Express (I), 1860s, Horse and wagon vignette	**195.00**
Mesaba Railway (I), 1920s	**16.00**
Metropolitan Cross Town Railroad (I), 1920s	**40.00**
Metropolitan Railroad Company (I), 1880s, Horse-drawn streetcar vignette	**65.00**
Michigan Electric Railway (I), 1920s, Electric train vignette	**30.00**
Michigan, Midland and Canada Railroad (I), 1800s	**15.00**
Michigan Southern and Northern Indiana Railroad (U), 1850s, Old train vignette	**45.00**
Michigan Southern and Northern Indiana Railroad (U), 1860s	**40.00**
Middleborough and Tauton Railroad (I), 1850s	**35.00**
Middlesex Railroad (U), 1880s, Ships in bay vignette	**20.00**
Milwaukee and Saint Paul Railway (I), 1870s, Large vignette	**90.00**
Minneapolis and Saint Louis Railroad (U), 1910s, Scrip certificate	**4.00**
Minneapolis, Saint Paul and Canadian Railroad (U), 1900s, Eagle vignette	**9.00**
Minneapolis, Saint Paul and Sault Sainte Marie Railway (I), 1930s, Train and signalman vignette	**20.00**
Minneapolis, Saint Paul Railroad (U), Woman on dock and train vignette	**10.00**
Minneapolis, Saint Paul, Rochester and Dubuque Electric Traction (I), 1910s, Horses with wings vignette	**37.00**

◀ ***Harlem River and Port Chester Railroad Company (I), 1860s,*** *State seal vignette* ***75.00***

◀ ***Huntington and Broad Top Mountain Railroad and Coal Company, the (I), 1860s,*** *Old steam train vignette, with stamps* ***110.00***

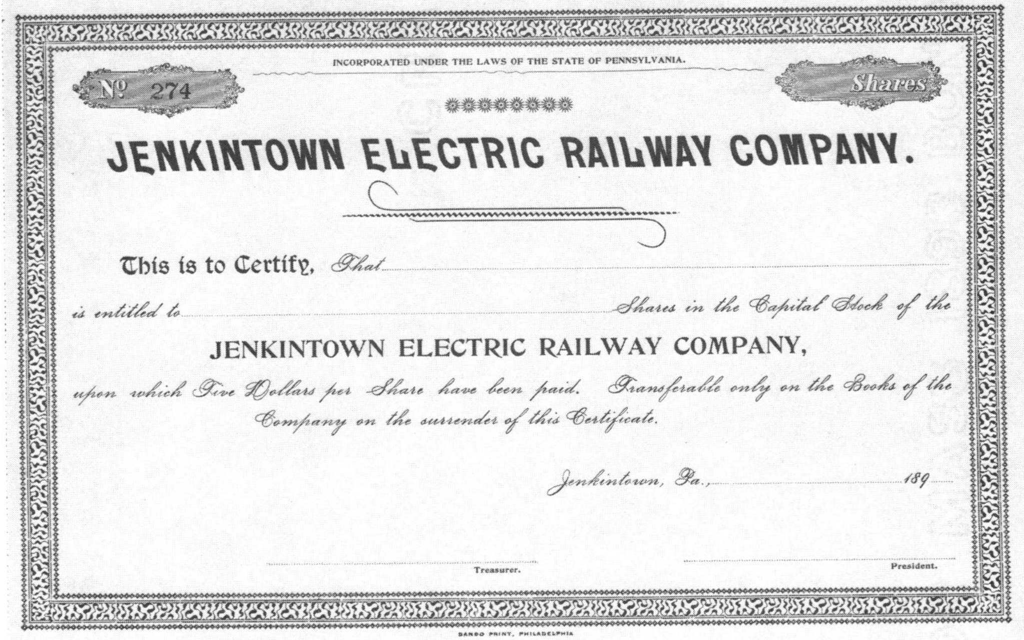

INCORPORATED UNDER THE LAWS OF THE STATE OF PENNSYLVANIA.

No. 274 Shares

JENKINTOWN ELECTRIC RAILWAY COMPANY.

This is to Certify, That ....

is entitled to .... Shares in the Capital Stock of the

JENKINTOWN ELECTRIC RAILWAY COMPANY,

upon which Five Dollars per Share have been paid. Transferable only on the Books of the Company on the surrender of this Certificate.

Jenkintown, Pa., ... 189...

.... Treasurer. .... President.

BANGO PRINT, PHILADELPHIA

AUTHORIZED ISSUE LIMITED TO $2,600,400.

No. 1195

STATE OF IOWA

THE KEOKUK AND DES MOINES RAILWAY COMPANY.

COMMON CAPITAL STOCK

SHARES $100 EACH.

This Certifies that A. W. Kilbourne & Co. is entitled to Twenty two Shares of One hundred Dollars each in the Common Capital Stock of the Keokuk and Des Moines Railway Company incorporated under the laws of the State of Iowa transferable only on the books of the Company in person or by Attorney upon the surrender of this Certificate.

The holder of the Common Stock will be entitled to dividends in each year after the payment of Interest and Eight per cent dividends to the holders of the Preferred Stock as provided for in the Certificate of the Preferred Stockholders and all surplus is to be divided pro rata between Preferred and Common Stockholders. Witness the hands of the President and Secretary of said Company at Keokuk Iowa, this 13th day of June A.D. 1898

SECRETARY PRESIDENT

CANCELLED BY

The Farmers Loan & Trust Company JUN 24 1901

Registered and Countersigned The Farmers Loan and Trust Company

Mississiquoi Valley Railroad (I), 1890s, Train and ship vignette	50.00
Mississippi and Missouri Railroad (I), 1850s, Train, Indians and riverboat vignette	110.00
Mississippi and Missouri Railroad (I), 1860s, Scrip certificate	28.00
Mississippi and Missouri Railroad (I), 1860s, Train, Indians and riverboat vignette	60.00
Mississippi and Missouri Railroad (U), 1800s, Trains, Indians, and riverboat vignette	30.00
Mississippi and Missouri Railroad (U), 1850s, Old train and Indians vignette	50.00
Mississippi and Missouri Railroad (U), 1860s, Old train vignette	35.00
Mississippi and Missouri Railroad (U), 1880s, Train, Indians and riverboat vignette	30.00
Mississippi Central Railroad (I-N), 1870s, Two trains, riverboat and cotton picker vignette, signed by A. M. West (president of the company)	225.00
Missouri, Kansas and Texas Railroad (I), 1880s, Cattle vignette	18.00
Missouri, Kansas and Texas Railroad (I), 1880s, Cattle vignette, with George Gould signature	125.00
Missouri, Kansas and Texas Railroad (I), 1890s, Old train vignette	15.00
Missouri, Kansas and Texas Railroad (I), 1900s, Train, roundhouse, British stamp	15.00
Missouri, Kansas and Texas Railroad (I), 1910s, Old train, man stoking boiler	14.00
Missouri, Kansas and Texas Railroad (I), 1920s, Two trains at station	12.00
Mobile and Alabama Grand Trunk (U), 1800s, Old funnel train at station vignette	25.00
Mobile and Montgomery Railroad (I),Train vignette	35.00
Mobile and Montgomery Railroad (U), 1870s, Old train and roundhouse vignette	24.00
Mobile and Ohio Railroad Company (I), 1850s	60.00
Mobile and Ohio Railroad Company (I), 1860s, Red seal, train vignette	55.00
Mobile and Ohio Railroad Company (I), 1860s, Gold seal, train vignette	65.00
Mobile and Ohio Railroad Company (I), 1870s, Certificate of deposit, train vignette	38.00
Mobile and Ohio Railroad Company (I), 1870s, Embossed seal, train vignette	42.00
Mobile and Ohio Railroad Company (I), 1880s, Train vignette	35.00
Mobile and Ohio Railroad Company (I), 1890s, Train vignette	30.00
Mobile and Ohio Railroad Company (U), 1870s, Two trains vignette	32.00
Mohawk and Ilion Horse Railroad (I), 1890s, Seal	50.00
Mohawk Valley Railroad (U), 1850s	45.00
Monon Railroad (I), 1950s, Man and woman vignette	5.00
Monongahela Valley Traction Company (U), 1900s, Streetcar vignette	40.00
Montana Railroad (I)	30.00
Montana Railroad (U)	8.00
Morris and Essex Railroad (I), 1940s	6.00
Morristown and Cumberland Cap Railroad (I), 1890s, Long train vignette	80.00
Mount Carbon and Port Carbon Railroad (I), 1890s, Train vignette	85.00
Mount Carbon and Port Carbon Railroad (I), 1930s	18.00
Mount Clemens and Lakeside Traction Company (U), 1890s, Eagle and globe	15.00
Muncie Belt Railroad (U), 1890s, Indiana, Eagle	20.00
Muscatine Western Railway Construction Company (U), 1800s, Train vignette	20.00
Nashville and Decatur Railroad Company (I), 1880s, Old steam train vignette and farm girl	45.00
Nashville and Decatur Railroad (I), 1950s, Train and farm girl vignette	10.00
Nashville and Florence Railroad Company (I), 1880s, Train vignette	60.00
Nashville, Chattanooga and Saint Louis Railroad (I), 1930s, Two trains at station vignette	20.00
Nashville, Chattanooga and Saint Louis Railroad (I), 1950s, Two trains at station vignette	18.00
Nassau Electric Railroad (I), 1890s, Seminude vignette	65.00
National Car Company (I), 1890s, Freight train and workers vignette	82.00
Naugatuck Railroad (I), 1850s, Small train vignette	115.00
Naugatuck Railroad (I), 1920s, Old train vignette	30.00
Navy Yard, Road Street and Fairmount Railway (U), 1860s, Horses and side vignette	43.00

◀ ***Jenkintown Electric Railway Company (U), 1890s,***	*7.00*
◀ ***Keokuk and Des Moines Railway Company, the (I), 1890s,*** *Two train vignette and Indians and surveyors*	*60.00*

No. Shares

STATE OF WISCONSIN

THE

LAKE SUPERIOR & SOUTHWESTERN RAILWAY COMPANY.

CAPITAL STOCK, $4,000,000. SHARES, $100 EACH.

This Certifies *that* ______________________________

the owner of ______________________________ *Shares of One Hundred Dollars each of the Stock of The Lake Superior & Southwestern Railway Company, transferable in person or by Attorney, on the books of the Company, at the Office of the Secretary, or at any Transfer Agency established by the Company, upon the surrender of this Certificate.*

______________ 188

Secretary ______________ *President*

LYKENS VALLEY Rail Road and Coal Company.

Number. 836 Shares. 7

VIRTUE LIBERTY AND INDEPENDENCE

LYKENS VALLEY RAIL ROAD AND COAL COMPANY.

SHARES $20 EACH.

Be it known, *That the Estate of Edward J Etting is entitled to* ~~~~~~~~ *Seven Shares in the Capital Stock of the* **LYKENS VALLEY RAIL ROAD AND COAL COMPANY,** *in Dauphin County, Pennsylvania. Transferable on the Books of the said Company at their Office, either in person or by Attorney.*

Witness the Seal of the Lykens Valley Rail Road and Coal Company, *in Dauphin County, Pennsylvania, at* **Philadelphia,** *this First day of Dec 1863*

President.

Treasurer.

John C. Clark, 60 Dock Street, Philadelphia.

Nebraska Railway (U), Train vignette	**32.00**
Negaunee and Palmer Railroad (I), 1880s	**65.00**
Negaunee and Palmer Railroad (U), 1880s	**15.00**
New Albany and Sandusky Railroad (U), 1800s, Train vignette	**35.00**
New Bedford Railroad (I), 1870s	**40.00**
New Haven and Centerville Street Railway (U), 1890s	**10.00**
New Haven and Derby Railroad Company (I), 1880s, Mortgage certificate	**40.00**
New Haven and Northampton (I), 1860s, Old train vignette with stamp	**95.00**
New Haven and Northampton (I), 1870s, Justice vignette	**75.00**
New Haven and Northampton (I), 1880s, Old train vignette	**50.00**
New Haven and Northampton (I), 1890s, Old train vignette	**40.00**
New Haven and West Haven Horse Railroad (I), 1880s, Horse streetcar vignette	**80.00**
New Haven and West Haven Horse Railroad (I), 1880s, Sailor at wharf vignette	**60.00**
New Jersey Junction Railroad 1800s, Old train vignette	**30.00**
New Orleans Great Northern Railroad Company (I), 1910s, Train vignette with stamps	**25.00**
New Orleans Great Northern Railroad Company (I), 1920s, Two trains vignette	**22.00**
New Orleans Great Northern Railroad Company (I), 1930s, Train vignette	**20.00**
New Orleans, Jackson and Great Northern Railroad (I), 1860s, Scrip	**15.00**
New Orleans, Mobile and Chicago (I), 1910s, Three trains in railroad yard vignette	**18.00**
New Orleans, Mobile and Northern (I), 1910s	**20.00**
New York and Boston Railroad (I), 1850s, Embossed seal plus old train and lake vignette	**135.00**
New York and Boston Railroad (I), 1860s, Train in country, seal vignette	**125.00**
New York and Coney Island Railroad (U), 1800s, Eagle and seal vignette	**75.00**
New York and Coney Island Railroad (U), 1890s, Map of Coney Island vignette	**65.00**
New York and Fort Lee Railroad (I), 1800s, Train and ship vignette	**40.00**
New York and Fort Lee Railroad (U), 1800s, Train and ship vignette	**18.00**
New York and Harlem Railroad (I), 1860s, Train and two men and dog (three vignettes) signed by William Vanderbilt	**900.00**
New York and New England Railroad (I), 1860s, Old train vignette	**175.00**
New York and New England Railroad (I), 1870s, Old train vignette	**45.00**
New York and New England Railroad (I), 1880s, Old train vignette	**40.00**
New York and New England Railroad (I), 1890s, Speeding train vignette	**35.00**
New York and New England Railroad (I), 1950s and 1960s, Train vignette	**20.00**
New York and New Jersey Railroad (U), 1900s, Streetcar vignette	**12.00**
New York and New Jersey Railroad (U), 1900s, Woman with dynamo vignette	**10.00**
New York and Northern Railroad (U), 1880s, Train vignette	**35.00**
New York and Oswego Midland Railroad (U), 1870s, State seal vignette, trustee certificate	**20.00**
New York and Providence and Boston Railroad (I), 1830s, Beautiful vignettes	**250.00**
New York and Western Pennsylvania Railway (I), 1890s, Train at station vignette	**42.00**
New York Cable Railways (I), 1880s	**30.00**
New York Central Railroad (U), 1800s, Eagle and seal vignette	**75.00**
New York Central Sleeping Car Company (I), 1870s	**85.00**
New York Central Sleeping Car Company (I), 1880s, Old train with boat vignette	**80.00**
New York Central Sleeping Car Company (I), 1880s, Train vignette	**75.00**
New York, Chicago and Saint Louis Railroad (I), 1940s, Two trains, workmen, and shack vignette	**5.00**
New York, Chicago and Saint Louis Railroad (I), 1950s and 1960s, Train vignette	**4.00**
New York, Chicago and Saint Louis Railroad (I), 1950s, Nickle plate road vignette	**4.00**
New York Consolidated Railroad (I), 1920s, Boats, ferry, Brooklyn Bridge	**32.00**
New York, Greenwood and Coney Island Railroad (I), 1880s, Train and ship vignette	**155.00**
New York, Lake Erie and Western Railroad (I), 1880s, Train vignette	**75.00**
New York, New Haven and Hartford Railroad 1950s, Trains vignette	**10.00**
New York, New Haven and Hartford Railroad, 1960s (I), Trains vignette	**10.00**

◀ ***Lake Superior and Southwestern (U), 1880s***	***15.00***
◀ ***Lykens Valley Rail Road and Coal Company (I), 1860s,*** *Horses vignette*	***95.00***

No. 11470 — 4 Shares

Metropolitan Rail Road Company

METROPOLITAN RAIL ROAD COMPANY. SHARES $50 EACH

Be it known, That Alice C. Pinkham — is Proprietor of — Four — Shares in the Capital Stock of the METROPOLITAN RAIL ROAD CO. of the par value of FIFTY DOLLARS, each amounting to the sum of — Two hundred — Dollars which has been paid in full, subject to the provisions of the Charter and the By Laws of the Company, the same being transferable by an Assignment in the Books of said Company upon a surrender of this Certificate. And when a transfer shall be made in the Books of the Company, and this Certificate surrendered a new one will be issued.

Dated at Boston, this twelfth day of November 1886

CANCELLED (Treasurer.) CANCELLED (President.)

Walker, Young & Co. 43 Kilby St. Boston.

MOBILE & OHIO RAILROAD COMPANY.

ASSENTED

ALABAMA, MISSISSIPPI, TENNESSEE & KENTUCKY.

AUTHORIZED CAPITAL $10.000.000.

NUMBER 5135 SHARES 100

Be it known that Thompson & Mairs are entitled to One Hundred Shares of the Capital Stock of the Mobile and Ohio Railroad Company, One hundred dollars per share having been paid on the same, said shares transferable on the books of the Company only by the above named Thompson & Mairs in person or by Attorney upon the surrender of this Certificate and subject to the power of Attorney herein referred to.

It is understood and declared that the ownership by the said and his assigns of the said shares of stock entitles them to all the rights and privileges which pertain to the ownership of the said shares, including the right to such dividends and profits as shall be ascertained and declared upon the capital stock of the said Company, and excepting that such ownership is subject to a power and authority heretofore granted by the owners of said shares to the Farmers' Loan & Trust Company in Trust for the benefit and security of the Preferred Income and Sinking Fund Debentures issued by said Railroad Company by virtue of which power and authority the said The Farmers' Loan & Trust Company and its successors will be entitled in person or by proxy to vote upon the said shares of stock at all the meetings of the stockholders of the said Company which may be hereafter for any purpose convened during the continuance of said trust and so to vote in the names of either the present or future holders of said shares or in the name of the said the Farmers' Loan & Trust Company or its successors or proxies.

In Witness whereof, the signature of the President and the countersignature of the Secretary and the seal of said Company are hereunto affixed this 24th day of March 1899

Countersigned and Registered FARMERS' LOAN & TRUST CO. Registrar.

CANCELLED BY THE Farmers' Loan & Trust Company AUG 20 1901

Secretary. President.

SHARES $100 EACH

New York, New Haven and Hartford Railroad (I), 1940s	20.00
New York, New Haven and Hartford Railroad (I-N), 1940s, Electric train vignette	27.00
New York, Ontario and Western Railroad (I), 1880s, Old train and ships vignette	60.00
New York, Ontario and Western Railroad (I), 1900s, Train, cows and boats vignette	36.00
New York, Ontario and Western Railway (I), 1920s, Train vignette	20.00
New York, Ontario and Western Railway (I), 1930s, Engine vignette	15.00
New York, Ontario and Western Railway (I), 1940s, Engine vignette	12.00
New York, Ontario and Western Railway (I), 1950s, Engine vignette	10.00
New York, Ontario and Western Railroad (U), 1880s, Old train and ships	14.00
New York, Pittsburgh and Chicago Railway (U), 1880s,	15.00
New York Railways (I), 1920s, Streetcar vignette	25.00
New York Railways (I), 1930s, Streetcar vignette	15.00
New York Railways Corporation (I), 1930s, Streetcar vignette	20.00
New York Railways Participation Company (I), 1920s, Streetcar vignette	45.00
New York, Susquehanna and Western Railroad (I), 1800s, Train vignette	150.00
New York, West Shore and Buffalo Railway (U), 1880s, Trains and ship vignette	49.00
New York, Westchester and Connecticut Traction (I), 1900s, Goddess vignette	28.00
New York, Westchester and Connecticut Traction (I), 1910s, Gold seal vignette	20.00
Newburg, Dutchess and Connecticut Railroad (I), 1890s	39.00
Newburgh and Ellenville Plank Road Company (U), 1850s	55.00
Newport News and Mississippi Valley Railroad (I), 1880s and 1890s, Signed by Huntington (Big Four) of Pacific Railroad	1,000.00
Newport News and Old Point Railway and Electric Company (U), 1800s	15.00
Newport News and Old Point Railway and Electric Company (U), 1910s	8.00
Niagara Falls Branch Railroad (U), 1800s, Old train vignette	40.00
Norfolk Southern Railroad (I), 1930s, Speeding train vignette	27.00
Northeastern Elevated Railway (I), 1890s, Small certificate	12.00
Northern Adirondack Extension Railroad (I), 1880s, Train at station vignette	80.00
Northern and Southern West Virginia Railroad (U), Train vignette	50.00
Northern and Southern West Virginia Railroad (U), 1870s, Train and boat vignette	30.00
Northern Indiana Railroad (U), 1850s,	33.00
Northern Pacific Railroad (I), 1900s, Covered wagon	11.00
Northern Pacific Railroad (I), 1910s, Train and two ladies vignette	25.00
Northern Pacific Railroad (U), 1860s, Eagle vignette	45.00
Northern Railroad (I), 1840s	100.00
Northern Railroad (I), 1850s	50.00
Northern Railroad (I), 1860s, Red seal with stamp, signed by Stearns	80.00
Northern Railroad (I), 1870s	30.00
Northern Railroad (I-N), 1870s	35.00
Norwich and Worcester Railroad (I), 1890s, Old train vignette, many stamps	40.00
Norwich and Worcester Railroad (I), 1920s, Preferred	25.00
Norwich and Worcester Railroad Company (I), 1930s, Train vignette	25.00
Norwich and Worcester Railroad Company (I), 1950s, Train vignette	20.00
Norwich and Worcester Railroad Company (I), 1960s, Eagle vignette	15.00

Oakland, Antioch and Eastern Railway (I), 1900s, Two interurban vignettes	25.00
Oakland, Antioch and Eastern Railway (I), 1910s, Interurban vignette	28.00
Ocean City Railroad (I), 1900s, Train vignette	45.00
Oconee and Western Railroad (I), 1890s, Train vignette	85.00
Oconee and Western Railroad (U), 1890s, Train vignette	15.00
Ogden Mine Railroad (I), 1890s, Old train, sailing ships vignette	35.00
Ogden Mine Railroad (I), 1920s, State seal, old train vignette	25.00

◀ ***Metropolitan Rail Road Company (I), 1880s,*** *Horse-drawn streetcar vignette* ***65.00***

◀ ***Mobile and Ohio Railroad Company (I), 1890s,*** *Train vignette* ***30.00***

United States of America
State of Connecticut
NEW HAVEN
No 71
No 71
AND Derby Railroad Company
Mortgage Certificate of Indebtedness
The New Haven and Derby Railroad Company
In Witness Whereof this Certificate by vote of the Board of Directors of said Company is signed by the President and attested by the Secretary of said Company on the first day of August 1888
President
Secretary
SFERABLE.
R. R. CO.
United States of America

Oklahoma Union Traction Company (I), 1910s, Eagle vignette	23.00
Old Colony and Fall River Railroad (I), 1850s, Train and ship vignette	70.00
Old Colony and Fall River Railroad (I), 1860s, Seal, with stamp	60.00
Old Colony and Newport Railway (I), 1860s, Seal with stamp	60.00
Old Colony and Newport Railway (U), 1860s, Train vignette	22.00
Old Colony Railroad (I), 1840s	95.00
Old Colony Railroad (I), 1850s, Red seal	75.00
Old Colony Railroad (I), 1870s, Train and ships vignette, signed by Stearns, red seal	65.00
Old Colony Railroad (I), 1870s, Train vignette	35.00
Old Colony Railroad (I), 1890s, Train and wagon vignette	30.00
Old Colony Railroad (U), 1880s, Transfer certificate	27.00
Omaha and Council Bluffs State Railway 1900s, Streetcars vignette	14.00
Omaha and Council Bluffs State Railway (I), 1950s, Old trolley car vignette	9.00
Omaha and Council Bluffs State Railway (U)	8.00
Omaha Transit Company (I), Old trolley car and horse and carriage vignette	7.00
Ontario Pacific Railway (U), 1880s	23.00
Oregon Branch Pacific Railroad (U), 1860s, Train vignette	39.00
Pacific Railroad (I), 1870s, Old train in mountain vignette	50.00
Pacific Railroad of Missouri (I), 1870s, Train vignette	75.00
Passaic Valley and Peapack Railroad (U), 1800s, Train and surveyors vignette	25.00
Payette Valley Extension Railroad (I-N), 1910s, Eagle vignette	18.00
Penn Yan and New York Railway (U), 1880s, Old train vignette	40.00
Pennock Battery Electric Light and Railway (I-N), 1890s	33.00
Pennroad Corporation (I), 1920s, Warrant	7.00
Pennsylvania and New York Canal and Railroad (U), 1870s, Train vignette	20.00
Pennsylvania and Ohio Electric Railway (I), 1920s, Streetcar vignette	12.00
Pennsylvania and Ohio Electric Railway (U), 1920s, Streetcar vignette	6.00
Pennsylvania Railroad (I), 1950s, State seal and train vignette	8.00
Peoples Passenger Railroad 1880s, Seal	14.00
Peoples Passenger Railroad (I), 1920s, Certificate of Deposit	6.00
Peoples Railroad (I), 1910s, Streetcar vignette	42.00
People's Traction of Pennsylvania (I), 1890s, Streetcar vignette	28.00
Peoria and Bureau Valley Railroad (I), 1850s, Old train vignette	125.00
Peoria and Bureau Valley Railroad (I), 1870s	75.00
Peoria and Bureau Valley Railroad Company (I), 1880s, Old train and Indians vignette	100.00
Peoria and Bureau Valley Railroad Company (I), 1890s	40.00
Peoria and Bureau Valley Railroad Company (I), 1900s	35.00
Peoria and Eastern Railway, 1890s, Train at station vignette	24.00
Peoria and Eastern Railway (U), 1900s, Train at station vignette	22.00
Peoria and Pekin Terminal Railway (I), 1900s, Train vignette	38.00
Peoria and Pekin Terminal Railway (U), 1900s	14.00
Pere Marquette Railroad (I), 1880s	30.00
Philadelphia and Gray's Ferry Passenger Railway Company (I), 1860s, Revenue stamps and seal vignette	62.00
Philadelphia and Gray's Ferry Passenger Railway Company (I), 1870s, Horsecar vignette	50.00
Philadelphia and Gray's Ferry Passenger Railway Company (I), 1920s , Horsecar vignette	15.00
Philadelphia and Reading Railroad (U), 1870s, With stamp	65.00
Philadelphia City Passenger Railway (I), 1870s, Two vignettes	75.00
Philadelphia City Passenger Railway (I), 1890s, Three vignettes and Independence Hall vignette	30.00
Philadelphia City Passenger Railway (I), 1910s, Independence Hall vignette	20.00
Philadelphia City Passenger Railway (U), 1870s	17.00

◀ ***New Haven and Derby Railroad (I), 1880's,*** *Mortgage Certificate* ***40.00***

Nashville & Decatur Rail Road Co.
NUMBER
5482
SHARES
AMERICAN NATIONAL BANK,
This Certifies that
owns
Shares
Twenty Five Dollars each of the Capital Stock of the
NASHVILLE & DECATUR RAILROAD COMPANY.
transferable only on the Books of the Company in person or by Attorney on the surrender of this Certificate.
Witness the Corporate Seal of the Company and the Signatures of the President and the Secretary hereto affixed.
Nashville, Tenn.
Secretary
President

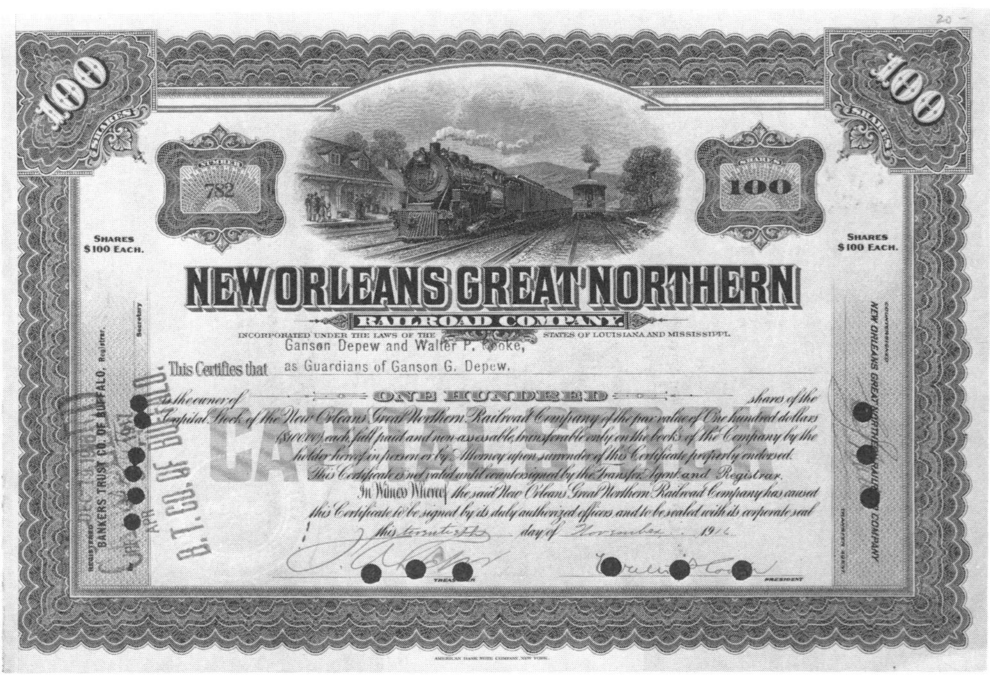

100
SHARES
782
100
SHARES $100 EACH.
SHARES $100 EACH.
NEW ORLEANS GREAT NORTHERN
RAILROAD COMPANY.
INCORPORATED UNDER THE LAWS OF THE STATES OF LOUISIANA AND MISSISSIPPI.
This Certifies that
Ganson Depew and Walter P. Cooke,
as Guardians of Ganson G. Depew.
is the owner of
ONE HUNDRED
shares of the Capital Stock of the New Orleans Great Northern Railroad Company of the par value of One hundred dollars ($100.00) each, full paid and non-assessable, transferable only on the books of the Company by the holder hereof in person or by Attorney upon surrender of this Certificate properly endorsed.
This Certificate is not valid until countersigned by the Transfer Agent and Registrar.
In Witness Whereof the said New Orleans Great Northern Railroad Company has caused this Certificate to be signed by its duly authorized officers and to be sealed with its corporate seal
this
day of
19
TREASURER
PRESIDENT
BANKERS TRUST CO. OF BUFFALO,
B. T. CO. OF BUFFALO
NEW ORLEANS GREAT NORTHERN RAILROAD COMPANY
AMERICAN BANK NOTE COMPANY, NEW YORK.

Philadelphia Rapid Transit Company (I), 1900s, Seal, train, streetcar, and bus vignette	18.00
Philadelphia Rapid Transit Company (I), 1910s, Trolley vignette	14.00
Philadelphia Rapid Transit Company (I), 1920s, Elevated, bus, and streetcar vignette	15.00
Philadelphia Rapid Transit Company (I), 1920s, Streetcar vignette	12.00
Philadelphia Rapid Transit Company (I), 1930s, Winged Mercury vignette	9.00
Philadelphia Thirteenth and Fifteenth Streets Passenger Railway (I), 1880s, Horses and train vignette	40.00
Philadelphia Traction Company (I), 1890s, Freight train vignette	48.00
Philadelphia Traction Company (I), 1900s, Streetcars vignette	30.00
Philadelphia Traction Company (I), 1900s, Waterworks vignette	30.00
Philadelphia Traction Company (I), 1920s, Freight train vignette	20.00
Philadelphia Transportation (I), 1940s, Winged figure vignette	12.00
Phillipsburg Horse Car Railroad (U), 1800s, Fancy old horse car vignette	65.00
Piedmont and Mountain View Railway (I), 1890s	55.00
Piedmont and Mountain View Railway (U), 1890s	20.00
Pine Creek Railway (I), 1880s–1910s, Old train vignette	55.00
Pine Creek Railway (I), 1880s, Old train vignette, signed by Cornelius Vanderbilt	800.00
Pittsburgh and Erie Railroad (U), 1800s, Two trains vignette	30.00
Pittsburgh and Erie Railroad (U), 1860s, Trains and two eagle vignettes	55.00
Pittsburgh and West End Traction Company, 1890s, Two streetcars vignette	45.00
Pittsburgh, Crafton and Mansfield Street Railway (I), 1890s, Pretty woman vignette	22.00
Pittsburgh, Lisbon and Western Railroad (I), 1900s, Train vignette	28.00
Pittsburgh, Marion and Chicago Railway Company (I), 1880s, Train at station vignette	40.00
Pittsburgh, Marion and Chicago Railway Company (U), 1880s, Old steam train vignette	20.00
Pittsburgh Traction Company (I), 1880s, Streetcar vignette	45.00
Pittsburgh Valley and Peapack Railroad (U), 1800s, Train and surveyor vignettes	28.00
Port Jarvis, Monticello and New York Railroad (I), 1900s, Seated woman vignette	32.00
Port Jarvis, Monticello and New York Railroad (U), 1880s, Train and farmer vignette	30.00
Portland and Rumford Falls Railway (I), 1890s, Train vignette	44.00
Portland Railroad (I), 1910s, Horse trolley vignette	50.00
Portland Railroad (I), 1920s–1940s, Horse trolley vignette	35.00
Port Reading Railroad (I), 1890s, Train vignette	80.00
Portsmouth Transit Company (U), Eagle vignette	8.00
Potosi and Rio Verde Railway (U), 1890s, Popular in silver mining areas	9.00
Providence, Warren and Bristol Railroad (I), 1850s	52.00
Puget Sound Commercial Company (U), 1870s	95.00
Pullman Company (I), 1900s, Portrait vignette	15.00
Pullman Company (I), 1920s, Portrait vignette	12.00
Pullman Palace Car Company (I), 1860s, With stamp, signed by Pullman	150.00
Pullman Palace Car Company (I), 1890s, Railroad car vignette	50.00
Quakertown Traction Company (U), 1890s, Old trolley	32.00
Raleigh and Gaston Railroad (I), 1850s, Old steam train vignette	150.00
Raleigh and Gaston Railroad (I), 1850s, Two vignettes, with stamps	100.00
Rantoul Railroad (I), 1900s–1930s	18.00
Reeding and Columbia Railroad (I), 1860s, Old train and seminude woman vignette	115.00
Richmond and West Point Terminal Railway and Warehouse (I), 1890s, Steamships vignette	75.00
Ridge Avenue Passenger Railway (I), 1900s, Horse streetcar vignette	40.00
Rio Grande Southern Railroad Company, The (U), 1890s	95.00

◀ ***Nashville and Decatur Rail Road Company (I), 1880s,*** *Old steam train vignette and farm girl* ***45.00***

◀ ***New Orleans Great Northern Railroad Company (I), 1910s,*** *Two train vignette with stamps* ***25.00***

BE IT KNOWN THAT
48569
JOHN C. MC GROARTY.
100
the proprietor of
Shares
IN THE CAPITAL STOCK OF THE
NEW YORK AND NEW ENGLAND
RAILROAD COMPANY
CAPITAL $20,000,000.
SHARES $100 EACH.
Transferable only on the Books of the said Company in person or by Attorney duly authorized at its Agency in New York upon the surrender of this Certificate.
In Witness whereof the Central Trust Company of New York, Transfer Agent authorized to sign and issue Certificates in New York by resolution of the Directors of the New York and New England Railroad Company passed April 1st 1881, signs this Certificate by its Secretary, and countersigns it by its Transfer Clerk, this
Countersigned by
Transfer Clerk.
Secretary.
CANCELLED
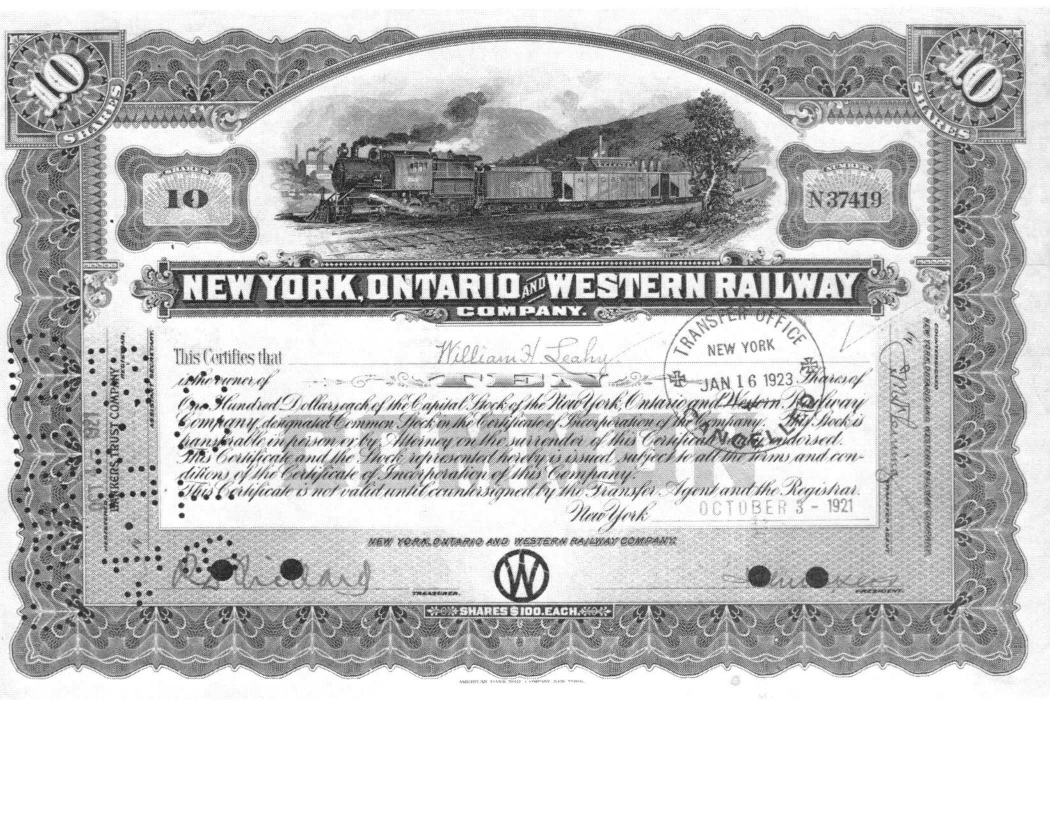
10
SHARES
N 37419
NEW YORK, ONTARIO AND WESTERN RAILWAY COMPANY.
This Certifies that
William H. Leahy
is the owner of
TEN
Shares of
One Hundred Dollars each of the Capital Stock of the New York, Ontario and Western Railway Company, designated Common Stock in the Certificate of Incorporation of the Company. This Stock is transferable in person or by Attorney on the surrender of this Certificate duly endorsed. This Certificate and the Stock represented hereby is issued, subject to all the terms and conditions of the Certificate of Incorporation of this Company.
This Certificate is not valid until Countersigned by the Transfer Agent and the Registrar.
New York
OCTOBER 3 - 1921
TRANSFER OFFICE
NEW YORK
JAN 16 1923
BANKERS TRUST COMPANY
NEW YORK, ONTARIO AND WESTERN RAILWAY COMPANY.
TREASURER.
PRESIDENT.
SHARES $100. EACH.

Rio Grande Southern Railroad Company, The (I), 1890s, Signed by President Mears	**260.00**
Rio Grande Southern Railroad Company, The (I), 1920s, Seated woman vignette, certificate of deposit	**20.00**
Rio Grande Southern Railroad Company, The (I), 1890s	**160.00**
Rochester and Lake Ontario Railroad (U), 1800s, Old train vignette	**40.00**
Rock Island and Eastern Illinois Railroad (U)	**6.00**
Rock Island Company (I), 1900s, Train and awaiting passenger vignette	**30.00**
Rocky River Railway (U), 1800s, Old funnel train vignette	**30.00**
Rome City Street Railway (U), 1880s, Horse trolley vignette	**28.00**
Rome, Watertown and Ogdensburg Railroad (U), 1800s, Niagara Falls vignette	**30.00**
Rome, Watertown and Ogdensburg Railroad (U), 1860s, Train vignette	**60.00**
Rome, Watertown and Ogdensburg Railroad (U), 1880s, Old train vignette	**40.00**
Rutland and Burlington Railroad (I), 1840s, Ship and old Tom Thumb Railroad vignette	**135.00**
Rutland and Noyan Railway (U), 1900s, Train vignette	**18.00**
Rutland Railroad (I), 1900s, Old train with two reclining ladies vignette	**24.00**
Saint Lawrence and Adirondack Railway (U), 1900s, Train and steamer vignette	**25.00**
Saint Louis, Jacksonville and Chicago Railroad (U), 1860s, Old train vignette	**38.00**
Saint Louis, Kansas City and Colorado (U), 1880s, Old train vignette	**30.00**
Saint Louis–San Francisco Railroad, (I) 1960s	**4.00**
Saint Louis–San Francisco Railroad (I), 1950s, Mercury and goddess vignette	**8.00**
Saint Louis–San Francisco Railroad (U), 1920s	**10.00**
San Francisco and Sacramento Railroad (I), 1920s, Eagle vignette	**15.00**
Sandy River and Rangeley Lakes Railroad, 1900s, Train vignette	**95.00**
Schoolcraft and Three Rivers Railroad (U), 1800s, Old train vignette	**24.00**
Schuylkill and Lehigh Valley Railroad (I), 1880s,, Three train vignettes	**65.00**
Schuylkill and Lehigh Valley Railroad (I), 1900s	**50.00**
Schuylkill and Lehigh Valley Railroad (U), 1800s, Three train vignettes	**35.00**
Scranton and Binghampton Railway (I), 1900s, Car vignette	**35.00**
Scranton Street Railway (I), 1870s, Horse trolley vignette	**48.00**
Sea Beach Railway (U)	**18.00**
Sea Train Lines, Inc., 1950s, Old train, ship, and Mercury vignette	**4.00**
Sea Train Lines, Inc., 1960s and 1970s, Man and two globes vignette	**3.00**
Seaboard Airline Railway (I), 1940s,	**12.00**
Seaboard Airline Railway (I-N), 1930s, Warrant	**12.00**
Seaboard–All Florida Railway (I), 1920s, Old auto, three presidents' signatures	**40.00**
Seaboard, Pennsylvania and Western (U), 1880s, Old train vignette, sailing ships vignette	**35.00**
Seaboard, Pennsylvania and Western Railroad Company (I), 1880s, Train and ships vignette	**75.00**
Seattle, Port Angeles and Lake Crescent Railway (U), Train vignette	**40.00**
Seattle, Port Angeles and Western Railroad (I)	**35.00**
Seattle, Port Angeles and Western Railroad (U), 1900s	**12.00**
Second and Third Street Passenger Railway Company (I), 1860s, Horse trolley vignette	**60.00**
Second and Third Street Passenger Railway Company (I), 1870s, Horse trolley vignette	**47.00**
Second and Third Street Passenger Railway Company (I), 1880s, Horse trolley vignette	**35.00**
Second and Third Street Passenger Railway (I), 1890s, State seal and horse trolley vignette	**30.00**
Second and Third Street Passenger Railway (I), 1900s, Horse trolley vignette, with stamps	**18.00**
Second and Third Street Passenger Railway Company (I), 1910, Seal vignette	**12.00**
Second and Third Street Passenger Railway Company (I), 1920s, Seal vignette	**11.00**
Second and Third Street Railway (I), 1880s, Horse trolley and seal vignette	**35.00**
Second and Third Street Railway (I), 1900s, Horse trolley and seal vignette	**25.00**
Second and Third Street Railway (I), 1920s, Horse trolley and seal vignette	**10.00**
Second and Third Street Railway (I), 1930s, Horse trolley and seal vignette	**8.00**

◀ ***New York and New England Railroad (I), 1890s,*** *Speeding train vignette* ***35.00***

◀ ***New York, Ontario and Western Railway (I), 1920s,*** *Train vignette* ***20.00***

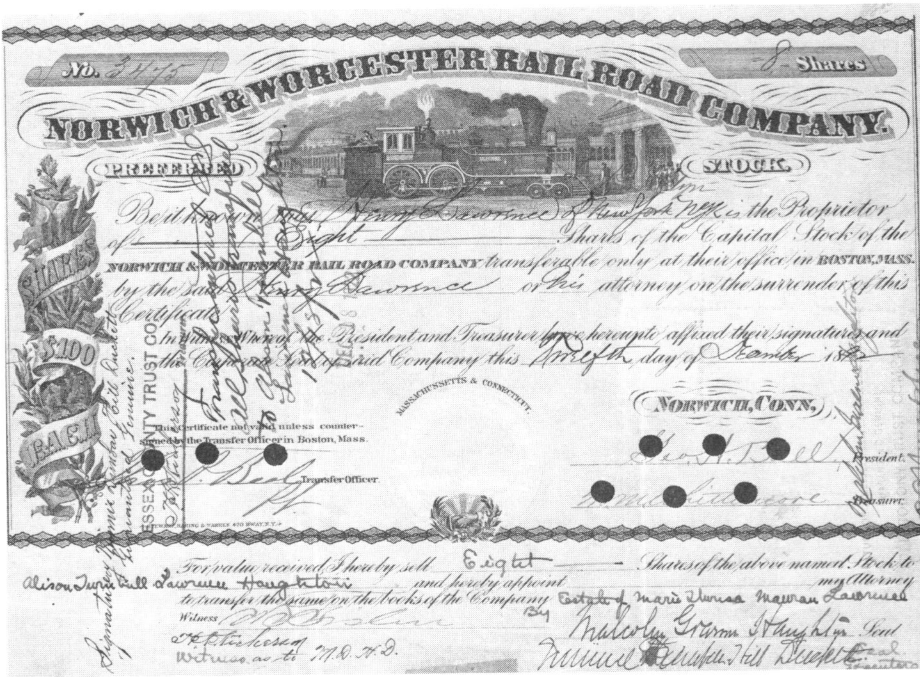
No. 3475
8 Shares
NORWICH & WORCESTER RAIL ROAD COMPANY.
PREFERRED
STOCK.
Be it known that Henry Lawrence of New York N.Y. is the Proprietor of Eight Shares of the Capital Stock of the NORWICH & WORCESTER RAIL ROAD COMPANY transferable only at their office in BOSTON, MASS. by the said Henry Lawrence or his attorney on the surrender of this Certificate.
In Witness Whereof the President and Treasurer have hereunto affixed their signatures and the Corporate Seal of said Company this twelfth day of December 18
SHARES $100 EACH
NORWICH, CONN.
This Certificate not valid unless countersigned by the Transfer Officer in Boston, Mass.
Transfer Officer.
President.
Treasurer.
For value received, I hereby sell Eight Shares of the above named Stock to
and hereby appoint my Attorney
to transfer the same on the books of the Company
Witness
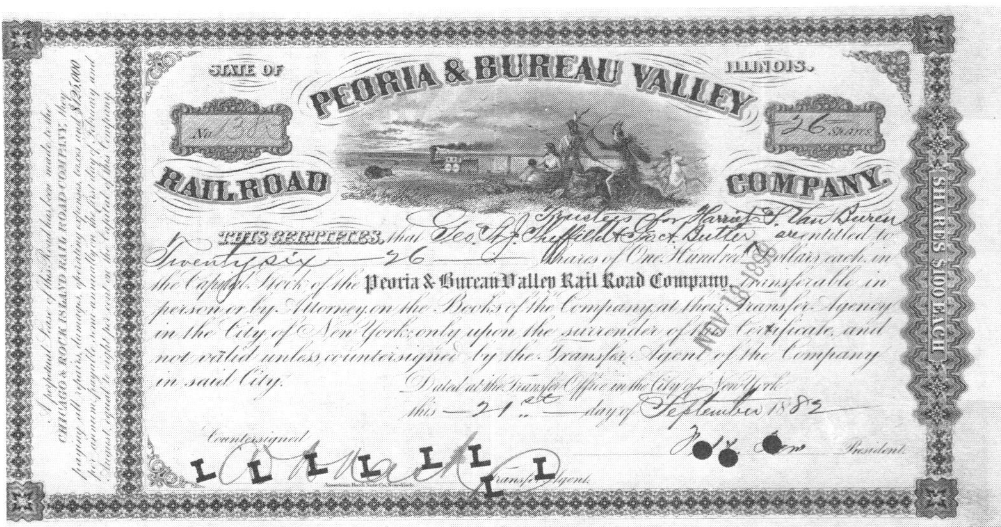
STATE OF ILLINOIS.
PEORIA & BUREAU VALLEY RAILROAD COMPANY.
No. 1383
26 Shares
THIS CERTIFIES, that Geo. H. J. Sheffield & Jas. A. Butler are entitled to Twenty six 26 Shares of One Hundred Dollars each in the Capital Stock of the Peoria & Bureau Valley Rail Road Company, transferable in person or by Attorney on the Books of the Company at their Transfer Agency in the City of New York, only upon the surrender of this Certificate, and not valid unless countersigned by the Transfer Agent of the Company in said City.
Dated at the Transfer Office in the City of New York this 21st day of September 1882
Countersigned
Transfer Agent.
President.
SHARES $100 EACH
A perpetual Lease of this Road has been made to the CHICAGO & ROCK ISLAND RAIL ROAD COMPANY, they paying all repairs, damages, operating expenses, taxes and $125,000 per annum, payable semi annually on the first day of February and August, equal to eight per cent on the Capital of this Company.

Sioux City and Pacific Railroad (U), 1800s, Five vignettes, including train, man and woman	40.00
Sixth Avenue Railroad (I), 1910s, Horse trolley vignette	34.00
Sixth Avenue Railroad (I), 1920s, Horse trolley vignette	21.00
Snohomish Valley Railway (U), 1900s, Eagle vignette	18.00
Somerset Railway (I), 1910s, Train vignette	28.00
Somerville Horse Railroad Company (I), 1860s	48.00
Somerville Horse Railroad Company (I), 1870s	37.00
Somerville Horse Railroad Company (I), 1880s	30.00
Somerville Horse Railroad Company (I), 1890s	27.00
Soo-Line Co-op (I), 1910s, Small certificate, with stamp	3.00
South and North Alabama Railroad (I), 1870s, Old train vignette	75.00
South Boston Railroad (I), 1880s	25.00
South Boston Railroad (U), 1880s	8.00
South Chicago and Southern Railroad (I), 1920s, Eagle vignette	30.00
South Western Railway Railroad Company, The (I), 1870s, Two old trains vignettes	55.00
South Western Railroad Company, The (I), 1880s, Old train vignette	50.00
South Western Railroad Company, The (I), 1890s, Woman with lamp vignette	30.00
Southern Indiana Express Company (I), 1890s	39.00
Southern Indiana Express Company (U), 1890s, State seal	12.00
Southern Indiana Railway (I), 1900s, Receivers certificate, speeding train vignette	45.00
Southern Pacific (I), 1930s, Warrant	7.00
Southern Pacific (U), 1890s	45.00
Southern Railway (I), Trust certificate with railroad maps	15.00
Southern Railway (I), 1900s, Train at station vignette	27.00
Southern Railway (I), 1930s, Train vignette	12.00
Southern Railway Company (I), 1910s, Train at busy station vignette	25.00
Southern Railway Company (I), 1920s, Train at busy station vignette	22.00
Southern Railway Company (I), 1940s, Train vignette	10.00
Southern Railway Company (I), 1950s and 1970s, Two men vignette	6.00
Southern Railway Equipment Company Trust of 1968 (I), Logo and railroad-crossing sign vignette	4.00
Southwestern Railroad Company, The (I), 1910s, Woman with lamp vignette	20.00
Southwestern Railroad Company, The (I), 1920s, Woman with lamp vignette	18.00
Spuyten-Duyvil and Port Morris Railroad (U), 1800s, New York	25.00
Stark Electric Railroad (I), 1920s, Goddess and world vignette	20.00
Stark Electric Railroad (I), 1930s, Goddess and world vignette	18.00
State Line and Sullivan Railroad (I), 1870s, Old train vignette	80.00
Staten Island Midland Railroad (U), 1890s, State seal, trolley vignette	110.00
Staten Island North and South Shore Railroad (I), 1880s, Old train vignette	90.00
Staten Island Railroad (I), 1860s, Old train and steamship vignette, two signatures by Jacob Vanderbilt	950.00
Stockbridge and Pittsfield Railroad (I), 1860s	55.00
Stoney Creek Railroad (U), 1800s, Train vignette	16.00
Stoney Creek Railroad (U), 1900s, Old train vignette	15.00
Sullivan Railroad (I), 1840s and 1850s, Old train vignette	210.00
Susquehanna and Clearfield Railroad (U), 1880s,	27.00
Swan Creek Railway (I), 1930s, Eagle, gold seal	25.00
Swan Creek Railway (U), 1800s, Train and ship vignette	60.00
Syracuse and Chenango Railroad (U), 1800s, Old train (large) vignette	32.00
Syracuse and Utica Railroad 1800s, Old train and ships, two vignettes	53.00

◀ ***Norwich and Worcester Railroad Company (I), 1890s,*** *Old train vignette, many stamps* ***40.00***

◀ ***Peoria and Bureau Valley Railroad Company (I), 1880s,*** *Old train and Indians vignette* ***100.00***

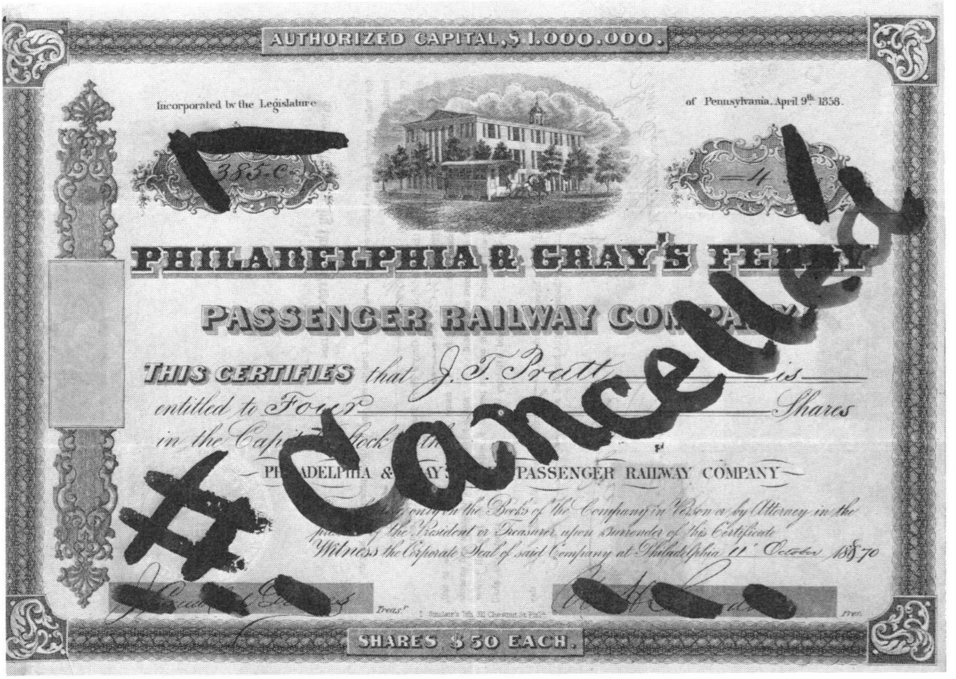

AUTHORIZED CAPITAL, $1.000.000.

Incorporated by the Legislature of Pennsylvania, April 9th 1858.

[redacted] 385-C

-4-

PHILADELPHIA & GRAY'S FERRY

PASSENGER RAILWAY COMPANY

THIS CERTIFIES that J. T. Pratt is entitled to Four Shares in the Capital Stock of the PHILADELPHIA & GRAY'S FERRY PASSENGER RAILWAY COMPANY transferable only on the Books of the Company in Person or by Attorney in the presence of the President or Treasurer upon surrender of this Certificate.

Witness the Corporate Seal of said Company at Philadelphia 11 October 1870

Cancelled

[redacted] Treas.r [redacted] Pres.

SHARES $50 EACH.

NORTHERN DIVISION

OF THE

PITTSBURG & ERIE RAILROAD.

SHARES

$50 EACH.

No.______ ______Shares.

THIS CERTIFIES That ______ is entitled to ______ Shares in the Capital Stock of the Rail Road called the NORTHERN DIVISION OF THE PITTSBURG AND ERIE RAILROAD, building by the Erie and North-East Railroad Company, under the Act of April 22, 1856, between the Lake Shore Railroad in the Township of Girard, Erie County, Pennsylvania, and Jamestown in the County of Mercer, Pennsylvania. Transferable only on the Books of the Company on surrender of this Certificate.

IN WITNESS WHEREOF is affixed the Corporate Seal of the Erie and North-East Railroad Company, at Erie, Pennsylvania, this ______ day of ______ 18__.

______ President.

______ Treasurer.

Printed at the Constitution Office, Erie, Pa.

Syracuse, Geneva and Corning Railway (U), 1800s, Railroad bridge over river 37.00
Syracuse, Ontario and New York Railway (U), 1880s, Train vignette 28.00

Tarkio Valley Railroad (U), 1880s, Nice railroad vignette 44.00
Taunton Branch Railroad (I), 1830s, Red seal 165.00
Taunton Branch Railroad (I), 1840s, Red seal 110.00
Taunton Branch Railroad (U), 1870s, Train vignette 35.00
Tennessee Northeastern (I), 1900s 35.00
Tenth and Eleventh Street Citizens Passenger Railroad (I), 1900s, State seal 11.00
Tenth and Eleventh Street Citizens Passenger Railroad (I), Two vignettes 15.00
Terre Haute, Indianapolis and Eastern Traction (I), 1930s, Streetcar vignette 35.00
Texas Central Railroad (I), 1890s–1900s, Train vignette 50.00
Thirteenth and Fifteenth Street Passengers Railway (I), 1880s, State seal and horses vignette 43.00
Thirteenth and Fifteenth Street Passengers Railway (I), 1890s 32.00
Thirteenth and Fifteenth Street Passengers Railway (I), 1910s, Horses, eagle on shield, and girl vignette 25.00
Thirteenth and Fifteenth Street Passengers Railway (I), 1920s, State seal and horses vignette 22.00
Thirteenth and Fifteenth Street Passengers Railway (I), 1930s, State seal and horses vignette 15.00
Tidewater Southern Railway (I), 1910s 18.00
Tiffin Street Railway (I), 1890s, Old streetcar vignette 27.00
Tivoli Hollow Railroad (U), 1890s, New York, 25.00
Toledo and Ohio Central Railway Company, The (U), 1800s, Bull vignette 15.00
Toledo and Ohio Central Railway Company, The (U), 1800s, Locomotive vignette 25.00
Toledo and Ohio Central Railway Company, The (U), 1900s 20.00
Toledo, Cincinnati and Saint Louis Railroad (I), 1880s, Ships vignette 60.00
Toledo, Delphos and Burlington Railroad (I), 1880s, Mine scene vignette 130.00
Toledo, Saint Louis and Western Railroad (I), 1900s, No vignette 10.00
Toledo, Saint Louis and Western Railroad (I), 1910s, Train vignette 25.00
Tonapah and Goldfield Railroad (U), 1900s, Nevada, Train at station vignette 80.00
Town of Vienna for New York and Oswego Midland Railroad (U), 1860s , Train vignette 160.00
Trans-Continental Transportation Company (I), 1880s 35.00
Transit Investment Corporation (I), 1930s and 1940s 10.00
Trenton Street Railway Company (I), 1900s, Streetcars and lady with lightning vignettes 30.00
Trenton Street Railway Company (U), 1890s, Streetcars and lady with lightning vignettes 22.00
Tunnel Railroad of Saint Louis (I), 1880s 39.00
Twenty-third Street Railway (I), 1890s and 1900s, Streetcar vignette 28.00
Twenty-third Street Railway (I), 1910s, Streetcar vignette 20.00
Twenty-third Street Railway (I), 1920s, Streetcar vignette 18.00
Twenty-third Street Railway (U), 1900s 10.00

Ulster and Delaware Railroad (U), 1800s, Train vignette 25.00
Union Passenger Railway Company of Philadelphia (I), 1860s, Trolley car vignette 42.00
Union Passenger Railway Company of Philadelphia (I), 1870s, Horse trolleys vignette 60.00
Union Passenger Railway Company of Philadelphia (I), 1870s, Imprinted stamp 125.00
Union Passenger Railway Company of Philadelphia (I), 1890s, Six vignettes (horse trolley) 40.00
Union Passenger Railway Company of Philadelphia (I), 1900s, Horse car vignette 30.00
Union Passenger Railway Company of Philadelphia (I), 1910s 25.00
Union Passenger Railway Company of Philadelphia (I), 1920s, Six vignettes (trolley cars) 20.00
Union Passenger Railway Company of Philadelphia (I), 1930s 8.00
Union Railroad Transfer and Stockyard Company (U), 1870s, Indiana, Large vignette 15.00
Union Railway Company (I), 1890s, Pennsylvania, Large eagle vignette 20.00
Union Traction Company (I), 1890s, Eagle vignette 20.00

◀ ***Philadelphia and Gray's Ferry Passenger Railway (I), 1870s,*** *Horsecar vignette* ***50.00***
◀ ***Pittsburgh and Erie Railroad (U), 1860s,*** *Train and two eagle vignettes* ***55.00***

THE RIO GRANDE SOUTHERN
RAILROAD COMPANY
Incorporated under the Laws of the State of Colorado
NUMBER
A391
100 SHARES
This is to Certify that O.A.OLMSTED
is the owner of ONE HUNDRED Shares of
Company, Denver, Colorado, this 31 day of JUL 1896
CANCELED
NEW CERTIF. No. 458
SECRETARY
PRESIDENT
50,000 SHARES OF $100 EACH

INCORPORATED UNDER THE LAWS OF THE STATE OF PENNSYLVANIA
SCHUYLKILL
AND LEHIGH VALLEY
RAILROAD COMPANY.
No 97
SHARES
Secretary
President
AMERICAN LOAN AND TRUST COMPANY
CAPITAL $2.000.000.

Union Traction Company (I), 1900s, Eagle vignette	14.00
Union Traction Company (I), 1910s and 1920s, Eagle vignette	12.00
Union Traction Company (I), 1920s, Certificate of deposit	10.00
Union Traction Company (I), 1930s, Eagle vignette	8.00
United Railways and Electric of Baltimore (I), 1890s, State seal	18.00
United Railways and Electric of Baltimore (I), 1900s, State seal	16.00
United Railways and Electric of Baltimore (I), 1910s, State seal	10.00
United States Car Company (I), 1890s, Old train vignette	95.00
United Smelters Railway and Copper Company (I-N), Train and mining vignette	50.00
United Traction Company (I), 1900s	12.00
United Traction Company (I), 1930s, Eagle vignette	10.00
Utah Western Railway Company (I), 1880s, Lady vignette	60.00
Utica and Mohawk Railroad (U), 1880s, Horse trolley vignette	20.00
Utica and Mohawk Valley Railway (U), 1900s, Horse trolley vignette	17.00
Utica and Schenectady Railroad (U), 1840s, Early train vignette	90.00
Utica and Schenectady Railroad (U), 1850s, Early train vignette	80.00
Utica and Waterville Railroad (U), 1800s	25.00
Utica Belt Line Railroad (U), 1800s, Old train vignette	45.00
Utica Belt Line Street Railway (U), 1890s, No vignette	10.00
Utica City Railroad (U), 1800s, Old streetcar vignette	28.00
Utica, Clinton and Binghamton Railroad Company (I), 1860s, Train vignette	55.00
Utica, Clinton and Binghamton Railroad Company (I), 1870s, Train vignette	45.00
Utica, Clinton and Binghamton Railroad Company (I), 1880s and 1890s, Train vignette	38.00
Utica, Clinton and Binghamton Railroad Company (I), 1900s, Train vignette	30.00
Vicksburg, Shreveport and Pacific Railroad (U), 1880s, Train vignette	35.00
Virginia Railway and Power Company (U), Two ladies with two streetcars vignette	8.00
Virginia Railway (I), Speeding train vignette specimen	25.00
Virginia Transit Company (I), 1940s, Eagle vignette	4.00
Wabash, Pittsburg Terminal Railway 1900s	18.00
Wabash Railroad (I), 1890s, Locomotive vignette	50.00
Wabash Railroad (I), 1900s, Flying eagle and three horse head vignette	28.00
Wabash Railroad (I), 1910s, Flying eagle and three horse head vignette	32.00
Wabash Railroad (I), 1930s, Train vignette	25.00
Wagner Palace Car Company (I), 1880s, Old train vignette	70.00
Wagner Palace Car Company (I), 1890s, Fractional certificate	12.00
Wagner Palace Car Company (I), 1890s, Old train vignette plus buildings. Certificate made out to Cornelius Vanderbilt.	210.00
Wagner Palace Car Company (I), 1890s, Old train vignette plus seal	65.00
Wagner Palace Car Company (I), 1890s, Three vignettes, train and buildings	60.00
Wampum and Stateline Railway (I), 1880s, Pennsylvania, Scarce	75.00
Ware River Railroad (U), 1900s, Portrait vignette	32.00
Warren and Vernango Railroad (U), 1800s, Two old trains vignette	60.00
Warren Railroad (I), 1940s, Certificate of deposit	4.00
Warren Railroad (U), 1850s, Mountain scene with railroad train vignette	42.00
Washington, Baltimore and Annapolis Electric Railroad (U), Streetcar vignette, also winged lady vignette	8.00
Waterloo, Cedar Falls and Northern (I), 1940s, No vignette	5.00
Waterloo, Cedar Falls Interurban Car (I), 1940s, Interurban vignette	8.00
Waterloo, Cedar Falls (I), 1950s, Electric train vignette	7.00
Waterloo, Cedar Falls Interurban Car (I), Electric donkey engine vignette	10.00
West End Angora and Park Passenger Railway, Two horses and car vignette	40.00

◀ ***Rio Grande Southern Railroad Company, The (I), 1890s***	***160.00***
◀ ***Schuylkill and Lehigh Valley Railroad (I), 1880s**, Three train vignettes*	***65.00***

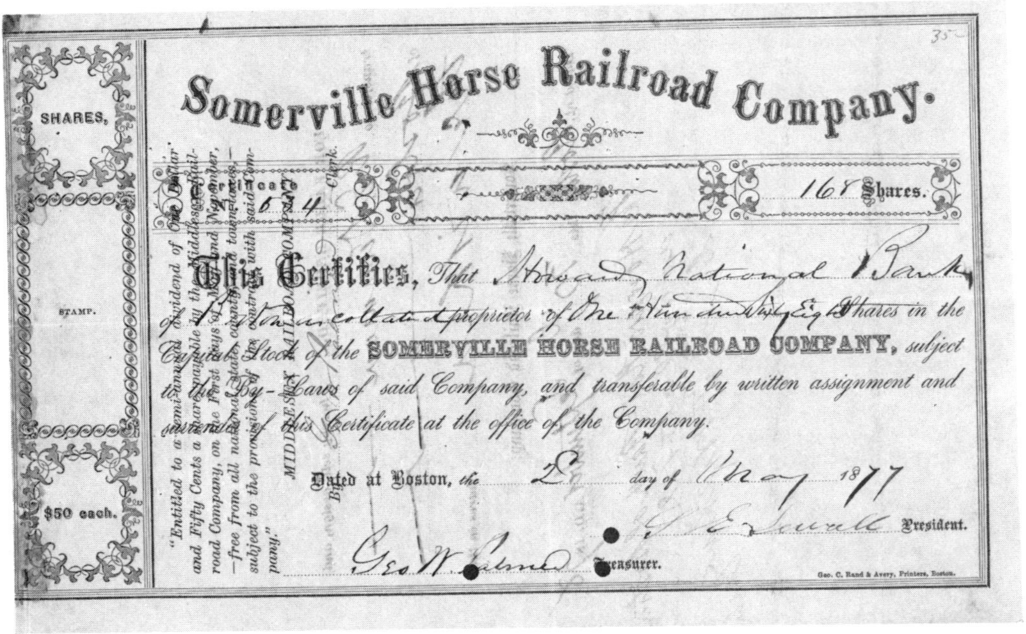

35

SHARES,

STAMP.

$50 each.

Somerville Horse Railroad Company.

Certificate 634 — 168 Shares.

"Entitled to a semi-annual dividend of One Dollar and Fifty Cents a share, payable by the Middlesex Railroad Company, on the first days of May and November, —free from all national, state, county and town taxes,— subject to the provisions of the contract with said company."

MIDDLESEX RAILROAD COMPANY,

By ... Clerk.

This Certifies, That Howard National Bank of Boston as collateral is proprietor of One Hundred Sixty Eight Shares in the Capital Stock of the **SOMERVILLE HORSE RAILROAD COMPANY**, subject to the By-Laws of said Company, and transferable by written assignment and surrender of this Certificate at the office of the Company.

Dated at Boston, the 2 day of May 1877

G. E. Jewell President.

Geo W. Palmer Treasurer.

Geo. C. Rand & Avery, Printers, Boston.

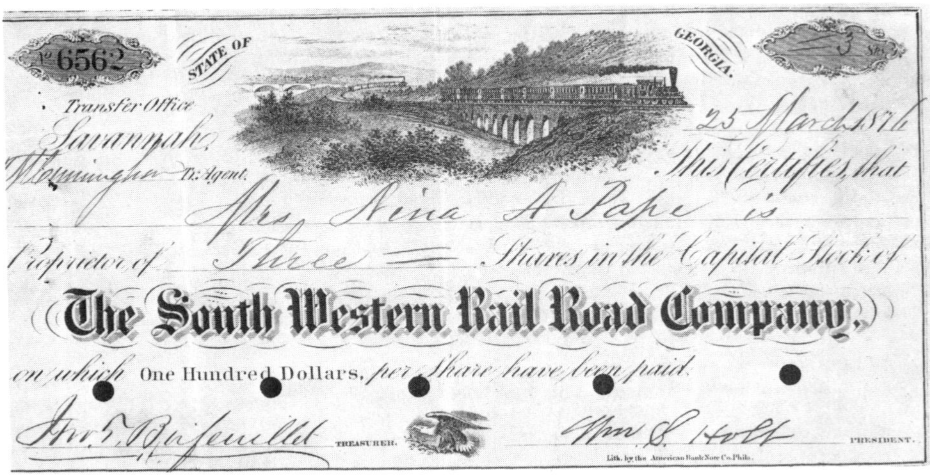

No 6562 — STATE OF GEORGIA. — 3 Shs

Transfer Office
Savannah,
W. Cummings Tr. Agent.

25 March 1876

This Certifies, that Mrs Nina A Pape is Proprietor of Three Shares in the Capital Stock of

The South Western Rail Road Company,

on which One Hundred Dollars, per Share have been paid.

Jno. T. Bosenillet TREASURER. — Wm. S. Holt PRESIDENT.

Lith. by the American Bank Note Co. Phila.

West End Street Railway (I), 1920s, Woman and Indian vignette	**6.00**
West End Street Railway Massachusetts (U), 1900s, State seal	**7.00**
West New Jersey Railroad (U), 1880s	**15.00**
West Philadelphia Passenger Railway Company (I), 1850s, Horse trolley vignette	**90.00**
West Philadelphia Passenger Railway Company (I), 1870s, Car barn in oval vignette	**35.00**
West Philadelphia Passenger Railway Company (I), 1880s, Signed by Widener	**45.00**
West Philadelphia Passenger Railway (I), 1880s, Horse streetcar vignette	**30.00**
West Philadelphia Passenger Railway (I), 1890s, Horse car approaching car barn vignette	**25.00**
West Philadelphia Passenger Railway (I), 1900s, Horse streetcar vignette	**20.00**
West Philadelphia Passenger Railway (I), 1910s, Signed by Widener	**30.00**
West Philadelphia Passenger Railway (I), 1920s, Horse streetcar vignette	**16.00**
West Philadelphia Passenger Railway (I), 1930s, Horse streetcar	**14.00**
West Shore and Ontario Terminal (U), 1880s, Steamboat vignette	**20.00**
West Shore Railroad (U), 1880s	**17.00**
Western Maryland (I), 1900s, Preferred certificate	**10.00**
Western Maryland (I), 1920s, Old train vignette	**10.00**
Western Maryland (I), 1930s, Steam train vignette	**5.00**
Western Maryland (I), 1940s	**4.00**
Western Maryland (I), 1950s and 1960s, New streamliner vignette	**3.00**
Western New York and Pennsylvania Railway (I), 1890s, Train vignette	**60.00**
Western Pacific Railroad (I), 1940s, Train vignette	**25.00**
Western Pacific Railroad (I), 1950s, Diesel train vignette	**7.00**
Western Railroad (I), 1840s, Border vignette and red seal	**110.00**
Western Railway Construction Company (U), 1870s, Old train vignette	**25.00**
Wharton Valley Railway (I), 1930s, Two figures vignette	**15.00**
Wheeling and Lake Erie Railway Company, The (I), 1940s, Train at mill and coal cars vignette	**12.00**
Whippany River Railroad (I), 1890s, State seal	**25.00**
White Water Railroad (U), 1800s, Old funnel train vignette	**35.00**
Wilkes-Barre Transit Corporation (I), 1950s, Eagle vignette	**3.00**
Williamsport and Clearfield Railroad (I), 1880s	**40.00**
Wilmington and Clearfield Railroad (I), 1880s	**40.00**
Wilmington and Northern Railroad (I), 1870s	**105.00**
Wilmington and Philadelphia Traction Company (I), 1900s, State seal vignette	**18.00**
Wilmington and Philadelphia Traction Company (I), 1910s, State seal vignette	**15.00**
Wilmington City Railway (I), 1890s, Two dogs and seal vignette	**37.00**
Wisconsin and Western Railroad (U), 1900s, No vignette	**5.00**
Wiscosset, Waterville and Farmington Railroad (I-N), 1900s	**60.00**
Wollkill Valley Railroad (U), 1800s, Old train vignette	**40.00**
Woodruff Sleeping and Parlor Coach Company (I), 1870s, Animals, two angels vignette, with stamp	**125.00**
Woodruff Sleeping and Parlor Coach Company (I), 1870s, Indian at harbor vignette	**95.00**
Woodruff Sleeping and Parlor Coach Company (I), 1880s, Animals, two angels vignette, with stamp	**85.00**
Worcester Consolidated Street Railway 1910s–1930s, Seal	**10.00**
Worcester Consolidated Street Railway (I), 1930s, Certificate of deposit	**40.00**
Yosemite Short Line Railway (I), 1900s	**85.00**
Youngstown and Suburban Railway (I), 1910s	**12.00**
Youngstown-Sharon Railway and Light (I), 1900s, Goddess and eagle vignette	**10.00**

◀ ***Somerville Horse Railroad Company (I), 1870s*** ***37.00***

◀ ***South Western Rail Road Company, The (I), 1870s,*** *Two old trains vignette* ***55.00***

NUMBER
3850
Preferred Stock
The Toledo and Ohio Central
Railway Company
This Certifies that
PREFERRED
Secretary
President.
SHARES
$100
EACH

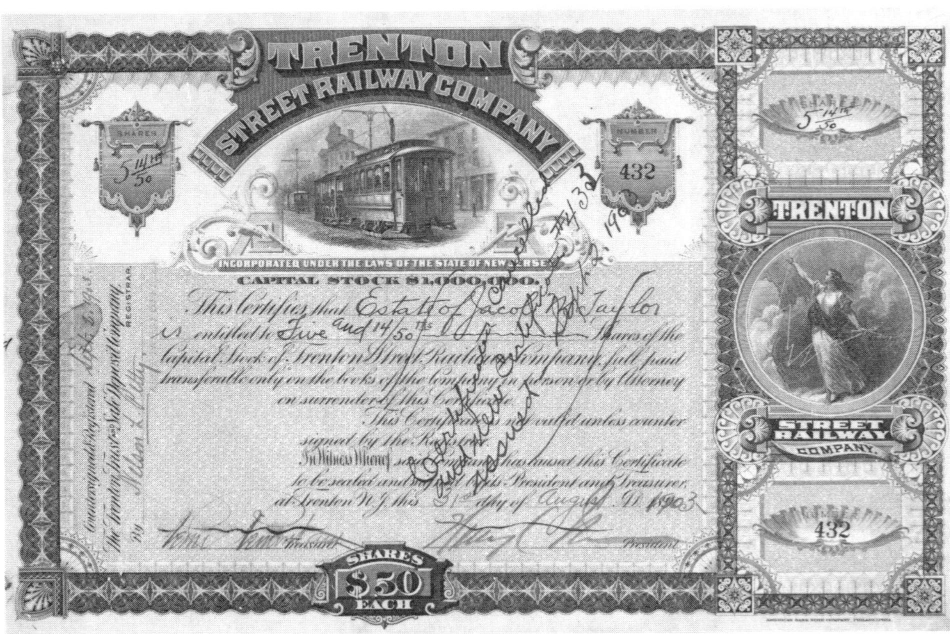
TRENTON
STREET RAILWAY COMPANY
SHARES
NUMBER
432
INCORPORATED UNDER THE LAWS OF THE STATE OF NEW JERSEY
CAPITAL STOCK $1,000,000.
TRENTON
STREET RAILWAY COMPANY
432
SHARES
$50
EACH

Bonds

Aberdeen, Huron and Southern Railroad (I), 1900s, Speeding train vignette	**85.00**
Aberdeen, Huron and Southern Railroad (I-N), 1900s, Speeding train vignette	**75.00**
Alabama and Chattanooga Railroad (I), 1860s, Train vignette	**175.00**
Alabama and Chattanooga Railroad (I-N), 1860s, Two train vignette	**275.00**
Alabama, Tennessee and Northern Railroad (I), 1910s	**33.00**
Albany and Schenectady Railroad (I), 1840s	**325.00**
Albany Railroad (I), 1870s	**145.00**
Allegheny and Kinsua Railroad Company (I), 1890s, Old train vignette	**58.00**
Allegheny Central Railroad (I), 1880s, Train and two vignettes	**125.00**
Altoona and Phillipsburg Connecting Railroad (I), 1890s, Two trains vignette	**115.00**
American and Chattanooga Railway Company (I), 1860s, Train vignette	**150.00**
Androscoggin and Kennebec Railroad (I), 1850s, Train vignette	**165.00**
Arkansas Central Railway Company (I), 1870s, Two vignettes, seal	**400.00**
Atlantic and Pacific Railroad (I), 1870s, Small trains vignette	**265.00**
Atlantic and Pacific Railroad (I), 1880s, Train vignette	**220.00**
Atlantic and Saint Lawrence Railroad (I), 1920s, Engine vignette	**70.00**
Aurora, Elgin and Chicago Railway (I), 1900s, Lady vignette with eagle electric cars on reverse, with stamps	**32.00**
Bainbridge, Cuthbert and Columbus (I), 1870s, Train and harbor vignette	**450.00**
Baltimore and Annapolis Short Line Railroad (I), 1900s, Streetcars vignette	**72.00**
Bartlett and Albany Railroad (I), 1880s, Train vignette	**125.00**
Bay City and East Saginaw Railroad, 1860s, Old train and two vignettes	**125.00**
Birmingham and Southeastern Railway (I), 1900s	**43.00**
Black Mountain Railroad (I), 1920s, Gold bond	**17.00**
Blue Ridge Railroad (I), 1860s, Old train vignette	**235.00**
Boston and New York Airline Railroad (I), 1920s, Train vignette	**28.00**
Boston and New York Central Railroad (U), 1850s, Three vignettes	**175.00**
Boston and Providence Railroad (I), 1840s, Train vignette	**260.00**
Boston and Providence Railroad (I), 1850s, Four trains vignette	**245.00**
Boston, Clinton, Fitchburg Railroad (I), 1860s, Old train vignette	**95.00**
Boston, Clinton, Fitchburg Railroad (I), 1870s, Three vignettes, with stamps	**350.00**
Boston Elevated Railway (U), 1910s, Elevated train vignette	**25.00**
Boston, Hartford and Erie Rail Road Company, The 1860s, Old train vignette, with station and workers. Signed by John Eldrige	**135.00**
Boston, Hartford and Erie Railroad Company, The (I), 1880s, With revenue stamps	**65.00**
Boston, Hartford and Erie Railroad Company, The (I-N), 1860s, Train vignette, revenue stamps	**95.00**
Boston, Hartford and Erie Railroad Company, The (U), 1800s, Woman vignette	**40.00**
Branchville and Bowman Railroad (I), 1890s, Old railroad train vignette	**225.00**
Broadway and Seventh Avenue Railroad (I), 1880s, Eagle vignette	**60.00**
Broadway and Seventh Avenue Railroad (I), 1890s, Reclining nudes vignette	**80.00**
Broadway Surface Railroad (I), 1880s, Broadway scene vignette	**100.00**
Broadway Surface Railroad (I), 1880s, Eagle vignette	**90.00**
Broadway Surface Railroad (I), 1890s, Eagle vignette	**55.00**
Broadway Surface Railroad (I), 1900s, Eagle vignette	**48.00**
Brooklyn and Brighton Beach Railroad (I), 1890s, Train vignette	**160.00**
Brooklyn and Brighton Beach Railroad (I-N), 1896, Train vignette	**175.00**
Brooklyn and Rockaway Railroad (I), , Horse trolley vignette, red seal	**250.00**

◀***Toledo and Ohio Central Railway Company, The, (U), 1900s***	***20.00***
◀***Trenton Street Railway Company (I), 1900s,*** *Streetcars and lady with lightning vignettes*	***30.00***

CHARTERED MARCH 25TH 1868.

AUTHORIZED CAPITAL $1,000,000.

SHARES $100 EACH.

UTICA, CLINTON AND BINGHAMTON RAIL ROAD CO.

No. 1828 — 200 — Shares.

This Certifies that John W Mac Lean entitled to Two hundred # Shares of the Capital Stock of the Utica, Clinton and Binghamton Rail Road Co. transferable only on the books of the Company in person or by duly authorized Attorney, on surrender of this Certificate.

Utica, N.Y. Nov 15 1927

Secretary — John W MacLean, President

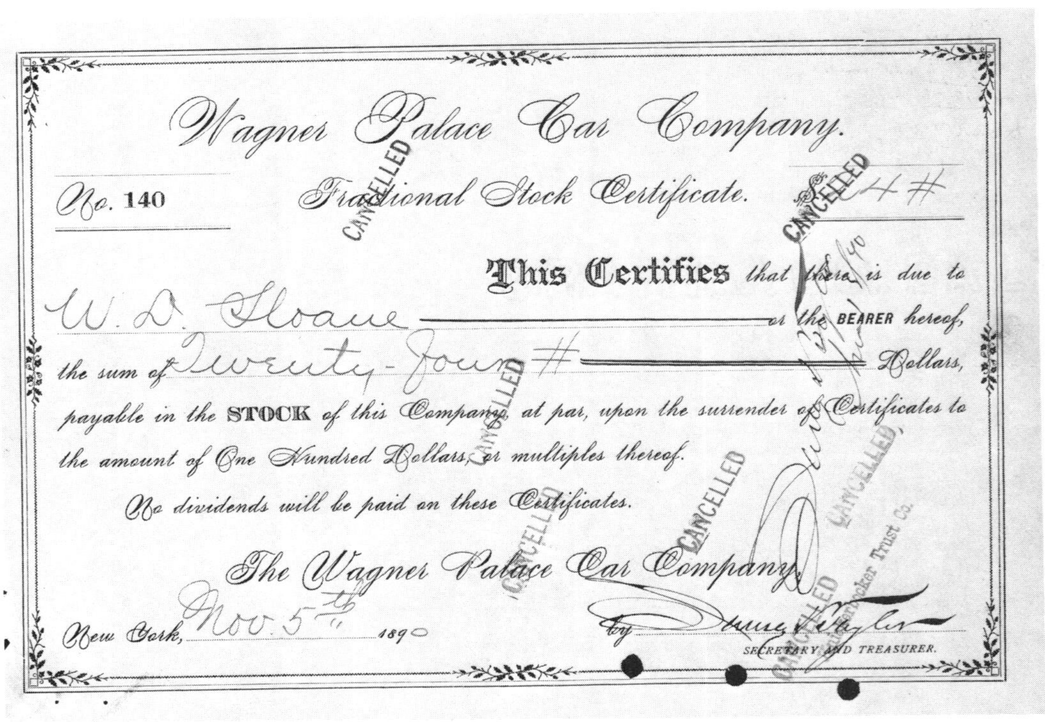

Wagner Palace Car Company.

No. 140 — Fractional Stock Certificate. $24#

CANCELLED

This Certifies that there is due to W. D. Sloane ———— or the BEARER hereof, the sum of Twenty-Four # ———— Dollars, payable in the **STOCK** of this Company, at par, upon the surrender of Certificates to the amount of One Hundred Dollars, or multiples thereof.

No dividends will be paid on these Certificates.

The Wagner Palace Car Company.

New York, Nov. 5th 1890

by ———— SECRETARY AND TREASURER.

CANCELLED Knickerbocker Trust Co.

Brooklyn Union Elevated Railroad (I), 1880s, Famous Brooklyn Bridge vignette	120.00
Buffalo and Susquehanna Railway (I), 1900s	60.00
Buffalo, Hamburg and Aurora Railway (I), 1900s, Old streetcar vignette	110.00
Buffalo, New York and Philadelphia Railroad (U), 1800s, Old train vignette	150.00
Burlington, Cedar Rapids and Minneapolis (U), Old train vignette	20.00
Burlington, Cedar Rapids and Minneapolis Railway (I), 1870s, Three trains vignette	75.00
Burlington Electric Railway (I), Soldier and streetcar vignette	85.00
Burlington Northern (I), 1970s, Equipment trust	6.00
Cairo and Norfolk Railroad (I), 1900s, Gold bond, train vignette	35.00
Cairo and Norfolk Railroad (I-N), 1900s, Gold bond, train vignette	95.00
Canada Southern Railway (U), 1870s, Two lovely ladies	75.00
Canada Southern Railway (U), 1880s, Old train vignette	70.0
Canada Southern Railway (U), 1880s, Signed by Cornelius Vanderbilt	275.00
Canon City and Cripple Creek Electric Railway (I), 1800s, Mountain scenery, seal	95.00
Canton, Aberdeen and Nashville Railroad Company (I), 1880s, Gold bond, train vignette	95.00
Cape Cod Central Railroad (I), 1860s,	110.00
Carolina, Clinchfield and Ohio Railway (I), 1900s, Train and workers vignette	42.00
Carolina, Clinchfield and Ohio Railway (I), 1920s, Old train and workers vignette	33.00
Carolina, Knoxville and Western Railway, 1880s, Speeding train vignette	95.00
Central New York and Western Railroad (I), 1890s, Train vignette	175.00
Central of Georgia Railway (I), 1880s, Train vignette	45.00
Central of Georgia Railway (I), 1890s, Train vignette	125.00
Central of Georgia Railway (I), 1910s, Old train, cotton workers vignette	65.00
Central of Georgia Railway (I), 1920s, Train vignette	38.00
Central of Georgia Railway (I), 1930s, Railroad vignette	30.00
Central of Georgia Railway (I), 1940s, Train vignette	20.00
Central Pacific Railroad (I), 1940s, Train vignette	20.00
Central Railroad and Banking Company of Georgia (I), 1860s, Two trains vignette	160.00
Charleston and Savannah Railroad (I), 1850s, Old train vignette	250.00
Chesapeake and Ohio Railroad (I), 1960s, Equipment trust, diesel locomotive vignette	5.00
Chicago and Alton Equipment Association (U),1900s, Bare-breasted woman in chariot vignette	7.00
Chicago and Alton Railroad (I), 1860s, Old train vignette	195.00
Chicago and Alton Railroad (I), 1890s, Five trains vignette	195.00
Chicago and Alton Railroad (I), 1900s, Old train vignette	75.00
Chicago and Southeastern Railway (I), 1880s, Old train vignette	155.00
Chicago and Southwestern Railway (I), 1890s, Train vignette	125.00
Chicago and Wisconsin Valley Street Railway (I-N), Gold bond	28.00
Chicago, Aurora and Elgin (I), 1920s	20.00
Chicago, Canada and Southern Railway (I), 1870s, Two ladies, U.S. shield vignette, red seal	225.00
Chicago, Indianapolis and Louisville Railroad (I), 1910s, Two trains vignette	23.00
Chicago, Milwaukee, Saint Paul and Pacific Railroad, Specimen bond	165.00
Chicago, Milwaukee, Saint Paul and Pacific Railroad, 1920s, Two trains vignette	125.00
Chicago, Northwestern Railway (I), 1960s	10.00
Chicago, Peoria and Saint Louis Railroad (I), 1900s, Gold bond, trains and workers vignettes	25.00
Chicago, Portage and Superior Railway (I), 1880s, Train and riverboat vignette	175.00
Chicago, Rock Island Railroad (I), 1860s, Train by lake vignette	55.00
Chicago, Rock Island Railroad (U), 1860s, Train by lake vignette	15.00
Chicago, Rock Island and Pacific Railway Company (I), 1870s	85.00
Chicago, Rock Island and Pacific Railway Company (I), 1880s	75.00
Chicago, Rock Island and Pacific Railway Company (I), 1890s	55.00

◀ ***Utica, Clinton and Binghamton Rail Road Company (I), 1900s,*** *Train vignette* ***30.00***

◀ ***Wagner Palace Car Company (I), 1890s,*** *Fractional certificate* ***12.00***

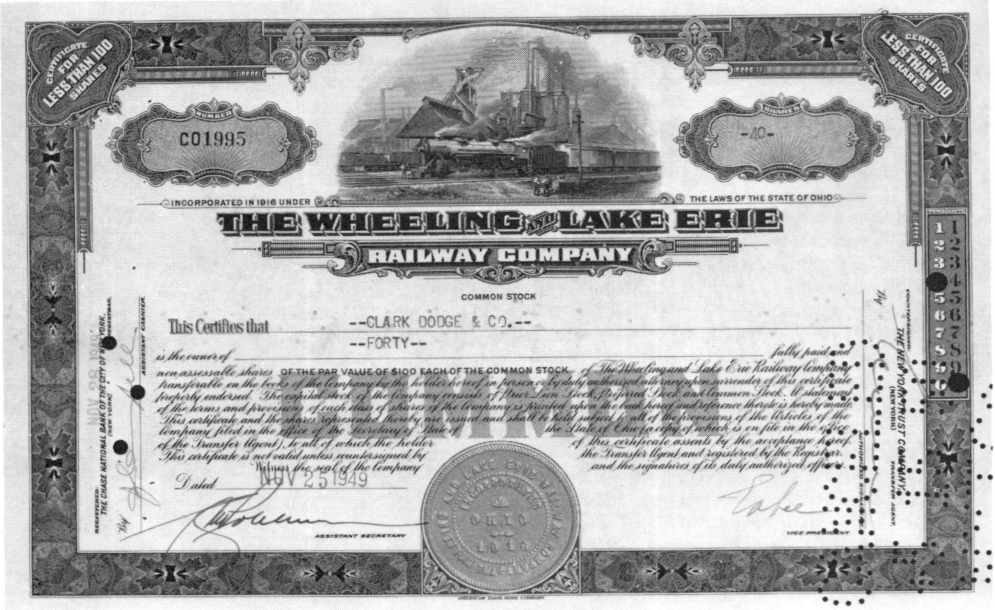
CERTIFICATE FOR LESS THAN 100 SHARES
C01995
-40-
INCORPORATED IN 1916 UNDER THE LAWS OF THE STATE OF OHIO
THE WHEELING AND LAKE ERIE
RAILWAY COMPANY
COMMON STOCK
This Certifies that --CLARK DODGE & CO.--
--FORTY--
is the owner of fully paid and non-assessable shares OF THE PAR VALUE OF $100 EACH OF THE COMMON STOCK of The Wheeling and Lake Erie Railway Company
Dated NOV 25 1949
ASSISTANT SECRETARY
VICE-PRESIDENT
THE CHASE NATIONAL BANK OF THE CITY OF NEW YORK
THE NEW YORK TRUST COMPANY
TRANSFER AGENT

100 SHARES
INCORPORATED UNDER THE LAWS OF THE STATE OF DELAWARE
Number A 48
100 Shares
Wilmington and Philadelphia
TRACTION COMPANY
Preferred Stock $1,500,000
Common Stock $5,000,000
Shares 100 Dollars Each.
This is to Certify that Scott & Co.,
is the owner of ONE HUNDRED Shares of the
Common Capital Stock of Wilmington and Philadelphia Traction Company
transferable only on the books of the Corporation by the holder hereof in person or by
Attorney upon surrender of this Certificate properly endorsed.
In Witness Whereof the said Corporation has caused this Certificate to
be signed by its duly authorized officers and to be sealed with the Seal of the
Corporation this third day of November A.D. 1910.
COMMON
TREASURER
PRESIDENT
COUNTERSIGNED AND REGISTERED
WILMINGTON TRUST COMPANY

Chicago, Rock Island and Pacific Railway Company (I), 1900s	**65.00**
Chicago, Rock Island and Pacific Railway Company (I), 1910s, Train vignette	**22.00**
Chicago, Rock Island and Pacific Railway Company (I), 1930s	**19.00**
Chicago, Rock Island and Pacific Railway Company (I), 1960s and 1970s	**3.00**
Chicago, Saint Louis and New Orleans Railroad (I), 1870s, Pelican vignette	**130.00**
Chicago Subway Company (I), 1900s	**50.00**
Chicago, Terre Haute and South Eastern Railroad (I), 1910s, Train vignette	**16.00**
Chicago, Terre Haute and South Eastern Railroad (I-N), 1910s	**24.00**
Chickasha Street Railway (I), 1910s, Streetcar vignette	**75.00**
Choctaw, Oklahoma and Gulf Railroad (U), 1900s, Indians watching train vignette	**75.00**
Cincinnati, Hamilton and Dayton Railroad (U), 1860s, Bond script	**30.00**
Cincinnati, Indianapolis, Saint Louis and Chicago Railroad (I), Train vignette	**50.00**
Cincinnati, Logansport and Chicago Railroad, 1850s, Old train vignette	**250.00**
Cincinnati, Union Terminal (U), 1900s, Specimen, old depot	**30.00**
Cincinnati, Washington and Baltimore Railroad, 1880s, Bond scrip	**12.00**
Citizen's Passenger Railway (I), 1860s, State seal	**50.00**
Cleveland and Canton Railroad (I), 1890s, Eagle vignette	**30.00**
Cleveland and Canton Railroad (I), 1890s, Train under bridge vignette	**56.00**
Cleveland, Cincinnati, Chicago and Saint Louis Railway (U) 1890s, Old train vignette	**40.00**
Cleveland, Painesville and Ashtabula Railroad (I), 1850s, Train vignette	**250.00**
Colorado and Southern Railway Company, The (I), 1900s, Gold note	**55.00**
Colorado, Midland Railway (I), 1890s, Train vignette at station in mountains	**250.00**
Colorado, Wyoming and Eastern Railway (I), 1910s, Train vignette	**70.00**
Columbus and Maysville Railway (I), 1870s, Train vignette	**175.00**
Columbus and Ninth Avenue Railroad (I), 1890s, Gold bond	**55.00**
Consolidated Railroads (I), 1910s, Train and workers vignette	**35.00**
Consolidated Railway Company (U), 1900s, Train vignette	**35.00**
Consolidated Railway Company (U), 1900s, Streetcar vignette	**25.00**
Danbury and Norwalk Railroad (U), 1900s, Train vignette	**25.00**
Darby and Yeadon Street Railway (I), 1900s, Streetcar and horse-drawn wagon vignette	**75.00**
Darby and Yeadon Street Railway (U), 1890s	**30.00**
Delaware and Hudson Railroad (I), 1960s, Two figures and large grain silo vignette	**12.00**
Deming, Sierra Madre and Pacific Railroad (I), 1880s, Gold bond, eagle vignette	**125.00**
Denver and Rio Grande 1920s	**28.00**
Denver and Rio Grande Western (I), 1920s, Two train vignette	**28.00**
Denver, Lakewood and Golden Railroad (I), Eagle vignette	**38.00**
Derby Street Railway Company (U), 1890s, Gold bond	**20.00**
Dorchester and Milton Branch Railroad (I), 1840s, Indian, seals vignette	**200.00**
Dorchester and Milton Branch Railroad (I), 1850s, Train vignette	**95.00**
Dorchester and Milton Branch Railroad (U), 1850s	**50.00**
Dubuque and Sioux City Railroad (I), 1860s, Train vignette	**275.00**
Duluth and Winnipeg Railroad (I), 1880s	**195.00**
Duluth and Winnipeg Railroad (U), 1880s, Train vignette	**150.00**
Duluth, Huron and Denver Railroad Company, The 1870s, Train at station, pixie, and Washington vignette	**265.00**
Duluth, Huron and Denver Railroad Company, The 1880s, Train at station, pixie, and Washington vignette	**250.00**
East Tennessee, Virginia and Georgia Railway (I), Gold bond, train vignette	**175.00**
Elizabethtown and Paducah Railroad (I), 1870s, Gold bond, three trains vignette	**175.00**

◀ ***Wheeling and Lake Erie Railway Company, The (I), 1940s,*** *Train at mill and coal cars vignette* ***32.00***

◀ ***Wilmington and Philadelphia Traction Company (I), 1910s,*** *State seal vignettes* ***15.00***

United States of America

States of New York and Pennsylvania

No. 255

The Allegheny and Kinzua Railroad Company

$1000 — $1000

First Mortgage Five per cent Gold Bond.

Know all men by these presents, That The Allegheny and Kinzua Railroad Company, a corporation created and existing under the Laws of the States of New York and Pennsylvania, for value received, promises to pay to the Central Trust Company of New York, as Trustee, or to the registered holder hereof, or in case this bond is not registered, to bearer, on the first day of February in the year hereinafter designated, at the office of said Trust Company in the City of New York, free of United States, State and Municipal taxes, the sum of **ONE THOUSAND DOLLARS** in gold coin of the United States of America, of or equal in weight and fineness to the present standard, with interest thereon from the first day of February A.D. one thousand eight hundred ninety at the rate of five per centum per annum, in like gold coin, payable semi-annually at the office of said Trust Company in the City of New York on the first days of February and August in each year, on the presentation and surrender of the coupons annexed hereto as they severally become due, and if any default shall be made in the payment of the interest upon this bond and such default shall continue for a period of six months, the whole amount of the principal sum of this bond shall thereupon become due and payable. This bond is one of a series of bonds of like tenor and date, consisting of five hundred bonds of one thousand dollars each, numbered consecutively from one to five hundred inclusive, the payment of the principal and interest whereof is equally and ratably secured by a First Mortgage or Deed of Trust bearing even date herewith, duly executed by said Railroad Company to the Central Trust Company of New York, in trust for the benefit of the holders of said bonds, upon all the railroad, property and franchises of said Railroad Company, including thirty thousand acres of timber land upon the construction and completion of the first forty-six miles of the railroad of said Railroad Company, and sixteen thousand acres of timber land in addition thereto upon the construction and completion of seventy miles of the railroad of said Railroad Company. Of the said series of bonds the bonds numbered from one to fifteen inclusive shall become due and payable February 1st 1894, and on the first day of February in each year thereafter, until all of said bonds shall be paid, the fifteen of said bonds then outstanding bearing the fifteen lowest consecutive numbers, shall likewise become due and payable until the first day of February 1924, when the remaining outstanding bonds shall become due and payable.

This bond shall pass by delivery unless the same has been registered in accordance with the provisions endorsed hereon. This bond shall not become valid until authenticated by the certificate endorsed hereon and signed by the said Trustee. In Witness Whereof, the said The Allegheny and Kinzua Railroad Company has caused its corporate seal to be hereunto affixed, and these presents to be signed by its President and Secretary this first day of February, A.D. one thousand eight hundred ninety.

The Allegheny and Kinzua Railroad Company

By

Lewis F. Wilson, SECRETARY — A. A. Bulles, PRESIDENT

Elkin and Allegheny Railway (I), Train vignette	60.00
Erie Railroad (I), 1940s, Man and woman vignette	12.00
Escanaba, Iron Mountain and Western Railroad (I), 1890s, Train and blacksmith vignette	110.00
Evansville and Crawfordsville Railroad (I), 1850s, Train vignette	135.00
Evansville and Indianapolis Railroad (U), 1870s, Three vignettes	165.00
Evansville and Terre Haute (I), 1880s, Old train vignette	135.00
Evansville and Terre Haute (I), 1890s, Old train vignette	110.00
Farmville and Powhatan Railroad (I), 1880s, Train vignette	95.00
Flint, Pere Marquette (I), 1860s, Two train vignettes	200.00
Flint, Pere Marquette Railroad (I), 1870s, Train on bridge vignette, with stamp	165.00
Flint, Pere Marquette Railroad (I), 1880s	90.00
Florida Midland Railway (I), 1880s, Alligator and train vignette	175.00
Florida Railway (I), 1900s, Gold bond, train vignette	50.00
Frankford, Tacony and Holmesburg Street Railway (I), 1910s, Gold bond, streetcar vignette	75.00
Frankfort and Shelbyville Electric Railway (I), 1910s, Gold note	12.00
Fruit Growers Equipment Trust, 1950s, Eagle vignette	4.00
Galveston, Houston and Henderson Railroad (I), 1850s, With attached forty-dollar share, issued in Amsterdam	265.00
Geary Street Park and Ocean Railroad (I), 1890s,	300.00
Georgia and Alabama Railway (U), 1890s, State seal	10.00
Georgia and Florida Railroad (U), 1920s, Specimen, speeding train	45.00
Glade Creek and Raleigh Railroad (I), 1890s, Gold bond	130.00
Grand Junction Railroad and Depot Company (I), 1850s, Harbor scene vignette	310.00
Grand Rapids, Holland and Lake Michigan Rapid Railway (I-N), Gold bond, trolley	100.00
Grand Rapids and Indiana Railroad (I), 1880s, Old train vignette	295.00
Grand Rapids and Indiana Railroad (I), 1890s, Old train vignette	210.00
Great Northern Railroad 1940s, Two old trains vignette	20.00
Great Northern Railroad 1960s, Equipment trust	5.00
Great Northern Railway (I), 1950s, Train vignette	15.00
Great Northern Railway (I), 1970s, Equipment trust	10.00
Greenburgh and Hempfield Electric Street Railway (I), 1890s	110.00
Greenville and Miami Railroad (I), 1850s	100.00
Gulf and Ship Island Railroad (I), 1880s, Mississippi, Old train at station with passengers vignette	110.00
Gulf, Florida and Alabama Railway (U), 1911, Specimen, train vignette	175.00
Gulf, Mobile and Northern Railroad (I), 1920	12.00
Harlem River and Port Chester Railroad (I), 1880s, Old train vignette	65.00
Harlem River and Port Chester Railroad (I), 1890s, Old train vignette	125.00
Harlem River and Port Chester Railroad (I), 1900s, Old train vignette	55.00
Hartford and Providence Railroad, 1850s, Blue seal	300.00
Hartford, Providence and Fishkill Railroad (I), 1850s	120.00
Hestonville, Mantua and Fairmont Railroad (I), 1890s, Extended bond, streetcar vignette	80.00
Holly, Wayne and Monroe Railroad (I), 1870s, Old train steam vignette, imprinted gold stamps	175.00
Houston and Great Northern Railroad (I), 1870s, Old funnel locomotive vignette	195.00
Houston and Great Northern Railroad (U),Gold bond, train vignette	95.00
Hudson and Berkshire Railroad (I), 1840s, Milford Eillmore signature	2,000.00
Hudson and Manhattan (U), 1910s, Train tunnel vignette	15.00
Illinois and Indiana Coal and Railway Company (I), Old train vignette	135.00
Illinois Central Railroad (I), 1850s, Old train vignette	45.00

◄ ***Allegheny and Kinzua Railroad Company (I), 1890s,*** *Old train vignette* ***58.00***

1000
NUMBER
436
1000
United States of America
Know all men by these presents that
THE BOSTON HARTFORD AND ERIE
RAIL ROAD COMPANY,
ACKNOWLEDGES ITSELF
INDEBTED UNTO DUDLEY S. GREGORY,
or Bearer in the sum of ONE THOUSAND DOLLARS
IN WITNESS WHEREOF this Company has caused its corporate seal to be hereto affixed and this Bond to be signed by its President and its Secretary.
Secretary
President
Trustee
Trustee
Trustee
M
M

Illinois Central Railroad (I), 1920s, Eagle vignette, gold bond	11.00
Indiana and Illinois Central Railway (I), 1870s, Seal, train and eagle vignette	175.00
Indiana Coal and Railway (I), 1880s, Trains vignette	175.00
Indiana, Illinois and Iowa Railroad 1900s, Train vignette	100.00
Indiana, Illinois and Iowa Railroad 1900s	75.00
Interborough-Metropolitan Collateral Trust (I), 1920s	20.00
International Railroad (I), 1870s, Seal and train vignette	250.00
International Railroad (U), 1870s, Gold bond, old train vignette	175.00
International Railroad of Texas (I), 1870s, Old train vignette	250.00
International Railroad of Texas (U), 1870s, Old train vignette	100.00
Ithaca, Auburn and Western Railway, 1870s, Old funnel train vignette	300.00
Jersey City Locomotive Works (I), 1850s, Old train vignette	175.00
Joliet and Chicago Railroad (I), 1850s	300.00
Kansas City and Olathe and Electric Railway (I), 1900s, Gold bond, streetcar vignette	90.00
Kansas City Northwestern Railroad Company, The (I), 1890s, Train vignette	60.00
Kansas City Railways (I), 1910s, Trolley and old auto vignette	50.00
Kansas City, Wyandotte and Northwestern Railroad (I), 1880s, Train vignette	70.00
Kentucky and Great Eastern Railway (I), 1870s, Battle scene and train vignette	80.00
Kentucky and South Atlantic Railway (I), 1880s, Old train vignette	165.00
Kentucky and Tennessee Railroad (I), 1870s, Train vignette	130.00
Kentucky Central Railroad (I), 1880s, Train vignette	210.00
Kentucky Railroad (I), 1900s, Gold bond, train at station vignette	30.00
Keokuk Mount Pleasant, and Muscatine Railroad (I), 1850s, Train, portrait vignette	285.00
Kings County Elevated Railroad (I)	125.00
Knoxville, Cumberland Gap and Louisville Railroad (I), 1880s, Old train vignette	235.00
La Salle County Electric Railroad (I), 1910s, Gold bond, electric train vignette	90.00
Lackawanna and Wyoming Valley Rapid Transit (U), Temporary, gold bond	16.00
Lackawanna Railroad (I), 1850s, Old train vignette	250.00
Lake Erie, Alliance and Southern Railway (I), 1880s, Old train vignette	250.00
Lake Ontario Shore Railroad (I), 1870s, Old train vignette	95.00
Lake Ontario Shore Railroad (I), 1880s, Old train vignette	85.00
Lake Shore and Michigan Southern Railway (I), 1920s, Two trains vignette	75.00
Lake Shore and Michigan Southern Railway (U), 1900s, Train vignette	85.00
Lake Superior and Southern Railroad (I), 1900s	28.00
Lake Superior, Southern of Michigan and Lake Superior Southern Railroad and Wisconsin (I), 1900s	30.00
Lancaster County Railroad (I), 1870s, Gold seal, train vignette	250.00
Lehigh Valley Railroad Company 1940s, Gold bond, old train and horse and wagon vignette	25.00
Lehigh Valley Railroad Company (I), 1900s, Train vignette	25.00
Lexington and Eastern Railway (I), 1890s, Old train vignette	240.00
Little Rock and Fort Smith Railroad (I), 1870s, Old train vignette	175.00
Little Rock, Pine Bluff and New Orleans Railroad (I), 1870s, Old train vignette	175.00
London, South Park and Leadville Railroad (I-N), 1880s, Colorado, Three vignettes	295.00
Los Angeles Consolidated Electric Railway Company (I-N), 1890s, Streetcar vignette	295.00
Louisiana and Missouri River Company (U), 1880s, Old train vignette	20.00
Louisville and Nashville Railroad (I), 1880s, Old train vignette	125.00
Manistee and Northeastern Railroad (I-N), 1880s, Michigan, Old train vignette	100.00
Mansfield and Framingham Railroad (I), 1860s, Old train vignette	350.00

◀ ***Boston, Hartford and Erie Rail Road Company, the, 1860s,*** *Old train vignette, with station and workers. Signed by John Eldridge* ***135.00***

TOTAL ISSUE $2,000,000.
1000
No 1,826.
1000
No 1,826.
Canton, Aberdeen & Nashville
RAIL ROAD COMPANY
GOLD BOND
PAYABLE 1922.
The Canton, Aberdeen and Nashville Rail Road Company acknowledges
itself indebted to the holder hereof in the sum of One thousand dollars,
weight and fineness, on the 1st day of December in the year 1922 in the City of New
York, and to pay interest thereon at the rate of five per cent per annum, payable
semi-annually in like Gold Coin, upon presentation and surrender of the coupons
hereto annexed, on the first days of June and December in each year as they
respectively become payable and so long as the principal remains unpaid, without
Company to Stuyvesant Fish and William J. Mauriac, as Trustees,
bearing even date herewith, to secure the payment of such Bonds, and when the
In Witness whereof the said Rail Road Company has
caused its common seal and the signatures of its President
and Secretary to be hereto affixed, the 1st day of December 1884.
Secretary.
President.
1000
1000

Marietta-Mineral Railway (I), 1880s, Old train vignette	**230.00**
Maysville and Lexington Railroad (I), Old train vignette	**300.00**
Memphis and Little Rock Railway (I), 1870s, Old train vignette	**110.00**
Memphis and Ohio Railroad (I), 1860s, Old train and six vignettes	**350.00**
Metropolitan Cross Town Railroad (I), 1880s, Company logo	**25.00**
Metropolitan Cross Town Railroad (I), 1890s, Horse trolley vignette	**100.00**
Michigan Central Railroad (I), Made out to others but signed by Cornelius Vanderbilt	**900.00**
Michigan Central Railroad Company (U), 1890s, Train	**50.00**
Michigan Central Railroad Company (U), 1900s, Two trains vignette	**34.00**
Minneapolis, Superior, Saint Paul and Winnepeg Railway (I), 1900s	**45.00**
Mississippi Central Railroad (I), 1870s, Gold bond, train vignette	**175.00**
Missouri Railroad (I), 1930s	**8.00**
Mobile and Girard Railroad (I), 1860s, Train vignette	**230.00**
Mobile and Girard Railroad (I), 1870s, Old train vignette	**75.00**
Mobile and Ohio Equipment Trust 1920s, Specimen, eagle vignette	**95.00**
Monongahela Valley Traction Company (U), 1900s, Streetcar vignette	**40.00**
Monterey and Fresno Railroad (I), 1890s, Old train vignette	**365.00**
Nassau Electric Railroad (I), 1900s, Streetcar vignette	**125.00**
Naugatuck Railroad (I), 1900s, Old train vignette	**38.00**
Nevada Southern Railway (I), 1890s, Seated figure vignette	**300.00**
New Bedford and Touton Railroad (I), 1860s,	**65.00**
New Bedford Railroad (I), 1870s, Train vignette	**75.00**
New Haven and Derby Railroad (I), 1870s, Train vignette	**55.00**
New Haven and Derby Railroad (I), 1880s, Train vignette	**50.00**
New Haven and Hartford (U), 1900s, Train vignette	**17.00**
New Haven and Northampton Railroad (U), 1900s, Train vignette	**20.00**
New Haven, Middletown and Willimatic Railroad (U), Train vignette	**25.00**
New Haven, Middletown and Willimatic Railroad (U), 1870s, Old steam train vignette	**50.00**
New Hope and Inyland Railroad (I), 1960s, Pennsylvania, Old train	**30.00**
New Orleans and North Eastern (I), Two trains vignette	**40.00**
New Orleans, Baton Rouge and Vicksburg Railroad (I), 1870s, Speeding train vignette	**285.00**
New Orleans Great Northern Railway (I), 1930s, Train vignette	**30.00**
New Orleans, Mobile and Chattanooga Railroad (I), 1860s, vignette plus five border vignettes	**600.00**
New Orleans, Mobile and Texas Railroad (I), 1870s, Red seal, two trains vignette	**250.00**
New Paltz and Highland Electric Railroad (I, 1890s), Streetcar vignette	**145.00**
New York and Boston Railroad (I), 1860s, Train with men working vignette	**260.00**
New York and Greenwood Lake Railway (I), 1870s, Bond scrip	**20.00**
New York and New England Railroad (I), 1880s, Train vignette	**70.00**
New York and New England Railroad (I), 1910s, Three trains vignettes	**30.00**
New York and New Haven Railroad (I), 1860s, Old train vignette	**160.00**
New York and Oswego Midland Railroad (I), 1860s, Town of Volney, train and two vignettes	**85.00**
New York and Oswego Midland Railroad (U), Train and three vignettes	**75.00**
New York, Boston and Montreal Railway (I), 1870s, Old train vignette	**325.00**
New York Cable Railway (I), Seal	**75.00**
New York Central and Hudson River Railroad (I), 1890s, Debt certificate, seminudes with eagle vignette	**90.00**
New York Connecting Railroad (I), 1910s, Bridge and ships vignette	**60.00**
New York, New Haven and Hartford Railroad (I), 1890s, Two females and train vignette	**35.00**
New York, New Haven and Hartford Railroad (I), 1900s, Train at station vignette	**25.00**
New York, New Haven and Hartford Railroad (I), 1910s, Three trains vignette	**30.00**

◀ ***Canton, Aberdeen and Nashville Rail Road Company (I), 1880s,*** *Gold Bond, train vignette* ***95.00***

UNITED STATES OF AMERICA

Number. 1629

Certificate for Ten BONDS.

THE Chicago, Rock Island and Pacific Railway Company

for a good and valuable consideration paid by [illegible] Company and Drexel, Morgan and Company, all of New York, hereby promises to deliver on or before the first day of January [illegible] to their order Ten of its First Mortgage Extension and Collateral Bonds numbered [illegible] to 23950 and secured by its First Extension and Collateral Mortgage, bearing date the fourth day of [illegible] One Thousand Eight Hundred and Eighty Four.

Said Bonds shall be certified by the United [illegible] Trust Company of New York, in accordance with the provisions of said Mortgage and shall be delivered to the holder of this Certificate duly endorsed by said firms upon demand made after said Bonds have been certified by said Trust Company upon the Treasurer or Assistant Treasurer of the Chicago, Rock Island and Pacific Railway Company at the office of said Company in the City of New York. When said Bonds shall be delivered, all [illegible] coupons shall be severed therefrom, but the Railway Company shall pay the holder hereof interest on the principal of the Bonds mentioned [illegible] rate of [illegible] per centum per annum accruing after the first day of January 188[illegible] and not covered by Coupons which remain upon the Bonds when delivered. If this Certificate shall not be surrendered [illegible] months from the date last above mentioned, the interest shall be paid semi annually computing from [illegible] at the office of said Railway Company in the City of New York. Payments of interest shall be endorsed on this Certificate.

In Witness Whereof, the Chicago, Rock Island and Pacific Railway Company has caused its corporate Seal to be impressed hereon and the signatures of its President and Secretary or Assistant Secretary to be affixed hereto this 14 day of May in the year One thousand eight hundred and eighty Eight.

[illegible] Secretary

R. R. Cable President

CANCELLED CHICAGO, R. ISLAND [illegible] JUL 10 1888

New York, New Haven and Hartford Railroad (U), 1890s, Two females and train vignette	20.00
New York, New Haven and Hartford Railroad (U), 1900s, Train over bridge vignette	20.00
New York, New Haven and Hartford Railroad (U), 1920s, Train, ship and streetcar vignette	20.00
New York, Ontario and Western Railroad (I), 1900s, Large train vignette	35.00
New York, Ontario and Western Railroad (I), 1920s, Equipment Trust, train vignette	25.00
New York, Ontario and Western Railway (I), 1920s	35.00
New York, Ontario and Western Railroad (I), 1930s, Train vignette	30.00
New York, Ontario and Western Railway (I), 1930s	22.00
New York, Ontario and Western Railway (I), 1940s	17.00
New York, Ontario and Western Railway (U), 1900s	25.00
New York, Pennsylvania and Ohio Railroad (I), 1880s, Scenic vignette, seal	150.00
New York, Pittsburgh and Chicago (I-N), 1880s, Two trains and sailboat vignette	150.00
New York, Rutland and Montreal Railway (I), 1880s, Old train vignette	90.00
New York, Susquehanna and Western Railroad (U), 1800s, Train vignette	50.00
North and South Carolina Railway (I), 1900s, Train vignette	30.00
North and South Carolina Railway (I), 1910s, Train vignette	30.00
Northern Electric (I), 1900s, Gold bond, interurban vignette	165.00
Northern Pacific Railroad (I), 1950s, Covered wagon vignette	12.00
Northern Pacific Railroad (I), 1950s, Trust, stagecoach vignette	16.00
Northern Pacific Railroad (I), 1960s, Diesel train vignette	10.00
Northern Pacific Railroad (I), 1970s	5.00
Northern Pacific Railroad (U), 1920s, Equipment trust	25.00
Northern Pacific Railway Equipment Trust (I), 1890s, View with logo vignette	90.00
Northern Pacific Railway Equipment Trust (I), 1960s, Equipment Trust Bond, Train vignette	10.00
Northern Pacific Railway Equipment Trust (U), 1920s, Equipment trust bond, specimen, train vignette	30.00
Northern Pacific Railway Equipment Trust (U), 1940s, Equipment trust bond, specimen, train vignette	25.00
North Lebanon Railroad (I), 1850s, Old train vignette	135.00
Ocean Shore Railway (I), 1900s, Old train vignette	40.00
Ohio and Mississippi Railway (I), 1870s, Eagle vignette	90.00
Okmulgee Northern Railway (I), 1910s, Gold bond, Indian vignette	45.00
Old Colony and Newport Railway Company (I), 1860s	45.00
Old Colony and Newport Railway Company (I), 1860s, Signed by Stearns and Choate	65.00
Old Colony and Newport Railway Company (U), 1860s	20.00
Old Colony Railroad (I), 1860s, Ship vignette	95.00
Old Colony Railroad (I), 1870s, Ship vignette	70.00
Old Colony Railroad (I), 1870s, Train vignette	75.00
Old Colony Railroad (I), 1880s, Train vignette	65.00
Old Colony Railroad (I), 1890s, Train vignette and gandy dancers	60.00
Old Colony Railroad (I), 1890s, Train and two ladies vignette	60.00
Old Colony Railroad (I), 1930s, Train vignette	35.00
Old Colony Railroad (U), 1870s, Railroad vignette	30.00
Old Colony Railroad (U), 1880s, Railroad vignette	32.00
Oswego and Rome Railroad (U), 1890s, Certificate for bond	25.00
Pacific Railroad (I), 1860s, Train with stamp vignette	495.00
Pennsylvania and Delaware Railway 1870s, Old train vignette	300.00
Pennsylvania Canal Company (I), 1870s, With stamp, train on bridge vignette	175.00
Pennsylvania, Slatington and New England Railroad (I), 1880s, Old train vignette	140.00
Penobscot and Kennebec Railroad (I), 1850s, Old train vignette	125.00
Peoria and Pekin Terminal Railway (I), 1900s, Huge vignette of inside of station	85.00
Philadelphia and Reading Railway (I), 1890s, Train vignette	30.00

◀ ***Chicago, Rock Island and Pacific Railway Company (I), 1880s*** ***75.00***

UNITED STATES OF AMERICA

$1000 $1000

The Colorado and Southern Railway Company

COLLATERAL TRUST NOTE No. 574

June 1st, 1904.

For value received, and on the first day of September, 1907, (without grace), The Colorado and Southern Railway Company, a corporation under the laws of Colorado, promises to pay to the bearer, or if registered, to the registered holder hereof, the sum of one thousand dollars, in gold coin of the United States of America, of or equal to the present standard of weight and fineness, at the office of Hallgarten & Co., in the City of New York, State of New York, and to pay interest thereon from the first day of June, 1904, until such principal sum shall be paid, at the rate of five (5) per centum per annum, payable at said office quarterly in like gold coin on each first day of September, December, March and June in each year on presentation, and surrender of the respective coupons for such interest hereto attached, as they severally mature.

This note is one of a series of 2,000 notes of like tenor, date and amount, numbered consecutively one to two thousand, both inclusive, issued and to be issued under and subject to and equally secured by the provisions of a Collateral Trust Agreement between the American Car and Foundry Company, the said Railway Company, and the St. Louis Union Trust Company, of St. Louis, Missouri, as Trustee, dated the first day of June, 1904, and deposited with said Trustee. For a description of the collateral pledged to secure the same, the nature and extent of the security, the rights of the holders of notes and the terms and conditions upon which the notes are issued and secured, reference is made to said Collateral Trust Agreement. This note shall pass by delivery unless registered in the owner's name upon the books of the Trustee, but after registration of ownership duly certified thereon, no transfer except on the books of the Trustee shall be valid until a transfer thereof upon said books to bearer, after which this note shall pass by delivery as at first, but shall continue subject to successive registrations and transfers to bearer, at the option of the holder.

This note may be paid at the option of the maker at any time before maturity, on any interest due date, upon three months' notice in writing duly served on the said Trustee, by depositing with the said Trustee on or before such interest due date, the amount of principal and interest due thereon to such interest due date, after which last named date interest thereon shall cease and the coupons therefor become void.

This note shall not become obligatory until the certificate endorsed hereon is signed by the said St. Louis Union Trust Company, of St. Louis, Missouri, Trustee.

In Witness Whereof, the said Railway Company has caused this note to be signed by its President and Assistant Secretary.

The Colorado and Southern Railway Company,

By ______________________
President.

____
Assistant Secretary.

TRUSTEE'S CERTIFICATE

This note is one of the series of notes described in the within mentioned agreement.

ST. LOUIS UNION TRUST COMPANY,
Trustee.

By ______________________
Vice President.

Philadelphia City Passenger Railway (I), 1890s, Signed by S. W. Pesnig, Packer, and Colket	**65.00**
Pittsburgh, Shawmut and Northern Railroad (I), 1900s, Large train vignette	**50.00**
Plymouth, Kankakee and Pacific Railroad (I), 1870s, Old train and seal vignette	**310.00**
Queen City Railway Company of Seattle (I-N), 1880s, Cable car vignette	**150.00**
Queen City Railway Company of Seattle, Gold bond, streetcar vignette	**190.00**
Rapid City, Black Hills and Western Railroad (I) , Gold bond, train vignette	**180.00**
Reading Company (I), 1900s, Gold bond, railroad train and harbor scene vignette	**35.00**
Richmond and York River Railroad (I), 1850s, Train and ship vignette	**320.00**
Richmond Passenger and Power Company (I), 1900s	**195.00**
Rio Grande Southern Railroad (I), 1920s, Seated lady vignette	**20.00**
Rock Island and Peoria and Northern Railroad (I), 1900s, Train at crossing vignette	**62.00**
Rock Island and Peoria Railroad (U), 1880s, Train at station vignette	**22.00**
Rock Island Southern Railroad (I), 1900s, Gold bond, train vignette	**110.00**
Rockford, Rock Island and St. Louis Railroad (I), 1860s, Revenue stamps, two train vignettes	**210.00**
Rome, Water Town and Ogdensburg Railroad (U), 1880s, Train vignette	**40.00**
Sacramento Northern Railroad (I), 1910s	**15.00**
Saint Francais County Railroad (I), 1910s, Gold bond with stamp	**40.00**
Saint Louis, Alton and Springfield Railroad (I), 1880s, Lady with shield	**350.00**
Saint Louis, San Francisco Railroad (I), 1940s, Old car, train, bus, plane, and Mercury vignette	**15.00**
Saint Louis, San Francisco Railway (U), 1920s, Gold bond, two ladies and log vignette	**10.00**
Sallisaw, Mcalister and Southern Railroad (I), 1910s	**18.00**
Salt Lake and Fort Douglas Railway (I), 1880s, Train vignette, signed by W. Young	**260.00**
Sandusky and Columbus Short Line Railway (I), 1890s, Train and buildings vignette	**185.00**
Sandy River and Rangeley Lakes (I), 1900s, Train vignette	**110.00**
Sante Fe, Liberal and Englewood Railroad (I), 1900s, Gold bond	**62.00**
Savannah and Charleston Railroad (I), 1860s, Old train vignette	**325.00**
Seaboard–All Florida Railway (I), 1920s, Old auto, three presidents' signatures vignette	**60.00**
Second Avenue Railroad (I), 1890s, Railway vignette	**48.00**
Selins Grove and North Branch Railroad (I), 1870s, Gold bond, ornate	**115.00**
Selma, Marion and Memphis Railroad (I), 1860s, Long train vignette, signed by Forrest	**355.00**
Sharpsville Railroad (I), 1880s, Seal vignette	**95.00**
Sierra Railway of California (I), 1890s, Steam train vignette	**100.00**
Sierra Railway of California (U), 1890s, Steam train vignette	**65.00**
Snohomish Valley Railway Company, The (U), 1900s, Electric car and lady in redwood tree vignette	**55.00**
Sodus Point and Southern Railroad (I), 1870s, Old train plus other vignettes	**115.00**
South Central Railroad (I), 1860s, Old train vignette	**125.00**
South Carolina Central Railroad (U), 1870s	**195.00**
South Carolina Railway (I), 1880s, Cotton pickers vignette	**125.00**
South Carolina Railway (I), 1880s, Tree and seal vignette	**80.00**
South Mountain Railroad (I), 1870s, Old train vignette	**160.00**
South Pennsylvania Railroad (I), 1880s	**25.00**
South Pennsylvania Railroad (U), 1880s	**15.00**
Southern Central Railroad (I), 1860s, New York, Two old funnel trains at station vignette	**140.00**
Southern Indiana Railroad (I), 1900s, Train vignette	**40.00**
Southern Indiana Railway (U), 1900s, Bond certificate	**12.00**
Southern Pennsylvania Iron and Railroad Company (I), 1870s, Three vignettes	**195.00**
Southern Railroad (I), 1920s, Several trains vignette	**42.00**

__Colorado and Southern Railway Company, The (I), 1900s,__ Gold Note ***55.00***

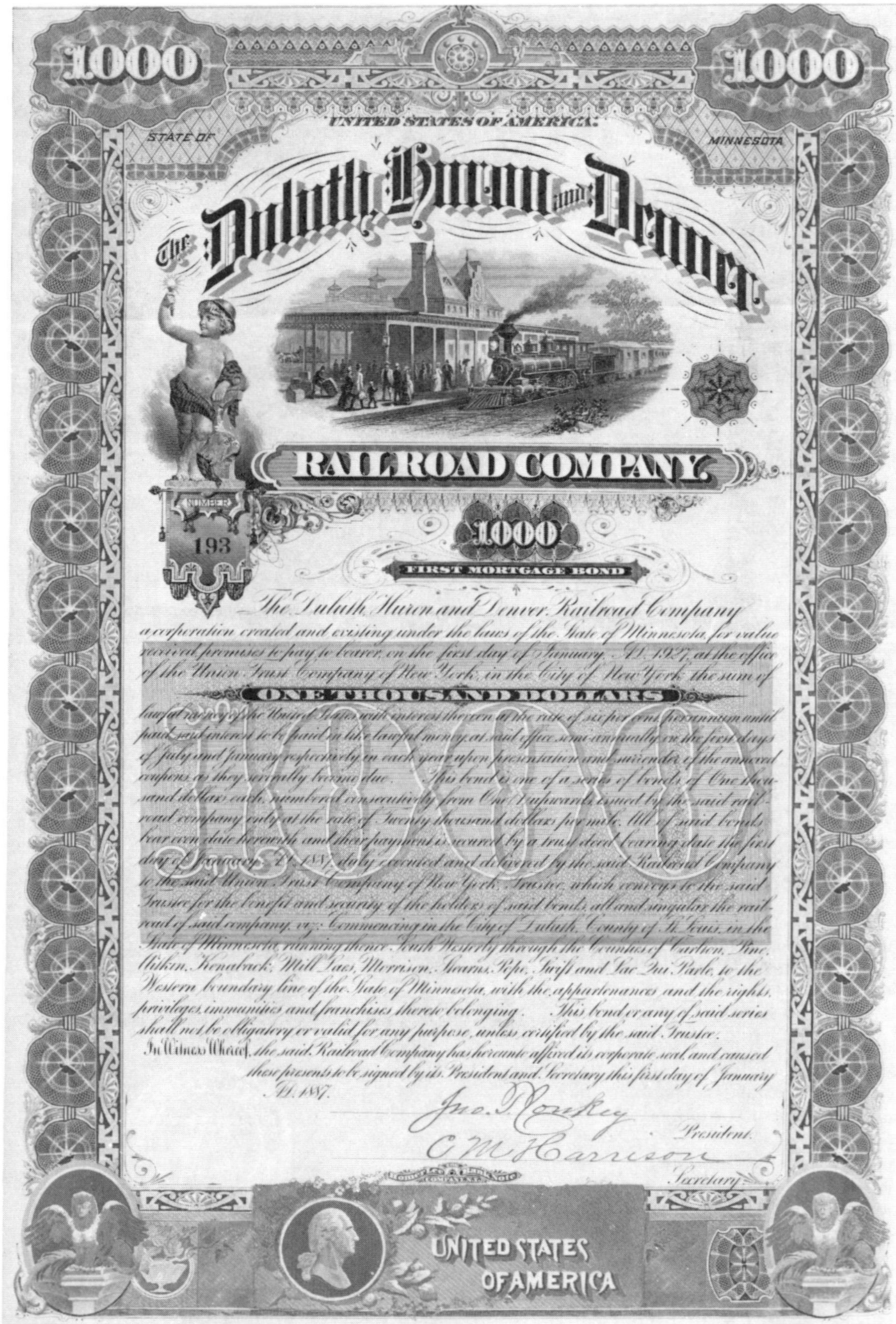

1000 1000

UNITED STATES OF AMERICA.

STATE OF MINNESOTA

The Duluth, Huron and Denver

RAILROAD COMPANY.

NUMBER 193

1000

FIRST MORTGAGE BOND

The Duluth, Huron and Denver Railroad Company a corporation created and existing under the laws of the State of Minnesota, for value received, promises to pay to bearer, on the first day of January, A.D. 1927, at the office of the Union Trust Company of New York, in the City of New York, the sum of

ONE THOUSAND DOLLARS

lawful money of the United States with interest thereon at the rate of six per cent per annum until paid, said interest to be paid in like lawful money at said office semi-annually on the first days of July and January respectively in each year upon presentation and surrender of the annexed coupons as they severally become due. This bond is one of a series of bonds of One thousand dollars each, numbered consecutively from One upwards, issued by the said railroad company only at the rate of Twenty thousand dollars per mile. All of said bonds bear even date herewith and their payment is secured by a trust deed bearing date the first day of January A.D. 1887, duly executed and delivered by the said Railroad Company to the said Union Trust Company of New York, Trustee, which conveys to the said Trustee for the benefit and security of the holders of said bonds, all and singular the railroad of said company, viz: Commencing in the City of Duluth, County of St. Louis, in the State of Minnesota, running thence South Westerly through the Counties of Carlton, Pine, Aitkin, Kenabeck, Mill Lacs, Morrison, Stearns, Pope, Swift and Lac Qui Parle, to the Western boundary line of the State of Minnesota, with the appurtenances and the rights, privileges, immunities and franchises thereto belonging. This bond or any of said series shall not be obligatory or valid for any purpose, unless certified by the said Trustee.

In Witness Whereof, the said Railroad Company has hereunto affixed its corporate seal, and caused these presents to be signed by its President and Secretary this first day of January A.D. 1887.

Jno. T. [illegible]
President.

C. M. Harrison
Secretary.

UNITED STATES OF AMERICA

Southern Railroad (I), 1930s, Several trains vignette	**38.00**
Southern Railroad (I), 1960s, Equipment trust bond	**4.00**
Springfield, Mount Vernon and Pittsburg Railroad (I), 1850s, Tiny train vignette	**150.00**
Staten Island Midland Railroad (I), 1890s, Trolley with state seal vignette	**250.00**
Staten Island Midland Railroad (U), 1890s, Trolley with state seal vignette	**135.00**
Steubenville and Indiana Railroad (I), 1850, Old train vignette	**95.00**
Sunbury and Erie Railroad (I), 1850s, Scarce	**190.00**
Talladega and Coosa Valley Railroad (I), 1880s	**225.00**
Talladega and Coosa Valley Railroad (U), 1880s	**235.00**
Tennessee North Eastern (I), 1900s, Gold bond	**32.00**
Tennessee Northern Railroad (I), 1900s, Black and gold seal vignette	**23.00**
Texas Electric Railway (I), 1910s, Streetcar and train vignette	**57.00**
Thirty-fourth Street Crosstown Railway (I), 1900s, Goddess vignette	**33.00**
Thirty-fourth Street Crosstown Railway (I), 1890s,	**79.00**
Toledo, Delphos and Burlington Railroad (I), Train vignette	**110.00**
Toledo, Peoria and Warsaw Railway (I), 1870s, Old train and seal vignette	**185.00**
Toledo, St. Louis and Western Railroad Company (I), 1900s, Gold bond, old train vignette	**60.00**
Toledo, Saint Louis and Western Railroad Company (U), 1900s, Train vignette	**25.00**
Town and Crown Point (I), 1860s, Bond for White Hall and Pittsburg Railroad, long train vignette	**220.00**
Town of Sandy Creek Railroad (I), 1870s, Bond for Syracuse Northern Railroad, train vignette	**110.00**
Town of Schroeppel (I), 1880s, Bond for Syracuse, Phoenix and Oswego Railroad, train vignette	**100.00**
Town of Volney, County of Oswego (I), 1860s, Bond for New York and Oswego Railroad, Cows vignette	**120.00**
Trans-Alaska Siberian Railway (I), 1900s	**75.00**
Troy and Lansingburgh Railroad (I), 1860s, Horse trolley vignette	**130.00**
Troy and Tiptonville Railroad (I), 1880s, Four small vignettes	**160.00**
Twenty-third Street Railway (I), 1910s, Gold bond, streetcar vignette	**75.00**
Ulster and Delaware Railroad (I), 1880s, Two ladies vignette	**48.00**
Union Passenger Railway Company of Philadelphia (I), 1870s, Horse trolleys, blacksmith, man and woman vignette	**150.00**
Union Passenger Railway Company of Philadelphia (U), 1870s, Horse trolleys, blacksmith, man, and woman vignette	**40.00**
Union Street Railway of Dover (I), 1890s, Orange-red seal vignette	**20.00**
Ver Cruz and Pacific Railroad (I), 1900s, Train and ships vignette	**45.00**
Vicksburg and Meridian Railroad (I), Old train vignette	**180.00**
Vicksburg and Nashville Railroad (I), 1870s, Four vignettes including two trains	**130.00**
Virginia and Truckee Railroad (I), 1870s, Gold bond, train in mountain scene vignette	**400.00**
Virginia Railway, The, 1940s, Steam train vignette	**20.00**
Virginia Railway, The (I), 1950s, Train vignette	**25.00**
Wabash-Pittsburgh Terminal Railway 1900s, Seal vignette	**65.00**
Washington and Old Dominion Railway (I), 1910s, Electric car vignette	**85.00**
Washington and Western Railroad (I), 1880s, Gold bond, old train vignette	**325.00**
Washington Virginia Railway (I), 1920s	**20.00**
West End Street Railway (U), 1900s, Streetcar vignette	**15.00**
West End Street Railway, Massachusetts (I), 1900s, Streetcar vignette	**20.00**

◀ ***Duluth, Huron and Denver Railroad Company, The, 1880s,*** *Train at station, pixie, and Washington vignette* ***250.00***

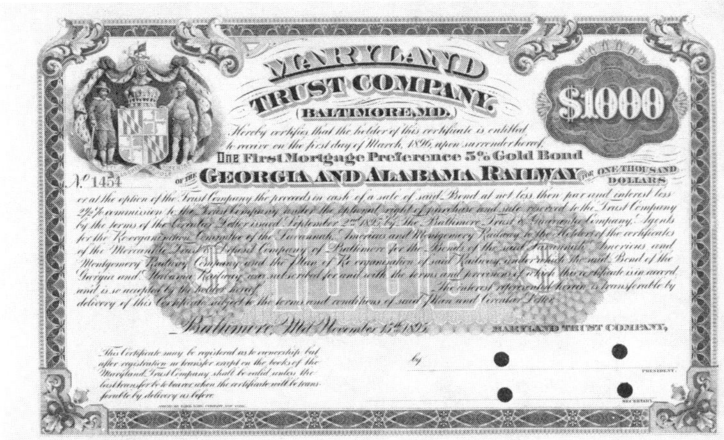

MARYLAND
TRUST COMPANY.
(BALTIMORE, MD.)
$1000
Hereby certifies that the holder of this certificate is entitled,
to receive on the first day of March, 1896, upon surrender hereof,
ONE First Mortgage Preference 5% Gold Bond
OF THE GEORGIA AND ALABAMA RAILWAY FOR ONE THOUSAND DOLLARS
No. 1454
Baltimore, Md. November 15th 1895
MARYLAND TRUST COMPANY,
by
PRESIDENT.
SECRETARY.

UNITED STATES OF AMERICA
STATE OF KANSAS
1000
2722
2722
The Kansas City Northwestern Railroad Company
FIRST MORTGAGE 5 GOLD BOND
Dated January First 1894
The Kansas City Northwestern Railroad Company
ONE THOUSAND DOLLARS
The Kansas City Northwestern Railroad Company.
by
VICE

Western Illinois and Iowa Railroad (I-N), 1900s, Streetcar vignette	60.00
Western Maryland (I), 1850s, Train vignette	175.00
Western Maryland (I), 1860s, Train, horses, and men vignette	165.00
Western Maryland (I), 1870s, Train vignette	125.00
Western Maryland (U), 1900s, Gold bond, speeding train vignette, signed and cancelled	12.00
Western Maryland Railroad, 1910s, Regular bond, John D. Rockefeller, not signed	100.00
Western Maryland Railroad (I), 1910s, Gold bond, speeding train vignette	65.00
Western North Carolina (I), 1870s	160.00
Western Pacific Railroad (I), 1900s, Train vignette	125.00
Western Pacific Railroad (I), 1930s, Train vignette	28.00
Western Pacific Railroad (I), 1940s, Train vignette	25.00
Western Railroad (I), 1830s, Massachusetts	160.00
Western Railroad (I), 1840s, Massachusetts	150.00
White Water Railroad (U), 1800s, Scrip coupon bond, old train vignette	40.00
Wichita Falls and North Eastern Railway (I), 1900s, Old train vignette	70.00
Wichita Falls and North Western Railway (I), 1900s, Steam train vignette	50.00
Wichita Falls and Southern Railway (I), 1900s, Large vignette of train and workers	95.00
Wilkes-Barre and Eastern Railroad (I), 1890s	35.00
Williamsport and Clearfield Railroad (I), 1880s	55.00
Wilmington and Manchester Railroad (I), 1860s, Old train vignette	285.00
Wilmington and Northern Railroad (U), 1880s, Old train vignette	65.00
Wilmington and Reading Railroad (I), 1870s	78.00
Winona and Southwestern Railway (I), 1880s, Seven large old trains and ladies vignettes	160.00
Wisconsin Interurban System (I), 1910s, Gold bond, state seal vignette	40.00
Wiscosset, Waterville and Farmington Railroad (I), 1900s, Old train vignette	50.00
Worcester Consolidated Street Railway (I), 1930s, Certificate of deposit for bond	3.00
Yazoo and Mississippi Valley Railroad (I), 1900s, Train at bottom vignette	85.00
Yosemite Short Line Railway Company (I), 1900s, Train and sheepherder vignettes	185.00

◀***Georgia and Alabama Railway (U), 1890s,*** *State seal* ***10.00***

◀***Kansas City Northwestern Railroad Company, The (I), 1890s,*** *Train vignette* ***60.00***

Nº C440
10,000
10,000
LEHIGH VALLEY RAILROAD
COMPANY
GENERAL CONSOLIDATED MORTGAGE GOLD BOND
TEN THOUSAND DOLLARS
REGISTERED
12TH
JUNE, 1944
Lehigh Valley Railroad Company
STATE OF PENNSYLVANIA
VICE PRESIDENT

110
UNITED STATES OF AMERICA
STATE OF MICHIGAN.
MICHIGAN CENTRAL RAIL ROAD COMPANY
REGISTERED 4 PER CENT.
SECURED BY
1000
GOLD BOND.
FIRST MORTGAGE ON THE PROPERTY OF THE TERMINAL RAILROAD COMPANY AT CHICAGO, ILLINOIS.
DUE 1941
The Michigan Central Rail Road Company, a corporation existing under the laws of the State of Michigan for Value Received,
promises to pay to
or assigns One Thousand Dollars
In Witness Whereof,
Union Trust Company of New York
President
Treasurer

OTHER TRANSPORTATION

Automotive

Ajax Rubber Company (I), 1920s, New York, Two allegorical figures, with company logo	**18.00**
American La France Fire Engine Company (I), 1920s, New York, Eagle vignette	**110.00**
American Motors Corporation (I), 1960s, Vignette of winged wheel with two men and woman	**10.00**
Armstrong Rubber Company (U), Specimen, workers and storage tanks vignette	**15.00**
Arsenal Motor Company (I), 1920s, Pennsylvania, Dealership	**20.00**
Auto Bus Belges (U), 1920s, Old busses in front of buildings vignette	**14.00**
Automobile Shares (I), 1940s, Group securities, eagle with ship and factory vignette	**38.00**
Auto-Train Corporation (I), 1970s, Florida, Company logo, seal	**3.00**
Baker Steam Motor Car (I), 1920s, Arizona, Allegorical vignette	**100.00**
Banner Motor Car Company (I), Winged Mercury with steering wheel vignette	**20.00**
Beggs Motor Car Company (I), 1910s,	**40.00**
Belmont Motors Corporation (U), 1900s, Lady vignette	**25.00**
Ben-Hur Motor Car Company (I-N), 1910s, Logo of car plus gladiator and chariot vignette	**100.00**
Ben-Hur Motor Car Company (I-N), 1910s, Western hemisphere vignette	**95.00**
Bonner Motor Car (I), 1920s, Driver with winged helmet vignette	**70.00**
Cadillac Automobile Company (I), 1920s, Massachusetts	**25.00**
China Motor Company (U), Panama	**5.00**
Chrysler Corporation (I-N), Two goddesses, radiator cap, cars, and trucks vignette	**30.00**
Columbia Wagon Company (I), 1890s, Pennsylvania	**50.00**
Continental Motors Corporation (I), 1920s and 1930s, Automobile motor vignette	**18.00**
Continental Motors Corporation (I), 1960s, Automobile motor vignette	**14.00**
Cooper Tire and Rubber Company (U), Specimen, company logo, figures vignette	**14.00**
Cornfield Wheel Company (I), 1910s, Michigan, Seal	**37.00**
Crawford Motor Company (I), 1920s, Pennsylvania, Three allegorical figures	**20.00**
Dill Tractor (I), 1920s, Arkansas, Eagle vignette	**55.00**
Duplex Tire Company (I), 1910s, Arizona, No vignette	**10.00**
Durant Motors (I), 1920s, Company logo on five-star shield in front of factory vignette	**110.00**
Durant Motors (I), 1920s, Two seminude figures with company logo "D" vignette	**85.00**
Durant Motors (I), 1930s, Angels, seal vignette	**65.00**
Elgin Motor Car Corporation (I), 1920s, Company logo	**110.00**
Falls Motor Corporation (I), 1910s	**95.00**
Flint Motor Car (I), 1920s, Michigan, Two ladies holding company logo in front of factory	**155.00**
Ford Foreign Motor Company (I), 1930s, Investment trust certificate, gold seal	**130.00**
Ford International Capital Corporation (I), 1960s, Bond, Henry Ford and antique car vignette	**12.00**
Ford Motor Company (I), 1960s, Vignette of Henry Ford and Model T car	**22.00**
Ford Motor Company (I), 1970s, Vignette of Henry Ford and model T car	**20.00**
Ford Motor Company (U), Vignette of Henry Ford and model T car	**19.00**
Ford Motor Company of Berlin (I), 1920s	**110.00**
General Motors Corporation (I), 1950s, Bond, vignette of streamliner, truck, and car	**15.00**

Lehigh Valley Railroad Company, 1940s, *Gold bond, old train and horse and wagon vignette*	***25.00***
Michigan Central Rail Road Company (U), 1890s, *Train*	***50.00***

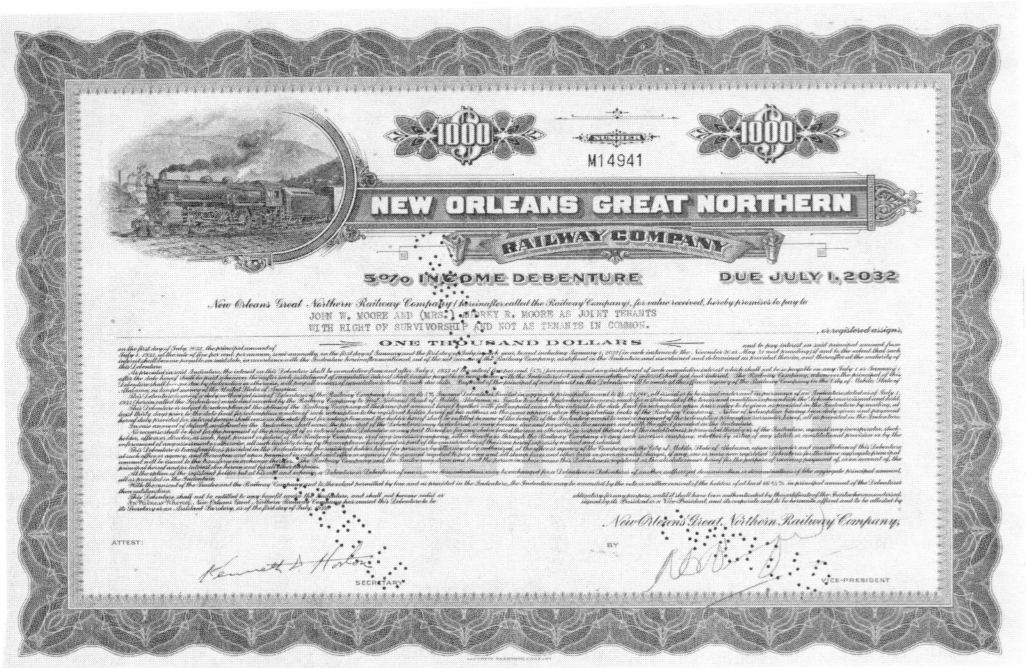
1000
NUMBER
M14941
1000
NEW ORLEANS GREAT NORTHERN
RAILWAY COMPANY
5% INCOME DEBENTURE
DUE JULY 1, 2032
JOHN W. MOORE AND (MRS.) AUDREY R. MOORE AS JOINT TENANTS
WITH RIGHT OF SURVIVORSHIP AND NOT AS TENANTS IN COMMON.
ONE THOUSAND DOLLARS
New Orleans Great Northern Railway Company,
ATTEST:
SECRETARY
BY
VICE-PRESIDENT

UNITED STATES OF AMERICA
1000
No. 00000
1000
No. 00000
NORTHERN PACIFIC RAILWAY EQUIPMENT TRUST OF 1922
FOUR AND ONE-HALF PER CENT EQUIPMENT TRUST GOLD CERTIFICATE
DATED AUGUST 15, 1922. — PAYABLE AUGUST 15, 1932.
AUTHORIZED ISSUE 4500 SHARES OF $1,000 EACH.
ONE THOUSAND DOLLARS
The First National Bank of the City of New York,
SPECIMEN
SPECIMEN

General Motors Corporation (U), Specimen, two seated figures with GM logo	75.00
Gove Motor Car Company (I), **1920s, Idaho**, Truck manufacturing, eagle vignette	75.00
Grant Motor Car (I), **1910s**, Winged Mercury with horn of plenty, books, and machinery vignettes	175.00
Grant Motor Car (I), **1920s**, Winged Mercury with horn of plenty, books, machinery vignettes	160.00
Greenwich Rubber Company (I), **1920s, Ohio**, Eagle vignette	8.00
Greyhound Motors Corporation (I), **1920s**, Factories, machinery, gold seal vignette	45.00
Harroun Motors Corporation (I), **1920s**	125.00
Hawkeye Cord Tire Company of Iowa (I), **1920s**, Green seal	22.00
Hawkeye Tire and Rubber (I), **1910s, Iowa**, Eagle vignette, gold seal	25.00
Hawkeye Tire and Rubber (I), **1920s, Iowa**, Eagle vignette, gold seal	22.00
Hudson Motor Car Company (I), **1920s**, Three different factory vignettes	40.00
Hudson Motor Car Company (I), **1930s**, Three different factory vignettes	35.00
Hudson Motor Car Company (I), **1940s**, Three different factory vignettes	30.00
Hudson Motor Car Company (I), **1950s**, Three different factory vignettes	20.00
Hutsell Motor Company (I), **1920s, Washington**, Eagle with flag vignette	43.00
Industrial Motors Corporation (I), **1920s Delaware**, Beautiful lady between two seminude men vignette	33.00
Jacquar Cars, Limited (I), **1970s**, No vignette	20.00
Kaiser-Frazer Corporation (I), **1940s and 1950s**	6.00
Kardell Tractor and Truck Company (I), **1920s**	63.00
Keely Motor Company (I), **1880s**, Seated woman with engine, portrait vignette	100.00
Kerosene Burning Carburetor Company (I), **1910s, Michigan**,	30.00
Lincoln Motor Company (I), **1920s**, Temporary certificate signed by W.C . Leland	20.00
Manufactured Rubber Company (U), **1900s**, Lady with two children vignette	12.00
Marmon Motor Company (I), **1930s**	155.00
McPhee Motor Company (U), **1900s, Virginia**, Winged Mercury holding steering wheel vignette	40.00
Metropolis Motor Company (I), **1910s**, Winged Mercury holding large steering wheel vignette	55.00
Mitchell Lewis Motors of Illinois (I), **1910s**, Bond	30.00
Moon Motor Car (I), **1930s**, Woman with moon tablet vignette	145.00
Moon Motor Car (U), Specimen, woman with moon tablet	130.00
Nash Kelvinator Corporation (I), **1950s**, Allegorical figure and factories	11.00
Nash Motors (I), **1910s**, Two ladies and child vignette	75.00
Nash Motors (I), **1920s**, Two ladies and child vignette	42.00
Nash Motors (I), **1930s**, Two ladies and child vignette	37.00
Nash Motors (U), **1900s**, Two ladies and child vignette	20.00
Nash-Pittsburgh Motors (I), **1920s, Pennsylvania**, Dealership certificate	30.00
Northway Motors (I), **1920s**, Lady portrait vignette	10.00
Olds-Fayette Motor Company (I), **1920s, Pennsylvania**, Child on globe vignette	45.00

◀ ***New Orleans Great Northern Railway Company (I), 1930s,*** *Train vignette*	***30.00***
◀ ***Northern Pacific Railway Equipment Trust (U), 1920s,*** *Equipment trust bond, specimen, train vignette*	***30.00***

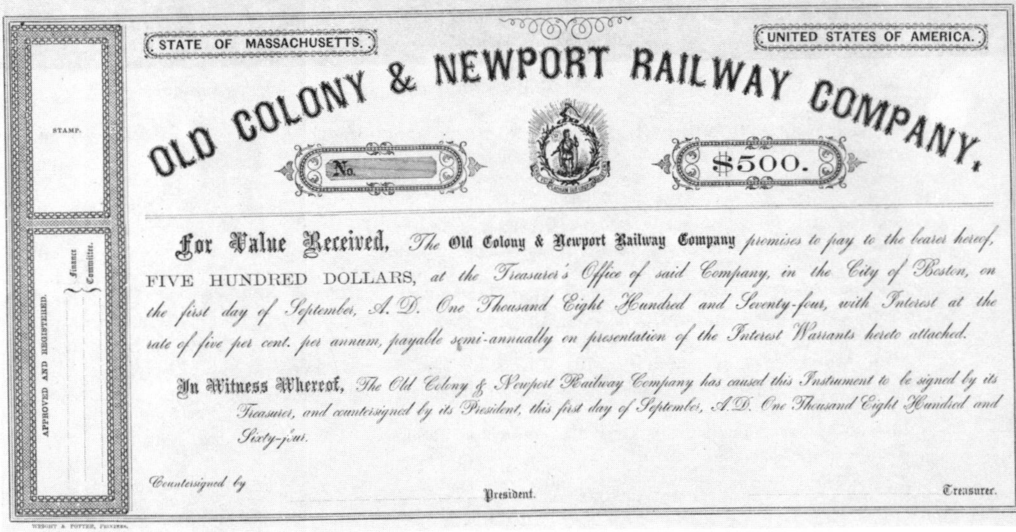

STATE OF MASSACHUSETTS.

UNITED STATES OF AMERICA.

OLD COLONY & NEWPORT RAILWAY COMPANY.

No.

$500.

STAMP.

APPROVED AND REGISTERED.

Finance Committee.

For Value Received, *The* **Old Colony & Newport Railway Company** *promises to pay to the bearer hereof,* FIVE HUNDRED DOLLARS, *at the Treasurer's Office of said Company, in the City of Boston, on the first day of September, A. D. One Thousand Eight Hundred and Seventy-four, with Interest at the rate of five per cent. per annum, payable semi-annually on presentation of the Interest Warrants hereto attached.*

In Witness Whereof, *The Old Colony & Newport Railway Company has caused this Instrument to be signed by its Treasurer, and countersigned by its President, this first day of September, A. D. One Thousand Eight Hundred and Sixty-four.*

Countersigned by

President.

Treasurer.

WRIGHT & POTTER, PRINTERS.

United States of America.

STATE OF ILLINOIS.

$1000

£200

The Rockford, Rock Island & St. Louis RAILROAD COMPANY

FIRST MORTGAGE BOND,

CONVERTIBLE & PAYABLE IN GOLD.

5499

5499

[illegible] is CANCELLED, subject to the provisions of the contract of [illegible]

Know all men by these presents, that The Rockford, Rock Island and St. Louis Railroad Company hereby acknowledges itself to owe to the Union Trust Company of New York, *or bearer, the sum of* ONE THOUSAND DOLLARS *in United States Gold Coin at par, to be paid at the Agency of the Company, in the City of New York, or the sum of* Two hundred Pounds Sterling *to be paid at an Agency of said Railroad Company in the City of London, England, at the option of the holder hereof, on the first day of August, one thousand nine hundred and eighteen, with interest on the said principal from the first day of August 1868, at the rate of* Seven per centum per annum, *in Gold Coin as aforesaid, free from any Government tax, at such Agency in the City of New York, or in the City of London, on the first days of February and August of each year, until the said principal shall be fully paid, on the presentation of the annexed coupons as they respectively become due.* [illegible]

$1000 or £200.

[illegible] *Two hundred Pounds Sterling* [illegible] *of even date herewith, secured by a deed of trust to the Union Trust Company* [illegible] *of this Company, Extending from the Town of* [illegible] *in the State of Illinois and all* [illegible] *and deed of trust.* [illegible] *payment of any interest coupon hereto attached,* [illegible] *for six months after maturity and demand of payment, or in case of the non-payment of any instalment required to be paid into the sinking fund provided for by the said deed of trust, if such default shall continue six months after said instalment shall have become payable, then and in either case the principal of this Bond shall become due in the manner provided in the deed of trust, and the said Company hereby expressly waives the benefit of every extension, stay or appraisement law which has been or may hereafter be enacted.*

[illegible] *of this Bond may at any time have the same converted into the Capital Stock of the said Company and be entitled to receive therefor Ten Shares of said Capital Stock on the surrender of this Bond with all unpaid Coupons thereto annexed. This Bond shall pass by delivery, or by transfer on the books of the Company in the City of New York. After the registration of ownership, certified hereon by the Transfer Agent, no transfer except on the books of the Company shall be valid unless the last transfer be to bearer, which shall restore transferability by delivery, and it shall continue subject to successive registrations and transfers to bearer, as aforesaid, at the option of the holder.*

This Bond shall not become obligatory unless the Certificate endorsed hereon is signed by the authorized Officer of the said Union Trust Company.

In Witness Whereof, *the said party of the first part has caused its Corporate Seal to be hereto affixed and these presents to be signed by its President and Treasurer and countersigned by its Secretary, on this Twenty third day of October A.D. 1868.*

Countersigned

President.

Secretary.

Treasurer.

Packard Motor Car (I), 1920s, Men and women vignettes 10.00
Pan Motor Company (I), 1920s, Automobile vignette 100.00
Peerless Motor Car Company (I), 1920s and 1930s, Train, building, and two allegorical figures vignettes 140.00
Pierce-Arrow Motor Car Company (U), 1920s, Eagle, gold seal, sailing ship 40.00
Portsmouth Automobile and Machine Company (I), 1910s, Ohio, Early model auto vignette 365.00

Rambler Auto Company of New England (U), 1910s, Massachusetts, State buildings vignette 55.00
Rambler Auto Company of New York (U), 1900s, Two ladies, train, and steamboat vignettes 65.00
Rambler Garage Company (U), 1900s, Eagle vignette 50.00
Reflex Auto-Light Corporation (I), 1920s, Indiana, Lady with shield 10.00
Reo Motor Car Company (I), 1920s, Females with winged logo signed by Scott (President of company) vignette 110.00
Reo Motors (U), 1900s, Michigan, Specimen, Company logo between two seminude men vignette 130.00
Revere Motor Car Company (I), 1910s, Torch vignette 80.00
Revere Motor Car Company (I), 1920s, Torch vignette 75.00
Richard Auto Manufacturing Company (I), 1910s, West Virginia, Touring car and eagle vignettes 160.00
Rickenbacker Motor Company (I), 1920s 100.00
Rolls-Royce of America (I), 1930s, Seated warrior with sword vignette 155.00

Sebring Tire and Rubber Company (I), 1910s, Ohio, Winged Mercury with steering wheel vignette 25.00
Severin Motor Company (I), Winged Mercury with steering wheel vignette 20.00
Sinclair Engine and Foundry, 1920s, Eagle vignette 30.00
Sinclair Motors (I), 1920s, Two allegorical vignettes 52.00
Standard Automobile Manufacturing (I), 1914, Vignette of open touring car 195.00
Star Motors (I), 1920s, Large vignette of star in front of factories and train 145.00
Steinmetz Electric Motor Car Company (I), 1920s, Eagle vignette 75.00
Sterling Engine Company (I), 1940s, Eagle on rock vignette 7.00
Stevens Duryea, Inc. (I), 1920s, Company logo vignette 70.00
Studebaker Brothers Manufacturing Company (U), 1900s, Indiana, Large auto-production plant vignette 85.00
Studebaker Corporation (I), 1920s, Blacksmith shop vignette 115.00
Studebaker Corporation (I), 1930s, Blacksmith shoeing horse vignette 105.00
Studebaker Corporation (U), Specimen, seated man holding auto piston, man working lathe, car designer at desk vignettes 25.00

Templar Motors Corporation (I), 1910s, Eagle vignette 70.00
Tire Mileage Recording Device Company (U), 1900s, California, Eagle vignette 14.00
Tractor Supply Company (I), 1960s, Female vignette 4.00
Tucker Corporation (I), 1940s 85.00

U.S. Automotive Corporation (I), 1920s, Minuteman with rifle vignette 95.00

Walker-Johnson Truck Company (I), 1920s, Eagle, Capitol vignette 22.00
Willys Corporation (I), 1920s, Certificate of deposit 8.00
Willys Corporation (I), 1930s, Fractional share 20.00
Willys-Overland Company (I), 1930s, Two figures with company logo 95.00

◀ ***Old Colony and Newport Railway Company (U), 1860s*** ***20.00***
◀ ***Rockford, Rock Island and St. Louis Railroad (I), 1860s,*** *Revenue stamps, two train vignettes* ***210.00***

5,000.
United States of America.
TOLEDO, ST. LOUIS AND WESTERN RAILROAD COMPANY.
No. A12
PRIOR LIEN 3½% GOLD BOND.
NORTHWESTERN MUTUAL LIFE INSURANCE COMPANY.
FIVE THOUSAND DOLLARS
$5000
STATE OF INDIANA
5,000.

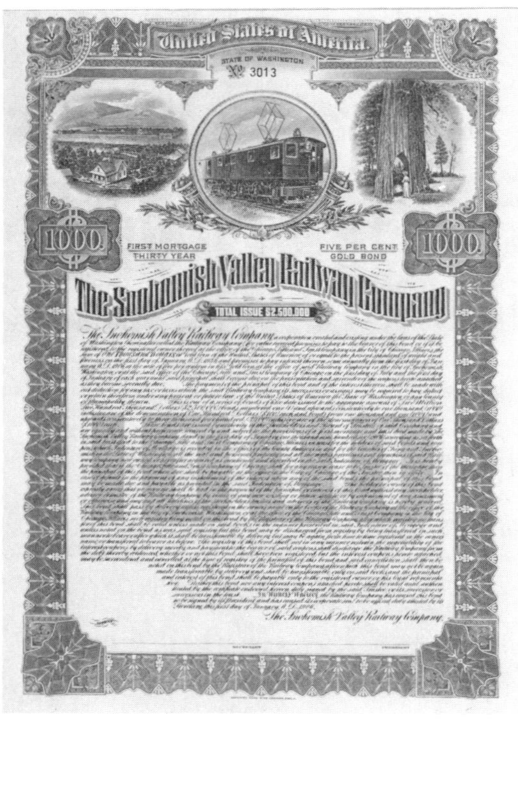
United States of America.
STATE OF WASHINGTON
No 3013
1000
FIRST MORTGAGE
THIRTY YEAR
FIVE PER CENT
GOLD BOND
1000
The Snohomish Valley Railway Company
TOTAL ISSUE $2,500,000
$1000

Willys-Overland Company (I), 1920s, Two seated figures with company logo vignette **105.00**
Winslow Motor Carriage Company (I), 1900s, State seal **150.00**
World's Fair Autocar Company (I), 1910s, Double-decker bus vignette, gold seal **265.00**
World's Fair Autocar Company (I), 1930s, Fraction share **15.00**

Yellow Truck and Coach Manufacturing Company (U), Specimen, woman seated in front of city skyline vignette **65.00**

◀ ***Toledo, St. Louis and Western Railroad Company (I), 1900s,*** *Gold bond, old train vignette* ***60.00***
◀ ***Snohomish Valley Railway Company, The (U), 1900s,*** *Electric car and lady in redwood tree vignette* ***55.00***

1000. 1000.

THE VIRGINIAN RAILWAY COMPANY

INCORPORATED UNDER THE LAWS OF THE COMMONWEALTH OF VIRGINIA

Nº M 32988

FIRST LIEN AND REFUNDING MORTGAGE BOND, SERIES B, 3%, DUE MAY 1, 1995

Nº M 32988

The Virginian Railway Company (hereinafter called the Railway Company), a corporation of the Commonwealth of Virginia, for value received, hereby promises to pay to bearer, or, if this Bond be registered as to principal, then to the registered holder hereof, on the 1st day of May, 1995 (unless before said date this Bond shall be called for redemption and payment duly provided for) the principal sum of

ONE THOUSAND DOLLARS,

and to pay interest on said principal sum from the date hereof at the rate of three per cent. (3%) per annum, semi-annually on the 1st day of May and the 1st day of November in each year until the payment of said principal sum, but until the maturity of this Bond only upon presentation and surrender of the coupons for such interest instalments as are evidenced thereby, hereto attached, as severally they mature. Both the principal of, premium if any, and interest on this Bond are payable at the office or agency of the Railway Company in the Borough of Manhattan, The City of New York, State of New York, in such coin or currency of the United States of America as at the time of payment is legal tender for the payment of public and private debts.

[illegible]

CORPORATE TRUSTEE'S CERTIFICATE

This Bond is one of the Bonds of the series designated therein described in the within-mentioned indenture.

CITY BANK FARMERS TRUST COMPANY, AS CORPORATE TRUSTEE,

By [signature] AUTHORIZED OFFICER.

The Virginian Railway Company,

By [signature] VICE PRESIDENT.

Attest: [signature] SECRETARY.

THE VIRGINIAN RAILWAY COMPANY INCORPORATED VIRGINIA

AMERICAN BANK NOTE COMPANY

WATER NAVIGATION

American Commercial Barge Line Company (U), Specimen, large riverboat and barge vignette 20.00
American Hawaiian Steam Ship Company (I), 1900s, New Jersy, Vignette of old sailing ship 30.00
American Ship and Commerce (I), 1930s, Harbor with two ships vignette 43.00
American Wave Power Company (I), 1900s, New Jersey, Steamship vignette 35.00
Aransas Pass Harbor Company (I), 1890s, Texas, Bond, map of gulf and bay 130.00
Aransas Pass Harbor Company (I), 1890s, Texas, Steamship vignette 80.00

Baltimore Shipbuilding and Dry Dock Company (I), 1900s, Maryland, Large ship in dry dock and shipbuilding works vignette 115.00
Blodget Canal Company (U), 1820s 75.00
Boston and Philadelphia Steamship Company (U), 1890s, Old sailing ship vignette 20.00
Boston, Newport and New York Steamboat Company (I), 1860s, Signature of Alexander Holmes and Oliver Ames 175.00
Boston Wharf Company (I), 1940s 4.00
Brooklyn Ferry Company of New York (I), 1900s, Gold bond 35.00

Chesapeake and Delaware Canal Company (I), 1880s 45.00
Chesapeake and Ohio Canal Company (I), 1840s, Six percent bond, embossed seal 165.00
Cotton Transportation Company (I), 1890s, Missouri, Barges in river vignette 55.00
Crowell and Thurlow Steamship Company (I), 1920s, Maine, Vignette of oceangoing freighter 55.00
Cunard Steamship Company (I), 1940s 20.00

Delta Canal Company (U), 1800s, Florida, Two vignettes of canal dredges 55.00
Detroit and Cleveland Navigation Company (I), 1930s, Ship vignette 20.00

East Boston Dry Dock Company (I), 1850s, Sailing ship in shipyard vignette 250.00
Erie Canal Bond (I), 1840s 375.00
Erie Canal Bond (I), 1850s and 1860s 350.00
Erie Canal Bond (I), 1870s 325.00

Franklin Canal (I), 1850s, Pennsylvania, Seven percent bond 225.00

Hazard Wharf Company of Baltimore City (U), 1900s, Maryland, Harbor scene 20.00

Kriks Mississippi Snag Fender Company Riverboat (U), 1840s, Mississippi, Two portraits, plus Mississippi riverboat vignette 210.00

Maryland Steamboat Company (I), 1810s, Maryland, Embossed seal 350.00
Mobile Docks Company (U), 1900s, Alabama 4.00
Morris Canal Company (I), 1880s 18.00

New Haven Steamboat Company (U), 1800s, Uncut sheet of four stock certificates 33.00
New York and New Jersey Company (U), 1890s, New Jersey, Ferryboat, sailing ships, and oarsmen in boat vignette 65.00

Old Colony Steamboat (I), 1870s, Old ship vignette 145.00
Old Colony Steamboat (I), 1880s, Ship, flags, seal with steamboat vignette 130.00

◀ ***Virginian Railway, The, 1940s**, Steam train vignette* ***20.00***

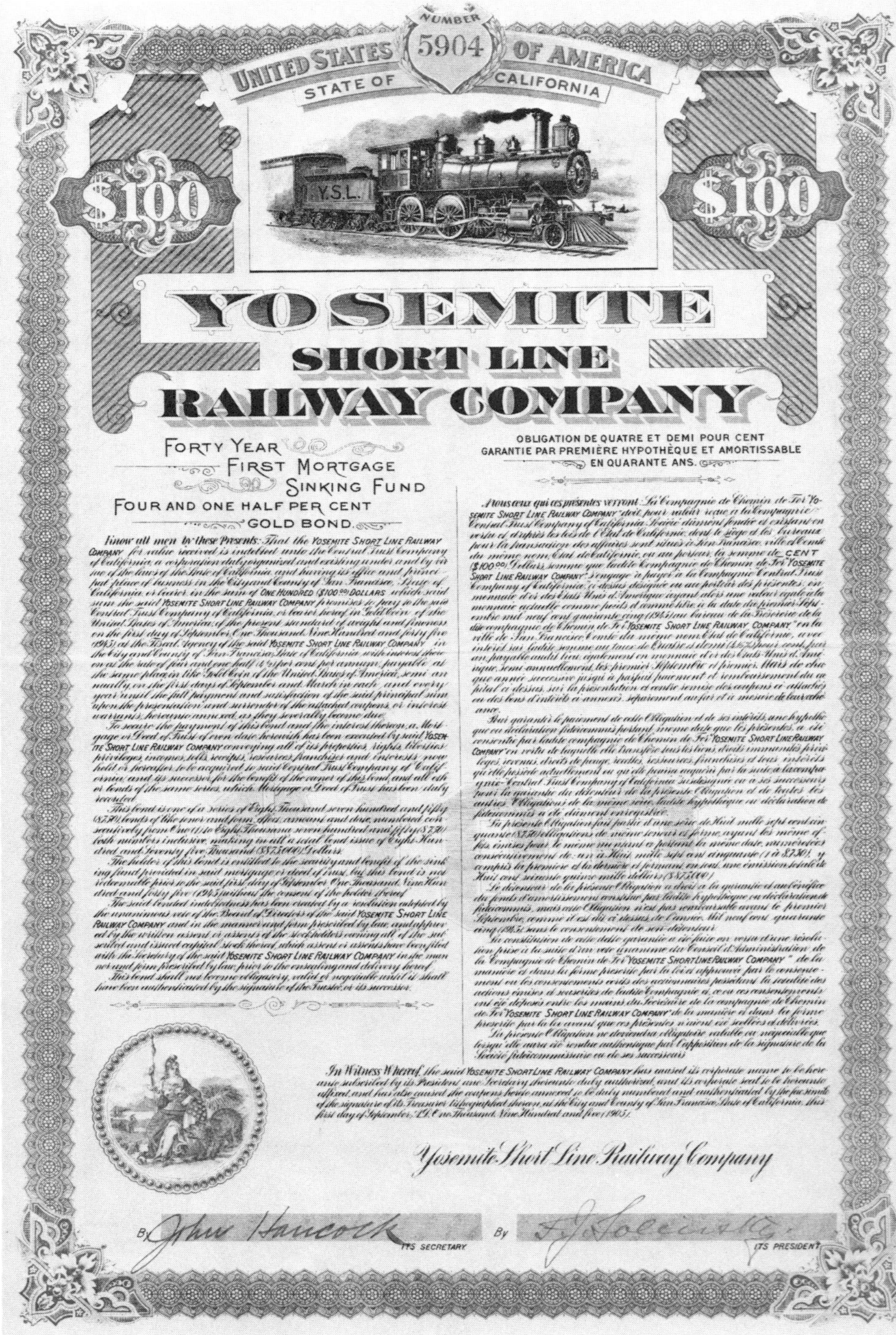

NUMBER 5904

UNITED STATES OF AMERICA

STATE OF CALIFORNIA

$100 $100

Y.S.L.

YOSEMITE SHORT LINE RAILWAY COMPANY

FORTY YEAR
FIRST MORTGAGE
SINKING FUND
FOUR AND ONE HALF PER CENT
GOLD BOND.

OBLIGATION DE QUATRE ET DEMI POUR CENT
GARANTIE PAR PREMIÈRE HYPOTHÈQUE ET AMORTISSABLE
EN QUARANTE ANS.

Know all men by these Presents: That the YOSEMITE SHORT LINE RAILWAY COMPANY for value received is indebted unto the Central Trust Company of California, a corporation duly organized and existing under and by virtue of the laws of the State of California, and having its office and principal place of business in the City and County of San Francisco, State of California, or bearer, in the sum of ONE HUNDRED ($100.00) DOLLARS which said sum the said YOSEMITE SHORT LINE RAILWAY COMPANY promises to pay to the said Central Trust Company of California, or bearer hereof, in Gold Coin of the United States of America, of the present standard of weight and fineness on the first day of September, One Thousand Nine Hundred and forty five (1945) at the Fiscal Agency of the said YOSEMITE SHORT LINE RAILWAY COMPANY in the City and County of San Francisco, State of California, with interest thereon at the rate of four and one half (4½) per cent per annum, payable at the same place in like Gold Coin of the United States of America, semi annually, on the first days of September and March in each and every year until the full payment and satisfaction of the said principal sum upon the presentation and surrender of the attached coupons, or interest warrants, hereunto annexed, as they severally become due.

To secure the payment of this bond and the interest thereon, a Mortgage or Deed of Trust of even date herewith has been executed by said YOSEMITE SHORT LINE RAILWAY COMPANY conveying all of its properties, rights, liberties, privileges, incomes, tolls, receipts, resources, franchises and interests, now held or hereafter to be acquired, to said Central Trust Company of California and its successor for the benefit of the owner of this bond, and all other bonds of the same series, which Mortgage or Deed of Trust has been duly recorded.

This bond is one of a series of Eight Thousand seven hundred and fifty (8750) bonds of like tenor and form, effect, amount and date, numbered consecutively from One (1) to Eight Thousand seven hundred and fifty (8750) both numbers inclusive, making in all a total bond issue of Eight Hundred and Seventy five Thousand ($875000) Dollars.

The holder of this bond is entitled to the security and benefit of the sinking fund provided in said mortgage or deed of trust, but this bond is not redeemable prior to the said first day of September One Thousand Nine Hundred and forty five (1945) without the consent of the holder thereof.

The said bonded indebtedness has been created by a resolution adopted by the unanimous vote of the Board of Directors of the said YOSEMITE SHORT LINE RAILWAY COMPANY and in the manner and form prescribed by law, and approved by the written assent or assents of the stockholders owning all of the subscribed and issued capital stock thereof, which assent or assents have been filed with the Secretary of the said YOSEMITE SHORT LINE RAILWAY COMPANY in the manner and form prescribed by law, prior to the ensealing and delivery hereof.

This bond shall not become obligatory, valid or negotiable until it shall have been authenticated by the signature of the Trustee, or its successor.

A tous ceux qui ces présentes verront: La Compagnie de Chemin de Fer "YOSEMITE SHORT LINE RAILWAY COMPANY" doit, pour valeur reçue à la Compagnie "Central Trust Company of California" Société dûment fondée et existant en vertu et d'après les lois de l'État de Californie, dont le siège et les bureaux pour la transaction des affaires sont situés à San Francisco, ville et Comté du même nom, État de Californie, ou au porteur, la somme de CENT ($100.00) Dollars somme que ladite Compagnie de Chemin de Fer "YOSEMITE SHORT LINE RAILWAY COMPANY" s'engage à payer à la Compagnie "Central Trust Company of California" ci-dessus désignée ou au porteur des présentes, en monnaie d'or des États Unis d'Amérique ayant alors une valeur égale à la monnaie actuelle comme poids et comme titre, à la date du premier Septembre mil neuf cent quarante cinq (1945) au bureau de la Trésorerie de la dite compagnie de Chemin de Fer "YOSEMITE SHORT LINE RAILWAY COMPANY" en la ville de San Francisco, Comté du même nom, État de Californie, avec intérêt sur ladite somme au taux de Quatre et demi (4½%) pour cent par an, payable audit lieu, également en monnaie d'or des États-Unis d'Amérique, semi-annuellement, les premier Septembre et premier Mars de chaque année successive jusqu'à parfait paiement et remboursement du capital ci-dessus, sur la présentation et contre remise des coupons ci-attachés ou des bons d'intérêts ci-annexés, séparément au fur et à mesure de leur échéance.

Pour garantir le paiement de cette Obligation et de ses intérêts, une hypothèque ou déclaration fidéicommis portant même date que les présentes, a été consentie par ladite compagnie de Chemin de Fer "YOSEMITE SHORT LINE RAILWAY COMPANY" en vertu de laquelle elle transfère tous les biens, droits immunités, privilèges, revenus, droits de péage, recettes, ressources, franchises et tous intérêts qu'elle possède actuellement ou qu'elle pourra acquérir par la suite, à la Compagnie "Central Trust Company of California" ci-dessus désignée ou à ses successeurs pour la garantie du détenteur de la présente Obligation et de toutes les autres Obligations de la même série, ladite hypothèque ou déclaration de fidéicommis a été dûment enregistrée.

La présente Obligation fait partie d'une série de Huit mille sept cent cinquante (8750) obligations de même teneur et forme, ayant les même effets, émises pour le même montant et portant la même date, numérotées consécutivement de un à Huit mille sept cent cinquante (1 à 8750), y compris la première et la dernière et formant en tout, une émission totale de Huit cent soixante quinze mille dollars ($875000).

Le détenteur de la présente Obligation a droit à la garantie et au bénéfice du fonds d'amortissement constitué par ladite hypothèque ou déclaration de fidéicommis, mais cette Obligation n'est pas remboursable avant le premier Septembre, comme il est dit ci-dessus, de l'année Mil neuf cent quarante cinq (1945) sans le consentement de son détenteur.

La constitution de cette dette garantie a été faite en vertu d'une résolution prise à la suite d'un vote unanime du Conseil d'Administration de la Compagnie de Chemin de Fer "YOSEMITE SHORT LINE RAILWAY COMPANY" de la manière et dans la forme prescrite par la loi et approuvée par le consentement ou les consentements écrits des actionnaires possédant la totalité des actions émises et souscrites de ladite Compagnie et, ce ou ces consentements ont été déposés entre les mains du Secrétaire de la compagnie de Chemin de Fer "YOSEMITE SHORT LINE RAILWAY COMPANY" de la manière et dans la forme prescrite par la loi avant que ces présentes n'aient été scellées et délivrées.

La présente Obligation ne deviendra obligatoire, valable ou négociable que lorsqu'elle aura été rendue authentique par l'apposition de la signature de la Société fidéicommissaire ou de ses successeurs.

In Witness Whereof, the said YOSEMITE SHORT LINE RAILWAY COMPANY has caused its corporate name to be hereunto subscribed by its President and Secretary thereunto duly authorized, and its corporate seal to be hereunto affixed, and has also caused the coupons hereto annexed to be duly numbered and authenticated by the facsimile of the signature of its Treasurer lithographed thereon, at the City and County of San Francisco, State of California, this first day of September, A.D. One Thousand Nine Hundred and five (1905).

Yosemite Short Line Railway Company

By *John Hancock* ITS SECRETARY

By *F. J. [illegible]* ITS PRESIDENT

Old Colony Steamboat (I), 1890s, Vignette of steamboat	75.00
Old Colony Steamboat Company (I), 1890s, Four and one-half percent bond, old double-stacked sidewheeler vignette	185.00
Old Colony Steamboat Company (U), 1890s	40.00
Oregon Improvement Company (I), 1880s, Ships vignette	100.00
Oregon Steam Navigation Company (I-N), 1870s, Sidewheeler ship vignette	210.00
Orinoco Steam Navigation Company of New York (I), 1850s, Figures in border	220.00
Orinoco Steam Navigation Company of New York (I), 1850s, Bond	160.00
Outboard Marine Corporation (I), 1960s, Three allegorical figures vignette	2.00
Pennsylvania Canal Company (I), 1870s, Riverboat vignette with stamp	145.00
Pere Marquette Transportation (I), 1890s, Gold bond, large steamship vignette	135.00
Philadelphia Maritime Exchange (I), 1880s, Ship vignette	110.00
Pioneer Steamship Company 1910s, Great Lakes freighter vignette	30.00
Pioneer Steamship Company (I), 1920s, Great Lakes freighter vignette	25.00
Portland and Booth Bay Steamboat Company (U), 1880s	24.00
Saint Petersburg Transportation Company (I), 1910s, Florida, Ships in harbor, train vignettes	38.00
Sea Train (I), 1920s	15.00
Sea Train Lines (I), 1940s, Eagle vignette	3.00
Sea Train Lines (I), 1950s and 1960s, Ship and train vignettes	4.00
Seafirst Company (I), 1970s, Bond, lady, ferryboat, harbor, and skyline vignettes	2.00
Sebago and Long Pond Steam Navigation Company (I), 1840s, Two vignettes of steamboats	185.00
Steamboat Helen (U), 1830s, New York	110.00
Submarine Signal Company (I), 1920s, Ship in stormy waters vignette, stamps	15.00
U.S. Shipbuilding Company (I), 1900s, New Jersey, Vignette of battleship	30.00
West Shore and Ontario Terminal Company (U), 1880s, Vignette of ships	45.00
Western Transit Company (U), 1880s, Sailing ship vignette	80.00

◀***Yosemite Short Line Railway Company (I), 1900s,*** *Train and sheepherder vignettes* ***185.00***

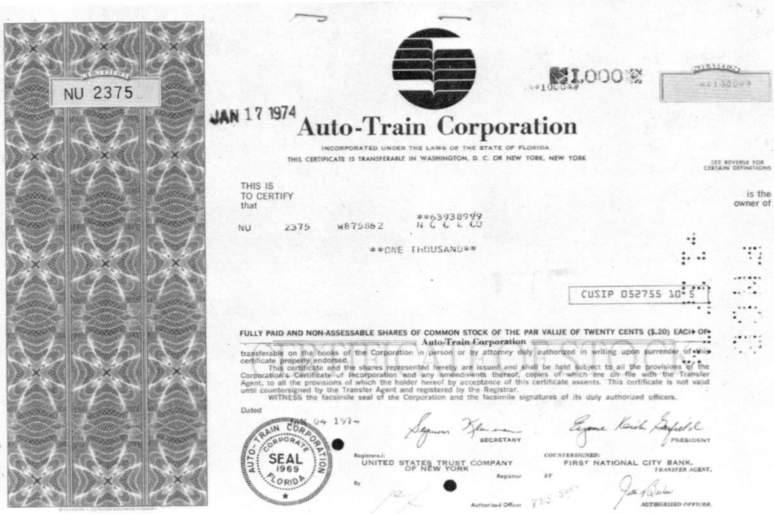
NU 2375

JAN 17 1974

$1,000

Auto-Train Corporation

INCORPORATED UNDER THE LAWS OF THE STATE OF FLORIDA

THIS CERTIFICATE IS TRANSFERABLE IN WASHINGTON, D. C. OR NEW YORK, NEW YORK

SEE REVERSE FOR CERTAIN DEFINITIONS

THIS IS TO CERTIFY that

is the owner of

NU 2375 W875862 **63938999 N C C & CO

ONE THOUSAND

CUSIP 052755 10 5

FULLY PAID AND NON-ASSESSABLE SHARES OF COMMON STOCK OF THE PAR VALUE OF TWENTY CENTS ($.20) EACH OF

Auto-Train Corporation

transferable on the books of the Corporation in person or by attorney duly authorized in writing upon surrender of this certificate properly endorsed.

This certificate and the shares represented hereby are issued and shall be held subject to all the provisions of the Corporation's Certificate of Incorporation and any amendments thereof, copies of which are on file with the Transfer Agent, to all the provisions of which the holder hereof by acceptance of this certificate assents. This certificate is not valid until countersigned by the Transfer Agent and registered by the Registrar.

WITNESS the facsimile seal of the Corporation and the facsimile signatures of its duly authorized officers.

Dated JAN 04 1974

AUTO-TRAIN CORPORATION CORPORATE SEAL 1969 FLORIDA

SECRETARY PRESIDENT

Registered: UNITED STATES TRUST COMPANY OF NEW YORK Registrar By Authorized Officer

COUNTERSIGNED: FIRST NATIONAL CITY BANK, TRANSFER AGENT, BY AUTHORIZED OFFICER.

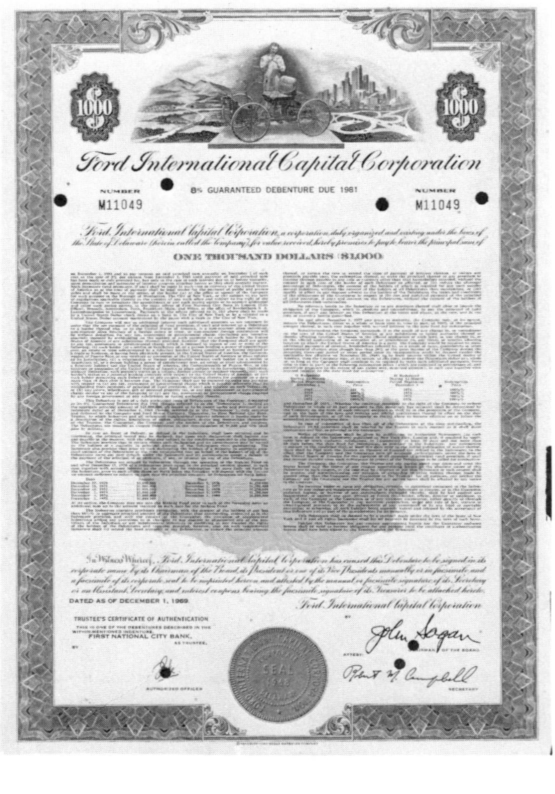
1000 1000

Ford International Capital Corporation

NUMBER M11049 8% GUARANTEED DEBENTURE DUE 1981 NUMBER M11049

Ford International Capital Corporation, a corporation duly organized and existing under the laws of the State of Delaware (herein called the Company), for value received, hereby promises to pay to bearer the principal sum of

ONE THOUSAND DOLLARS ($1,000)

In Witness Whereof, Ford International Capital Corporation has caused this Debenture to be signed in its corporate name by its Chairman of the Board, its President or one of its Vice Presidents manually or in facsimile, and a facsimile of its corporate seal to be imprinted hereon and attested by the manual or facsimile signature of its Secretary or an Assistant Secretary, and interest coupons bearing the facsimile signature of its Treasurer to be attached hereto.

DATED AS OF DECEMBER 1, 1969.

Ford International Capital Corporation

TRUSTEE'S CERTIFICATE OF AUTHENTICATION

THIS IS ONE OF THE DEBENTURES DESCRIBED IN THE WITHIN-MENTIONED INDENTURE. FIRST NATIONAL CITY BANK, AS TRUSTEE,

BY AUTHORIZED OFFICER

SEAL 1968

BY CHAIRMAN OF THE BOARD

ATTEST: SECRETARY

AIRCRAFT

Aerospace-Science Fund (I), 1960s, Eagle vignette	4.00
Aircraft Acceptance Corporation (I), 1960s, Eagle vignette	5.00
Autoplane Development Company of Nevada (I), 1930s, Flying eagle vignette	55.00
Aviation Corporation (I), 1940s, Eagle and map of United States vignette	6.00
Aviation-Electronics-Electrical Equipment (I), 1960s, Eagle vignette	4.00
Aviation Shares (I), 1960s, Steamship, trains, and old factory vignettes	4.00
Douglas Aircraft (U), 1900s, Specimen, globe separated by two allegorical figures vignette	45.00
Eastern Airlines (U), Specimen, kneeling man with company logo vignette	45.00
Fairchild Engine and Airplane Corporation (I), 1950s, Man, woman, and winged horse vignette	8.00
Flywarm Corporation of America (I), 1920s, Nevada, Large eagle vignette	42.00
Lincoln Aircraft Company (I), 1920s, Portrait of Lincoln vignette	80.00
Moore Aircraft Corporation (I), 1930s, Nevada, Flying eagle vignette	40.00
New York City Airport, Inc. (U), Specimen, old airport with old flying transport plane vignette	90.00
North American Aviation, Inc. (U), Specimen, flying Mercury with transport plane vignette	80.00
Pan-American World Airways (I), 1950s, Eagle, two hemispheres, allegorical figures vignettes	20.00
Pan-American World Airways (I), 1950s, Four and three-quarters percent bond, eagle, two hemispheres, allegorical figures vignettes	12.00
Peeksill Hydro-Aeroplane Company (U), 1910s, Airplane vignette	55.00
Pickwick Airways (I), 1920s, Standing woman on mountain with two flying transports vignettes	78.00
Resort Airlines (I), Eagle vignette	5.00
Robinson Airlines Corporation (I-N), 1940s, New York	20.00
Robinson Airlines Corporation (U), 1940s, New York	6.00
Tradewinds Airlines (U), Eagle vignette	6.00
Transcontinental and Western Air, Inc. (U), Specimen, perched eagle by bay vignette	55.00
Transinternational Airlines (U), 1900s, Nevada, Specimen, company logo vignette	30.00
Transworld Airlines (I), Eagle and plane vignette	27.00
Universal Aero-Transportation Company (U), 1910s, Arizona, Eagle and early aircraft vignette	25.00
United Aircraft Corporation (I), 1960s, Bond, planes, skyline vignette	5.00
United Airlines (I), Bond, winged Mercury with winged wheel vignette	5.00

◀ ***Auto-Train Corporation (I), 1970s, Florida,*** *Company logo, seal*	***3.00***
◀ ***Ford International Capital Corporation (I), 1960s,*** *Bond, Henry Ford and antique car vignette*	***12.00***

100 SHARES

No. D2622

INCORPORATED UNDER THE LAWS OF THE STATE OF NEVADA, AUGUST 9, 1945

100 Shares

COMMON STOCK

KAISER-FRAZER CORPORATION

5,000,000 SHARES - PAR VALUE $1.00 EACH

THIS CERTIFICATE IS TRANSFERABLE IN THE CITY OF NEW YORK, DETROIT, MICH., OR SAN FRANCISCO, CAL.

This Certifies that **SAM M. LESHTZ** is the owner of

ONE HUNDRED

Full Paid and Non-Assessable Shares, of the Par Value of One Dollar ($1.00) each, of the Common Stock of

KAISER-FRAZER CORPORATION

transferable in person or by duly authorized attorney upon surrender of this Certificate, properly endorsed. This Certificate is issued subject to all the terms of the Corporation's Articles of Incorporation as amended and By-Laws as amended (copies of which are on file at the office of the Transfer Agent), to which reference is hereby made with the same effect as if they were herein set forth in full and to all the provisions of which the holder hereof by acceptance of this Certificate assents.

This Certificate is not valid until countersigned by the Transfer Agent and registered by the Registrar.

WITNESS the seal of the Corporation and the signatures of its duly authorized officers.

Dated OCT 11 1945

KAISER-FRAZER CORPORATION INCORPORATED AUGUST 9, 1945 NEVADA

KAISER-FRAZER CORPORATION

SECRETARY. PRESIDENT.

REGISTERED: DETROIT TRUST COMPANY, REGISTRAR. BY AUTHORIZED OFFICER.

COUNTERSIGNED: NATIONAL BANK OF DETROIT, TRANSFER AGENT. BY AUTHORIZED OFFICER.

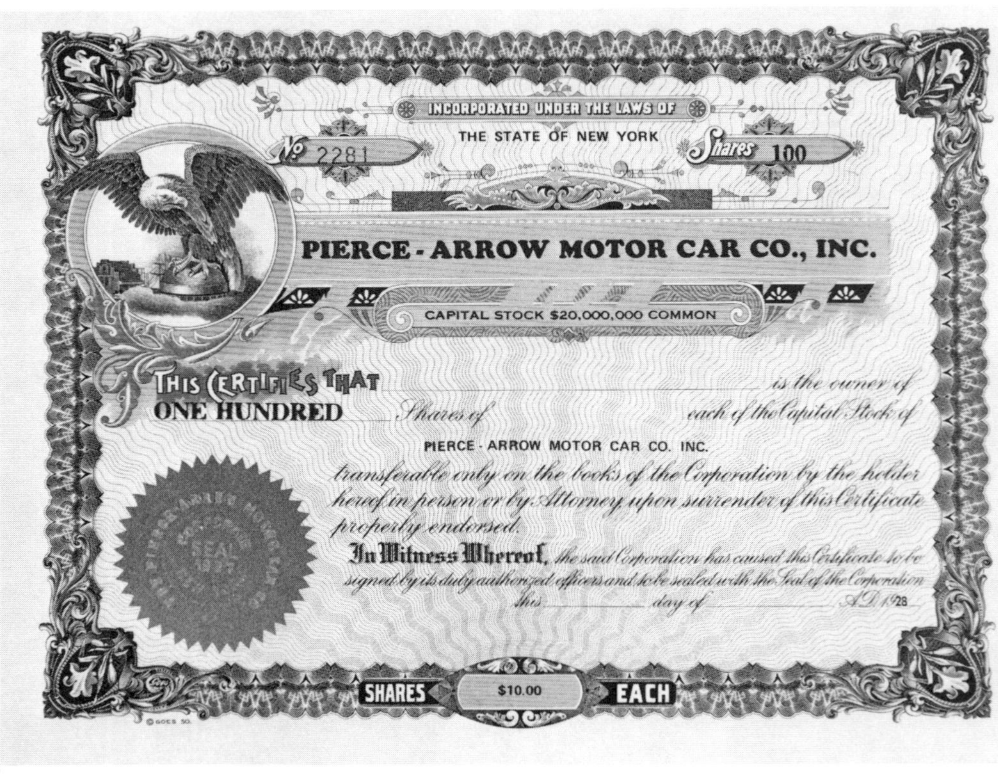

INCORPORATED UNDER THE LAWS OF THE STATE OF NEW YORK

No 2281

Shares 100

PIERCE - ARROW MOTOR CAR CO., INC.

CAPITAL STOCK $20,000,000 COMMON

THIS CERTIFIES THAT is the owner of

ONE HUNDRED Shares of each of the Capital Stock of

PIERCE - ARROW MOTOR CAR CO. INC.

transferable only on the books of the Corporation by the holder hereof in person or by Attorney upon surrender of this Certificate properly endorsed.

In Witness Whereof, *the said Corporation has caused this Certificate to be signed by its duly authorized officers and to be sealed with the Seal of the Corporation this day of A.D. 1928*

SHARES $10.00 EACH

© GOES 50.

CITY, COUNTY, AND STATE GOVERNMENTS

Alachua County (I), 1930s, Alabama, Five and one-half percent road and bridge bond, palm tree, Indian maiden, and ship vignette	**52.00**
Albany, City of (I), 1810s, Bond, embossed seal	**310.00**
Altoona, City of (I), 1880s, Bond, city by river, old train vignette	**35.00**
Altoona, City of (I), 1890s, Bond, city by river, state seal vignette	**25.00**
America, Confederate States of (I), 1860s, Eight percent bond, two ladies with sailing ship vignette	**62.00**
America, Confederate States of (I), 1860s, Eight percent bond, two ladies with sailing ship vignette	**55.00**
America, Confederate States of (I), 1860s, Eight percent bond, portrait and old city scene, reclining woman at bottom	**45.00**
America, Confederate States of (I), 1860s, Eight percent bond, portrait vignette	**78.00**
America, Confederate States of (I), 1860s, Eight percent bond, three figures surround portrait vignette	**80.00**
America, Confederate States of (I), 1860s, Fifth series six percent bond, mounted soldier vignette, two females in border	**30.00**
America, Confederate States of (I), 1860s, Four percent bond, sailing warships vignette	**63.00**
America, Confederate States of (I), 1860s, Seven percent bond, portrait of General Lee	**40.00**
Arkansas State Levee Bond (I), 1870s, Seven percent bond, riverboats on Mississippi River, seal vignette	**260.00**
Arkansas State Levee Bond (I), 1870s, Seven percent bond, sidewheeler and log raft vignette	**320.00**
Arkansas, State of (I), 1860s, Eight percent war bond state seal vignette	**49.00**
Arkansas, State of (I), 1860s, Seven percent railroad bond (Memphis and Little Rock Railroad)	**185.00**
Atlantic City, City of (I), 1890s, Five percent water gold bond, state seal, train and ship vignette	**90.00**
Bridgeport, City of (I), 1950s, Connecticut, Two and three-tenths percent school bond, large eagle vignette	**6.00**
Bristol, Borough of, 1960s, Pennsylvania (I), Three and three-fourths percent general fund bond, state seal vignette	**4.00**
Broome County, War Loan (I), 1860s, New York, Seven percent war bond, eagle vignette	**160.00**
Colorado Springs, City of (I), 1900s, Colorado, Four percent refunding bond	**40.00**
Colorado Springs, City of (I), 1900s, Public improvement gold bond, allegorical figure	**44.00**
Colorado Springs, City of, 1920s, Six percent paving and improvement gold bond (Series Number 69)	**22.00**
Connecticut, State of (I), 1780s, Interest-bearing note	**60.00**
Connecticut, State of (I), 1780s, Six percent bond	**210.00**
Connecticut, State of, U.S. Loan Office (I), 1790s, Certificate of loan	**475.00**
Cumberland County Power and Light (U), 1920s, Maine, Four and one-half percent gold bond, specimen	**70.00**
Delaware State of (I), 1900s, Six percent water improvement gold bond number four, state seal	**10.00**
Denver, City and County of (I), 1920s, Moffat Tunnel gold bond, state seal	**6.00**

◀ ***Kaiser-Frazer Corporation (I), 1940s and 50s*** ***6.00***

◀ ***Pierce-Arrow Motor Car Company (U), 1920s**, Eagle, gold seal, sailing ship* ***40.00***

Exhibit C

BN34291

LESS THAN 100 SHARES

NUMBER

SHARES

LESS THAN 100 SHARES

SC

STUDEBAKER CORPORATION

INCORPORATED UNDER THE LAWS OF THE STATE OF MICHIGAN

THIS CERTIFICATE IS TRANSFERABLE IN THE CITY OF NEW YORK OR IN THE CITY OF CHICAGO

THIS CERTIFIES THAT

IS THE OWNER OF

SEE REVERSE FOR CERTAIN DEFINITIONS

TENS	UNITS
1	1
2	2
3	3
4	4
5	5
6	6
7	7
8	8
9	9
0	0

FULLY PAID AND NON-ASSESSABLE SHARES OF THE COMMON STOCK, PAR VALUE $5 PER SHARE OF

Studebaker Corporation (hereinafter and on the back hereof sometimes called the Corporation) transferable on the books of the Corporation by the holder hereof in person or by duly authorized attorney, upon surrender of this certificate properly endorsed. This certificate and the shares represented hereby are issued and shall be held subject to all the provisions of the Articles of Incorporation, as amended, and the By-laws, as amended, of the Corporation and all amendments and supplements thereto (copies of which are on file with the Transfer Agent), to all of which each holder of this certificate, by acceptance hereof, assents. This certificate is not valid unless countersigned by the Transfer Agent and registered by the Registrar.

In Witness Whereof, Studebaker Corporation has caused facsimiles of the signatures of its proper officers and a facsimile of its corporate seal to be hereto affixed.

Studebaker Corporation

Dated:

S. B. Feuer
SECRETARY

B A Burlingame
PRESIDENT

STUDEBAKER CORPORATION SEAL

REGISTERED:
THE CHASE MANHATTAN BANK
REGISTRAR
BY
SPECIMEN
AUTHORIZED SIGNATURE

COUNTERSIGNED:
FIRST NATIONAL CITY BANK
TRANSFER AGENT
BY
SPECIMEN
AUTHORIZED OFFICER

© SECURITY-COLUMBIAN BANKNOTE COMPANY

No. 730

Shares

CERTIFICATE OF DEPOSIT

FOR

EIGHT PER CENT. CUMULATIVE CONVERTIBLE FIRST PREFERRED STOCK OF

WILLYS CORPORATION

UNDER AN AGREEMENT DATED FEBRUARY 3, 1921, BETWEEN HOWARD BAYNE, U. N. BETHELL, STEDMAN BUTTRICK, THOMAS B. GANNETT, ROBERT E. HUNTER, LECLANCHÉ MOEN AND ROBERT L. MONTGOMERY, COMMITTEE: FIRST PREFERRED STOCKHOLDERS OF WILLYS CORPORATION: AND COLUMBIA TRUST COMPANY, DEPOSITARY.

COLUMBIA TRUST COMPANY

NEW YORK CITY

Hereby certifies that *it has received from* Roger C Johnson

TWO *shares of stock as above stated, in trust subject to the terms and conditions of and deliverable as stated in the above mentioned agreement.*

The holder hereof assents to and is bound by the provisions of said agreement by receiving this certificate and is entitled to receive all the securities, benefits and advantages to which the depositor of said shares is or may become entitled pursuant to the provisions of said agreement. The interest represented by this certificate is assignable, subject to the terms and conditions of said agreement, by transfer upon books kept by this Company for that purpose, by the holder hereof in person or by attorney, upon the surrender of this certificate duly endorsed for transfer.

New York,

COLUMBIA TRUST COMPANY, DEPOSITARY,

By *Assistant Secretary.*

REPUBLIC BANK NOTE COMPANY

Edison County War Bond (I), 1860s, Seven percent bond, state seal 100.00
Essex County Volunteer War Bond (I), 1860s, New York, Seven percent bond, blue seal 80.00
Essex County Volunteer War Bond (I), 1860s, New York, Seven percent bond, red seal 90.00

Fallon, City of (I), 1911, Nevada, Sewer bond 85.00
Fallon, City of (I), 1911, Nevada, Water works bond 85.00
Fifth Louisiana Levee District (I), 1910s, Five percent bond, two ladies vignette 35.00
Fort Wayne, City of (I), 1920s, P. B. Aviation bond, radial-engine plane vignette 45.00
Fort Wayne, City of (I), 1930s, Four and one-fourth percent bond, buffalo and hunter vignette 8.00

Georgia, State of, County of Baldwin (U), 1860s, Bond 44.00
Georgia, State of (I), 1870s, Seven percent gold bond, two portraits and several figure vignettes 260.00

Indianapolis (I), 1920s, Four and one-half percent hospital bond, gold seal 9.00
Indianapolis (I), 1930s, Two percent city hall refunding bond 6.00
Indianapolis (I), 1950s, One and three-quarters percent airport bond, eagle vignette 5.00
Indiana, State of, County of Shelby (I), 1860s, Six percent bond, portrait, stamps 90.00

Jasper, County of (I), 1910s, Mississippi, Bond, Mossville School District, Eagle vignette 9.00
Jasper, County of (I), 1920s, Road bond, eagle vignette 8.00
Jasper, County of (I), 1930s, Five and three-quarters percent school bond, eagle with shield vignette 4.00
Jasper, County of (I), 1940s, Three and one-half percent school bond, eagle vignette 2.00
Jersey City, City of (I), 1880s, New Jersey, Six percent funded debt bond, passenger steamer vignette, state seal 83.00
Jersey City, City of (I), 1900s, One-thousand-dollar general gold bond, state seal 12.00
Jersey City, City of (I), 1910s, School gold bond 6.00
Jersey City, City of (I), 1920s, Gold bond signed by "Boss" Hagen 25.00
Jersey City, City of (I), 1930s, Four and one-half percent school refunding bond, state seal 4.00
Jersey City (I), 1930s, Bond with signature of Frank Hague 25.00
Jersey City, City of (I), 1940s, Four and one-half percent refunding gold bond, state seal 3.00
Jersey City, City of (I), 1940s, Street assessment bond 3.00
Jersey City, City of (I), 1960s, Vignette of state 5.00

Kansas, State of (I), 1870s, Bond, two vignettes 225.00
Kansas, State of (I), 1880s, Eight bond, scenic vignette 210.00
Kansas, State of (I), 1930s, School bond 7.00

Lakeshore City (I), 1960s, New Mexico, Sanitation district bond 15.00
Lawrence City (I), 1950s, Alabama, Gas tax antic bond 3.00
Lawrence County (I), 1950s, Alabama, Tax warrant 2.00
Letchfield, Town of (I), 1860s, Volunteer fund bond with stamps 66.00
Lewisboro, Town of (U), 1860s, New York, Seven percent military bond, eagle with national shield vignette 75.00
Lincoln, County of (I), 1930s, Oregon, Six percent refunding gold bond, large eagle vignette 5.00
Los Angeles, City of (I), 1920s, Four percent waterworks bond, large vignette of two seated women (seminude) with city seal, ships, and waterfall vignette 75.00
Los Angeles, City of (I), 1920s, Sewage disposal bond, large city official seal, other vignettes 17.00

◀ ***Studebaker Corporation (U),*** *Specimen, seated man holding auto piston, man working lathe, car designer at desk vignettes* ***25.00***
◀ ***Willys Corporation (I) 1920s,*** *Certificate of deposit* ***8.00***

Incorporated under the Laws of the State of New Jersey
No. 555
100 Shares
American-Hawaiian Steam Ship Company
This Certifies that George W. Wickersham
is entitled to One Hundred Shares
of the Capital Stock of the American-Hawaiian Steam Ship Company, transferable
only on the books of the Company in person or by Attorney on surrender
of this Certificate properly endorsed.
Witness the Seal of the Company and the signatures of the President
and Treasurer, this 17th day of April 1906
TREASURER.
PRESIDENT.
CAPITAL STOCK $3,500,000.
FULL PAID AND UNASSESSABLE
CANCELLED
MAY

INCORPORATED UNDER THE LAWS OF
OHIO.
CAPITAL STOCK
$3,000,000.00
NUMBER
1811
7
SHARES
THE PIONEER STEAMSHIP COMPANY
MENTOR SPECIAL DISTRICT,
LAKE COUNTY, OHIO.
This Certifies that J. W. SPEDDY is the owner of
SEVEN Shares of One Hundred Dollars each of the Capital Stock of
THE PIONEER STEAMSHIP COMPANY,
transferable only on the Books of the Corporation in
person or by Attorney on surrender of this Certificate.
In Witness Whereof the duly authorized officers of this Corporation have
hereunto subscribed their names and caused the corporate Seal to be hereto affixed at
Mentor Special District Lake County, O. this 8th day of March A.D. 1923
Secretary
President
SHARES
$100
EACH
COUNTERSIGNED
CENTRAL NATIONAL BANK SAVINGS & TRUST CO.
TRANSFER AGENT.
MAR 8 1923
STOCK TRANSFER
REGISTERED
CENTRAL NATIONAL BANK SAVINGS & TRUST CO.
REGISTRAR
REGISTERED
C.N.B.S.&T.CO.
AUDITING DEPT

Los Angeles, City of (I), 1920s, Street improvement bond 30.00
Los Angeles, City of (I), 1930s, Bond, waterworks vignette 25.00
Louisiana, State of (I), 1870s, Eight percent bond for railroad signed by Gov. H. C. Warmouth 360.00
Louisiana, State of (I), 1880s, Four percent bond, riverboats vignette 295.00
Louisiana, State of (I), 1890s, Baby bonds 5.00
Louisiana, State of (I), 1890s, Bond, state capitol building vignette 33.00
Louisiana, State of (I), 1890s, Consolidated bond, state building vignette 40.00
Louisiana, State of (I), 1890s, Consolidated 4 percent bond, signed by Gov. M. J. Foster, building and trees vignette 60.00
Louisiana, State of (I), 1930s, One-thousand-dollar refunding bond, pelican vignette 14.00

Maryland, State of (I), 1770s, Six percent bond 525.00
Maryland, State of (I), 1890s, Six percent bond, barrels and pail vignette 80.00
Massachusetts Bay (I), 1770s, Six percent note bond 510.00
Massachusetts Bay (I), 1770s, Six percent note bond, war committee 595.00
Massachusetts Bay, State of (I), 1770s, Six percent bond, soldier with sword vignette 725.00
Massachusetts Bay, State of (I), 1770s, Six percent bond, pine tree vignette 650.00
Massachusetts, Commonwealth of (I), 1780s, Six percent bond 650.00
Massachusetts, Commonwealth of (I), 1950s, August and October bond, eagle vignette 4.00
Massachusetts, Commonwealth of (I), 1950s, Capital outlay loan, eagle vignette 28.00
Massachusetts, Commonwealth of (I), 1950s, Eight and one-half percent highway flood relief bond, eagle vignette 3.00
Miami Beach, City of (U), 1960s, Improvement bond, eagle vignette, city seal 4.00
Minnesota, State of (I), 1890s, Six percent bond, farming vignette 110.00
Minnesota, State of (U), 1920s, Four and three-quarters percent bond, specimen, state seal 60.00
Mississippi, State of (I), 1830s, Five percent bond, two seated ladies, two eagles, and ships vignettes 325.00
Mississippi, State of (I), 1870s, State capitol building vignette 185.00
Missouri Defense Bond (I), 1860s, Red on blue 185.00
Missouri Defense Bond (I), 1860s, Red on tan 210.00
Monroe, County of (I), 1860s, New York, Indebtedness bond, female vignette 35.00
Montana State Warrant (I), 1890s, Standing lady vignette 35.00
Montana Territory (I), 1860s, Sailor vignette 175.00
Mossville, Mississippi (I), 1930s, Four percent bond 3.00
Muskegan Heights, City of (I), 1950s, Three and three-fourths percent highway bond, eagle vignette 6.00

Nashville, City of (I), 1860s, Tennessee, Eight percent bond, state capitol building vignette 110.00
Nevada State Bond (I), 1870s, Train and mountain scene 135.00
Nevada, State of (I), 1880s, State controllers warrant, train and miners vignette 35.00
Nevada State Warrant (I), 1880s, Orphan home fund 42.00
New Bergen, Township of (I), 1940s, New Jersey, Refunding bond, state seal 7.00
New Hampshire, State of (I), 1780s, Loan office certificate 425.00
New York, City of (I), 1850s and 1860s, Central Park assessment fund, city seal, signed by Major Wood 100.00
New York, City of (I), 1860s, Assessment fund bond, city hall vignette 110.00
New York, City of (I), 1860s, Revenue bond, vignette of city hall 150.00
New York, City of (I), 1860s, Tax repayment bond, city hall vignette, red seal 85.00
New York, City of (I), 1870s, City improvement stock, Indian and merchant with canoe and ships vignette 125.00

◀ ***American-Hawaiian Steam Ship Company (I), 1900s, New Jersey,*** *Vignette of old sailing ship* ***30.00***
◀ ***Pioneer Steamship Company, 1910s,*** *Great Lakes freighter vignette* ***30.00***

CERTIFICATE FOR LESS THAN 100 SHARES

CAPITAL $2,000,000.

NOT OVER TWENTY-FIVE SHS.

Number 2642

-25- Shares

INCORPORATED UNDER THE LAWS OF THE STATE OF MAINE

SUBMARINE SIGNAL COMPANY.

This Certifies that JOSEPH W. POWELL ----- is entitled to ----- TWENTY FIVE ----- Shares of the Capital Stock of the Submarine Signal Company transferable on the books of the Company by the holder hereof in person or by Attorney or by assignment properly endorsed hereon and upon surrender of this Certificate.

SHARES $25 EACH

In Witness Whereof the said Company has caused its corporate seal to be hereto affixed and this certificate to be signed by its President and Treasurer this JUN 22 1922 day of A.D. 19

TREASURER. PRESIDENT.

OLD COLONY TRUST COMPANY, REGISTRAR

STATE STREET TRUST COMPANY, (BOSTON) TRANSFER AGENT

FULL PAID AND NON-LIABLE

AMERICAN BANK NOTE COMPANY, NEW YORK & BOSTON

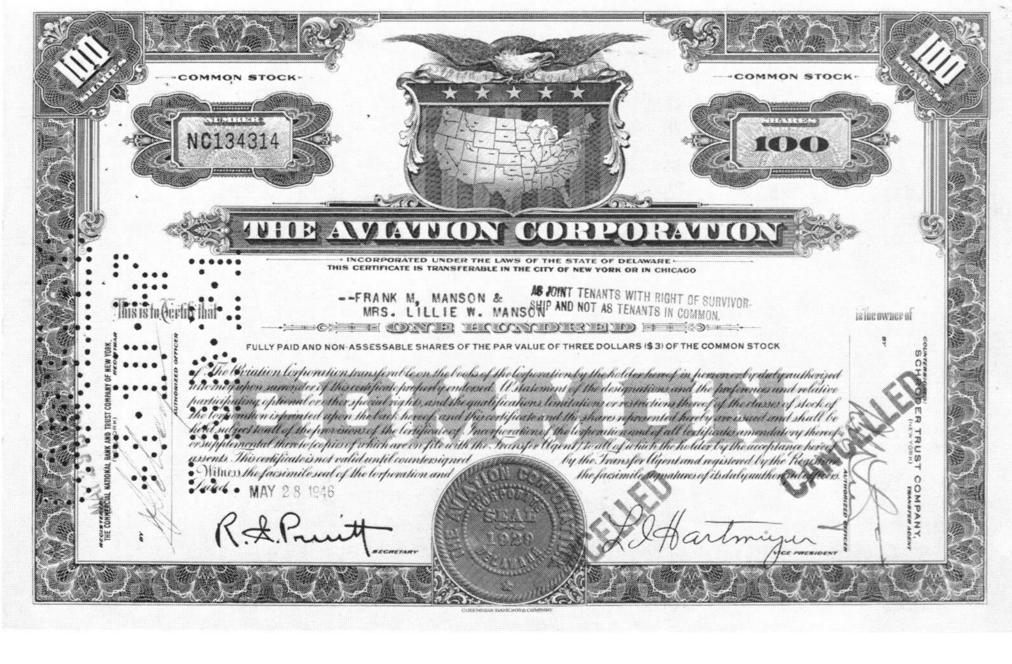

100 SHARES

COMMON STOCK

NUMBER NC134314

SHARES 100

THE AVIATION CORPORATION

INCORPORATED UNDER THE LAWS OF THE STATE OF DELAWARE

THIS CERTIFICATE IS TRANSFERABLE IN THE CITY OF NEW YORK OR IN CHICAGO

This is to Certify that --FRANK M. MANSON & MRS. LILLIE W. MANSON AS JOINT TENANTS WITH RIGHT OF SURVIVORSHIP AND NOT AS TENANTS IN COMMON. is the owner of

ONE HUNDRED

FULLY PAID AND NON-ASSESSABLE SHARES OF THE PAR VALUE OF THREE DOLLARS ($3) OF THE COMMON STOCK of The Aviation Corporation transferable on the books of the Corporation by the holder hereof in person or by duly authorized attorney upon surrender of this certificate properly endorsed. A statement of the designations and the preferences and relative participating, optional or other special rights, and the qualifications, limitations or restrictions thereof of the classes of stock of the Corporation is printed upon the back hereof, and this certificate and the shares represented hereby are issued and shall be held subject to all of the provisions of the Certificate of Incorporation of the Corporation and of all certificates amendatory thereof or supplemental thereto (copies of which are on file with the Transfer Agent) to all of which the holder by the acceptance hereof assents. This certificate is not valid until countersigned by the Transfer Agent and registered by the Registrar.

Witness the facsimile seal of the Corporation and the facsimile signatures of its duly authorized officers.

Dated MAY 28 1946

SECRETARY VICE PRESIDENT

THE AVIATION CORPORATION CORPORATE SEAL 1929 DELAWARE

CANCELLED

COUNTERSIGNED: SCHRODER TRUST COMPANY, (NEW YORK) TRANSFER AGENT

REGISTERED: THE COMMERCIAL NATIONAL BANK AND TRUST COMPANY OF NEW YORK, REGISTRAR

COLUMBIAN BANK NOTE COMPANY

New York, City of (I), 1870s, City parks improvement stock seal 50.00
New York, City of (I), 1870s, Improvement and assessment bonds 50.00
New York, City of (I), 1870s, Revenue bond, vignette of city hall 140.00
New York, City of (I), 1890s, Hotel license, excise certificate 135.00
New York, City of (I), 1890s, Saloon liquor license 150.00
New York, City of, Insurance Company, 1920s, New York, Skyline vignette 5.00
New York, County of (I), 1860s, Revenue bonds, city hall vignette 80.00
New York, County of (I), 1860s, Seven percent bond, red seal 90.00
New York, County of (I), 1870s, Seven percent bond, red seal 85.00
New York, State (I), 1810s, Seven percent stock bond 225.00
New York, State of (I), 1830s, Erie Canal improvement five percent loan 260.00
New York, State of (I), 1830s, Five percent stock, Black River Canal 265.00
New York, State of (I), 1830s, New York, Chenango Canal five percent bond, two cherubs vignette 265.00
New York, State of (I), 1830s, New York, Chenango Canal Five percent bond, two figures with eagle vignette 260.00
New York, State of (I), 1840s, Seven percent canal department stock debt 210.00
New York, State of (I), 1840s, Five and one-half percent stock, comptrollers office 210.00
New York, State of (I), 1850s, Six percent canal revenue certificate 255.00
New York, State of (I), 1860s, Certificate of indebtedness, signed by Civil War Governor R. E. Fenton 45.00
New York, State of (I), 1860s, Seven percent civil war bounty bond 145.00
New York, State of (I), 1860s, Seven percent stock bond, comptroller's office 150.00
New York, State of (I), 1960s, General revenue bond, Power Authority 4.00
Newark Ohio Waterworks (I), 1880s, New York, Six percent bond, prehistoric scene and water tower vignette 40.00
Newbury County (South Carolina) (U), Two and nine-tenths percent road bond, eagle vignette 4.00
Norfolk, City of (I), 1870s, Eight percent street paving bond 70.00
North Bergen Township of, State of New Jersey (I), 1920s, Improvement note, state seal vignette 4.00
North Carolina, State of (I), 1860s, Six percent bond, state capitol building vignette 185.00
North Carolina, State of (U), 1900s, Four percent bond specimen, two seated figures with state seal vignette 75.00
North Danville, Town of (U), 1880s, Virginia,, Train and landscape vignette 75.00

Oklahoma, State of (U), 1910s, Building fund bond, state seal 12.00
Ontonagon Town Site Company (U), 1880s, Michigan, State seal 12.00
Orange, City of (I), 1950s, Bond, housing authority, woman with houses vignette 2.00
Owensboro Waterworks (I), 1880s, Kentucky, Five percent bond, eagle vignette 40.00

Panama Pacific Exposition Bond (I), 1910s, San Francisco bond to finance world exposition, waterfront scene with winged messenger vignette 95.00
Passaic, County of (I), 1930s, New Jersey, Road, bridge, and building bond, figure holding winged wheel vignette 3.00
Passaic, County of, Board of Education in the Township of Wayne (I), 1950s and 1960s, New Jersey, Bonds 2.00
Pennsylvania, Commonwealth of (I), 1790s,Three percent bond 520.00
Pennsylvania, Commonwealth of (I), 1790s, Unfunded debt 500.00
Pennsylvania, Commonwealth of (I), 1850s, Five percent bond; portraits, man and woman figures, and seal vignette 310.00

◀ ***Submarine Signal Company (I), 1920s***, *Ship in stormy waters vignette, stamps* ***15.00***
◀ ***Aviation Corporation, the (I), 1940s***, *Eagle and map of United States vignette* ***6.00***

REGISTERED
REGISTERED
1000
1000
RM27200
UNITED AIRCRAFT CORPORATION
RM27200
4½% SUBORDINATED DEBENTURE, DUE OCTOBER 1, 1992
(CONVERTIBLE ON OR BEFORE OCTOBER 1, 1977, UNLESS PREVIOUSLY REDEEMED)
United Aircraft Corporation, a corporation duly organized and existing under the laws of the State of Delaware (herein referred to as the "Company"), for value received, hereby promises to pay to
---HARVARD & CO---
or registered assigns, the principal sum of
ONE THOUSAND DOLLARS
Reference is made to the further provisions of this Debenture set forth on the reverse hereof. Such further provisions shall for all purposes have the same effect as though fully set forth at this place.
This Debenture shall not be valid or become obligatory for any purpose until the certificate of authentication hereon shall have been signed by the Trustee under the Indenture referred to on the reverse hereof.
In Witness Whereof, United Aircraft Corporation has caused this Debenture to be executed in its corporate name by the facsimile signature of its Chairman, its President or one of its Vice Presidents and impressed or imprinted with its corporate seal or a facsimile thereof, attested by the manual or facsimile signature of its Secretary or an Assistant Secretary.
United Aircraft Corporation
DATED:
TRUSTEE'S CERTIFICATE OF AUTHENTICATION
This is one of the Debentures described in the within-mentioned Indenture.
FIRST NATIONAL CITY BANK,
AS TRUSTEE,
BY
AUTHORIZED OFFICER
ATTEST:
BY
SECRETARY
PRESIDENT

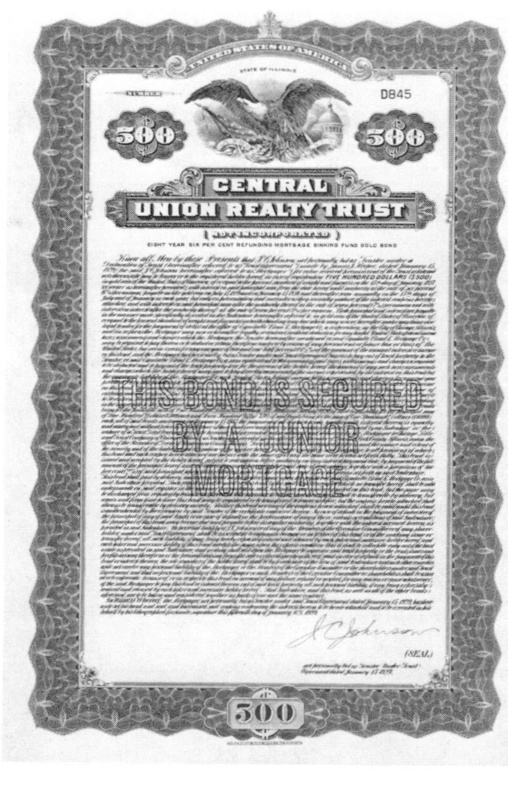

UNITED STATES OF AMERICA
STATE OF ILLINOIS
D845
500
500
CENTRAL
UNION REALTY TRUST
EIGHT YEAR SIX PER CENT REFUNDING MORTGAGE SINKING FUND GOLD BOND
FIVE HUNDRED DOLLARS ($500)
THIS BOND IS SECURED
BY A JUNIOR
MORTGAGE
(SEAL)
500

Pennsylvania, Commonwealth of, District of Richmond (**I**), **1850s**, Six percent bond, Standing woman with anchor and gears in front of train and Harbor City, six vignettes and portraits in border **320.00**
Pennsylvania, Corporated, District of, Philadelphia County (**I**), **1850s**, Six percent bond, two portraits, three seated women and eagle vignette **315.00**
Pennsylvania State Treasurer Warrant (**I, 1850s**), Farm scene, two corner figures vignettes **55.00**
Philadelphia, City of (**I**), **1850s**, Five percent bond, Indians vignette, embossed seal **95.00**
Philadelphia, City of (**I**), **1850s**, Many vignettes, including portraits of Washington and Franklin, train **100.00**
Philadelphia, City of (**I**), **1850s**, Six percent bond, many vignettes **90.00**
Philadelphia, City of (**I**), **1860s**, Six percent bond, Independence Hall, embossed seal vignette **90.00**
Philadelphia, City of (**I**), **1870s**, Six percent bond, Independence Hall, embossed seal vignette **60.00**
Philadelphia, City of (**I**), **1880s**, Four percent bond, City Hall and portraits, plus woman and portraits in corner **160.00**
Philadelphia, City of (**I**), **1880s**, Six percent bond, city hall and portraits, plus woman and portraits in corner **195.00**
Philadelphia, City of (**I**), **1890s**, Sewer and repaving bond **42.00**
Philadelphia, City of (**I**), **1900s**, Three percent bond, portrait plus two seated figures vignette **155.00**
Philadelphia, City of (**I**), **1910s**, City hall vignette and portrait **35.00**
Poplar Bluff, City of (**I**), **1910s**, Five percent funding bond, eagle vignette **8.00**
Poughkeepsie, City of (**I**), **1860s**, Six percent bond, Women, soldiers, and eagle vignette **70.00**
Poughkeepsie, City of (**I**), **1870s**, Seven percent sewer bond, Indian women and eagle vignette **45.00**
Poughkeepsie, City of (**I**), **1870s**, Seven percent water bond **72.00**
Poughkeepsie, City of (**I**), **1880s**, Four and one-half percent second bounty bond, signed by Mayor E. White **55.00**
Providence, City of, and Providence Plantations (**U**), **1800s**, Old city vignette **50.00**
Providence, City of (**I**), **1890s**, Pilgrims and Indians vignette, plus two additional vignettes at sides **55.00**
Providence, City of (**I**), **1900s**, Bond, pilgrims and Indians vignette **38.00**
Providence, City of (**I**), **1910s**, Bond, pilgrims and Indians vignette **25.00**
Providence, City of (**I**), **1930s**, Two and three-fourths percent bond, P. W. A. muncipal dock bond, pilgrims and Indians vignette **20.00**
Providence, City of (**U**), **1880s**, State capitol vignette **26.00**

Rawlins County, 1920s, Kansas, Four and three-fourths percent school bond **5.00**
Rensselaer, County of (**I**), **1900s**, Three and one-half percent highway improvement bond, two ladies with state seal vignette **42.00**
Rensselaer County Toll Road Bond (**I**), **1900s**, Three percent bond, eagle with flag vignette **28.00**
Rhode Island, State of (**Providence**) (**I**), **1890s**, Four percent highway loan bond, Indians and Pilgrims vignette **35.00**
Richmond Water Company (**I**), **1880s, Maine** Five percent bond, water fountain with aqueduct vignette **45.00**
Rose Hill (**I**), **1940s, Mississippi**, Three and one-fourth percent school bond, eagle with seal vignette **2.00**

San Francisco Airport (**I**), **1950s**, Bond, vignette of four-engined aircraft **25.00**
San Francisco, City and County of (**I**), **1850s**, One-thousand dollar funded debt bond, courthouse vignette **260.00**
San Francisco, City and County of (**I**), **1850s**, Six percent bond, city hall vignette **120.00**
San Francisco, City and County of (**I**), **1860s**, Five hundred dollar bond, bay scene, unloading ship, mayor's signature **485.00**

◀ ***United Aircraft Corporation (I), 1960s,*** *Bond, planes, skyline vignette* ***5.00***
◀ ***Central Union Realty Trust (I), 1920s,*** *Six percent bond, eagle, flag, and capitol dome vignette* ***8.00***

INCORPORATED UNDER THE LAWS OF THE STATE OF ILLINOIS

NUMBER 5

SHARES 142

Fourteen Thirty Chicago Avenue Building Corporation

AUTHORIZED CAPITAL STOCK 900 SHARES WITHOUT PAR VALUE

This Certifies that C. H. SEARLE is the owner of One Hundred Forty-Two - - - - - - - - - - - - - - shares, fully paid and non-assessable, *except as on the reverse hereof otherwise provided, of the Capital Stock of* **Fourteen Thirty Chicago Avenue Building Corporation,** *transferable only on the books of the Corporation by the owner in person or by duly authorized attorney, upon surrender of this Certificate properly endorsed.*

This certificate is issued subject to all provisions of the Certificate of Incorporation and of the By-Laws of the Corporation (as from time to time amended) and as well, the terms and conditions referred to on the reverse of this Certificate, and the owner, for himself, his legal representatives, heirs at law and immediate and remote assigns, by receiving delivery of this Certificate, conclusively evidences his agreement thereto and acquiescence therein.

Witness *the Seal of the Corporation and the signatures of its duly authorized officers this* 11th *day of* October *A. D. 19*[illegible]

E. A. Heidman
Asst SECRETARY

Victor C. Carlson
PRESIDENT

DWIGHT & M. H. JACKSON, CHICAGO

San Francisco, City and County of (I), 1860s, Five-thousand dollar seven percent bond, sailing ships in San Francisco Harbor, embossed seal **180.00**
San Francisco, City and County of (I), 1860s, One-thousand dollar seven percent bond, embossed seal **110.00**
San Francisco, City and County of (I), 1900s, Five percent fire protection bond, large battleship scene **43.00**
San Francisco, City and County of (I), 1940s, Airport bond, airplane vignette **23.00**
San Francisco, City and County of (I), 1940s, Juvenile court bond, eagle vignette **14.00**
San Francisco, City and County of (I), 1940s, Two and one-half percent sewer bond, workers laying sewer lines vignette **10.00**
San Francisco, City and County of (I), 1950s, Two and one-fourth percent hospital bond, Laguna Harbor home vignette **6.00**
San Francisco, City and County of (I), 1950s, Two and three-fourths percent school bond, eagle vignette **6.00**
San Francisco City Bond (I), 1850s, Six percent bond, city hall vignette **380.00**
San Francisco, City of (I), 1850s, Five hundred dollar bond, San Francisco Bay vignette and four others, signed by Van Ness **420.00**
San Francisco, City of (I), 1860s, Five hundred dollar seven percent bond, ships in harbor vignette **175.00**
San Francisco, City of (I), 1860s, One thousand dollar seven percent bond, Mother Earth vignette, embossed seal **110.00**
San Francisco, City of (I), 1900s, Four and one-half percent water bond, cascading water vignette **28.00**
San Francisco, City of (I), 1900s, Water supply and one-half percent bond, embossed seal, water reservoir vignette **18.00**
San Francisco, City of (I), 1910s, Five percent exposition bond, angel vignette **22.00**
San Francisco, City of (I), 1910s, Five percent street railway bond, trolley and early autos vignette **28.00**
San Francisco, City of (I), 1910s, Four percent water bond, waterfall and river vignette **40.00**
San Francisco, City of (I), 1920s, Five percent school gold bond, *The Thinker* vignette **14.00**
San Francisco City Stock (I), 1850s, Ten percent bond, Embarcadero waterfront vignette **110.00**
San Francisco, County of (I), 1850s, Bond, George Washington vignette **270.00**
San Francisco Fire Protection (I), 1900s, Eight percent bond, Warships in harbor vignette **30.00**
San Francisco Garbage System (I), 1900s, Five percent bond, ships in harbor vignette **30.00**
San Francisco Municipal Bond (I),1900s, Three and one-half percent bond **30.00**
San Francisco School Bond (I), 1870s, One thousand dollar seven percent bond, city hall vignette **110.00**
Santa Clara, County of (I), 1870s, Seven percent bond, vignette of domed county building **210.00**
Schuylkill Water Company (U), 1880s, Waterfalls, embossed seal vignette **15.00**
South Bend, City of (I), 1950s, Sewage works revenue Bond, eagle vignette **4.00**
South Carolina (I), 1830s, Five percent bond **95.00**
South Carolina (I), 1830s, Five percent stock certificate of 250 pounds sterling, steamer with seated woman vignette **85.00**
South Carolina (I), 1860s, Six percent bond palmetto tree or vignette of George Washington **85.00**
South Carolina (U), 1860s, Six percent bond, palmetto tree vignette **35.00**
South Carolina (U), 1860s, Six percent stock certificate, error in printing: $30–$35 **110.00**
South Carolina (I), 1870s, Deficiency stock certificate, palm tree and farm scene **40.00**
South Carolina (I), 1870s, Fifty dollar deficiency bond, palm tree vignette **50.00**
South Carolina (I), 1870s, Six percent bond, Allegorical figures and cotton boll vignette **55.00**
South Carolina (U), 1870s, Six percent bond, Allegorical figures and cotton boll vignette **30.00**

◀ ***Fourteen Thirty Chicago Avenue Building Corporation (I), 1920s,*** *Eagle on rock vignette* ***2.00***

UNITED STATES OF AMERICA
STATE OF ILLINOIS
100
100
NUMBER
202
ROSELAND BLOCK
SOUTHWEST CORNER MICHIGAN AVENUE AND 111TH STREET, CHICAGO, ILLINOIS.
SIX PER CENT. FIRST MORTGAGE GOLD BOND
Know all Men by these Presents:
ROSELAND BLOCK
JULY, 1933.
$3.00
NUMBER
202
CHICAGO TITLE AND TRUST CO.
BY
ITS CASHIER
No.16
No.18
No.19
ROSELAND BLOCK
JAN. 1934.
$3.00
NUMBER
202
No.17
of said taxes, assessments and charges so required to be deducted and to pay out of the mortgaged property to or for the account of the holder hereof the amount of any such taxes, assessments and charges which the holder hereof may have to pay directly on account of the income represented by the interest on this bond, but the aggregate liability of the Mortgagor for such United States federal income taxes, assessments and charges for any one year provided for by this paragraph shall not exceed two per cent (2%) of the amount of the annual interest on this bond.
This bond is one of a series of five hundred eight (508) bonds, numbered consecutively from one (1) to five hundred eight (508), both inclusive, of like form, tenor and effect, except as to denomination, number and date of maturity thereof, amounting in the aggregate to the principal sum of Two Hundred Fifty Thousand Dollars ($250,000)
manner to bearer, and thereafter it shall be transferable by delivery, but again and from time to time this bond may be registered or be transferred to bearer as before, but the coupons hereto attached shall always be transferable by delivery merely.
Neither this bond nor any of the coupons hereto attached shall be valid until this bond is authenticated by the execution by said Trustee of the certificate endorsed hereon. In case of default in the payment of interest or of the principal of any of said bonds or in case of default in the performance of any of the covenants or conditions of said Indenture, the principal of this bond may become due and payable before its regular maturity, together with the interest accrued hereon, as provided in said Indenture.
No personal liability of the Mortgagor shall be asserted or be enforcible because or in respect of this bond, or of the making, issue or transfer thereof, all such liability, if any, being hereby expressly waived by each taker and holder hereof, and each successive holder of this bond accepts the same upon the express condition, that it shall be collectible only out of said mortgaged property, as provided in said Indenture and for by recourse to the guaranty of this bond by Fred. Bernstein and Steck L. Bernstein, endorsed hereon.
Said Indenture and this bond, as well as all of the other bonds aforesaid, are to be taken and considered together as parts of one and the same contract.
IN WITNESS WHEREOF the Mortgagor, as Trustee under the said Trust Agreement dated April 17, 1923, and not individually, has caused these presents to be signed by its President or Vice-President, and its corporate seal to be hereunto affixed, and to be attested by its Secretary or Assistant Secretary, and has caused said coupons evidencing the interest hereon to be hereto attached and to be executed in its behalf by the lithographed fac simile signature of its Cashier, this first day of July, A.D. 1925.
Liberty Trust and Savings Bank, as Trustee under the Trust Agreement dated April 17, 1923, known as Trust Number 308, and not individually,
Attest:
BY
ITS SECRETARY.
ITS PRESIDENT.
CENTRAL BANKNOTE COMPANY
CHICAGO.

South Carolina, State of (I), **1800s**, Six percent loan, vignettes of sailing ships, seated woman, old soldier, and portrait of Washington **80.00**
South Carolina, State of (U), **1800s**, Consolidated stock issue, portrait of Washington, sailing ship, cotton picker, and figures vignettes **45.00**
South Carolina, State of (U), **1800s**, Six percent stock bond, seated women and cotton boll vignettes **28.00**
Stamford,City of (I), **1960s**, Bond Specimen **5.00**

Texas, Late Republic of (I), **1850s**, Public debt **120.00**
Texas, Republic of (I), Eight percent bond, cattle, steamboat vignette, five stars at bottom **60.00**
Texas, Republic of (I), **1840s**, Certificate of stock, two vignettes of man and woman **185.00**
Toledo, City of (I), **1960s**, Bond, eagle vignette **2.00**

United States Centennial International Exhibition (I), **1870s**, Many vignettes of people who built the United States during the first 100 years **1250.00**
United States, Treasury of (I), **1790s**, Three percent bond, Alexander Hamilton's signature as secretary of the treasury **1600.00**

Vallejo City Water Company (U), **1860s, California**, Early vignette of Vallejo, plus fountains and birdbath **30.00**

Wayne, Township of (I), **1950s**, State seal **2.00**
West Hoboken (I), **1890s**, Five percent improvement redemption bond, state seal and beehive vignette **35.00**
Westport, Town of (I), **1920s, Connecticut**, school bond **14.00**

Yonkers, City of, Tax relief bond, assessment of street paving issues, horses and coach in front of vignette **5.00**
Yonkers, City of (I), Consolidated bond, allegorical figures, eagle vignette **65.00**
Yonkers, City of (U), **1890s**, School bond **12.00**

◀***Roseland Block** (I), **1920s**, Six percent gold bond, large eagle vignette* ***5.00***

NUMBER
360

$100 $100

UNITED STATES OF AMERICA

STATE OF ILLINOIS

SIX AND ONE-HALF PER CENT

FIRST MORTGAGE REAL ESTATE GOLD BOND

The Wynlake Crest Apartments

SECURED BY FIRST MORTGAGE ON LAND AND BUILDING
LOCATED AT 4717 WINTHROP AVENUE,
CHICAGO, ILLINOIS.

The undersigned, MICHAEL L. E. JENSEN and ANNA R. JENSEN, his wife, for value received, hereby promise to pay to the bearer (or the registered owner) hereof, on the **FIFTEENTH DAY OF MAY, 1939,** the sum of

ONE HUNDRED DOLLARS ($100.00)

together with interest thereon from the date hereof at the rate of six and one-half per cent per annum, payable semi-annually on the fifteenth day of May and November in each year, and at maturity hereof, on the presentation and surrender of the attached interest coupons as they severally become due. Both said principal and interest are payable in gold coin of the United States of America, of the present standard of weight and fineness, at the office of ERNEST W. J. HUGHES & CO., in the City of Chicago, and bear interest after maturity at the highest rate for which it is now legal to contract. The undersigned are held and firmly bound unto the bearer (or the registered owner) hereof, for the payment of said principal and interest as herein specified, and they bind themselves, their heirs, executors and administrators for the payment of said sums to said bearer (or the registered owner) hereof.

This bond is one of a series of Five Hundred Seventy-Four (574) bonds of like date and tenor, (except as to number, maturity and denomination) numbered consecutively from One (1) to Five Hundred Seventy-Four (574), both inclusive, Two Hundred Forty-Five (245) of said bonds being for the sum of One Hundred Dollars ($100) each, Two Hundred Sixty-Seven (267) of said bonds being for the sum of Five Hundred Dollars ($500) each, and Sixty-Two of said bonds being for the sum of One Thousand Dollars ($1,000) each, amounting in the aggregate to the sum of Two Hundred Twenty Thousand Dollars ($220,000.00) and secured by a Trust Deed of even date herewith, executed by MICHAEL L. E. JENSEN and ANNA R. JENSEN, his wife, to CHICAGO TITLE AND TRUST COMPANY of Chicago, Illinois, as Trustee, upon the following described real estate, to-wit: Lot Twelve (12) in the Subdivision of Lots One Hundred Fifty (150) to One Hundred Fifty-Seven (157), both inclusive, in the William Deering Surrenden Subdivision in the West Half (W1/2) of the North East Quarter (NE1/4) of Section 17, Township 40 North, Range 14, East of the Third Principal Meridian, in Cook County, Illinois; together with all buildings, improvements and appurtenances thereunto attached or belonging, now or hereafter upon said premises, including all furniture, furnishings, fittings, equipment, window screens, curtain fixtures, window shades, door screens, furnaces, ranges, gas and electric light fixtures, and steam and other apparatus, and any and all other fixtures which may be placed in any building erected or hereafter standing upon said premises, together with all the rents, issues and profits which shall hereafter accrue from said premises, which said rents, issues and profits are hereby conveyed and assigned to said Trustee and to its successors in Trust.

This bond shall pass by delivery unless registered as to the principal hereof upon the books of said ERNEST W. J. HUGHES & CO. but after registration duly endorsed hereon, no transfer except upon said books shall be valid unless the last registration shall be made to bearer. The coupons hereto attached, however, shall always be transferable by delivery. This bond shall not become valid or obligatory until authenticated by the signature of the CHICAGO TITLE AND TRUST COMPANY, Trustee, to the certificate on the back hereof. The liability of the undersigned hereon shall continue in its original force until the principal and interest are paid in full. All of the bonds and interest coupons attached thereto herein described are equally in all things secured by said Trust Deed without any preference or priority whatsoever of the lien thereof in favor of any one or more of said bonds or coupons over any one or more of the others.

Said Trust Deed and this bond are parts of the same contract and are to be construed together.

It is further expressly agreed that if default be made in the payment of interest or principal of any of said bonds, or if default is made in the performance of any of the covenants in the said Trust Deed contained, the principal of this bond may become due and payable before its regular maturity, together with interest accrued thereon, as provided in said Trust Deed.

The right is hereby reserved by the undersigned to pay before maturity, any or all of said bonds from time to time outstanding and unpaid, on any semi-annual interest day, by the payment of principal, accrued interest and a premium of three (3) per cent of the principal of the bonds so paid and on giving sixty (60) days previous written notice, as prescribed in said Trust Deed, provided, however, that said bonds so prepaid, shall be paid in the reverse of their numerical order.

And, further to secure the payment of the principal and interest of this bond, we and each of us do hereby jointly and severally, authorize irrevocably, Charles R. Young, or any attorney of any court of record, to appear for us or either or any of us in such court during term time or vacation, at any time after this bond becomes due, whether by election as aforesaid, or by the regular maturity thereof, and confess a judgment without process against us or either or any of us in favor of the legal holder of this bond, for such amount as may appear to be unpaid thereon, together with interest, costs and reasonable attorney's fees, and hereby waive and release all errors which may intervene in such proceeding and consent to an immediate execution upon said judgment, and that no writ of error or appeal shall be prosecuted upon said judgment, nor any bill in equity filed to interfere with the operation of the same, hereby ratifying and confirming all that said attorney may lawfully do by virtue hereof.

IN WITNESS WHEREOF, said MICHAEL L. E. JENSEN and ANNA R. JENSEN, his wife, have hereunto set their hands and affixed their seals, and have caused the interest coupons hereto attached to be executed with their lithographed signatures at Chicago, Illinois, this fifteenth day of May, 1929.

Michael L. E. Jensen (SEAL)   Anna R. Jensen (SEAL)

CENTRAL BANKNOTE COMPANY

BANKS

America, Bank of (I), 1850s, Eagle, ship, and old train vignette	**80.00**
America, Bank of (I), 1930s, Eagle, ship and old train vignette	**20.00**
American International Savings and Loan Association (I), 1960s	**3.00**
American Trust Company (I), 1920s, Eagle vignette, seal	**4.00**
Andover National Bank, The (I), 1890s, Portrait, state seal, and view of capitol building with horses and carriages, plus stamp	**38.00**
Andover National Bank (I), 1910s, Massachusetts, Portrait, state seal, and view of capitol building with horses and carriage vignette	**25.00**
Arkansas, Real Estate Bank of, State of (I), 1830s, Copy of certificate	**260.00**
Associates Investment Company (I-N), One thousand dollar four-three-eighths percent bond, company logo	**5.00**
Atlanta, Lowry National Bank of (I), 1910s, Georgia, Eagle vignette, embossed seal	**22.00**
Atlanta National Bank (I), 1870s, Georgia, Eagle vignette	**50.00**
Atlantic Avenue Bank (I), 1920s	**6.00**
Azures Dairy Bank (I), 1920s, Embossed seal	**5.00**
Baltimore, Drovers and Mechanics Bank of (I), 1930s, Arm and hammer, and cow vignettes	**40.00**
Baltimore, National Marine Bank of (I), 1920s, Maryland, Early steamboat with sails vignette	**15.00**
Bankers Trust, New York Corporation (I), Reclining woman vignette	**5.00**
Barnstable Bank (I), 1830s, Maine	**85.00**
Barnstable Bank (I), 1840s	**60.00**
Barnstable Bank (I), 1850s	**55.00**
Barnstable Bank (I), 1860s	**30.00**
Bath, First National Bank of, Maine (I), 1900s, State seal	**40.00**
Bath, Lincoln National Bank of (I), 1880s, Maine, Capitol building vignette	**63.00**
Bath, Lincoln National Bank of (I), 1900s, Capitol building vignette	**45.00**
Bethel, National White River Bank of (I), 1870s, Vermont, Pedestrians, horses, carriages, and capitol building vignette	**60.00**
Boston, Atlantic National Bank of (I), 1930s, Sailing ships vignette	**40.00**
Boston, Investment Trust of (I), 1960s, State building vignette	**2.00**
Boston, National Union Bank of (I), 1880s, Massachusetts, Large capitol building vignette	**50.00**
Boston, National Union Bank of (I), 1890s, Massachusetts, Large capitol building vignette	**30.00**
Boston Personal Property Trust (I), 1960s, Eagle vignette	**1.00**
Boston, Rockland-Atlas National Bank of (I), 1950s, Vignette of man with world on his back	**10.00**
Boston, Second National Bank (I), 1920s	**20.00**
Boston, Second National Bank of (I), 1900s, Capitol building, Indian maiden, and seated lady vignettes	**42.00**
Boston, Second National Bank of (I), 1910s, Capitol building, Indian maiden, and seated lady vignettes	**20.00**
Boston, Second National Bank of (I), 1920s, Capitol building, Indian maiden, and seated lady vignettes	**12.00**
Bridgeton Saving Fund and Building Association (I), 1860s, With revenue stamp	**63.00**
Briggs National Bank and Trust Company (I), 1930s, New York, Eagle and gold seal vignette	**6.00**
Briggs National Bank and Trust Company (I), 1940s, Eagle and gold seal vignette	**5.00**
Briggs National Bank of Clyde (U), 1870s, Two vignettes (old sailing ship)	**20.00**
Broadway National Bank of Boston (I), 1890s	**20.00**
Brooklyn, First National Bank of (I), 1860s, Woman with eagle vignette, also seated lady vignette	**40.00**
Brownville, First National Bank of (U), 1870s, Cows and girl vignettes	**15.00**
Builders Loan and Fund Corporation (U), 1850s, Vignette of large house	**35.00**
Builders Loan and Fund Corporation (U), 1860s, Massachusetts, Old bank building vignette	**30.00**

◀ ***Wynlake Crest Apartments (I), 1920s**, 6 and one-half percent gold bond, large eagle vignette* ***4.00***

NUMBER NC5991

SHARES 100

100 SHARES

INCORPORATED UNDER THE LAWS OF THE STATE OF DELAWARE

AMERICAN NATURAL GAS CORPORATION

COMMON STOCK, WITHOUT PAR VALUE

THIS CERTIFICATE IS TRANSFERABLE EITHER IN NEW YORK, N.Y., OR IN CHICAGO, ILL.

This Certifies that --LEONARD J. KLECZKA--

is the owner of One Hundred full paid and non assessable Shares of the Common Stock without par value of American Natural Gas Corporation transferable in person or by duly authorized attorney upon the surrender of this Certificate properly endorsed.

A statement of the designations, preferences, rights ... of the Preferred Stock and of the Common Stock ... Corporation as amended ... thereto and to the provisions of the Certificate of Incorporation of the Corporation as amended and of the by-laws of the Corporation. ... with the Transfer Agent ... signed by the Transfer Agent and registered by the Registrar. Witness the seal of the Corporation and the signatures of its duly authorized officers.

"The Certificate of Incorporation ... 1931, to provide that holders of $7 Cumulative Preferred Stock ... should have ordinary voting powers ... Cumulative Voting ..."

Dated OCT 21 1931

ASSISTANT TREASURER

VICE-PRESIDENT

COUNTERSIGNED THE NEW YORK TRUST COMPANY, TRANSFER AGENT. ASSISTANT SECRETARY.

REGISTERED: CENTRAL HANOVER BANK AND TRUST COMPANY, REGISTRAR. AUTHORIZED OFFICER. OCT 22 1931

HAMILTON BANK NOTE, NEW YORK

INCORPORATED UNDER THE LAWS OF STATE OF DELAWARE

No 3667

Shares ***300***

Century Natural Gas & Oil Corporation

TOTAL AUTHORIZED ISSUE THREE MILLION (3,000,000) SHARES

PAR VALUE TEN CENTS (10c) EACH

THIS CERTIFIES THAT ****ROSETTA D. FARRELL**** is the owner of ***Three Hundred*** Shares of the Capital Stock of

Century Natural Gas and Oil Corporation Fully Paid and Non-Assessable

transferable only on the books of the Corporation by the holder hereof in person or by Attorney upon surrender of this Certificate properly endorsed.

In Witness Whereof, the said Corporation has caused this Certificate to be signed by its duly authorized officers and to be sealed with the Seal of the Corporation this 19th day of May A.D. 1952

SECRETARY-TREASURER

PRESIDENT VICE-PRESIDENT

SHARES 10c EACH

COUNTERSIGNED: CENTURY NATURAL GAS & OIL CORPORATION, TRANSFER AGENT, BY SECRE.

REGISTERED: CENTURY NATURAL GAS & OIL CORPORATION, REGISTRAR, BY ASST. TREASURER.

© GOES 59

Bullion and Exchange Bank (I), 1880s, Nevada	100.00
Bullion and Exchange Bank (I), 1890s, Nevada	80.00
Bullion and Exchange Bank (I), 1900s, Nevada	50.00
Bullion and Exchange Bank (U), 1880s, Nevada	22.00
California, Bank of (I), 1870s, Small certificate	25.00
Carbon Building and Loan Association (I), 1910s, Three vignettes	4.00
Carbon Building and Loan Association (I), 1920s, Old house vignette	3.00
Carolina Savings Bank (U), 1870s, South Carolina, Dog in front of safe vignette	33.00
Carson City Savings Bank (U), Nevada, Eagle vignette	10.00
Carson City Savings Bank of America (I), Train vignette	30.00
Centerville National Bank (I), 1860s, Eagle with flag vignette with revenue stamp	80.00
Central Farmers' Trust Company (I), 1930s, Eagle with shield vignette	3.00
Chandler, Bank of (I), 1920s, Arizona, Eagle vignette	6.00
Charleston, Bank of (I), 1830s, Two women, palm tree, sailing ships, and seal vignettes	160.00
Charleston, Bank of (I), 1840s, Two women, palm tree, sailing ships, and seal vignettes	100.00
Charleston, Bank of (I), 1850s, Two women, palm tree, sailing ships, and seal vignettes	80.00
Charleston, Bank of (I), 1860s, Two women, palm tree, sailing ships, and seal vignettes	70.00
Charleston, Bank of (I), 1870s, Palm trees vignette	55.00
Chester Bank and Saving Fund (I), 1880s	20.00
China Agency and Trading Company (I), 1910s, California, Chinese characters	20.00
Citizen's Trust and Deposit Company of Baltimore (I), 1890s, Dog in front of large safe vignette	50.00
City Bank Farmer's Trust (North American Trust Shares) (I), 1950s, Eagle, ship, train and tank cars vignettes	5.00
Continuous Transit Securities Company (I-N), 1920s	3.00
Cooperstown, First National Bank of (I), 1920s, Lady with flag, hunter with rifle, eagle and figures with eagle vignette	8.00
Cooperstown, First National Bank of (I), 1930s, Lady with flag, hunter with rifle, eagle, and figures with eagle vignettes	7.00
Culver City, First National Bank of (I), 1920s, California, Allegorical figures	10.00
Cumberland, Second National Bank of (U), 1900s, Seated lady vignette	9.00
Dallas, State Savings Bank (I), 1870s, Texas, Indian maiden with star on rock, gold seal vignettes	80.00
Delaware County Trust, Safe Deposit and Title Insurance Co. (I), 1890s, Ships vignette, plus Pennsylvania	15.00
Delaware County Trust, Safe Deposit and Title Insurance Company (I), 1890s, No vignette	9.00
Detroit Mortgage Corporation (I), 1920s, Embossed seal	8.00
Dime Savings Institution (I), 1860s, Vignette of dog	25.00
Eastman College Bank (I), 1880s, New York, Vignette of large old college building and carriage	110.00
Empire Loan and Trust Company (I), 1890s, One thousand dollar bond	33.00
Emporia Mutual Loan and Savings Association (I), 1880s	10.00
Equitable Trust Company (I), 1870s, Seven percent mortgage bond, seated female vignette	30.00
Exeter Bank (I), 1850s, Train vignette	35.00
Farmers and Exchange Bank (I), 1850s, South Carolina, Overseer on horse in cotton field vignette	160.00
Farmers Loan and Trust (I), 1900s	4.00

◀***American Natural Gas Corporation (I-N), 1930s,*** *Two sexy ladies, derrick, well head, and shack vignette*	***10.00***
◀***Century Natural Gas and Oil Corporation (I), 1950s,*** *Oil field vignette*	***8.00***

No.M 21830
No.M 21830
1,000
1,000
EL PASO NATURAL GAS COMPANY
5¼% CONVERTIBLE DEBENTURE DUE SEPTEMBER 1, 1977
(Convertible through August 31, 1967 unless called for previous redemption)
ONE THOUSAND DOLLARS ($1,000)
IN WITNESS WHEREOF,
EL PASO NATURAL GAS COMPANY,
TRUSTEE'S CERTIFICATE OF AUTHENTICATION
CITY BANK FARMERS TRUST COMPANY,
EL PASO NATURAL GAS COMPANY CORPORATE SEAL 1928 DELAWARE
President
Secretary

NUMBER NUMÉRO H40707
100
SHARES ACTIONS
IMPERIAL OIL LIMITED
INCORPORATED UNDER THE LAWS OF CANADA
AUTHORIZED CAPITAL 160,000,000 SHARES WITHOUT NOMINAL OR PAR VALUE
CONSTITUÉE EN VERTU DES LOIS DU CANADA
CAPITAL AUTORISÉ DE 160,000,000 D'ACTIONS SANS VALEUR NOMINALE OU AU PAIR
THIS IS TO CERTIFY THAT
CECI CERTIFIE QUE
-MC LEOD YOUNG WEIR INC-
CUSIP 453038 10 8
ONE HUNDRED
JUL 2 - 1971
ASSISTANT-SECRETARY
SECRÉTAIRE ADJOINT
CHAIRMAN OF THE BOARD
PRÉSIDENT DU CONSEIL

Franklin-American Trust (I), 1930s, Missouri, Embossed seal	**5.00**
Freeland Ville Bank (I), 1920s, Large eagle, green or orange seal vignette	**5.00**
Frontier National Bank (I), 1880s, Eastport, Maine, Capitol building	**25.00**
Gastonia, Citizen's National Bank of (U), North Carolina, Eagle vignette	**3.00**
Globe National Bank (I), 1890s, Maine, Globe vignette	**15.00**
Guaranty Trust Company of Detroit (I), 1920s, Gold bond, vignette of bank building	**4.50**
Hatfield National Bank and Trust (U), Warrant	**2.00**
Helena, First National Bank of (U), 1890s, Montana	**14.00**
Hoboken, First National Bank of (I), 1860s, Capitol building vignette with revenue stamp	**70.00**
Hoboken, First National Bank of (I), 1870s, Capitol building vignette	**55.00**
Hoboken, First National Bank of (I), 1880s, Capitol building vignette	**40.00**
Hoboken, First National Bank of (I), 1890s, Capitol building vignette	**20.00**
Hoboken, First National Bank of (I), 1920s, Capitol building vignette	**10.00**
Hoboken, First National Bank of (I), 1930s, Capitol building vignette	**6.00**
Hollywood, Bank of (U), 1920s, Embossed seal	**10.00**
Independence Trust Shares (I), 1930s, Independence Hall and Liberty Bell vignettes	**5.00**
Independence Trust Shares (I), 1940s, Independence Hall and Liberty Bell vignettes	**5.00**
Industrial Finance Corporation "Morris Plan," (I), 1920s and 1930s, Two seated figures with tools, world globe vignettes	**3.00**
Invincible Building and Loan Association of Westwood, N.J. (I), 1920s, New Jersey, Family home vignette	**6.00**
Irving Trust Company (I), 1930s, Allegorical figures, train, and boats vignette	**8.00**
Irving Trust Company (I), 1940s, Seated woman, old train, and paddle steamer vignettes	**7.00**
Irving Trust Company (I), 1950s, Seated woman, old train, and paddle steamer vignettes	**6.00**
Jamaica, West River National Bank of (I), 1870s, Vermont, Three vignettes including boy on a horse	**50.00**
Jamestown, Bank of, Jamestown, New York (I), Specimen, vignette of bank building	**22.00**
Jersey, State Bank of (I), 1950s, Eagle on rock holding arrows vignette	**3.00**
Kensington National Bank of Philadelphia (I), 1870s, Three vignettes with revenue stamp	**45.00**
Kentucky, Bank of (I), 1840s, Two portraits, two scenes of children, woman, and eagle vignettes	**110.00**
Kentucky, Bank of (I), 1860s, Woman with eagle, blacksmith, and seated lady vignettes	**80.00**
Kentucky, Bank of (I-N), 1840s, Rare, beautiful woman vignette	**100.00**
Lancaster, Farmer's Bank of (I), 1810s	**265.00**
Langdon Bank (I), 1850s, New Hampshire, Embossed seal	**75.00**
Long Island National Bank of New York, The (I), 1920s, Eagle vignette, many stamps	**6.00**
Los Angeles, Seaboard National Bank of (I), Specimen, large four-funnel ship vignette	**45.00**
Love Joy's Wharf Trust (I), 1920s, Massachusetts	**3.00**
Lowry National Bank of Atlanta (I), 1910s, Large eagle vignette	**16.00**
Lynn, Central National Bank of (I), 1930s, Massachusetts, Eagle, teepee with squaw, and ship vignette	**25.00**
Lynn, Manufacturer's National Bank of (I), 1890s, Massachusetts, Horses, carriages, and banks vignette	**25.00**
Lynn, Manufacturer's National Bank of (I), 1910s, Massachusetts, Horses, carriages,and banks vignette	**20.00**

◀ ***El Paso Natural Gas (I), 1950s,*** *Five and one-fourth* ***5.00***

◀ ***Imperial Oil Limited (I), 1970s,*** *Large logo* ***2.00***

NUMBER 4537

INCORPORATED UNDER THE LAWS OF THE STATE OF DELAWARE

SHARES *5000*

King Petroleum Corporation

FULL PAID — CAPITAL $1,000,000 — NON-ASSESSABLE

This Certifies that --JOHN F. COWAN--
is the owner of FIVE THOUSAND* * * * * * * * * * Shares of the Capital Stock of
KING PETROLEUM CORPORATION
transferable only on the books of this Corporation in person or by Attorney upon surrender of this Certificate properly endorsed.

IN WITNESS WHEREOF, the said Corporation has caused this Certificate to be signed by its duly authorized officers and its Corporate Seal to be hereunto affixed this day of MAR 2 1920 A.D. 19

ASST. SECRETARY — VICE-PRESIDENT

SHARES $1.00 EACH

COUNTERSIGNED: SECURITY TRANSFER & REGISTRAR CO.

MAR 4 1920

PREFERRED SIX PER CENT CUMULATIVE STOCK

NUMBER 3762

INCORPORATED UNDER THE LAWS OF THE STATE OF WEST VIRGINIA, U.S.A.

SHARES *400* — 400

CAPITAL STOCK $10,000,000.

PREFERRED STOCK $5,000,000.
COMMON STOCK $5,000,000.

THE NATIONAL CONSOLIDATED OIL COMPANY.

This is to Certify that B. F. Snyder
is the owner of Four hundred
fully paid and non-assessable shares of the par value of One Dollar each, in the Preferred Capital stock of THE NATIONAL CONSOLIDATED OIL COMPANY, transferable only in person or by Attorney upon the books of said Corporation, upon surrender of this certificate. The holders of the Preferred stock shall be entitled to receive, when and as declared, from the surplus or net profits of the Corporation, yearly dividends at the rate of six per centum per annum, payable semi-annually on dates to be fixed by the Board of Directors. The dividends on the Preferred stock shall be cumulative and shall be payable before any dividends on the Common stock shall be paid or set apart, so that if in any year dividends amounting to six per cent shall not have been paid thereon, the deficiency shall be payable before any dividends shall be paid upon or set apart for the Common stock. Whenever all cumulative dividends on the Preferred stock for all previous years shall have been declared and shall have become payable, and the accrued semi-annual installments for the current year shall have been declared, and the Company shall have paid such cumulative dividends for previous years and such accrued semi-annual installments, or shall have set aside from its surplus or net profits a sum sufficient for the payment thereof, the Board of Directors may declare equal dividends on the Common and Preferred stock alike, payable then or thereafter out of any remaining surplus or net profits. In the event of any liquidation or dissolution or winding up (whether voluntary or involuntary) of the Corporation, the holders of the Preferred stock shall be entitled to be paid in full both the par amount of their shares and the unpaid dividends accrued thereon, and after the payment to the holders of the Preferred stock of its par value, and the unpaid accrued dividends thereon, the remaining assets and funds shall be divided equally and paid to the holders of the Common and Preferred stock alike according to their respective shares.

The Preferred stock and the Common stock may be increased as provided by the laws of West Virginia. This certificate is not valid without the signatures of the Transfer Agent and Registrar of Transfers.

IN WITNESS WHEREOF, the duly authorized officers of this Corporation have hereunto subscribed their names and caused the corporate seal to be hereto affixed this day of APR 2 1902 A.D. 19

SECRETARY. — PRESIDENT.

SHARES $1.00 EACH

Registered this day of 19 Knickerbocker Trust Company, Registrar. By SECRETARY.

Countersigned By Transfer Agent. SECRETARY.

APR 2 1902

Manufacturer's and Trader's Bank (I), 1890s, Six nice vignettes	120.00
Manufacturer's and Trader's Bank (I), 1900s, Six nice vignettes	70.00
Manufacturer's National Bank (I), 1910s, Massachusetts, Large old bank building with horse and carriages vignette	25.00
Marine National Bank (I), 1880s, New York, Ship in heavy seas vignette	135.00
Maryland, Farmer's Bank of (I), 1800s, Embossed seal	365.00
Maryland Trust Company (U), 1900s, State seal	10.00
Massachusetts Investors Trust (I), 1940s, Old state building vignette	3.00
Massachusetts Investors Trust (U), Old state building vignette	2.00
Merchants and Manufacturer's Bank (I), 1860s, Connecticut, Portrait of woman, antlered deer vignettes with revenue stamp	90.00
Methuen, The National Bank of (I), 1890s, Massachusetts, Capitol building with stagecoach and riders vignettes	40.00
Methuen, The National Bank of (I), 1900s, Massachusetts, Capitol building with stagecoach and riders vignettes	25.00
Methuen, The National Bank of (I), 1910s, Maine, Capitol building vignette	10.00
Miner's and Merchant's Bank (U), South Carolina	10.00
Mitten Bank Securities Corporation (I), 1920s, Pennsylvania	15.00
Mitten Bank Securities Corporation (I), 1930s, Pennsylvania	12.00
Morris Canal and Banking Company (I), 1840s, Certificate	80.00
Morris Canal and Banking Company (I), 1850s, New Jersey, Canal scenes, seal	70.00
Morris Canal and Banking Company (I), 1860s, Reclining seminudes, seated women, and canalboat vignettes	120.00
Mortgage Bank and Financial Administration (I), 1960s, Bond, girl vignette	8.00
New Haven, Second National Bank of (I), 1930s, Bank building	6.00
New York, First Fulton National Bank of (I), 1860s, New York, Man sitting against bust, in foreground of ship and city vignette	135.00
Norfolk, First National Bank of (I), 1870s, Seated woman, old sailor, and anchor vignettes with stamps	85.00
North Pennsylvania Bank (U), Eagle vignette	3.00
Oakland Mortgage and Finance Company (I-N), 1930s, California, Large three-story home vignette	8.00
Occidental Finance and Mortgage Company (I), 1910s, California, Eagle vignette, seal	6.00
Ohio Union Loan (I), 1860s, Ohio, Vignettes of Ben Franklin and safe	255.00
Old Colony State Bank (I), New York, State seal	8.00
Old Colony State Bank (U), 1920s, New York, State seal	4.00
Oriental Bank (I-N), 1910s, New York, Figure with globe, steamship, sailing ship, and fountain vignettes	25.00
Pajaro Valley Bank (I), 1880s, California, Bank logo	30.00
Pajaro Valley Bank (I), 1890s, Calfornia, Bank logo	22.00
Pajaro Valley National Bank (I), 1910s, Company logo and name in clouds	13.00
Pajaro Valley National Bank (I), 1920s, Company logo and name in clouds	10.00
Palisades Trust Company (I), 1950s, Certificate of deposit, Palisades and Hudson River scene	2.00
Palisades Trust Company (U), 1950s, Certificate of deposit, Palisades and Hudson River scene	1.00
Pennsylvania, Bank of (I-N), 1850s, Pennsylvania, State seal, portrait of William Penn, train, and harbor canal scene	115.00

◀ ***King Petroleum Corporation (I-N), 1920s,*** *Huge oil field vignette* ***10.00***

◀ ***National Consolidated Oil Company, The (I-N), 1900s,*** *Large oil field vignette, with stamps* ***14.00***

NUMBER 1673

SHARES - 10 -

PRODUCING ROYALTIES POOL, Inc.

INCORPORATED UNDER THE LAWS OF DELAWARE

CAPITALIZATION $500,000.00 COMMON PAR VALUE $1.00 / $500,000.00 PREFERRED PARTICIPATING

This Certifies that A. H. Moore is the owner of EXACTLY TEN shares of the Preferred Capital stock of Producing Royalties Pool, Inc., fully paid and non-assessable of a par value of One Dollar, transferable only on the books of this Corporation, in person or by attorney upon surrender of this Certificate properly endorsed. Holders of Preferred stock will receive a fixed cumulative dividend at the rate of eight percent per annum, payable quarterly on the 15th day of January, April, July and October. After payment of dividends at the rate of eight percent, the Preferred stock will participate to the extent of fifty percent of all net earnings distributed as dividends by the corporation. The Preferred shares are non-voting but Preferred, both as to assets and dividends and may be retired in whole or part on any dividend date at par, plus accrued dividends.

In Witness Whereof, The said Corporation has caused this certificate to be signed by its duly authorized officers and its Corporate Seal to be hereunto affixed

this Eleventh day of ________ A. D. 1929

SEC'Y PRES.

PREFERRED

SHARES $ EACH

© GOES 70

INCORPORATED UNDER THE LAWS OF

STATE OF INDIANA

No 3

Shares 1

Reece Oil Company

CAPITAL STOCK $20,000.00

THIS CERTIFIES THAT Donald Baker is the owner of One (1) Shares of the Capital Stock of

REECE OIL COMPANY

transferable only on the books of the Corporation by the holder hereof in person or by Attorney upon surrender of this Certificate properly endorsed.

In Witness Whereof, the said Corporation has caused this Certificate to be signed by its duly authorized officers and to be sealed with the Seal of the Corporation

this 21st day of November A.D. 1921

William Reece PREST.

Donald Baker Secy TREAS.

SHARES $100.00 EACH

© GOES 89

Pennsylvania Safe Deposit and Trust (U),1880s, City of Philadelphia	**15.00**
Portland National Bank (I), 1900s, Maine, State seal of Maine	**7.00**
Royal National Bank of New York (I), 1960s, Bank logo, seal	**3.00**
Second Street Trust, State Street (I), 1950s, Old courthouse with clock vignette	**3.00**
Skowhegan, First National Bank of (I), 1890s, Maine	**10.00**
South Carolina Loan and Trust (I), 1860, Embossed seal	**85.00**
South Carolina Loan and Trust (I), 1870s, Soldier and state seal vignette	**85.00**
South Carolina Loan and Trust (I), 1880s, Allegorical figures, seal vignette	**80.00**
South Danvers National Bank (I), 1860s, Massachusetts, Portrait plus revenue stamp	**115.00**
Springfield, First National Bank of (I), 1870s, Train and farmer vignette	**75.00**
Springfield, First National Bank of (I), 1880s, Kentucky, Three vignettes of train, river, farmer, and sheep	**65.00**
State Street Bank and Trust Company (I), 1960s, Old courthouse with clock vignette	**2.00**
Straus Safe Deposit Company (I), 1920s, Illinois, Bond, woman with child, seal vignette	**12.00**
Stuart Central Farmer's Bank (I), 1920s, Eagle with shield vignette	**5.00**
Sutro Mortgage Investment Trust (I), 1970s, Company logo, seal	**1.00**
Thomaston, Georges National Bank of (I), 1910s, Maine, Maine state seal	**30.00**
Thomaston National Bank (I), 1870s, Maine , Deer and dog vignette	**50.00**
Thomaston National Bank (I), 1900s, Maine, Deer and dog vignette	**40.00**
Thomaston National Bank (I), 1910s, Maine, Pine tree and seal vignette	**30.00**
Times Square Trust (I), 1930s, New York, Eagle vignette	**6.00**
Tioga National Bank and Trust Company (I), 1920s, State seal of Pennsylvania	**8.00**
Tioga National Bank and Trust Company (I), 1930s, State seal of Pennsylvania	**5.00**
Troy, National Bank of (I), 1880s, New York, Eagle with flag, gold seal vignette	**15.00**
Union Deposit and Trust (I), 1910s, Colorado	**8.00**
Union Deposit and Trust (I), 1920s, Colorado	**6.00**
Union National Bank (I), 1860s, Pennsylvania, Eagle and lady vignette	**68.00**
Union National Bank (I), 1870s, Pennsylvania, Eagle and seated lady vignette	**50.00**
Union National Bank (I), 1880s, Pennsylvania, Eagle and lady vignette	**40.00**
United States Bank of, 1920s, Eagle vignette and seal	**10.00**
United States Bank of, 1930s, Eagle vignette and seal	**7.00**
United States, Bank of (I), 1920s, New York, Large eagle vignette	**15.00**
United States, Bank of (I), 1930s, Eagle with logo	**12.00**
United States National Bank (I), 1930s, California, Capitol, seal	**5.00**
United States National Bank (U), 1920s, California, Capitol, seal	**6.00**
Valley Thrift Corporation, The (I), 1930s, Green embossed seal	**3.00**
Venice, First National Bank of (I), 1920s, California, Capitol building vignette	**10.00**
Victoria Bond Holders Corporation (I), 1930s, New York	**7.00**
Waverly Co-operative Bank (I-N), Massachusetts, Vignette of a house	**10.00**
West Hollywood, Bank of (I), 1930s	**10.00**
Westminister, First National Bank of (I), 1870s, Maryland, Eagle and farmers vignettes	**80.00**
Williamson Securities (U), New York, State seal	**2.00**
Williamson, State Bank of (I), 1910s, New York, Sailing ship, eagle vignette	**6.50**
Wilmington and Brandywine, National Bank of (I), 1880s, Large capitol building, woman with flying eagle vignettes	**54.00**
Wilmington Trust (U), Delaware, Two men with shield and steamboat vignette	**3.00**
Wilshire National Bank (I), 1920s, California, Embossed seal	**8.00**

Producing Royalties Pool, Inc., (I-N), 1920s, Eagle vignette ***4.00***
Reece Oil Company (I-N), 1920s, Indiana, Oil field vignette ***10.00***

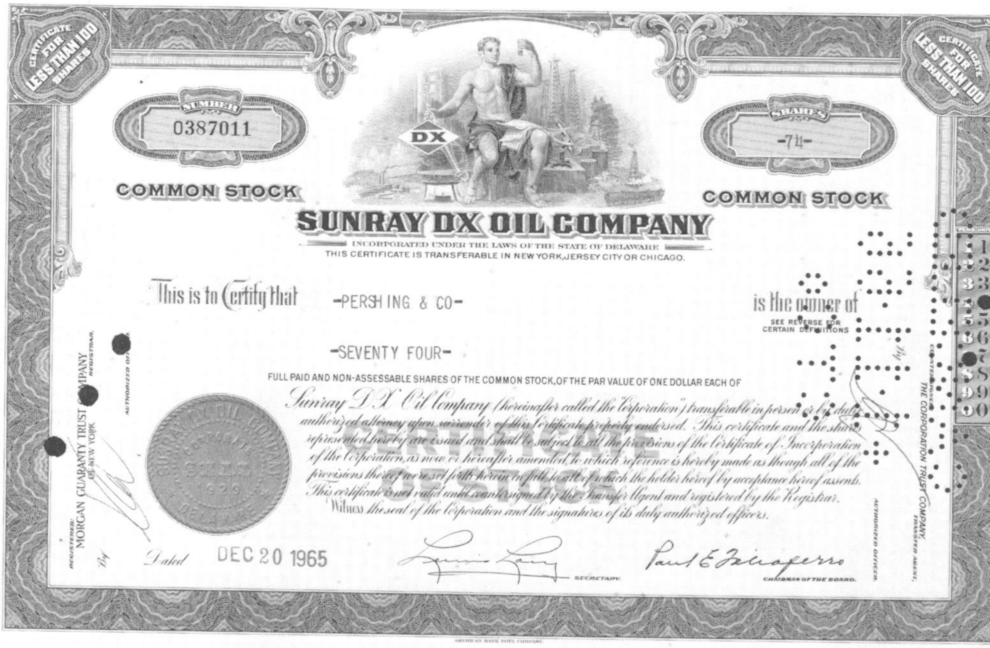
CERTIFICATE FOR LESS THAN 100 SHARES

NUMBER 0387011

SHARES -74-

COMMON STOCK

SUNRAY DX OIL COMPANY

INCORPORATED UNDER THE LAWS OF THE STATE OF DELAWARE

THIS CERTIFICATE IS TRANSFERABLE IN NEW YORK, JERSEY CITY OR CHICAGO.

This is to Certify that -PERSHING & CO- is the owner of

SEE REVERSE FOR CERTAIN DEFINITIONS

-SEVENTY FOUR-

FULL PAID AND NON-ASSESSABLE SHARES OF THE COMMON STOCK, OF THE PAR VALUE OF ONE DOLLAR EACH OF

Sunray D.X. Oil Company (hereinafter called the Corporation) transferable in person or by duly authorized attorney upon surrender of this Certificate properly endorsed. This certificate and the shares represented hereby are issued and shall be subject to all the provisions of the Certificate of Incorporation of the Corporation, as now or hereafter amended, to which reference is hereby made as though all of the provisions thereof were set forth herein in full, to all of which the holder hereof by acceptance hereof assents. This certificate is not valid until countersigned by the Transfer Agent and registered by the Registrar.

Witness the seal of the Corporation and the signatures of its duly authorized officers.

Dated DEC 20 1965

SECRETARY. CHAIRMAN OF THE BOARD.

REGISTERED: MORGAN GUARANTY TRUST COMPANY OF NEW YORK, REGISTRAR. BY AUTHORIZED OFFICER.

COUNTERSIGNED: THE CORPORATION TRUST COMPANY, TRANSFER AGENT. BY AUTHORIZED OFFICER.

CERTIFICATE OF STOCK

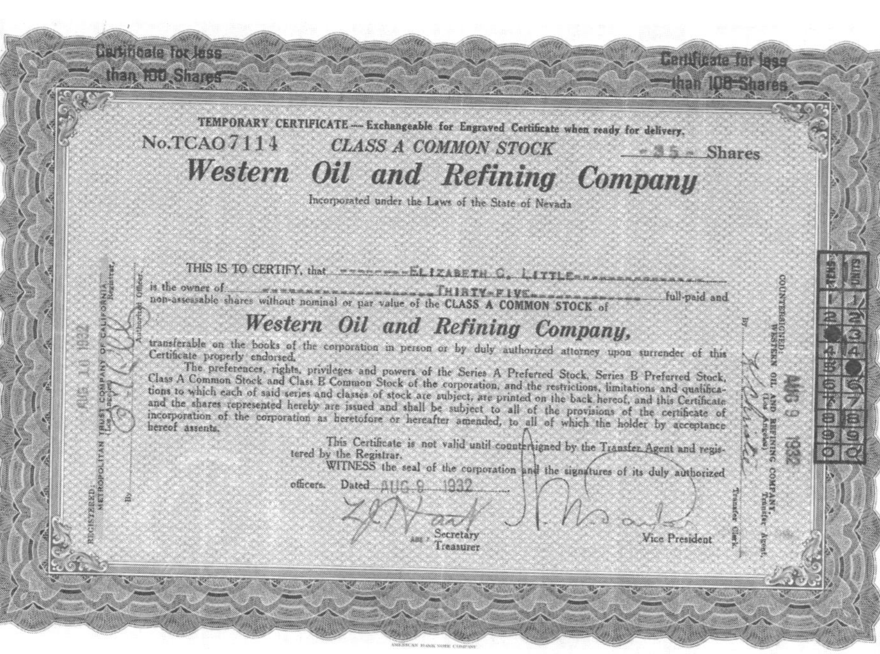
Certificate for less than 100 Shares

TEMPORARY CERTIFICATE — Exchangeable for Engraved Certificate when ready for delivery.

No. TCAO7114 CLASS A COMMON STOCK -35- Shares

Western Oil and Refining Company

Incorporated under the Laws of the State of Nevada

THIS IS TO CERTIFY, that ELIZABETH C. LITTLE is the owner of THIRTY-FIVE full-paid and non-assessable shares without nominal or par value of the CLASS A COMMON STOCK of

Western Oil and Refining Company,

transferable on the books of the corporation in person or by duly authorized attorney upon surrender of this Certificate properly endorsed.

The preferences, rights, privileges and powers of the Series A Preferred Stock, Series B Preferred Stock, Class A Common Stock and Class B Common Stock of the corporation, and the restrictions, limitations and qualifications to which each of said series and classes of stock are subject, are printed on the back hereof, and this Certificate and the shares represented hereby are issued and shall be subject to all of the provisions of the certificate of incorporation of the corporation as heretofore or hereafter amended, to all of which the holder by acceptance hereof assents.

This Certificate is not valid until countersigned by the Transfer Agent and registered by the Registrar.

WITNESS the seal of the corporation and the signatures of its duly authorized officers. Dated AUG 9 1932

Secretary Treasurer Vice President

REGISTERED: METROPOLITAN TRUST COMPANY OF CALIFORNIA, Registrar. AUG 10 1932

COUNTERSIGNED: WESTERN OIL AND REFINING COMPANY, Transfer Agent. AUG 9 1932 Transfer Clerk.

Oil and Gas Exploration

Aetna Petroleum (I), 1920s, Oil wells, train vignette	12.00
Allen Oil (I), 1910s, Wyoming, Eagle vignette, seal	5.00
Amalgamated Mining and Oil (I), 1900s, Arizona Territory, Bond, oil field vignette	32.00
American Indian Oil and Gas Company (I), 1910s, Oklahoma, Oil field vignette	23.00
American Natural Gas (I), 1930s, Two allegorical figures	3.00
American Natural Gas Corporation (I-N), 1930s, Two sexy ladies, derrick, well head, and snack vignette	10.00
American Refineries (I-N), 1900s, South Dakota, Oil gushers, trains, and oil tanks vignettes	14.00
Amico Oil and Land (I), 1910s, Arizona, Train and oil field vignette	15.00
Amico Oil Company of Kansas (I), 1910s, Oil field vignette	15.00
Auburn Oil and Gas (I), 1920s	10.00
Bankers Equitable Royalty and Producing (I-N), 1920s, Oil derricks and tank cars vignette	8.00
Bankers Oil Company (I-N), 1900s, South Dakota, train and workers in oil fields vignette	13.00
Bateman Oil (I), 1930s, Embossed seal	3.00
Bay State Gas Company (I-N), 1890s, Indian vignette	24.00
Beaver Oils, Ltd. (I), 1910s, train and derricks vignette	14.00
Berkimer County Mining and Petroleum Company of New York (I), 1860s, Oil derrick vignette	185.00
Birmingham, East Birmingham and South Pittsburg Gas (I), 1860s, Gasworks vignette	135.00
Black Diamond Oil (I), 1910s, Bond, embossed seal	17.00
Blacklick and Conemaugh Petroleum and Mining (U), 1860s, Oil field workers	28.00
Bolsa-Chica Oil (I), 1920s, California, Gusher vignette	10.00
Bolsa-Chica Oil (I), 1940s, California, Vignette of lady, oil fields, and harbor	6.00
Boston Mexican Petroleum Trustees (I), 1920s	22.00
Brookline Oil (I), 1930s, California, Truck and oil field vignette	7.00
Buckeye Petroleum and Mining (I), 1860s, California, Oil field vignette	250.00
Buena Vista Oil Company (I), 1860s, New York, Oil derrick vignette, with stamp	195.00
Buick Oil (I), 1910s, Train and oil derricks vignette	14.00
Burt Tex Pool Oil Company (I), 1910s, California, Many oil wells vignette	15.00
California Combined Oil Company (I), 1900s, California, Vignettes of trains, oil gushers, derricks, and storage tanks	15.00
California Combined Oil Company (I-N), 1900s, California, Vignettes of trains, oil gushers, derricks, and storage tanks	23.00
Calpetro Producers Syndicate (U), 1920s, California, Gushing wells in oil fields and train vignettes	7.00
Cambria Oil (I), 1920s, Huge certificate, large eagle, and large oil gushers vignette	25.00
Campbell Oil (I-N), 1920s, Texas, Embossed seal	4.00
Canadian Export Gas and Oil (I), Seated woman between oil wells vignette	2.00
Century Consolidated Oil (I), 1920s, Large oil field vignette, green seal	20.00
Century Natural Gas and Oil Corporation (I), 1950s, Oil field vignette	8.00
Century Natural Gas and Oil Corporation (I), 1960s, Eagle vignette with stamp	2.00
Century Petroleum Corporation (I-N), 1910s, Oil gusher and tanks vignette	23.00
Chambers Oil and Gas (I), 1940s, train and oil derrick vignette	5.00
Cherry Run and Pithole Oil (I), 1860s, New York, Oil derricks and tanks vignette	115.00

◀*Sunray Oil Company (I), 1960s, Chemist, oil derricks, and tank cars vignette* ***2.00***

◀***Western Oil and Refining Company (I-N), 1930s*** ***3.00***

INCORPORATED UNDER THE LAWS OF THE STATE OF TEXAS
No 14351
Shares -30-
WORLD OIL COMPANY
CAPITAL $1,600,000.00
This Certifies that A. H. MOORE is the owner of
EXACTLY THIRTY EXACTLY Shares of the Capital Stock of
WORLD OIL COMPANY
transferable only on the books of the Corporation by the holder hereof in person or by Attorney, upon surrender of this Certificate properly endorsed.
In Witness Whereof, the said Corporation has caused this Certificate to be signed by its duly authorized officers and to be sealed with the seal of the Corporation this JUN 29 1926 day of A. D. 192
SECRETARY
PRESIDENT
Shares $1.00 Par

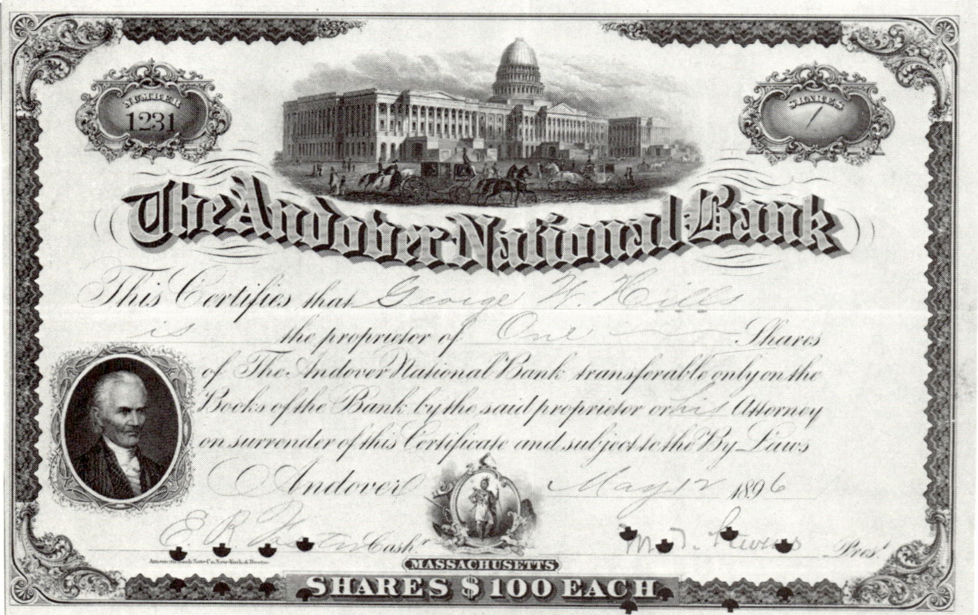
1231
The Andover National Bank
This Certifies that George W. Hills
is the proprietor of One Shares
of The Andover National Bank transferable only on the Books of the Bank by the said proprietor or his Attorney on surrender of this Certificate and subject to the By Laws
Andover May 12 1896
Cash.
Pres.
MASSACHUSETTS
SHARES $100 EACH

Cincinnati, Utah and Wyoming Oil Company (I), 1900s, South Dakota, Oil gushers, seal vignette 15.00
Cities Service Company (I), 1930s, Three vignettes of oil derrick and ships 10.00
Clarno Basin Oil (I), 1930s, Oregon, Gushing oil wells vignette 10.00
Coalinga Aladdin Oil of California (I), 1900s, Arizona 20.00
Columbia Gas System (I), Girl with torch in front of oil field vignette 3.00
Columbian Gas (I), 1950s and 1960s, Gas fields vignette 4.00
Columbian Oil, Asphalt and Refining (I-N), 1900s, Arizona, Oil derricks and horse tank cars vignette 22.00
Consolidated Oil of Oklahoma (I), 1900s, Arizona, Eagle vignette 14.00
Consolidated Petroleum Oil Company (I), 1860s, New York, Oil derrick and allegorical figures vignette 220.00
Constant Refining Company (I-N), 1920s, Gold bond, large eagle and small train vignette 14.00
Crescent Oil and Refining (I), 1910s, Arizona, Oil derricks, seal vignette 12.00
Crown Oil Company (I), 1910s, Arizona, No vignette 8.00
Cypress Petroleum of California (I-N), 1920s, Train and oil derricks vignette 25.00

Dixie Chief Oil Company (I-N), 1920s, Oil derrick and oil cars vignette 12.00

Eames Oil Processing (I), 1870s, State seal vignette 40.00
Eames Petroleum Iron Company (I), 1880s, Woman with eagle vignette 15.00
El Paso Natural Gas (I), 1950s, Five and one-fourth percent bond, large eagle vignette 5.00
Ellis-Mexia Oil Company (I-N), 1920s, Colorado 6.00
Entex Oil Company 1970s, Lady holding globe, company logo, and pipelines vignette 3.00
Erie County Oil Company (I), 1860s, New York, Two vignettes with stamp 235.00
Esmeralda Oil and Gas (I-N), 1910s, Three vignettes of oil derricks and train 10.00
Evangeline Oil Company (I), 1920s, Many oil gushers vignette 20.00

Ferris-O'Brien-Wyoming Oil (I), 1910s, Oil field and gushers vignettes 12.00
First National Development Corporation (I-N), 1930s, Nevada, Oil field vignette 10.00
Flathead Petroleum (I), 1910s, Washington, Company logo 10.00

German-American Oil and Gas (I-N), 1910s, Gushing oil wells vignette 13.00
Getty Oil Company (I), 1950s, Oil derricks vignette 10.00
Getty Oil Company, 1970s (I), Oil field and workers vignette 4.00
Glendale Oil Company (U), 1860s, Oil derrick, train, and seated lady vignettes 20.00
Glenrock Oil Company (I-N), 1920s, Large oil fields vignette 35.00
Greene Oil and Refining (I), 1920s, Arizona 5.00

Hammond Oil Company (I), 1860s, New York, Oil field, pumping station, and Indian maiden vignettes 140.00
Harris Consolidated Petroleum (I), 1920s, Eagle vignette, embossed seal 4.00
Henrietta Oil and Refining (I-N), 1900s, Texas, Eagle and oil gusher vignette 20.00
High Gravity Oil Company (I), 1910s, Oil field vignette 15.00
Houston Oil, Oil derricks and oil truck vignette 8.00
Hudson Oil and Gas (I), 1920s, Oil derricks and oil tanks vignette 15.00
Hudson Oil and Gas (I-N), 1920s, Oil derricks and tanks vignette 18.00
Humble Oil and Refining (I), 1950s, Vignette of ship, cracking plant, and oil derricks 10.00

Imperial Oil Limited (I), 1970s, Large logo 2.00
Independence Oil Company (I), 1900s, Texas, Oil fields and tanks vignette, seal 14.00

◀ ***World Oil Company (I-N), 1920s, Texas,*** *Embossed seal* ***6.00***
◀ ***Andover National Bank, the (I), 1890s,*** *Portrait, state seal, and view of capitol building with horses and carriages, plus stamp* ***38.00***

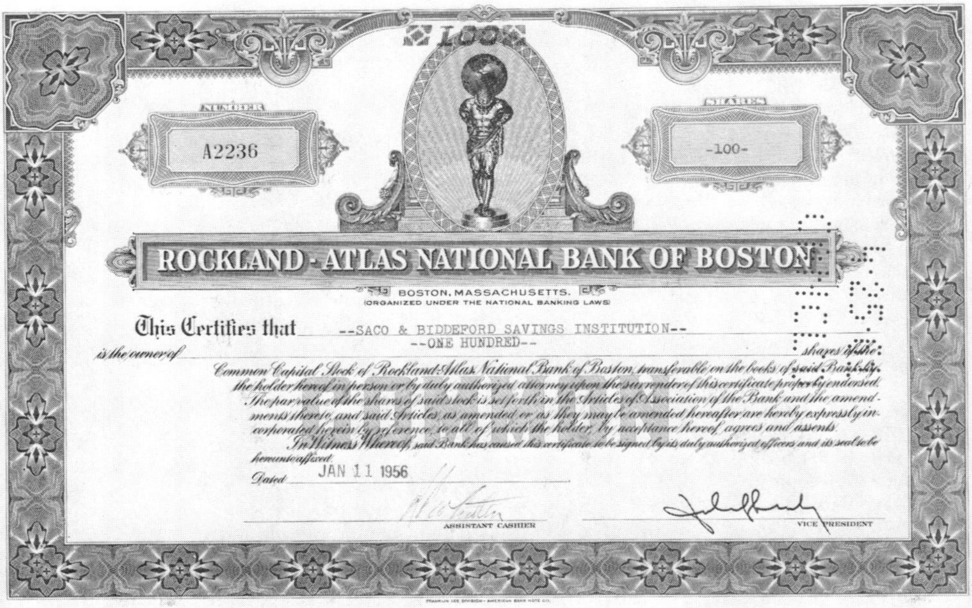

NUMBER A2236

SHARES -100-

ROCKLAND - ATLAS NATIONAL BANK OF BOSTON

BOSTON, MASSACHUSETTS.
(ORGANIZED UNDER THE NATIONAL BANKING LAWS)

This Certifies that --SACO & BIDDEFORD SAVINGS INSTITUTION--

is the owner of --ONE HUNDRED-- shares of the

Common Capital Stock of Rockland-Atlas National Bank of Boston, transferable on the books of said Bank by the holder hereof in person or by duly authorized attorney upon the surrender of this certificate properly endorsed. The par value of the shares of said stock is set forth in the Articles of Association of the Bank and the amendments thereto, and said Articles, as amended or as they may be amended hereafter are hereby expressly incorporated herein by reference, to all of which the holder, by acceptance hereof, agrees and assents.

In Witness Whereof, said Bank has caused this certificate to be signed by its duly authorized officers and its seal to be hereunto affixed.

Dated JAN 11 1956

ASSISTANT CASHIER

VICE PRESIDENT

NUMBER 102

SHARES -5-

Central Farmers' Trust Company

West Palm Beach, Florida

This Certifies that JAMES H. PERKINS

is the owner of FIVE full paid shares of One Hundred Dollars each of the Capital Stock of Central Farmers' Trust Company, a Corporation existing under the laws of the State of Florida, transferable only on the books of the Corporation in person or by attorney on surrender of this certificate properly endorsed.

In Witness Whereof, the Corporation has caused this certificate to be signed by its duly authorized officers and its corporate seal to be hereunto affixed, at West Palm Beach, Florida, this September 8, 1933 19

Secretary

President

Inspiration Oil and Refining (U), **Arizona**, Oil field vignette 7.00
Intercontinent Petroleum (I), **1920s** 4.00
International Oil of New Orleans (I-N), **1900s**, Oil derricks and horse-drawn tank cars vignette 17.00
Invincible Oil (I), **1920s**, Train and oil gushers vignette 15.00
Invincible Oil (U), **1920s**, Train and oil gushers vignette 5.00
Ixl Oil and Refining (I), **1910s**, **Colorado**, Oil gushers vignette 10.00

Kanawha River Oil Company (I), **1860s**, **West Virginia**, Oil derricks vignette 245.00
Karthaus and Salt Lick Oil Company (I), **1860s**, **Pennsylvania**, Oil derricks vignette with stamps 190.00
Kerr-McGee Oil (I), **1950s**, Five and one-fourth percent bond, oil field vignette 9.00
Kerr-McGee Oil (I), **1950s**, Oil scenes and woman vignette 7.00
Keystone Oil Company (U), **1900s**, **Arizona Territory**, Eagle vignette 8.00
Kimbly Oil and Refining (I-N), **1910s**, Eagle and oil fields vignette 9.00
King Petroleum Corporation (I), **1920s**, Oil field vignette 7.00
King Petroleum Corporation (I-N), **1920s**, Huge oil field vignette 10.00
Koss Royalty (I-N), **1920s**, **Texas**, Large vignette of oil fields 15.00

Lee Oil and Natural Gas (I), **Maryland**, Lady and lion vignette 3.00
Lehigh and Wyoming Oil Company (U), **1860s**, Oil derrick scene 85.00
Leonard Oil Development (I-N), **1940s**, Gushing oil well vignette 9.00
Lexa Oil Corporation (I), **1950s**, Oil gusher vignette 10.00
Louisiana Oil Company (I-N), **1900s**, **Arizona Territory**, Eagle vignette 20.00
Lucky Dime Oil Company (I), **1900s**, **Texas**, Train with oil derricks vignette and seal 15.00

McPartlan-Smackover Lease Syndicate (I-N), **1920s** 4.00
Mahoning Oil Company (I), **1860s**, **Pennsylvania**, Oil derrick vignette 175.00
Mammoth Cave Petroleum and Mining (I), **1860s**, **Kentucky**, Oil derrick and train vignette 300.00
Mammoth Oil Products (I), **1910s**, Oil field vignette 16.00
Maple Farm Oil Company (I), **1860s**, **Pennsylvania**, Oil derricks and tanks in mountains vignette 95.00
Maracaibo Oil Exploration (I), **1950s**, Seated lady with two men vignette 3.00
Mid-Continent Petroleum (I), **1910s**, Two oil field vignettes 15.00
Mid-Mesa Oil (U), Oil well vignette 5.00
Mission Development (I), **1950s** 5.00
Missouri, Kansas and Texas Oil Company (I), Embossed seal 12.00
Mobil Oil Corporation (I), **1970s**, Seminude lady with torch and flying horse logo vignette 5.00
Mojo Oil and Refining (I), **1920s**, **Indiana**, Oil field vignette 10.00
Monarch-Greybull Oil (I), **1910s**, **Washington**, Oil derrick vignette 12.00
Monongah Oil (I), **1910s** 10.00
Mountain States Oil (I-N), **1910s**, **Wyoming**, Mountain scene 12.00
Mud Creek Valley Oil Company (I), **1860s**, **New York**, Oil derrick and sheds vignette and stamp 300.00
Muncie Natural Gas and Land Improvement Company (I), **1890s**, **Indiana**, Gas well gusher, embossed seal 50.00

Napa Petroleum (I), **1860s**, Capitol stock, standing woman vignette, with revenue stamp 215.00
National Consolidated Oil Company, The (I-N), **1900s**, Large oil field vignette, with stamps 14.00
New England Gas and Oil Corporation (I), **1900s**, Oil field vignette 22.00

◀ ***Boston, Rockland-Atlas National Bank of (I), 1950s,*** *Vignette of man with world on his back* ***10.00***
◀ ***Central Farmers' Trust Company (I), 1930s,*** *Eagle with shield vignette* ***3.00***

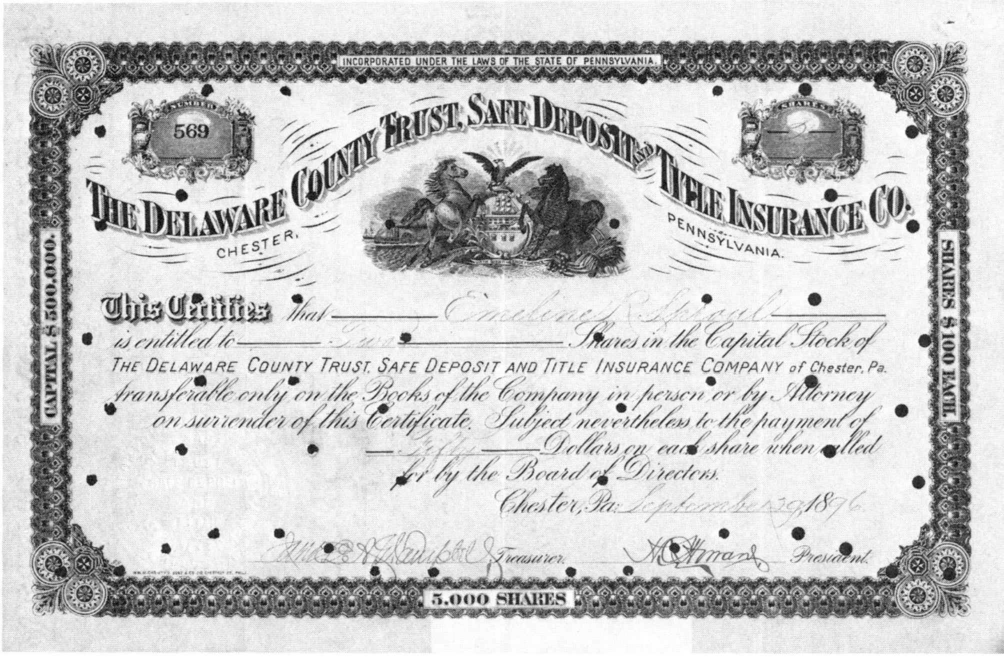
INCORPORATED UNDER THE LAWS OF THE STATE OF PENNSYLVANIA.
569
THE DELAWARE COUNTY TRUST, SAFE DEPOSIT AND TITLE INSURANCE CO.
CHESTER, PENNSYLVANIA.
CAPITAL $500,000.
SHARES $100 EACH.
This Certifies that
is entitled to Shares in the Capital Stock of
THE DELAWARE COUNTY TRUST, SAFE DEPOSIT AND TITLE INSURANCE COMPANY of Chester, Pa.
transferable only on the Books of the Company in person or by Attorney
on surrender of this Certificate. Subject nevertheless to the payment of
Dollars on each share when called
for by the Board of Directors.
Chester, Pa. September 30, 1896
Treasurer.
President.
5,000 SHARES
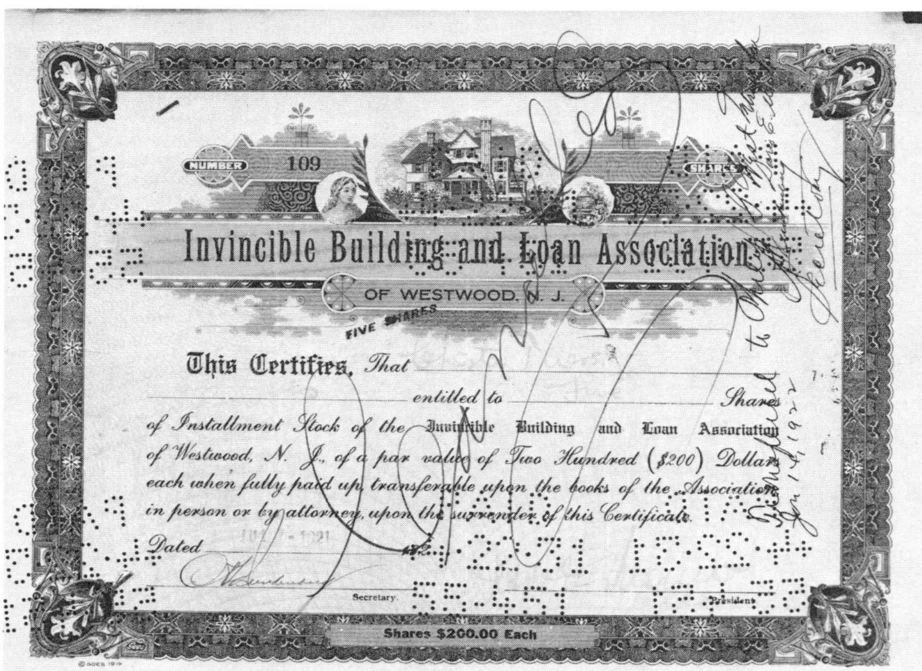
NUMBER
109
SHARES
Invincible Building and Loan Association
OF WESTWOOD, N. J.
FIVE SHARES
This Certifies, That
entitled to
Shares
of Installment Stock of the Invincible Building and Loan Association
of Westwood, N. J., of a par value of Two Hundred ($200) Dollars
each when fully paid up, transferable upon the books of the Association
in person or by attorney, upon the surrender of this Certificate.
Dated
Secretary.
President.
Shares $200.00 Each

New England Oil Corporation (I), 1920s, Ships and railroad cars vignette	13.00
Newport Texas Oil and Pipe Line (I), 1900s, Texas, Two oil field vignettes	24.00
Nicaragua Oil (I), 1920s, Nevada, Oil derricks vignette	9.00
Noble Farm Petroleum Company (I), 1860s, Pennsylvania, Oil derrick vignette, stamp	235.00
Norman Oil (I), 1920s, Bond train and oil derricks vignette	43.00
North Star Oil Company (I), Nevada, Eagle on mountain vignette	3.00
North Texas Central Oil (I), 1920s, Workers at oil derrick vignette	17.00
Northern Consolidated Oil and Mining Number Two (I), 1900s, Oil field vignette	28.00
No-Wood River Oil (I-N), 1880s, Wyoming Territory, Oil rigs, tanks, trains	100.00
Nyvatex Oil Corporation (I), 1950s, Texas, Eagle and company logo vignette	2.00
Oil and Gas Company (I-N), 1910s, Kansas, Large vignette of gushers, storage tanks, and buildings	12.00
Oil Creek and Caldwell Branch Petroleum Company (U), Pennsylvania, Oil derrick vignette	84.00
Oil Creek Petroleum Company (I), 1860s, New York, Oil derrick, train, and figures vignette	195.00
Oil Creek Petroleum Company (U), 1860s, California, Derricks scene	80.00
Oil Field Lease Syndicate (I-N), Large oil field scene	14.00
Oklahoma Oil Company (I), 1910s	10.00
Oltex Oil (I-N), 1920s, Oil gushers, derricks, and train vignette	8.00
Orange Oil Production (U), 1920s, Texas, Star in wreath vignette	5.00
Pacific Union Oil (I), 1900s, California, Oil field, gold seal	28.00
Palmer Union Oil (I), 1920s, Oil field vignette	7.00
Palmer Union Oil (U), 1920s, Oil field vignette	4.00
Panhandle Eastern Pipe Line Company (I), 1970s, Oil derricks, tanks and valves, and skyline vignette	2.00
Paramount Oil and Gas (I), 1910s, Nevada, Oil gusher vignette	7.00
Paramount Royalty Syndicate (I-N), 1920s, Oil gushers, derricks, and train vignette	8.00
Penn Osage Oil (I-N), 1910s, Oil gusher vignette	17.00
Phoenix Oil Company (I), 1860s, Pennsylvania, Eagle, derrick, and two figures vignette	300.00
Phoenix Oil Company (U), 1930s, Oil field, tank cars	7.50
Pithole and Kanawha Oil (U), 1860s, Pennsylvania, Two horses vignette	13.00
Producers and Refiners (I-N), 1920s, Oil rig and tank vignette	19.00
Producing Royalties Pool, Inc. (I-N), 1920s, Eagle vignette	4.00
Producing Royalties Pool, Inc. (I-N), 1920s, Lighted torch vignette	4.00
Progress Oil and Gas (I), 1910s, Gushing oil derrick vignette	20.00
Quaker 777 Oil (I), 1910s, Oil derricks and gusher vignette	28.00
Quaker State Oil Refining (U), Specimen, oil well, buildings, and tank cars vignette	15.00
Queen Oil (I-N), 1910s, Oil derricks, train, and gushers vignette	10.00
Quimby Farm Oil Company (I), 1860s, Oil derricks vignette, revenue stamp	135.00
Red Arrow Oil and Gas Company (I), 1910s, Arizona, Oil derricks and gusher vignette, gold seal	20.00
Red Bank Oil Company (I), 1950s, Eagle vignette	3.00
Reece Oil (I), 1920s, Indiana, Oil field vignette	8.00
Reece Oil Company (I-N), 1920s, Indiana, Oil field vignette	10.00
Republic Refining Company (I), 1920s, Bond, eagle vignette, gold seal	12.00

◀ ***Delaware County Trust, Safe Deposit and Title Insurance Co. (I), 1890s,*** *No vignette*	***9.00***
◀ ***Invincible Building and Loan Association of Westwood, N.J. (I), 1920s, New Jersey,*** *Family home vignette*	***6.00***

NUMBER 713

SHARES 5

THE LONG ISLAND NATIONAL BANK OF NEW YORK

THIS CERTIFIES that Samuel J Gold in Trust for Minnie Gold

is the owner of Five (5) shares

of the par value of One Hundred Dollars each in the Capital Stock of the

THE LONG ISLAND NATIONAL BANK OF NEW YORK

transferable only on the books of the said Bank, by the said holder, in person or by attorney, upon surrender of this Certificate properly endorsed.

WITNESS the signatures of the President and the Cashier, and the seal of the said Bank, this 19th day of May 1928

Cashier. President.

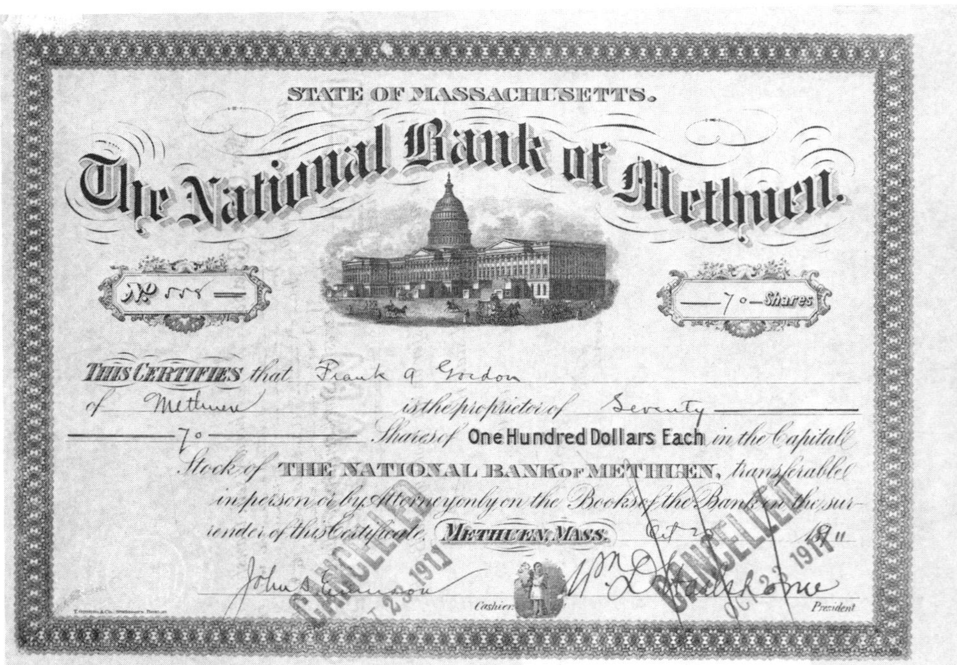
STATE OF MASSACHUSETTS.

The National Bank of Methuen.

№ 558

70 Shares

THIS CERTIFIES that Frank A Gordon of Methuen is the proprietor of Seventy 70 Shares of One Hundred Dollars Each in the Capital Stock of THE NATIONAL BANK OF METHUEN, transferable in person or by Attorney only on the Books of the Bank on the surrender of this Certificate. METHUEN, MASS. Oct 2 1911

CANCELLED OCT 23 1911

Cashier President

Revere Oil Company (I), 1920s	**10.00**
Rice Ranch Oil (I-N), 1920s, Oil derricks and gushers vignette	**15.00**
Rocky Hill Oil and Gas (I), 1920s, State capitol building vignette	**10.00**
Root Oil Company (I), 1920s, Indiana, Oil field vignette	**12.00**
Rosa Renavides Syndicate (I-N), 1920s, Texas	**5.00**
Ross Oil Company (I), 1860s, Pennsylvania, Derrick, portrait vignette, plus stamp	**150.00**
Rumsey Petroleum Company (I), 1920s, Oklahoma	**5.00**
Rumsey Petroleum Company (I), 1920s, Oklahoma, Scrip certificate	**3.00**
Saint Urain Petroleum (I), 1930s, Two oil well vignettes	**6.00**
Sandy River Petroleum Prize Company (I), 1860s, New York, Oil derricks vignette, plus stamp	**180.00**
Sawyer Petroleum (I), 1960s, Arizona, Large eagle vignette	**2.00**
Schuylkill and Oil Creek Oil Company (I), 1860s, Revenue stamp	**95.00**
Security Oil Company (I-N), 1910s, Oil wells and storage tanks vignette	**15.00**
Sedalia and California Oil Company (I-N), 1900s, Oil derricks vignettes	**28.00**
Shenango Oil Company (I), 1860s, Pennsylvania, Oil derrick with tanks and train vignette	**110.00**
Ship Channel Oil Company (I), 1920s, Indiana, Eagle vignette	**10.00**
Sierra Refining Company (I), 1920s, Eagle vignette	**3.00**
Signal Petroleum Company (I-N), Oil well vignette, two wells in border	**6.00**
Sinclair Oil Reclamation (I-N), 1920s, Iowa, Seated woman vignette	**10.00**
Socony Mobil, Inc. (I), 1950s, Lady with flaming torch between two worlds vignette	**5.00**
Socony Mobil Oil (I), 1960s, Certificate, goddess and gloves vignette	**3.00**
Socony Mobil Oil (I), 1960s, Four and one-half percent bond, goddess with two hemispheres vignette	**12.00**
Socony Vacuum Corporation (I), 1930s, Seminude woman between two globes vignette	**10.00**
Solid Rock Oil Company (I), 1900s, Train and oil field vignette	**24.00**
South American Oil (U), 1920s, Train and oil derrick vignette	**7.00**
Southern Oil and Transport (I-N), 1920s, Train, oil rigs, and tanks vignette	**20.00**
Standard Oil (I), 1870s, Vignette of capitol building, signed by John D. Rockefeller and made out to others	**750.00**
Standard Oil Company of Mexico (I), 1900s, South Dakota, Large oil field with tank train vignette	**75.00**
Standard Oil of New Jersey (I), 1950s, Oil rig workers vignette	**18.00**
Standard Oil of New Jersey (U), 1950s, Bond, specimen, woman with globe and oil scenes	**28.00**
Star Petroleum (I), 1900s, Texas, Embossed seal	**10.00**
Success Oil Company (I), 1900s, Texas, Oil fields	**20.00**
Sun Oil Company (I), 1960s, New Jersey, Man and woman with company logo vignette	**1.00**
Sunray Oil Company (I), 1960s, Chemist, oil derricks, and tank cars vignette	**2.00**
Superior Oil Company (I), 1950s, Bond	**3.00**
Sycamore Oil Company (I), 1860s, Oil derricks, and oil tank vignette	**140.00**
Tarr and Scott Farm Oil Company (I), 1860s, Pennsylvania, Oil derricks, boats, portrait, and eagle vignette, plus stamp	**245.00**
Texas Crescent Oil Company (I), 1910s, Oil derricks and gushers vignette	**12.00**
Texiana Petroleum (I), 1920s, Colorado	**12.00**
Thrift Royalty Company (I-N), 1920s, Texas, Oil gusher vignette	**7.00**
Tidewater Associated Oil (U), 1930s, Specimen, oil industry scenes	**30.00**
Tower and McKanna (U), 1920s, Oil field vignette	**5.00**

◀ ***Long Island National Bank of New York, The (I), 1920s,*** *Eagle vignette, many stamps*	***6.00***
◀ ***Methuen, The National Bank of (I), 1910s, Maine,*** *Capitol building vignette*	***10.00***

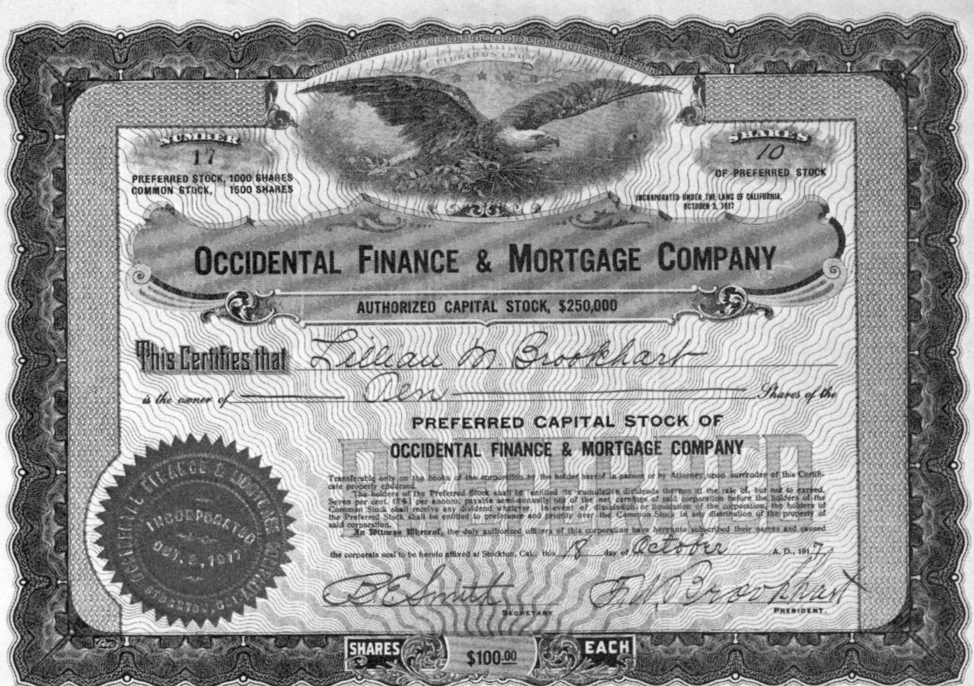

NUMBER 17

PREFERRED STOCK, 1000 SHARES
COMMON STOCK, 1500 SHARES

SHARES 10

OF PREFERRED STOCK

INCORPORATED UNDER THE LAWS OF CALIFORNIA, OCTOBER 3, 1917

OCCIDENTAL FINANCE & MORTGAGE COMPANY

AUTHORIZED CAPITAL STOCK, $250,000

This Certifies that Lillian M. Brookhart

is the owner of Ten Shares of the

PREFERRED CAPITAL STOCK OF

OCCIDENTAL FINANCE & MORTGAGE COMPANY

Transferable only on the books of the corporation by the holder hereof in person or by Attorney upon surrender of this Certificate properly endorsed.

The holders of the Preferred Stock shall be entitled to cumulative dividends thereon at the rate of, but not to exceed, Seven per cent. (7%) per annum, payable semi-annually out of the net earnings of said corporation before the holders of the Common Stock shall receive any dividend whatever. In event of dissolution, or liquidation of the corporation, the holders of the Preferred Stock shall be entitled to preference and priority over the Common Stock in any distribution of the property of said corporation.

In Witness Whereof, the duly authorized officers of this corporation have hereunto subscribed their names and caused the corporate seal to be hereto affixed at Stockton, Cal., this 18 day of October A. D., 1917

B. E. Smith, SECRETARY — F. M. Brookhart, PRESIDENT.

SHARES $100.00 EACH

ATWOOD PRINTING CO., MASONIC TEMPLE STOCKTON, CAL.

INCORPORATED UNDER THE BANKING LAW OF THE STATE OF NEW YORK

100 SHARES

NUMBER 12545

SHARES 100

The Bank of United States

CAPITAL STOCK $20,875,000 PAR VALUE OF SHARES $25.00 EACH

This is to Certify that -SAUL SINGER- is the owner of

One Hundred

fully paid shares of the capital stock of The Bank of United States, transferable upon conditions specified on the reverse side hereof and only on the books of the Bank, in person or by duly authorized attorney, upon the surrender of this certificate properly endorsed.

This certificate is not valid until registered by the Registrar.

Witness the seal of the Bank and the signatures of its duly authorized officers

Dated: DEC 10 1930

CASHIER. VICE PRESIDENT.

REGISTERED: THE CHASE NATIONAL BANK OF THE CITY OF NEW YORK, REGISTRAR, BY ASSISTANT CASHIER

THIS CERTIFICATE CANNOT BE TRANSFERRED WITHOUT TRANSFERRING AT THE SAME TIME THE ATTACHED CERTIFICATE FOR BANKUS CORPORATION STOCK.

HAMILTON BANK NOTE COMPANY, NEW YORK.

Trans Ocean Gulf Oil (I), 1960s, Bond	6.00
Transit Oil and Gas (I-N), 1960s, Arizona, Gusher in oil field vignette	15.00
Triumph Oil Company (I), 1860s, Pennsylvania, Oil derricks vignette, plus stamp	285.00
Tug River Natural Gas (I), 1930s, Drilling vignettes	6.00
Tuxpam Star Oil (I), 1910s, Oil gusher vignette	12.00
Uncle Sam Oil (I), 1910s, Arizona Territory, Oil fields with gusher vignette	30.00
Uncle Sam Oil (I-N), 1900s, Arizona Territory, Oil gushers vignette	40.00
Uncle Sam Oil (I-N), 1910s, Kansas, gold bond	20.00
Union Consolidated Oil (I-N), 1900s, West Virginia, Eagle, train, buffalo, and shield vignette	15.00
Union Oil and Coal Company (I), 1870s, Pennsylvania, Oil derrick and tank vignette, plus seal	145.00
Unita Oil and Exploration Company, (I), 1920s, Oil gushers, refineries, and tank scenes	12.00
United Oil Corporation (I), 1950s, Oil well, train, and woman vignette	7.00
United Plains Oil (I), 1960s, Oklahoma, Big star vignette	5.00
Victoria Oil (I-N), 1910, Train, oil derricks, and tanks vignette	18.00
Victory Oil (I), 1920s, Colorado, Gushers, train, and refineries scene, embossed seal	12.00
Washington Natural Gas and Oil (I), 1900s, Oil derricks vignette	14.00
Wayland Oil and Gas (I-N), 1910s, West Virginia, Figure and industrial scene	15.00
Western Oil and Refining Company (I-N), 1930s	3.00
Western Oil, Land and Engineering (I), 1900s, Arizona, Train and oil field vignette	15.00
Westfield Petroleum (I), 1910s, Oklahoma, Huge oil field scene	20.00
White Throne Oil (U), 1920s, Utah, Oil wells vignette	5.00
Williams Bros. (I), 1960s, Bond, seminude chemist, oil derricks, tanks, and shut-off valve vignette	5.00
Williston Basin Oil Exploration (I), 1950s, Utah, Eagle vignette	1.50
Williston Basin Oil Exploration (I), 1950s, Utah, Goddess vignette	2.00
World Oil (I), 1920s, Texas, Embossed seal	5.00
World Oil (I-N), 1920s, Texas, Texas star vignette	8.00
Wyoga Gas and Oil (I), 1930s, Eagle and shield vignette, embossed seal	6.00
Y Oil and Gas (I), 1920s, Wyoming	3.00
Zapata Producing and Refining	12.00

Occidental Finance and Mortgage Company (I), 1910s, California, *Eagle vignette, seal*	***6.00***
United States, Bank of, 1930s, *Eagle vignette and seal*	***7.00***

No. 9 — 5 — SHARES

INCORPORATED UNDER THE LAWS OF THE STATE OF PENNSYLVANIA

Valley Thrift Corporation

This Certifies that, *Benjamin Goodman*
is the owner of *FIVE* Shares of the Capital Stock of

VALLEY THRIFT CORPORATION

fully paid and non-assessable, transferable only in person or by attorney upon the books of the said corporation, upon surrender of this certificate properly endorsed.

1. The stock represented by this Certificate is Preferred Stock of the Valley Thrift Corporation, and is entitled to an annual dividend of 6 per cent. payable out of the net profits of the corporation before any dividend is paid upon any common stock of said corporation. Should the net profits at any time be insufficient to pay said preferred dividend, either in whole or in part, any unpaid portion thereof shall become a charge against the net profits of said corporation before any dividends are paid upon the common stock, and shall remain a charge upon such net profits until any deferred preferred dividends shall have been fully paid.

2. The dividends to become due and payable upon this stock shall be paid on the first day of January, April, July and October of each year and the same shall be payable to the stockholders of record on the fifteenth day of the month preceding that in which the dividend becomes payable.

3. The holder of this stock certificate by his acceptance hereof, agrees to each and all of the provisions as set forth hereon and in paragraphs 4 and 5 upon the back of this certificate.

In Witness Whereof, the said Corporation has caused this certificate to be signed by its duly authorized officers and its Corporate seal to be hereunto affixed this 1st
day of November A. D. 1930.

TREASURER — PRESIDENT

SHARES 100 EACH

STATE OF PENNSYLVANIA

THE FUNDED LOAN OF **The City of Altoona.** IT IS HEREBY CERTIFIED THAT

NUMBER 213

The City of Altoona is indebted to ~~*Trustee for James J. Hazuria*~~
in the sum of ~~*Two Thousand*~~ *dollars lawful money of the United States of America. Redeemable at the option of said City on and after the first day of July A.D. 1901, and payable at the office of the Treasurer of the City of Altoona on the first day of July A.D. 1906, with interest at the rate of* **FOUR** *per cent per annum payable semi-annually on the first day of January and July, at such place in the City of Philadelphia as shall be designated by the semi-annual notice of the Treasurer of the City of Altoona, to be given for that purpose in one of the daily newspapers of the City of Philadelphia. This bond is registered in the name of the owner thereof, on the books of the Treasurer of the City of Altoona and is transferable on said books in person or by Attorney in sums of one hundred dollars or any multiple thereof. This bond is issued under authority of an Act of General Assembly of the Commonwealth of Pennsylvania approved the 14th day of April A.D. 1882 and an Ordinance of said City of Altoona approved the 31st day of May A.D. 1886 and is free of all taxes.*

In Witness whereof *the Mayor of said City of Altoona has hereunto affixed his signature and the Corporate Seal of said City, and the Controller of said City has countersigned the same.*

Dated Altoona, Pa.

City Controller. — *Mayor.*

REAL ESTATE

Arapahoe Cattle and Land Company (I), 1880s, Colorado, Large vignette of cow with calf 110.00

Berkeley Development (U), 1890s, Street scene 38.00
Boston and Montana Development Company (I), 1910s, Indian chief vignette 50.00
Boston and New York Chichasaw Land Company (I), 1830s, Indian vignette 225.00
Boston Chamber of Commerce Realty Trust (I), 1920s, Massachusetts, Old office building and autos vignette 4.00
Boston Metropolitan Buildings, Voting Trust 1.00
Broadway Halsted Building Corporation (I), 1920s, Seven percent real estate gold bond 3.00
Builder's Investment Group (I), 1970s, Seated girl before panoramic view 1.00

Cairo Trust Company (I), 1870s, Illinois, Land speculation certificate 20.00
Central Canal and Land Company (I), Wyoming Territory, Farm scene 195.00
Central Land Company (U), 1800s, California, Dog in foreground of building vignette 15.00
Central Union Realty Trust (I), 1920s, Six percent bond, eagle, flag, and capitol dome vignette 8.00
Chopin Theater Building (I), 1910s, Six percent bond 4.00
Citrus Belt Land Company (I), 1910s, Warrior vignette 6.00
Clarke Estate Company (I), 1920s, Gold bond, medical arts building, Kansas City, Missouri, vignette 12.00
Commercial Exchange Building (I), 1920s, California, Gold bond 4.00

Dakota Farm Mortgage Company (U), 1880s, Real estate bond, farmer working with horses, dog, eagle, and standing woman vignettes 195.00
Danielson Masonic Building Association (I), 1920s, Connecticut, Three percent bond 12.00
Danielson Masonic Building Association (I), 1940s, Connecticut, Three percent bond 10.00
Denver Land and Water Company (I), 1890s, Bond, eagle and figures vignette 25.00

El Capitan Land and Cattle Company (I), 1880s, New Mexican Territory, Vignette of horned steer 130.00

Fifteen Park Row Corporation (I), 1930s, New York, Gold bond, eagle vignette 3.00
First Real Estate Bond (I), 1920s 2.00
Foss Bond and Mortgage, Real Estate Collateral (I), 1920s, Five percent gold bond 3.00
Fourteen Thirty Chicago Avenue Building Corporation (I), 1920s, Eagle on rock vignette 2.00
Franklin County Land Office (U), Missouri, Eagle vignette 1.00

Gastonia Insurance and Realty Company (U), 1930s, North Carolina, Eagle vignette 2.00
Gulf Guaranty Land and Title Company, 1960s, Seven percent bond, eagle vignette 2.00

Hilldale Building Corporation (I), 1920s, Seven percent gold bond, large eagle vignette 3.00

Industrial Land Company (U), 1900s, Alabama, Eagle vignette, gold seal 2.00

Jarvis-Conklin Trust Company (I), 1880s, Missouri, Real estate mortgage Seven percent bond, farmers plowing vignette, sea at bottom 295.00

Kesef Realty (I), 1920s, Eagle, two allegorical figures, state seal, embossed green seal 4.00

La Marr Hotel (I), 1930s, Five percent bond 3.00

◀ ***Valley Thrift Corporation, The (I), 1930s,*** *Green embossed seal* ***3.00***
◀ ***Altoona, City of (I), 1880s,*** *Bond, city by river, old train vignette* ***35.00***

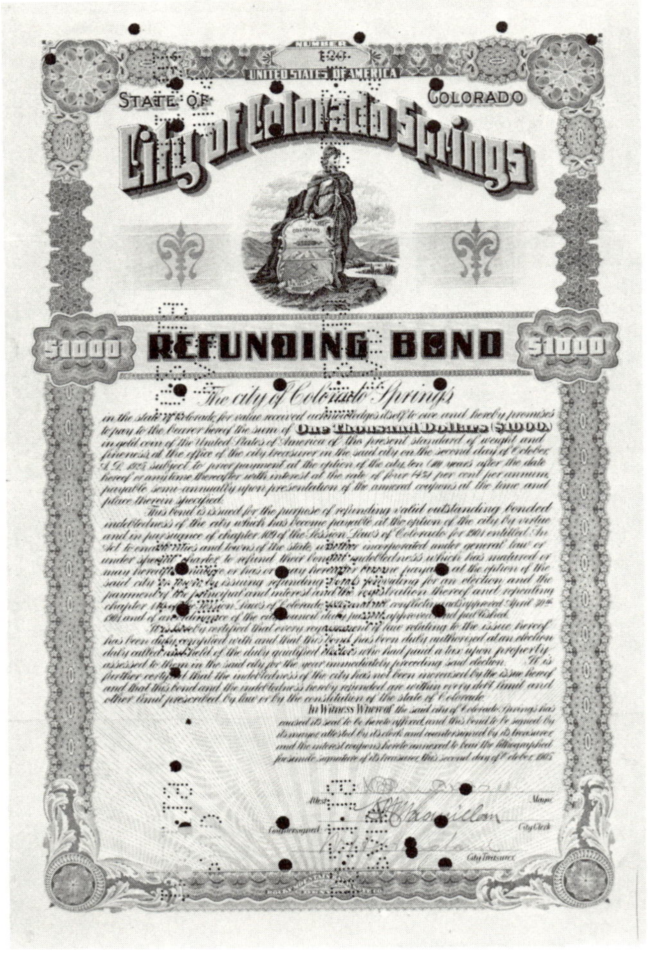

NUMBER

124

UNITED STATES OF AMERICA

STATE OF COLORADO

City of Colorado Springs

$1000 REFUNDING BOND $1000

The city of Colorado Springs

in the state of Colorado for value received acknowledges itself to owe and hereby promises to pay to the bearer hereof the sum of **One Thousand Dollars ($1000)** in gold coin of the United States of America of the present standard of weight and fineness at the office of the city treasurer in the said city on the second day of October A.D. 1925 subject to prior payment at the option of the city ten (10) years after the date hereof or anytime thereafter with interest at the rate of four (4%) per cent per annum payable semi-annually upon presentation of the annexed coupons at the time and place therein specified.

This bond is issued for the purpose of refunding valid outstanding bonded indebtedness of the city which has become payable at the option of the city by virtue and in pursuance of chapter 109 of the Session Laws of Colorado for 1901 entitled "An Act to enable cities and towns of the state, whether incorporated under general law or under special charter to refund their bonded indebtedness which has matured or may hereafter mature or has or may hereafter become payable at the option of the said city or town by issuing refunding bonds providing for an election and the payment of the principal and interest and the registration thereof and repealing chapter [illegible] of the Session Laws of Colorado [illegible] and all conflicting acts approved April 30th 1901 and of an ordinance of the city council duly passed, approved and published.

It is hereby certified that every requirement of law relating to the issue hereof has been duly complied with and that this bond has been duly authorized at an election duly called and held of the duly qualified electors who had paid a tax upon property assessed to them in the said city for the year immediately preceding said election. It is further certified that the indebtedness of the city has not been increased by the issue hereof and that this bond and the indebtedness hereby refunded are within every debt limit and other limit prescribed by law or by the constitution of the state of Colorado.

In Witness Whereof the said city of Colorado Springs has caused its seal to be hereto affixed and this bond to be signed by its mayor attested by its clerk and countersigned by its treasurer and the interest coupons hereto annexed to bear the lithographed facsimile signature of its treasurer this second day of October 1905

Mayor

Attest

City Clerk

Countersigned

City Treasurer

Lake Terrace Apartments (I), **1920s, Illinois**, Gold bond, eagle vignette 5.00
Loews Boston Theaters (I), **1920s** 8.00

Madison Clark Building (I), **1920s**, Bond, eagle vignette 5.00
Madison Clark Building (I), **1920s**, Gold bond, coat of arms vignette 6.00
Madison River Improvement Company (I), **1900s**, Large eagle, train, and ship vignette 8.00
Monarch Timber (I), **1900s, Idaho**, Large eagle vignette 7.00

Newhall Land and Farming (I), **1970s**, Pretty girl under tree in summertime vignette 1.00
North American Land Company (I), **1790s**, Robert Morris signatures 495.00
North Western Development Company (I), **1900s, Maine**, Five percent gold bond 63.00

One William Street Fund (I), **1950s and 1960s, Maryland**, Entry to building vignette 2.00
Owner's Realty Company (I), **1930s**, Six percent gold bond 3.00

People's Homestead Company 1880s, Warranty deed option bond 30.00
Puget Sound Commercial Company (U), **1870s**, Two large waterfront vignettes 120.00

Ramsen Realty Company (U), **1900s, New York**, State seal 3.00
Realty Investment Bond (I), **1890s** 4.00
Realty Syndicate (I), **1890s, California** 5.00
Realty Syndicate (I), **1890s, California**, Bond 5.00
Realty Syndicate Paid Up Certificate, 1890s 5.00
Red Hook Building Company (I), **1830s, New York**, Blacksmith vignette 140.00
Reppard Land, Lumber and Saw Mill (I), **1880s** 30.00
Reynolds-Alaska Development Company (I), **1910s, Washington**, Standing and seated figures with flag, train, and ship vignette 42.00
Rocky Ford Canal, Reservoir, Land, Loan and Trust Company (I), **1910s**, Gold bond 5.00
Roseland Block (I), **1920s**, Six percent gold bond, large eagle vignette 5.00

San Diego Land and Town Company 1890s, Maine, Indiana in front of city vignette, seal 44.00
Scandinavian Realty Company (U), **1920s, Michigan**, Lady vignette 3.00
Seventy-Fifth Street Land Association (I-N), **1910s** 4.00
State-Lake Office Building and Theatre (I), **1910s**, Six percent real estate gold bond, with stamp 6.00
Summer Street Trust (I), **1920s, Massachusetts** 1.00

Texas Association (U), **1800s**, Trinity River Ranch in Texas, cowboy on horse vignette 695.00
Third Avenue Corporation (I), **1930s, New York**, Seated man and woman, oil tank, factory, and train vignettes 3.00

Union Realty and Investment (I), **1910s**, Bond with documentary stamp 2.00
United States Land Company (I), **1880s**, 14.00
Urbain, L. and N., Leasehold Estate, 1920s, Six and one-half percent gold bond, with stamp 4.00
Utman Farms (I), **1910s, Wisconsin**, Real estate gold bond with stamp 9.00

Van Alst Land (I), **1920s**, Six percent gold bond, lighted torch vignette 3.00

Wahnetah Land and Improvement Company (U), **1800s, New York**, Indian, Indian maiden, and horse (three vignettes) 18.00
Webb and Knapp Real Estate (I), Vignette of United Nations Buildings 10.00
West Iron Gate Land Company (U), **1890s, Virginia**, River between mountains vignette 39.00

◀ ***Colorado Springs, City of (I), 1900s, Colorado,*** *Four percent refunding bond* ***40.00***

No. 474 UNITED STATES OF AMERICA. No. 474

$1000 STATE OF NEW JERSEY $1000

CITY OF JERSEY CITY

FOUR PER CENT SCHOOL BONDS

— GOLD —

Know all Men by these Presents that The Mayor and Aldermen of Jersey City, a municipal corporation of the State of New Jersey, does hereby for value received acknowledge itself to be indebted and firmly bound unto or bearer in the sum of **One Thousand Dollars** gold coin of the United States of America of the present standard of weight and fineness to be paid at the Office of the City Treasurer of Jersey City on the First day of May One thousand nine hundred and thirty seven with interest thereon at the rate of four per cent per annum payable in like gold coin on the first days of every May and November hereafter until this bond is paid on presentation and surrender of the proper coupon hereto annexed. This bond is executed and issued in conformity with a resolution passed for that purpose on April fifth 1907, by the Board of Finance of Jersey City and approved by the Mayor of said City on April sixth 1907, under an Act of the Legislature of the State of New Jersey entitled An Act to establish a thorough and efficient system of free public schools and to provide for the maintenance, support and management thereof, approved October nineteenth 1903. This bond is exempt from taxation under the Laws of the State of New Jersey.

In Witness Whereof, this Bond is signed by the Mayor of Jersey City and sealed with the corporate seal of the said The Mayor and Aldermen of Jersey City, attested by the City Clerk and countersigned by the City Comptroller this First day of May One thousand nine hundred and seven.

Mayor.

Attest

City Clerk.

COUNTERSIGNED

City Comptroller.

INTERNATIONAL BANK NOTE Co. N.Y.

Western Townsite Company of Montana (U), 1900s, Eagle vignette 6.00
Western Townsite Company of Washington (U), 1900s, Eagle vignette 7.00
Wynlake Crest Apartments, The (I), 1920s, Six and one-half percent gold bond, large eagle vignette 4.00

◀ ***Jersey City, City of, (I), 1900s,*** *One thousand dollar school gold bond, state seal* ***12.00***

UNITED STATES OF AMERICA

NUMBER 57

DOLLARS $500

STATE OF OREGON

County of Lincoln

REFUNDING GOLD BOND

SERIES "K"

County of Lincoln, STATE OF OREGON, FOR VALUE RECEIVED, PROMISES TO PAY TO BEARER, THE SUM OF

FIVE HUNDRED DOLLARS

ON THE FIRST DAY OF JULY, 1936, IN GOLD COIN OF THE UNITED STATES, ON PRESENTATION AND SURRENDER OF THIS OBLIGATION, WITHOUT GRACE, WITH INTEREST THEREON FROM THE DATE HEREOF UNTIL REDEEMED, OR UNTIL THE TIME OF THE SEMI-ANNUAL INTEREST PAYMENT NEXT ENSUING THE PUBLICATION OF NOTICE BY THE TREASURER OF LINCOLN COUNTY, OREGON THAT THIS BOND WILL BE TAKEN UP AND CANCELLED AND THAT INTEREST THEREON WILL CEASE AT THE INTEREST PAYMENT PERIOD NEXT FOLLOWING SUCH PUBLICATION, AT THE RATE OF 6% PER ANNUM, PAYABLE SEMI-ANNUALLY IN LIKE GOLD COIN ON THE 1st DAY OF JANUARY AND JULY IN EACH YEAR, ON THE PRESENTATION AND SURRENDER OF THE PROPER COUPONS HERETO ANNEXED, PRINCIPAL AND INTEREST PAYABLE AT THE FISCAL AGENCY OF THE STATE OF OREGON IN NEW YORK CITY.

THIS BOND IS ONE OF A SERIES OF LIKE DATE AND TENOR, EXCEPT AS TO MATURITY AND AMOUNT, AGGREGATING $32,400, PAR VALUE, ISSUED FOR THE PURPOSE OF

RETIRING MATURING LINCOLN COUNTY, OREGON BONDS IN AN EQUAL AMOUNT, UNDER AND PURSUANT TO CHAPTER 43 OF THE GENERAL LAWS OF OREGON FOR 1933.

IT IS HEREBY CERTIFIED THAT EVERY REQUIREMENT OF LAW RELATING TO THE ISSUANCE OF THIS SERIES OF BONDS HAS BEEN DULY COMPLIED WITH AND THAT THIS BOND IS WITHIN EVERY DEBT AND OTHER LIMIT PRESCRIBED BY THE CONSTITUTION OR LAWS OF THE STATE OF OREGON.

FOR THE FULFILLMENT OF THE CONDITIONS OF THIS OBLIGATION THE FULL FAITH AND CREDIT OF LINCOLN COUNTY, OREGON IS HEREBY IRREVOCABLY PLEDGED.

In Testimony Whereof, LINCOLN COUNTY, OREGON HAS CAUSED THE SEAL OF ITS COUNTY COURT TO BE HERETO ANNEXED AND THIS BOND TO BE SIGNED BY ITS COUNTY JUDGE AND ITS COUNTY CLERK, AND THE ANNEXED COUPONS TO BEAR FAC-SIMILE SIGNATURES OF SAID OFFICERS, THIS FIRST DAY OF JULY, 1933.

Lincoln County, Oregon

ATTEST:

COUNTY CLERK

BY

COUNTY JUDGE

© GOES 316

INDUSTRIES

A and P Company (I), 1920s, Issued to others but still signed by George Hartford, president of the company **12.00**
A and P Company (I), 1920s, Issued to president of company and signed by president, George Hartford **20.00**
A and P Tea Company, The Great, (I), 1970s, Maryland, Two winged ladies with company logo vignette **.85**
A. M. Byers Company (I), Pennsylvania, Man vignette **1.00**
Adams Nickel Plating and Manufacturing (U), 1870s, No vignette **9.00**
Adirondack Company (I), 1870s, New York, Seven percent gold bond, red seal, woman standing over globe with train in the distance **215.00**
Air Products and Chemical Inc. (I), 1970s, Seated man, tank cars, and modern buildings vignette **1.00**
Air Products and Chemical, Inc. (I), 1970s, Seminude man, factory, tank, trucks, and train vignette **2.00**
Aircraft Acceptance Corporation (I), 1960s, Ohio, Eagle vignette **3.00**
Akzona, Inc. (I), 1970s, Seated woman with globe and winged wheel vignette **1.00**
Alabama-Mississippi Investment and Development (U), 1900s, Mining and mountain scenes **8.00**
Alden Industries, Inc. (I), 1960s, Company building logo **.50**
Alden Type Setting and Distributing Machine (I), 1860s, New York, Old printing machine vignette and two portraits **170.00**
Alden Type Setting and Distributing Machine (U), 1860s, Old printing machine vignette and two portraits **40.00**
Algonquin Club (I), 1890s, Maine, Bond **65.00**
All City Insurance (I), 1870s, New York, United States map vignette **1.00**
Allegheny Corporation, Specimen, nude man with wheel vignette **5.00**
Alles and Fisher, Inc. (I),1920s, Massachusetts, Two cigars in vignette **5.00**
Allied Chemical (I), 1950s and 1960s, Seated woman between two men with lab equipment vignette **3.00**
Allied Chemical and Dye (I), 1940s, **3.00**
Allied Chemical and Dye (I), 1950s, Three and one-half percent bond, seated lady with globe **3.00**
Allied Kid Company (I), 1940s, Seated ladies and goats vignette **15.00**
Allied Stores (I), 1960s, Seated lady vignette **1.00**
All-State Credit Corporation (I), 1960s, Woman and two men vignette **2.00**
Aluminum Company of Canada (I), 1950s, Workmen and world globe vignette **2.00**
American and European Crystalized Egg Company (I), 1870s, No vignette **37.00**
American and Foreign Power Company, Inc. (I-N), 1930s, Warrant **3.00**
American Asbestos and Fireproofing Company (I), 1900s, Gold bond, phoenix in flames vignette **23.00**
American Book–Stratford Press (I), 1970s, New York, Eagle vignette **1.00**
American, British and Continental Corporation (I), 1920s and 1930s , Warrior with sword, figure with scales, kneeling woman vignette **3.00**
American Can Company (I), 1960s, Four and three-quarters percent bond, four allegorical figures with large winged wheel vignette **2.00**
American Caramel Company (U), 1890s, Eagle and coat of arms vignette **9.00**
American Caramel Company (I), 1910s, Eagle and coat of arms vignettes **9.00**
American Centrifugal Concrete Company (I-N), 1911, American territory, Goddess, Indians, and city vignette **35.00**
American Cities (I), 1910s, Topless lady vignette **14.00**
American Colortype Company (I), 1940s, Warrant **1.00**

◂ ***Lincoln, County of (I), 1930s, Oregon,*** *Six percent refunding gold bond, large eagle vignette* ***5.00***

NUMBER

84

1000 $ 1000

UNITED STATES OF AMERICA
STATE OF MICHIGAN
COUNTY OF MUSKEGON

CITY OF MUSKEGON HEIGHTS

MOTOR VEHICLE HIGHWAY FUND BOND

KNOW ALL MEN BY THESE PRESENTS that the CITY OF MUSKEGON HEIGHTS, County of Muskegon, State of Michigan, for value received hereby promises to pay to the bearer hereof the sum of

ONE THOUSAND DOLLARS

on the FIRST DAY OF MARCH, A.D., 1962,

with interest thereon from the date hereof until paid at the rate of three and three-quarters (3¾) per cent per annum, payable on September 1, 1957, and semi-annually thereafter on the first day of March and September of each year, upon presentation and surrender of the proper interest coupons hereto annexed, as they severally become due. Both principal of and interest on this bond are hereby made payable in lawful money of the United States of America at THE SPRING LAKE STATE BANK, Spring Lake, Michigan, and for the prompt payment of this bond, both principal and interest, the full faith, credit and resources of the City of Muskegon Heights are hereby irrevocably pledged.

This bond is one of a series of one hundred eighty (180) bonds of even date and like tenor, except as to rate of interest and date of maturity, aggregating the principal sum of $180,000.00, numbered consecutively in direct order of maturity from 1 to 180, both inclusive, issued pursuant to authority of Act 175, Public Acts of Michigan, 1952, and pursuant to resolution duly and regularly adopted by the City Council on March 4, 1957, as amended, for the purpose of paying part of the cost of constructing the Norton-Glade Expressway, and improving Summit Avenue from Harrison Avenue to Woodcliffe Street in said City.

This bond and the interest thereon are payable from the proceeds of State-collected taxes returned to the City of Muskegon Heights for road purposes pursuant to law; and the resolution authorizing the issuance and sale of said bonds contains an irrevocable appropriation of the amount necessary to pay the principal of and interest on this bond and the series of bonds of which this is one from moneys derived from such State-collected taxes returned to the City for highway purposes which have not been heretofore specifically allocated and pledged for the payment of indebtedness, or in case of the insufficiency of said State-returned funds, said principal and interest are payable from the general funds of the City of Muskegon Heights.

It is hereby certified and recited that all acts, conditions and things required to be done, exist and happen, precedent to and in the issuance of said series of bonds of which this is one, in order to make them valid and binding obligations of said City of Muskegon Heights, have been done, exist and have happened in regular and due form and time as required by law, and that the total indebtedness of said City, including the series of bonds of which this is one, does not exceed any constitutional, charter or statutory limitation.

IN WITNESS WHEREOF, the City of Muskegon Heights, County of Muskegon, State of Michigan, by its City Council, has caused this bond to be signed in the name of said City by its Mayor and to be countersigned by its City Treasurer and its corporate seal to be hereunto affixed, and has caused the annexed interest coupons to be executed with the facsimile signatures of said Mayor and City Treasurer, all as of the first day of March, A.D., 1957.

Countersigned:

Charles H Redman
City Treasurer

CITY OF MUSKEGON HEIGHTS

By Basil [illegible]
Mayor

NORTHERN BANK NOTE CO. CHICAGO

American Commonwealth Power Company (I), 1930s, Goddess plus factory and oil refinery vignette 8.00
American Commonwealth Power Corporation (I-N), 1930s, Goddess, power plant, and oil refinery vignettes 10.00
American Electric Power (I), 1960s, New York, Man with globe, woman with torch, and company logo vignettes 1.00
American Express (I), 1960s, New York, Portrait vignette 5.00
American Express Company (I), 1850s, Type I 1970.00
American Express Company (I), 1850s, Type II 1400.00
American Express Company (I), 1850s, Type III, train vignette 1450.00
American Express Company (I), 1860s, Type IV, signed by Wells and Fargo 800.00
American Express Company (I), 1860s, Type V, signed by Henry Wells, president of the company 750.00
American Express Company (I), 1870s, Type VI, Vignette of dog 485.00
American Express Company (I), 1960s, Type VII, Roman soldier vignette 5.00
American Financial and Home Stead (I), 1870s, Eagle, seminude lady, dog, and seal vignette 85.00
American Founders Corporation (I), 1920s, Maryland, Vignette of Washington and Jefferson, eagle, and Washington Monument 3.00
American Founders Corporation (I), 1930s, Maryland, Vignette of Washington and Jefferson, eagle, and Washington Monument 2.00
American General Corporation (I), 1930s and 1940s, Company logo 2.00
American General Insurance Company (I), 1970s, Texas, George Washington picture 4.00
American Hay and Cotton Press (I), 1860s, New York, Large vignette showing men, horse, and two level working press, also vignettes of farmers and cotton field 215.00
American International Corporation (U), 1920s, New York, Allegorical figures on each side of the western hemisphere 2.00
American League Baseball of Saint Louis (I), 1940s, (Old Saint Louis Browns), signed by Bill DeWitt 235.00
American Light and Traction (I), 1940s, Lady with electric torch vignette 1.50
American Locker Company (I), 1930s, Trustee certificate 2.00
American Locker Company (I), 1940s, Outline map of United States, eagle vignette 5.00
American Machine and Foundry (I), New Jersey, Man with gear and sledgehammer vignette 2.00
American Merchants Union Express (I), 1860s, William Fargo, president 420.00
American Natural Gas (I), 1930s, Two ladies vignette 5.00
American Natural Gas (I), 1950s and 1960s, Pipeline map from Houston to Detroit vignette 2.00
American Natural Resources (I), 1960s and 1970s, Two men with company logo vignette 1.00
American News Company (I), 1960s, Newsboy between two allegorical figures vignette 6.00
American Pneumatic Service (I), 1920s, Eagle vignette 4.00
American Radiator Company (U), 1920s, Specimen, bond, reclining woman vignette 10.00
American Reclamation Company (I), 1910s, Arizona, Colorful certificate, Indian, buffalo, eagle, flag, and shield vignette 6.00
American Safety Device (I), 1920s, Vignettes of building, bridges, and safety items 9.00
American Safety Device (I), 1930s, Vignettes of building, bridges, and safety items 5.00
American Safety Equipment (I), 1970s, Large vignette 2.00
American Sugar (I), 1960s, New Jersey, Three allegorical figures with tools and equipment vignette .85
American Superpower Corporation (I), 1920s, Old and new power stations and mountains vignette 5.00
American Telephone and Telegraph, 1930s, Specimen, five percent gold Bond, man with telephone to ship, plane, and overseas vignette 25.00
American Telephone and Telegraph (I), 1940s, Globe and old phones vignette 6.00

◀ ***Muskegan Heights, City of (I), 1950s,*** *Three and three-fourths percent highway bond, eagle vignette* ***6.00***

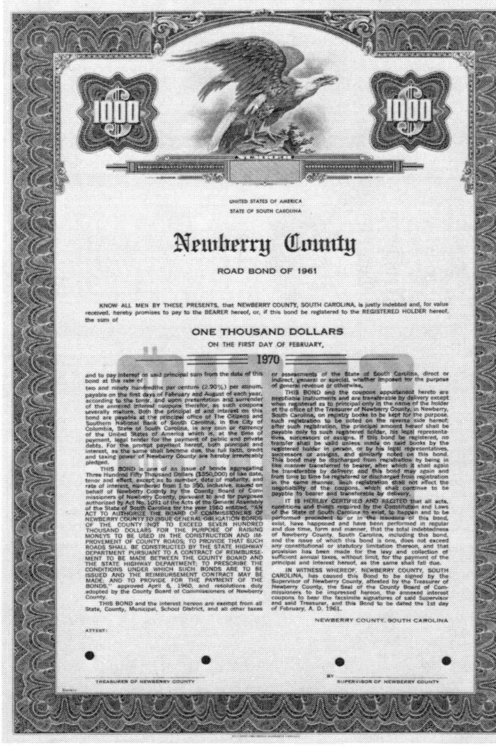

UNITED STATES OF AMERICA

STATE OF SOUTH CAROLINA

Newberry County

ROAD BOND OF 1961

KNOW ALL MEN BY THESE PRESENTS, that NEWBERRY COUNTY, SOUTH CAROLINA, is justly indebted and, for value received, hereby promises to pay to the BEARER hereof, or, if this bond be registered to the REGISTERED HOLDER hereof, the sum of

ONE THOUSAND DOLLARS

ON THE FIRST DAY OF FEBRUARY,

1970

and to pay interest on said principal sum from the date of this bond at the rate of two and ninety hundredths per centum (2.90%) per annum, payable on the first days of February and August of each year, according to the tenor, and upon presentation and surrender of the annexed interest coupons therefor, as such coupons severally mature. Both the principal of and interest on this bond are payable at the principal office of The Citizens and Southern National Bank of South Carolina, in the City of Columbia, State of South Carolina, in any coin or currency of the United States of America which is, at the time of payment, legal tender for the payment of public and private debts. For the prompt payment hereof, both principal and interest, as the same shall become due, the full faith, credit and taxing power of Newberry County are hereby irrevocably pledged.

THIS BOND is one of an issue of bonds aggregating Three Hundred Fifty Thousand Dollars ($350,000) of like date, tenor and effect, except as to number, date of maturity, and rate of interest, numbered from 1 to 350, inclusive, issued on behalf of Newberry County by the County Board of Commissioners of Newberry County, pursuant to and for purposes authorized by Act No. 1091 of the Acts of the General Assembly of the State of South Carolina for the year 1960 entitled, "AN ACT TO AUTHORIZE THE BOARD OF COMMISSIONERS OF NEWBERRY COUNTY TO ISSUE GENERAL OBLIGATION BONDS OF THE COUNTY NOT TO EXCEED SEVEN HUNDRED THOUSAND DOLLARS FOR THE PURPOSE OF RAISING MONEYS TO BE USED IN THE CONSTRUCTION AND IMPROVEMENT OF COUNTY ROADS; TO PROVIDE THAT SUCH ROADS SHALL BE CONSTRUCTED BY THE STATE HIGHWAY DEPARTMENT PURSUANT TO A CONTRACT OF REIMBURSEMENT TO BE MADE BETWEEN THE COUNTY BOARD AND THE STATE HIGHWAY DEPARTMENT; TO PRESCRIBE THE CONDITIONS UNDER WHICH SUCH BONDS ARE TO BE ISSUED AND THE REIMBURSEMENT CONTRACT MAY BE MADE; AND TO PROVIDE FOR THE PAYMENT OF THE BONDS," approved April 6, 1960, and resolutions duly adopted by the County Board of Commissioners of Newberry County.

THIS BOND and the interest hereon are exempt from all State, County, Municipal, School District, and all other taxes or assessments of the State of South Carolina, direct or indirect, general or special, whether imposed for the purpose of general revenue or otherwise.

THIS BOND and the coupons appurtenant hereto are negotiable instruments and are transferable by delivery except when registered as to principal only in the name of the holder at the office of the Treasurer of Newberry County, in Newberry, South Carolina, on registry books to be kept for the purpose, such registration to be noted on the reverse side hereof; after such registration, the principal amount hereof shall be payable only to such registered holder, his legal representatives, successors or assigns. If this bond be registered, no transfer shall be valid unless made on said books by the registered holder in person, or by his legal representatives, successors or assigns, and similarly noted on this bond. This bond may be discharged from registration by being in like manner transferred to bearer, after which it shall again be transferable by delivery; and this bond may again and from time to time be registered or discharged from registration in the same manner. Such registration shall not affect the negotiability of the coupons, which shall continue to be payable to bearer and transferable by delivery.

IT IS HEREBY CERTIFIED AND RECITED that all acts, conditions and things required by the Constitution and Laws of the State of South Carolina to exist, to happen and to be performed precedent to or in the issuance of this bond, exist, have happened and have been performed in regular and due time, form and manner, that the total indebtedness of Newberry County, South Carolina, including this bond, and the issue of which this bond is one, does not exceed any constitutional or statutory limitation thereon, and that provision has been made for the levy and collection of sufficient annual taxes, without limit, for the payment of the principal and interest hereof, as the same shall fall due.

IN WITNESS WHEREOF, NEWBERRY COUNTY, SOUTH CAROLINA, has caused this Bond to be signed by the Supervisor of Newberry County, attested by the Treasurer of Newberry County, the Seal of the County Board of Commissioners to be impressed hereon, the annexed interest coupons to bear the facsimile signatures of said Supervisor and said Treasurer, and this Bond to be dated the 1st day of February, A. D. 1961.

NEWBERRY COUNTY, SOUTH CAROLINA

ATTEST:

TREASURER OF NEWBERRY COUNTY

BY

SUPERVISOR OF NEWBERRY COUNTY

United States of America

No. 167

STATE OF NEW JERSEY

COUNTY OF HUDSON

$8-694 18/100

Township of North Bergen

TEMPORARY IMPROVEMENT NOTE

The Township of North Bergen, *in the County of Hudson in the State of New Jersey, for value received, promises to pay the Steneck Trust Company, Hoboken, New Jersey, or bearer hereof, the sum of* Eight Thousand, Six Hundred Ninety Four 18/100 **Dollars,** *on the* Fourteenth *day of* November 1921, *with interest thereon from the date hereof at the rate of* six (6%) *per centum per annum, payable* at Steneck Trust Co., Hoboken, N.J.

Both principal and interest of this Note are payable in gold coin of the United States of America of or equal to the present standard of weight and fineness at the Steneck Trust Company, Hoboken, New Jersey.

This Note is issued pursuant to Chapter 252 *of the Laws of* 1916 *of the State of New Jersey, the acts amendatory thereof and supplemental thereto, and a resolution adopted by the Township Committee of said Township on the* Seventh *day of* April 1921, *for the purpose of temporarily financing* [illegible] 28-29-30-32-33-34 & 35 Hudson & Palisade Aves.

It is hereby certified and recited that all conditions, acts and things required by the Constitution or Statutes of the State of New Jersey to exist, be performed or happen precedent to or in the issuance of this Note, exist, have been performed and have happened and that this Note, together with all other indebtedness of said Township, is within every debt and other limit prescribed by the Constitution or Statutes of said State.

In Witness Whereof, *The Township Committee, of the TOWNSHIP OF NORTH BERGEN, in the County of Hudson, in the State of New Jersey, has caused this Note to be signed in its corporate name by the Mayor and Chairman and Treasurer of the Township and the seal of said Township to be hereto affixed and attested by the Township Clerk this* Eleventh day of April, 1921.

The Township of North Bergen in the County of Hudson

PAID

STENECK TRUST COMPANY HOBOKEN, N.J.

Attest:

TOWNSHIP CLERK

MAYOR AND CHAIRMAN

TREASURER

THOMAS AGLAN & SONS, NEW YORK

American Telephone and Telegraph (I), **1950s**, Globe vignette	**5.00**
American Telephone and Telegraph (I), **1950s**, Winged Mercury vignette	**3.00**
American Telephone and Telegraph (I), **1960s**, Vignette of Alexander G. Bell, new of city	**3.00**
American Telephone and Telegraph (I), **1970s**, Portrait of Bell, oil derrick, and buildings vignettes	**5.00**
American Turpentine and Tar (U)	**3.00**
AMF (I), **1960s**,	**2.00**
AMF, Inc. (I), **1970s**, Factories and seated man with tools vignette	**1.00**
Ampet Carpet (I), **1950s**, Woman between blacksmith and draftsman vignette	**1.00**
Analogue Controls (I), **1960s**	**1.50**
Ancient Accepted Scottish Rite (U), **1800s**, Emblem of cross, eagle, swords vignette	**8.00**
Anderson Management (I),	**.65**
Ansonia Clock Company (I), **1910s**, **Connecticut**, Seal	**27.00**
Appalachian Power Company (I), **1960s and 1970s**, Eagle	**1.50**
Aracata National Corporation (I), **1960s**, Lady in clouds vignette	**.75**
Arastock Potato Company (U), Eagle, small train vignette	**1.00**
Arcturus Radio Tube Company (I-N), **1930s**, Man holding radio tube vignette	**14.00**
Art House, Inc. (U), **1900s**, Two allegorical figures, beehive, two globes, and museum vignette	**1.00**
ASA G. Neville Glass Company (I), **1890s**, Glassblower at work, state seal vignette	**105.00**
Ashland Industries Corporation (I), **1920s**, Seated lady with tools, ship, and train vignette	**4.00**
Associated Corporation of America (I), **1970s**, Eight and one-half percent bond, seated man and woman, and company logo vignette	**2.00**
Associated Gas and Electric Company (I), **1930s**	**7.00**
Associated Gas and Electric Company (I-N), **1930s**, Goddess and two naked children vignette	**10.00**
Associated Pharmacists (I-N), **1920s**, Large membership certificate with two eagles and world vignette	**6.00**
Associates Investment Company (I), **1960s**, Four and three-eighths percent bond, company logo between two figures vignette	**8.00**
Association for Mutual Investment (I), **1930s**, **Massachusetts**	**1.00**
Atlantic City Racing Association (I), **1940s**, Bond	**10.00**
Atlantic Department Stores (I), **1970s**, **New York**	**1.00**
Atlantic Fruit and Sugar Company (I), **1920s**, Eight percent bond, lady holding globe, winged wheel, anchor and ship vignette	**32.00**
Atlantic Fruit and Sugar Company (I), **1930s**	**23.00**
Atlantic Mutual Fire and Marine Insurance Company (I), **1870s**, Sailing ship vignette, with stamp	**110.00**
Atlantic Mutual Insurance Company (I), **1870s**, Eagle with ships, revenue stamp	**110.00**
Atwood Grapefruit Company (I), **1940s**, Female and seal vignette	**12.00**
Atwood Grapefruit Company (I), **1950s**, Woman vignette	**10.00**
Austin Hotel Company (I), **1920s**, **Illinois**, Eagle vignette	**6.00**
Austin Hotel Company (I), **1930s**, **Illinois**, Eagle vignette	**5.00**
Auto City Brewing Company (U), **Michigan**, Specimen, two seated ladies with eagle and company logo vignette	**27.00**
Auto Train Corporation, Train seats vignette	**1.50**
Automatic Retailers of America (I), **1960s**, Winged gear and allegorical figures vignette	**1.00**
Automatic Traffic Regulator (I-N), Eagle and gold seal vignette	**3.00**
Autosonics (I), **1960s**, Large eagle vignette	**.65**
B. F. Goodrich (I), **1970s**, **New York**, Vignette of plantation and worker	**2.00**

◀ ***Newberry County (South Carolina) (U),*** *Two and nine-tenths percent road bond, eagle vignette* ***4.00***

◀ ***North Bergen, Township of, State of New Jersey (I), 1920s,*** *Improvement note, state seal vignette* ***4.00***

No 493

UNITED STATES OF AMERICA

STATE OF NEW JERSEY

The Board of Education of the Township of Wayne, in the County of Passaic

SCHOOL DISTRICT BOND

THE BOARD OF EDUCATION OF THE TOWNSHIP OF WAYNE, IN THE COUNTY OF PASSAIC, a school district of the State of New Jersey, situate in said County of Passaic, hereby acknowledges itself indebted and for value received promises to pay to the bearer of this bond, or if it be registered to the registered owner, the sum of

ONE THOUSAND DOLLARS ($1,000)

ON THE FIRST DAY OF APRIL,

1974

upon presentation and surrender of this bond, and to pay interest on such sum, from the date of this bond until it matures, at the rate of four and fifteen hundredths per centum (4.15%) per annum payable semi-annually on the first days of April and October in each year in accordance with the tenor of the respective coupons therefor annexed hereto, and upon presentation and surrender of said coupons as they severally mature or, if this bond be registered as to both principal and interest, to the registered owner. Both principal of and interest on this bond will be paid in lawful money of the United States of America, at the office of New Jersey Bank and Trust Company, Haledon, New Jersey.

This bond is transferable by delivery, except if registered as to principal otherwise than to bearer. At the request of the holder this bond will be registered as to principal in his name on the books of said School District kept for that purpose in the office of its Secretary, such registration to be noted on the back of this bond, and thereafter, until registered transfer to bearer, no transfer of this bond shall be valid unless made on said books and similarly noted hereon. Such registration, however, shall not affect the negotiability of the coupons which shall continue to be payable to bearer and transferable by delivery. At the request of the registered owner this bond upon presentation at said office will be converted into a bond registered as to both principal and interest, by the execution of the conversion certificate on the back of this bond and by removing and cancelling the unmatured coupons hereto annexed, and thereafter both principal and interest shall be payable only to the registered owner. At the written request of the registered owner this bond, if it has been duly registered as to both principal and interest, will, at the expense of such owner and upon surrender hereof at said office, be reconverted into a bond payable to bearer and coupon in form by the preparation and substitution of a new bond, signed or executed by such of its officers then in office as said Board of Education shall designate and of the same tenor as this bond at the time of its issuance, with coupons annexed for any interest thereafter payable on this bond until its maturity.

This bond is one of an authorized issue of bonds, which are of like tenor except as to maturity, and is issued pursuant to Title 18, Education, of the Revised Statutes of the State of New Jersey, particularly Chapter 7 thereof, and by virtue of a proposal adopted by the affirmative vote of a majority of the legal voters present and voting at a special district meeting held on November 19, 1957, and of resolutions adopted by the Board of Education.

The full faith and credit of said School District are hereby irrevocably pledged for the punctual payment of the principal of and interest on this bond according to its terms.

It is hereby certified and recited that all conditions, acts and things required by the Constitution or statutes of the State of New Jersey to exist, to have happened or to have been performed precedent to or in the issuance of this bond, exist, have happened and have been performed, and that the issue of bonds of which this is one does not exceed any limitation imposed thereon by said Constitution or statutes.

IN WITNESS WHEREOF, THE BOARD OF EDUCATION OF THE TOWNSHIP OF WAYNE, IN THE COUNTY OF PASSAIC, has caused this bond to be signed in its name by its President, and its corporate seal to be hereunto affixed, and this bond and said seal to be attested by its Secretary, and each of the coupons hereto annexed to be authenticated by the facsimile signature of said Secretary, and this bond to be dated the first day of October, 1958.

THE BOARD OF EDUCATION OF THE TOWNSHIP OF WAYNE, IN THE COUNTY OF PASSAIC

ATTEST:

William H. DeYoung
Secretary

By Bernard Brody
President

COLUMBIAN BANK NOTE COMPANY

B.P.O.E. (I), 1920s, Bond, elk vignette 12.00
B. T. Mortgage Investors (I), 1970s, Girl vignette 2.00
Babcock and Wilcox Company (I), 1950s, Company logo 5.00
Babcock and Wilcox Company (I), 1960s, Two seated men, company logo vignette 1.00
Backer, J. B., Inc. (U), 1980s, Warrant certificate 3.00
Baltimore American Insurance Company of New York (I), 1920s and 1930s, Knight on horseback vignette 4.00
Baltimore American Insurance Company of New York (I), 1930s, Company logo vignette 4.00
Baltimore and Fredrick-town Road (I), 1800s 325.00
Baltimore and Yorktown Turnpike Road Company (I), 1880s, Horse trolley covered wagon, farmer, and sailor vignette 85.00
Baltimore Orioles, Inc. 1980s, Ball, bats, and bird vignette 45.00
Baltimore Refrigerating and Heating Company (I), 1900s, Gold bond, refrigerating and heating plant vignette 14.00
Bankers Trust, New York (I), Reclining lady in front of mountain vignette 3.00
Barrows Iron and Land Company (I), 1900s, Eagle vignette 12.00
Bausch and Lomb Optical Company (I), 1920s, New York, Six percent gold bond, seated lady vignette 42.00
Bay Bridge Company (U), 1800s, Maryland, Vignette of city 39.00
Bay State Gas (I-N), 1900s, Massachusetts, State seal vignette 9.00
Beacon Chocolate Company (I), Certificate of deposit, gold bond, no vignette 2.00
Beacon Manufacturing Group (U), 1960s, Six percent bond, eagle vignette 1.00
Bell and Howell (U), Illinois, Specimen, two seated figures with company logo vignette 22.00
Belmont Iron Works, The (I), 1950s, Horse and ship seal vignette, many stamps 2.00
Berkshire Gas Company (I), 1960s, Eagle vignette .75
Bessmer Company (I), 1870s, New Jersey, Little girl portrait vignette 55.00
Bethelem Steel Corporation (I-N), 1930s, Three and one-half percent bond, warrant 3.00
Big Horn Timber (I), 1900s, Idaho, Eagle on globe vignette 30.00
Big Horn Timber (U), 1900s, Idaho, Eagle on globe vignette 15.00
Billings and Spencer Company (I), 1900s, Connecticut, Vignette of large building 5.00
Bloomfield and Montclair Crystal Ice Company (I), 1890s, Vignette of old icemaking machine 80.00
Bodie and Hawthorne Telephone and Telegraph (I), 1890s, California, (Bodie mine) 80.00
Bond Stores (I), 1950s and 1960s, Maryland, Nude man turning wheel vignette 3.00
Borg Warner (I), 1970s, Seated man with wheel vignette 1.00
Boston and Worcester Electric Companies (I), 1900s, Two angels vignette 20.00
Boston Personal Property Trust (I), 1960s, Eagle vignette .75
Boston Rubber Company (I), 1890s, Massachusetts 8.00
Boston Water Power Company (I), 1860s, Red seal 62.00
Boston Water Power Company (I), 1900s, Massachusetts, Two figures with old train and sailboats vignettes 38.00
Bourne Mills (I), 1940s, Portrait vignette 6.00
Braceville Coal Company (U), 1800s, No vignette 4.00
Bradford Hospital (I), 1890s, State seal vignette 80.00
Breakfast Brownies Company (U), 1900s, Montana, Brownies and cereal box vignette 17.00
Brewers Malting Corporation (I), 1910s, Six percent gold bond, eagles vignette 10.00
Bridges Telephone (I), 1900s, Oklahoma Territory, Lightning vignette 44.00
Bridges Telephone (I), 1900s, Oklahoma Territory, Lightning vignette, red seal 53.00
Bristol-Myers Company (U), Specimen, bond, company logo vignette 4.00
Broadway Joe's (I), 1960s, Joe Namath and company logo vignette 3.00
Bronx Refrigerator (I), 1910s, With many stamps, state seal 5.00
Brooklyn Tabernacle (I), 1890s, New York, Five percent bond, three seated figures vignette 325.00
Brooklyn Union Gas Company (I), 1960s, New York, Four and three-eighths percent bond, standing lady with globe vignette 8.00

◀ ***Wayne, Town of, County of Passaic, Board of Education (I),*** *State seal* ***2.00***

$5000 $5000

NUMBER

UNITED STATES OF AMERICA
STATE OF CONNECTICUT

City of Stamford

URBAN REDEVELOPMENT BOND, ISSUE OF 1963
AUTHORIZED ISSUE $500,000

The City of Stamford, Connecticut, a municipal corporation duly established by law, for value received, promises to pay the bearer of this bond, but only on presentation and surrender hereof,

ON THE FIRST DAY OF JANUARY,

1983

the principal sum of

FIVE THOUSAND DOLLARS

and pay interest thereon from the date of this bond until it shall mature at the rate of two and eighty hundredths per centum (2.80%) per annum, payable semi-annually on the first day of January and July in each year, but only upon presentation and surrender of the annexed interest coupons as they severally mature. Principal and interest are payable at The Chase Manhattan Bank, in the City of New York, New York, or, at the option of the holder, at The Fairfield County Trust Company, in the City of Stamford, Connecticut, in lawful money of the United States of America.

This bond is one of an issue of bonds of like date, tenor and effect except as to number and maturity, issued upon the faith and credit of the City of Stamford, under and pursuant to and in full compliance with the Charter of the City and the Connecticut General Statutes, for the purpose of financing public improvements and other municipal works of a permanent character in said City, all duly authorized and included in the capital budget and capital projects program for the fiscal year beginning July 1, 1962.

IT IS HEREBY CERTIFIED, RECITED AND DECLARED that each and every act, condition and thing required to be done, to have happened and to be performed precedent to and in the issuance of this bond and the issue of which it forms a part has been done, has happened and has been performed in full and strict compliance with the Constitution and statutes of the State of Connecticut, and this bond and the issue of which it forms a part are within every debt and other limit prescribed by law, and the full faith and credit of the City of Stamford are hereby irrevocably pledged to the punctual payment of the principal of and interest on this bond according to its terms.

IN WITNESS WHEREOF, the City of Stamford has caused its corporate seal to be hereto affixed and this bond to be signed in its name and behalf by the facsimile signature of its Mayor and countersigned by its Controller and the coupons hereto annexed to be authenticated by the facsimile signature of its Controller this first day of January, 1963.

CITY OF STAMFORD, CONNECTICUT
By

SPECIMEN

Mayor

COUNTERSIGNED:
By

SPECIMEN

Controller

SECURITY-COLUMBIAN BANKNOTE COMPANY

Brookside Mills (I), **1910s, Tennessee**, Vignette of factories	**20.00**
Brookside Mills (I), **1920s and 1930s, Tennessee**, Vignette of factories	**15.00**
Brotherhood Investment Company (I-N), 1920s	**2.00**
Brown and Bigelow (U), Specimen, two seated ladies with company logo vignette	**5.00**
Brunswick-Blake-Callender Company (I), Subscription warrant, no vignette	**1.00**
Buena Vista Plantation (I-N), 1900s, Plantation scene, gold seal	**15.00**
Buffalo Dry Dock Company (U), **West Virgnia**, Vignette of Niagara Falls	**9.00**
Buffalo Iron Company (I), **1900s, Tennessee**, Proxy with stamp	**4.00**
Buffalo Niagara Electric Corporation (I), **New York**, Two and three-quarters percent bond, man vignette	**6.00**
Buffalo Pipe Line Company (U), **1800s, New York**, Vignettes of buffalos, oil wells, and storage tanks	**8.00**
Buffalo Steam Engine Works (I), **1850s**, Green seal	**125.00**
Building Products (I), **1930s**	**.75**
Bulova Watch Company (U), **New York** , Specimen, seminude girl in front of watchface vignette	**35.00**
Bureau County Minerals (U), **1900s**, No vignette	**25.00**
Burk Pipe Lines and Refining (I), **1920s, Texas**, No vignette	**6.00**
Bush Service Corporation (I), **1930s**, Seated woman with winged wheel vignette, port city in background, railroad	**3.00**
Butler Brothers (I), **1920s, Illinois**, Company catalogue, steam engine, and clerks vignettes	**5.00**
Butte and Montana Commercial Company (I), **1890s**, Train, ships, and eagle vignette, embossed seal	**35.00**
Butte City Water Company (I), **1890s**, Waterfall with city in background vignette	**34.00**
California Controllers Warrant (I), **1880s**, Train and seated lady and state building vignette	**110.00**
California Fertilizing Company (U), **1870s, California**, Two vignettes of fruit and trees, company logo	**25.00**
Caloris Manufacturing (I), **1900s**, Two globes with cartridge vignette	**45.00**
Calumet and Hecla, Inc. (U), **1900s**, Specimen, Indians around cooking campfire vignette	**22.00**
Cambridge Garage (I), **1930s**, Five percent income bond, eagle vignette	**2.00**
Canada General Fund (I), **1950s**, Map of Canada vignette	**1.50**
Carlo Darwin Insurance (I)	**.75**
Carnegie Life Insurance of America (I), Eagle vignette	**1.00**
Carolina Insurance Company, The (I), **1920s and 1930s, North Carolina**, Females and company logo, vignette, with stamps	**9.00**
Carolina Power and Light (I), **1970s**, Vignettes of dam, woman with globe, and man with turbine	**3.00**
Corona Typewriter Company (I), **1920s**, Vignette of typewriter	**25.00**
Carroon and Reynolds, Inc. (I), **1930s**, Two kneeling women, globes, and company logo vignettes	**3.00**
Cartridge T. V. Insurance (I), **Delaware**, Multicolored log vignette	**1.00**
Cartridge Television (I-N), 1970s, Three-color logo vignette	**2.00**
Cavalier Motion Picture Company (I), **1920s**, Mounted rider, gold seal vignette	**55.00**
Cavanagh-Dobbs, Inc. (I), **1930s**, Man and woman with company logo vignette	**2.00**
Cedar Rapids, Iowa City and Southern Construction Company (I), **1910s**, Seated lady with shield and wreath vignette	**3.00**
Celanese Corporation of America (I), **1960s**, Two men with company logo vignette	**2.00**
Central Bridge Corporation (I), **1820s, New Hampshire**, No vignette	**145.00**
Central Farmer's Corporation (U), **1900s, Florida**	**1.00**
Central Mills (I), **1940s, Ohio**, Bond, eagle vignette	**4.00**
Central Public Service Corporation (I), **1930s, Maryland**, Vignette of man	**4.00**
Century Ribbon Mills, Inc. (I), **1930s**, Bare-breasted seated woman with winged wheel vignette	**4.00**

Stamford, City of (I), 1960s, Bond specimen* — *5.00

No. D 1801

$1000 $1000

CITY AND COUNTY OF SAN FRANCISCO

SCHOOL BOND - 1948

SERIES D

The City and County of San Francisco, a municipal corporation organized and existing under the Constitution and laws of the State of California, hereby acknowledges itself indebted and for value received, promises to pay to the bearer (or if this bond be registered, to the registered holder hereof), on the 1st day of December, 1959.

ONE THOUSAND (1,000) DOLLARS

together with interest thereon at the rate of — ONE AND THREE-FOURTHS — *percent, per annum until payment of said principal sum in full, payable semi-annually on the 1st day of June and the 1st day of December of each year. Unless this bond is registered such interest, prior to maturity, shall be payable only on presentation and surrender of the proper interest coupons hereto attached as they respectively become due. Both the principal of and interest on this bond are payable in lawful money of the United States of America, at the office of the Treasurer of said City and County or, at the option of the holder hereof, at the Fiscal Agency of said City and County of San Francisco in the City and State of New York.*

This bond is issued under and pursuant to the Constitution and statutes of the State of California, and under and pursuant to the ordinances and proceedings of said City and County duly adopted and taken and a vote and assent of more than two-thirds of all qualified electors of said City and County voting at a special election duly called and held for that purpose.

It is hereby certified, recited and declared that all acts, conditions and things required by law to exist, happen and to be performed precedent to and in the issuance of this bond have existed, happened and been performed in due time, form and manner as required by law, and that the amount of this bond, together with all other indebtedness of said City and County does not exceed any limit prescribed by the Constitution or statutes of said State, and that the provision has been made as required by the Constitution and statutes of said State for the collection of an annual tax sufficient to pay the principal of, and interest on, this bond as the same becomes due. The full faith and credit of said City and County are hereby pledged for the punctual payment of the principal and interest of this bond.

This bond may be registered in the manner provided by law and thereafter the principal hereof and interest hereon shall be payable only to such registered owner.

In Witness Whereof, said City and County of San Francisco has caused this bond to be executed under its corporate seal, signed by its Mayor and its Treasurer, and countersigned by the Clerk of the Board of Supervisors, and has caused the interest coupons hereto attached to be signed by the Treasurer of said City and County, and this bond to be dated the 1st day of December 1952.

COUNTERSIGNED:

John R. McGrath

CLERK OF THE BOARD OF SUPERVISORS

JOHN J. GOODWIN, TREASURER

PAID

MAYOR.

DEPUTY CLERK

John J. Goodwin

TREASURER.

COLUMBIAN BANK NOTE CO.

Chapple Publishing Company (I), 1910s, Beehives vignette, gold seal	12.00
Chesebrough-Ponds, Inc. (U), Specimen, seated woman and globe vignette	5.00
Chicago Cotton Manufacturing Company (U), 1870s, Factory vignette and revenue stamp	43.00
Chicago Livestock Exchange (I), 1890s, Vignette of cow	63.00
Chicago Livestock Exchange (I), 1900s, Damaged	10.00
Chicago Livestock Exchange (I), 1900s, Vignette of cows	52.00
Chicago Realty Shares (I), 1930s, City street scene	8.50
China Mutual Insurance Company (I), 1920s, Vignettes of Chinese junks, ship, and sailor	75.00
Chino Odd Fellows Hall Association (U), **1890s, California**	8.00
Cincinnati Union Stockyard Company (I), 1880s, Stockyards, three freight trains, and large cow head vignettes	25.00
Citizens' Gas Light Company (I), 1890s, Bond, woman with light vignette	20.00
Citizens' Light, Heat and Power (I), 1890s, Virginia, Bond, ships in bay, and seal vignette	70.00
Citizens' Underwriters (I), 1940s, Eagle vignette	4.00
City Associates (I), 1920s, No vignette	1.00
City Dairy Company (I), 1920s, Maryland, Eagle vignette	4.00
Clark Equipment Overseas Finance Corporation (U), Specimen, bond, seated man with tools vignette	15.00
Clark Fluid (I), 1910s, Large eagle with arrows, gold seal vignette	2.00
Clark Wireless Telephone and Telegraph Company (I), 1910s, Arizona, Eagle vignette	55.00
Clay Commercial Telephone Company (I), 1890s, New Jersey, Lady with two cherubs vignette, brown seal	110.00
Cleveland and Sandusky Brewing Company (I), 1930s, Ohio, Seated woman vignette	37.00
Cleveland Gas, Light and Coke Company (I), 1880s, Storage tank vignette	55.00
Cleveland Gas, Light and Coke Company (I), 1890s, Power station vignette	48.00
C N A Overseas Capital (I), 1970s, Bond	5.00
Coal Investment (U), Eagle	1.00
Cohoes Company (I-N), 1860s, New York, Woman and baby sitting on a bale vignette	50.00
Cohu Electronics, Inc. (I), 1970s, Eagle, globe, and shield vignette	.75
Coldak Corporation (I), 1920s, Delaware, Girl at birdbath vignette	.75
Coleman, J and V (I), 1920s, Four percent gold bond	3.00
Collins and Aikman (I), 1960s, Woman standing between seated man and woman vignette	.75
Collins and Aikman (I), 1970s, Two women and man vignette	.75
Colonial Dairy Company (I), 1950s, Illinois, Large vignette of dairy, farm, and cows	6.00
Colorado Southern Irrigation Company (I), 1900s, Gold bond, three ladies vignette	15.00
Colt Patent Firearms (I), 1940s, Horse, crossed pistols, and seal vignette	22.00
Colt's Manufacturing (I), 1950s, Rearing horse and crossed rifles vignettes	22.00
Columbia Gas System Inc., The (I), 1970s, Seminude lady with torch, oil derricks in rear	3.00
Columbia Graphophone Manufacturing Company (I), 1920s, Angels vignette, company logo and seal	38.00
Comet Transport Corporation (I), 1970s, Nevada, Large eagle, gold seal vignette	1.00
Commercial Appliance Corporation (I), 1960s	.50
Commercial Cable Company (I), 1890s, Interim bond, vignette of map of Atlantic Ocean with cables	30.00
Commercial Cable Company (I), 1890s, New York, Map of Atlantic cable, embossed seal	18.00
Commercial Credit (I), 1960s, Note	1.00
Commercial Credit (I), 1960s, Four and three-fourths percent bond, eagle vignette	2.00
Common Stock Fund (I), Ocean liner, trains, truck, and eagle vignettes	2.00
Common Stock Fund (I), 1960s, Eagle on mountaintop vignette	.75
Computer Applications, Inc. (I), 1960s, Delaware, Woman with two globes vignette	1.00
Comstock Tunnel (I), 1880s, Four percent gold bond, eagle vignette	45.00
Connecticut Fire Insurance Company, The (I), 1870s, State seal, eagle vignette	28.00

◀ ***San Francisco, City and County of (I), 1950s,*** *Two and three-fourths percent school bond, eagle vignette* ***6.00***

NUMBER

401

$ 1000

$ 1000

UNITED STATES OF AMERICA
STATE OF INDIANA
COUNTY OF ST. JOSEPH

CITY OF SOUTH BEND

SEWAGE WORKS REVENUE BOND

The City of South Bend, in St. Joseph County, State of Indiana, for value received, hereby promises to pay to the bearer, or if this bond be registered then to the registered holder, solely out of the special revenue fund hereinafter referred to, the principal amount of

ONE THOUSAND DOLLARS

on the FIRST DAY OF OCTOBER, 1958,

and to pay interest thereon from the date hereof until the principal is paid, at the rate of ——— three ——— per cent (3%) per annum, payable on the first days of April and October of each year, beginning on Octo[illegible] 1, 1954, u[illegible] presentatio[illegible]d surrend[illegible]f the anne[illegible] coupon[illegible] they seve[illegible] become [illegible].

Both [illegible]ncipal and [illegible]terest of th[illegible]bond are p[illegible]able in law[illegible] money of the United States of America at the First Bank and Trust Company of South Bend, in the City of South Bend, Indiana, or, at the option of the holder, at the Harris Trust and Savings Bank, in the City of Chicago, Illinois.

This bond is one of an authorized issue of Eight Thousand Five Hundred (8,500) bonds of the City of South Bend, of like date, tenor and effect, except as to numbering, interest rate, and dates of maturity, in the total amount of Eight Million Five Hundred Thousand Dollars ($8,500,000.00), numbered from One (1) to Eight Thousand Five Hundred (8,500) inclusive, issued for the purpose of providing funds to pay the cost of sewage treatment works, as authorized by an Ordinance adopted by the Common Council of the City of South Bend, Indiana, on the eighth day of February, 1954, entitled "An Ordinance concerning the construction and operation by the City of South Bend, Indiana, of sewage treatment works, the issuance of revenue bonds to provide the cost thereof, the collection, segregation and distribution of the revenues of said works, the safeguarding of the interests of the holders of said bonds, and other matters connected therewith," and in strict compliance with the provisions of Chapter 61 of the Acts of the Indiana General Assembly for the year 1932 (Special Session) and the acts amendatory thereof and supplemental thereto.

Pursuant to the provisions of said Act and said Ordinance, the principal and interest of this bond and all other bonds of said issue are payable solely from the Sewage Works Sinking Fund (created by said ordinance) to be provided from the net revenues (herein defined as gross revenues after deduction only for the payment of the reasonable expenses of operation, repair and maintenance) of the sewage treatment works of the City of South Bend, including the works constructed or acquired by the use of the proceeds of this bond and the issue of which it is a part, and all additions and improvements thereto and replacements thereof subsequently constructed or acquired. This bond shall not constitute an indebtedness of the City of South Bend, within the meaning of the provisions and limitations of the constitution of the State of Indiana, and the City shall not be obligated to pay this bond or the interest thereon except from said special fund provided from said net revenues.

The City of South Bend irrevocably pledges the entire net revenues of said sewage treatment works to the prompt payment of the principal and interest of the bonds issued on account of the construction of said sewage treatment works, of which this is one, and all bonds on a parity therewith, and covenants that during the period in which the works are being constructed and prior to the completion thereof, it will cause to be fixed, maintained and collected such rates and charges for services to be rendered by the works in an amount sufficient to meet the interest on the bonds prior to the completion of the works, and further covenants that after the completion of the works it will cause to be fixed, maintained and collected such rates and charges for services rendered by said works as are sufficient in each year for the payment of the proper and reasonable expenses of operation, repair and maintenance of said works, to provide for proper depreciation, and for the payment of the sums required to be paid into said sinking fund under the provisions of said Act. In the event the City of South Bend, or the proper officers thereof, shall fail or refuse to so fix, maintain and collect such rates or charges, or if there be a default in the payment of the interest on or principal of this bond, the holder of this bond shall have all of the rights and remedies provided for in said Chapter 61, Acts of 1932 (Special Session), and the acts amendatory thereof and supplemental thereto, including the right to have a receiver appointed to administer the works and to charge and collect rates sufficient to provide for the payment of this bond and the interest thereon.

The City of South Bend further covenants that it will set aside and pay into its Sewage Works Sinking Fund a sufficient amount of the net revenues of said works to meet (a) the interest on this bond and the other bonds of the issue herein referred to, and all bonds on a parity therewi[illegible] such in[illegible]t shall fa[illegible]e, (b) the [illegible]cessary fis[illegible] agency [illegible]ges for pa[illegible] the bonds [illegible] interest, [illegible] principal [illegible] this bon[illegible]d the othe[illegible]nds of said [illegible]e, and all [illegible]s on a par[illegible] therewith, as the same are payable, and (d) an additional amount as a margin of safety, which margin, together with any unused surplus of such margin carried forward from the preceding year, shall equal not less than ten per cent (10%) of all other amounts so required to be paid into said sinking fund. Such required payments shall constitute a first charge upon all the net revenues of said works.

If any bond or interest coupon shall not be presented for payment or redemption on the date fixed therefor, the City may deposit in trust with the First Bank and Trust Company of South Bend in the City of South Bend, Indiana, an amount sufficient to pay such bond or interest coupon or the redemption price thereof, as the case may be, and thereafter the holder shall look only to the funds so deposited in trust with said bank for payment and the City shall have no further obligation or liability in respect thereto.

This bond and all other bonds of said issue shall have all the qualities and incidents of negotiable instruments under the Negotiable Instruments Law of the State of Indiana. This bond may be registered as to principal at the office of the City Controller of the City of South Bend, Indiana, in the name of the owner hereof, and such registration noted hereon by said City Controller. Thereafter, no transfer hereof shall be valid unless made at said office by the registered owner in person or by his duly authorized attorney and similarly noted hereon, but this bond may be discharged from registration by being in like manner transferred to bearer and may again from time to time be registered or transferred to bearer as before. Such registration shall not restrict or affect the negotiability of the interest coupons hereto attached by delivery only, but such interest coupons shall always be payable to bearer.

The bonds of this issue maturing on April 1, 1960, and thereafter shall be redeemable at the option of the City, in whole or in part, on October 1, 1959, or at any interest payment date thereafter, in their inverse numerical order, at face value, together with the following premiums:

4% if redeemed on October 1, 1959,
or thereafter on or before April 1, 1965;
3% if redeemed on October 1, 1965,
or thereafter on or before April 1, 1971;
2% if redeemed on October 1, 1971,
or thereafter on or before April 1, 1977;
1% if redeemed on October 1, 1977,
or thereafter prior to maturity;

plus in each case accrued interest to the date fixed for redemption. Notice of such redemption shall be published one time at least thirty days prior to the date fixed for redemption in a newspaper or financial journal published in each of the following named cities: South Bend, Indiana; Chicago, Illinois; and New York, New York. A like notice shall be sent by mail to the holders of such bonds as are then registered. Interest on bonds so called for redemption shall cease on the redemption date fixed in said notice, if funds are available at the place of redemption to pay the redemption price on the date so named or when presented for payment.

It is hereby certified and recited that all acts, conditions and things required to be done precedent to and in the execution, issuance and delivery of this bond have been done and performed in regular and due form as provided by law.

IN WITNESS WHEREOF, the City of South Bend, in St. Joseph County, State of Indiana, has caused this bond to be signed in its corporate name by its duly elected, qualified and acting Mayor, countersigned by its City Controller, its corporate seal to be hereunto affixed, and attested by its duly elected, qualified and acting City Clerk, and the interest coupons hereto attached to be executed by placing thereon the facsimile signature of said City Controller, all as of the first day of April, 1954.

CITY OF SOUTH BEND,

By John A. Scott Mayor

Countersigned

By [illegible] City Controller

Attest:

[illegible] City Clerk

Connecticut Fire Insurance Company, The (I), 1890s, State seal, eagle vignette 23.00
Connecticut Fire Insurance Company, The (I), 1960s, Connecticut 2.00
Connecticut Fire Insurance Company, The (I-N), 1900s, Company logo 7.00
Connecticut Insurance Company (I), 1906, To Hartford Orphan Asylum 12.00
Consolidated Edison Company (I), 1940s, Five percent bond, view of New York City vignette 15.00
Consolidated Edison Company of New York (I), 1940s, Three percent bond, vignette of New York, two seated figures, and lighted tower with clocks 7.00
Consolidated Edison Company of New York (I), 1950s, Five percent bond, vignette of New York 6.00
Consolidated Edison Company of New York (I), 1960s, Four and three-quarters percent bond, lighted tower between two figures vignette 8.00
Consolidated Gas (I), 1960s .65
Consolidated Investment Trust (I), 1960s, Eagle vignette .75
Consolidated Telephone Company (I), 1880s, Eagle vignette 95.00
Consolidated Telephone Company of Pennsylvania (I), 1900s, Female with telephone vignette, five percent gold bond 85.00
Consolidated Terminal Corporation (U), Washington, D.C., No vignette 2.00
Construction Materials Corporation (I), 1930s, Large vignette of freighter being loaded in ship canal and other ships 11.00
Consumer Growth Capital, Inc.(U), Minnesota, Eagle vignette 1.00
Consumer Ice Company (I), 1910s, No vignette 8.00
Consumer Ice Company (I), 1920s, Eagle vignette 10.00
Consumers' Discount Corporation (U), Texas, Star and wreath vignette 2.00
Consumers Power Company (I), Maine, Two and seven-eighths percent bond, generator and power lines vignette 11.00
Continental Express (U), 1900s, Montana 5.00
Continental Telephone International Finance (I), 1970s, Bond 6.00
Continental Timber Company (U), 1900s, Eagle vignette 15.00
Continental Wireless Telephone and Telegraph (I), 1900s 50.00
Continuous Transit Securities (I), 1920s, New York, Company logo 3.00
Controls Company of America (I), 1960s, Man with wheel vignette 2.00
Co-op Dairy (I), 1920s 2.00
Co-op Dress Association (I), 1880s, New York, Sailor, Indian, and eagle vignette 42.00
Co-op Pure Milk Association (U), Farm scene and house vignette 1.00
Copeland Commercial Photo (I) .75
Copper Metals Company (I), 1910s, Six percent gold bond 10.00
Corroon-Reynolds (I), 1930s, Two kneeling women with two globes vignette 3.00
Corroon-Reynolds (I), 1950s, Two kneeling women with two globes vignette 2.00
Corrugated Container Company (I), 1960s, Ohio 3.00
Cosmopolitan Electric Underground Telephone and Telegraph Electric Light Company of Camden, New Jersey (I), 1880s, Vignette of lady telegraph operator 55.00
Cottaraugus and Buffalo Plank Road Company (I), 1850s, Old stagecoach with four horses vignette 215.00
Cox Realization Company of Houston, Texas (I-N), 1920s, Seal with Texas star 14.00
Crescent Corporation (U), Specimen, Winged Mercury, ship, plane, train and cars vignettes 5.00
Crown-Zellerbach Corporation (I), Man, woman, and company logo vignette 2.00
Crusader Industry (I), 1970s, Nevada, Lighted torch vignette 1.00
Crystal Ice Manufacturing and Cold Storage (I), 1900s, Large vignette of Indian chief with sailing ship in background 15.00
Cuba Company (I), 1920s, New Jersey, Sugarcane workers vignette 6.00
Cuban Cane Products (I), 1930s, Delaware, Gold bond, train vignette 20.00
Cudahy Packing (U), 1900s, Specimen, portrait of cow, signed 20.00

◀ ***South Bend, City of, (I), 1950s**, Sewage works revenue, bond, eagle vignette* ***4.00***

Number 14 | Dollars 1000

UNITED STATES OF AMERICA

State of Missouri
County of Butler

City of Poplar Bluff
FUNDING BOND

Know all Men by these Presents, *That the* **City of Poplar Bluff,** *in the State of Missouri acknowledges itself to owe, and, for value received, hereby promises to pay bearer*

ONE THOUSAND DOLLARS

in lawful money of the United States of America, on the **First Day of July, A. D. 1933,** *together with interest thereon from the date hereof at the rate of* **Five and One-half Per Centum** (5½%) **Per Annum,** *payable semi-annually on the* **First Day of January and of July** *of each year, as evidenced by and payable upon presentation and surrender of the annexed interest coupons as they each severally become due. Both principal and interest of this bond are payable at the Banking House of the* **Continental and Commercial National Bank, in the City of Chicago, Illinois.**

This Bond *is one of a series of bonds of like date, tenor and effect, except as to numbers, denominations and maturities, issued by the City of Poplar Bluff, Missouri, for the purpose of funding its valid and legal outstanding indebtedness represented by a judgment, which debt has been liquidated and reduced to judgment in a court of competent jurisdiction, under and by virtue of and in full compliance with the Constitution and laws of the State of Missouri, including the provisions of an act of the General Assembly of Missouri, of 1917, entitled: "An Act to empower cities of the third class to issue bonds for outstanding indebtedness of the City, which has been reduced to judgment, and providing for a sinking fund for the payment thereof, with an emergency clause," approved March 27, 1917, and of an ordinance duly, regularly and legally passed and adopted by the City Council of said City. Said City is hereby firmly bounden and held, and its full faith, credit and resources are hereby irrevocably pledged for the prompt payment of the principal and of the installments of interest hereof as they respectively become payable.*

It is Hereby Certified, Recited and Declared, *that due provisions for the prompt payment of the installments of the interest and of the principal of this bond have been made.*

It is Further Certified and Recited, *that all acts, conditions and things required to be done, to happen and be performed precedent to and in the issuance of this bond have been legally and properly done, have happened and been performed in regular and due form, time and manner as required by law; that the total indebtedness of said City, including this bond, does not exceed any constitutional or statutory limitations.*

In Testimony Whereof, *the* **City of Poplar Bluff,** *in the State of Missouri, by its City Council, has caused its corporate seal to be hereto affixed, and this bond to be signed by the Mayor, attested by the Clerk thereof, and the coupons hereto annexed to be executed with the lithographed fac-simile signatures of said officials, and this bond to be dated the first day of July, A. D. 1918.*

CITY OF POPLAR BLUFF, MISSOURI,

Attest:

H. H. Wilcox
Clerk.

By J. W. Berryman
Mayor.

Cutler Hammer International Finance, Inc. (I), **1970s**, Bond, electric supplies vignette 1.00
Cyro-Therm, Inc. (I), **1960s**, Woman between two worlds, train and buildings vignette .85

D. M. Osborne and Company (U), **1800s, New York**, Three vignettes of farmers working with horses 88.00
Dairy League Co-op Corporation (U), **New York**, Specimen, cow vignette 30.00
Damarra Manufacturing (I), **1900s, Arizona Territory**, Female with electricity vignette 10.00
Dane, Stern and Wood, Inc. (I), **1930s**, Eagle vignette 10.00
Data Control Systems (I), **1960s**, Rocket and tower 2.00
Databyte, Inc. (U), Eagle vignette 2.00
Davega Stores (I), **1960s, New York**, Skyline vignette 6.00
Davis Sewing Machine Company (I), **1870s**, Allegorical figures vignette 73.00
Davis Sewing Machine Company of Watertown, New York (I), **1860s**, Two figures with eagle vignette, revenue stamp 80.00
Dayco Corporation, Orbiting electrons and girl vignette 1.00
Delaware County Trust Company (I), **1930s, Pennsylvania**, Two horses and eagle vignette 4.00
Delaware Mutual Safety Insurance Company (I), **1870s, Pennsylvania**, Two ladies seated in front of riverboat and sailing ship, Indian warrior, and portrait of man vignettes 165.00
D'Esterre Estate (I), **1910s**, Gold bond 4.00
Detroit and Canada Tunnel Company (I), **1920s**, Flag-covered ladies vignette 22.00
Detroit and Canada Tunnel Company (I), **1930s**, Flag-covered ladies vignette 20.00
Detroit Autocleno Mfg. Co. (I-N), Train vignette, gold seal, stamps 15.00
Dewey and Almy Chemical (I), **1940s, Massachusetts**, Eagle vignette 2.00
Dewey and Almy Chemical (I), **1950s**, Globe between two ladies vignette 2.00
Dewey Portland Cement (I), **1940s and 1950s, West Virginia** 1.00
Diamond Disc Shop (I), **1910s, New York**, Signed by Charles Edison 75.00
Diebold Venture Capitol Corporation (I), **1970s**, Woman with atoms vignette 1.00
Dillingham Corporation (I), **1970s**, Nine and three-quarters percent bond, man, dam, bridge, and buildings vignettes 2.00
Dixon Chemical Industries (I), **1950s and 1960s, New Jersey**, Tank car, and truck, and factory vignette 2.00
Doerr, A. A. Mercantile (U), **1900s**, Eagle vignette 3.00
Dominion Diamond Company (I), **New York**, Eagle vignette 2.00
Dourte Manufacturing Company 1910s, Gold seal 4.00
Dover Corporation (U), **1970s**, Seated lady with globe, company logo vignette 1.00
Dow-Corning (I), Bond vignette of research lab 3.00
Dow-Corning (I), **1970s**, Certificate, vignette of research lab .75
Drury's Tailoring (U), Eagle vignette 2.00
Dunluth and Dubuque Bridge Company (I), **1860s**, Eight percent bond, train-crossing bridge vignette 125.00
Duquesne Light Company (U), Specimen, bond, woman with light and generator vignette 3.00
Duquesne Light Company (U), **1950s**, Specimen, stock certificate, lady holding light vignette 3.00

Eagle General Corporation (I), **1970s**, Eagle vignette 1.00
Eagle Lock Company (I), **1890s, New York**, Eagle with flag vignette 10.00
Eagle Lock Company (I), **1910s**, Eagle with flag vignette 8.00
Eagle Lock Company (I), **1930s and 1940s**, Eagle with flag vignette 4.00
Eames Petroleum Gold and Smelting (I), **1880s, New York**, Two seated figures with eagle vignette 55.00
Eames Petroleum Iron Company (I), **1880s, New York** 8.00
Eastern Electric Light and Storage Battery (I-N), Stylized light bulb 20.00
Eastern Steel Company (I), **1920s**, Horses and seal vignette 10.00

◀ ***Poplar Bluff, City of (I), 1910s,*** *Five and one-half percent funding bond, eagle vignette* *8.00*

$1000 $1000

NUMBER 839

UNITED STATES OF AMERICA

STATE OF NEW JERSEY

The Board of Education of the Township of Wayne, in the County of Passaic

SCHOOL DISTRICT BOND

THE BOARD OF EDUCATION OF THE TOWNSHIP OF WAYNE, IN THE COUNTY OF PASSAIC, a school district of the State of New Jersey, situate in said County of Passaic, hereby acknowledges itself indebted and for value received promises to pay to the bearer of this bond, or if it be registered to the registered owner, the sum of

ONE THOUSAND DOLLARS ($1,000)

ON THE FIRST DAY OF MAY,

1974

upon presentation and surrender of this bond, and to pay interest on such sum, from the date of this bond until it matures, at the rate of three and forty-five hundredths per centum (3.45%) per annum payable November 1, 1965 and semi-annually thereafter on the first days of May and November in each year in accordance with the tenor of the respective coupons therefor annexed hereto, and upon presentation and surrender of said coupons as they severally mature or, if this bond be registered as to both principal and interest, to the registered owner. Both principal of and interest on this bond will be paid in lawful money of the United States of America, at the Haledon office of the New Jersey Bank and Trust Company, in the Borough of Haledon, New Jersey.

This bond is transferable by delivery, except if registered as to principal otherwise than to bearer. At the request of the holder this bond will be registered as to principal in his name on the books of said School District kept for that purpose in the office of its Secretary, such registration to be noted on the back of this bond, and thereafter, until registered transfer to bearer, no transfer of this bond shall be valid unless made on said books and similarly noted hereon. Such registration, however, shall not affect the negotiability of the coupons which shall continue to be payable to bearer and transferable by delivery. At the request of the registered owner this bond upon presentation at said office will be converted into a bond registered as to both principal and interest, by the execution of the conversion certificate on the back of this bond and by removing and cancelling the unmatured coupons hereto annexed, and thereafter both principal and interest shall be payable only to the registered owner. At the written request of the registered owner this bond, if it has been duly registered as to both principal and interest, will, at the expense of such owner and upon surrender hereof at said office, be reconverted into a bond payable to bearer and coupon in form by the preparation and substitution of a new bond, signed or executed by such of its officers then in office as said Board of Education shall designate and of the same tenor as this bond at the time of its issuance, with coupons annexed for any interest thereafter payable on this bond until its maturity.

This bond is one of an authorized issue of bonds, which are of like tenor except as to maturity, and is issued pursuant to Title 18, Education, of the Revised Statutes of the State of New Jersey, particularly Chapter 7 thereof, and by virtue of a proposal adopted by the affirmative vote of a majority of the legal voters present and voting at a special district meeting held on October 9, 1963, and of resolutions adopted by the Board of Education, and as validated by virtue of the provisions of Chapter 13 of the Laws of 1964 of said State.

The full faith and credit of said School District are hereby irrevocably pledged for the punctual payment of the principal of and interest on this bond according to its terms.

It is hereby certified and recited that all conditions, acts and things required by the Constitution or statutes of the State of New Jersey to exist, to have happened or to have been performed precedent to or in the issuance of this bond, exist, have happened and have been performed, and that the issue of bonds of which this is one does not exceed any limitation imposed thereon by said Constitution or statutes.

IN WITNESS WHEREOF, THE BOARD OF EDUCATION OF THE TOWNSHIP OF WAYNE, IN THE COUNTY OF PASSAIC, has caused this bond to be signed in its name by its President and its corporate seal to be hereunto affixed, and this bond and said seal to be attested by its Secretary, and each of the coupons hereto annexed to be authenticated by the facsimile signature of said Secretary, and this bond to be dated the first day of May, 1965.

THE BOARD OF EDUCATION OF THE TOWNSHIP OF WAYNE, IN THE COUNTY OF PASSAIC

ATTEST: William H. DeYoung

SECRETARY

BY George H. Schroeder

PRESIDENT

Eastern Tanning Company (U), **Massachusetts**, Indian and harbor vignette 7.00
Eaton and Howard Balanced Fund (I), **1950s**, 3.00
Eaton Howard (I), **1960s**, Woman justice between two men vignette .65
Eckard (Jack) Corporation (I), **1970s**, Two seated workmen and company logo vignette 1.00
Eckmar Corporation (I), **1960s**, Christmas decorations, deer, and so forth vignette .75
Eckmar Corporation (I), **1960s**, Christmas packages and company logo vignette .75
Edison Cement Corporation (I), **1930s**, Debenture note, no vignette, payable to Thomas Edison, executor for Edison's will 65.00
Edison Electric Illuminating Company (I), **1880s, New Jersey**, Generator with light vignette 140.00
Edison Kinetophone Company (U), **1910s**, Eagle vignette 23.00
Edison New York (I), **1940s**, Bond 4.00
Edison Phonographs Ltd. (U), **1900s**, Eagle vignette 27.00
Edison Portland Cement Company (I), **1890s**, Vignette of Thomas Edison 65.00
Edison Portland Cement Company (I), **1900s**, Vignette of Thomas Edison 60.00
Edison Portland Cement Company (I), **1900s**, With signature of Edison on front and back of certificate with stamp 750.00
Edison Splitdorf Corporation (I-N), **1940s** 28.00
Edison Storage Battery Company (I),**1900s**, Woman in clouds superimposed on map of North America, signed by Thomas Edison 995.00
Edison Storage Battery Company (I), **1910s**, Signed by Thomas A. Edison as president of the company 775.00
Edison Storage Battery Supply Company (I), **1910s**, Eagle vignette, signed by Thomas A. Edison as president of the company 685.00
Edison, Thomas A., Inc. (I), **1920s, New Jersey**, No vignette, but signed three times by Charles Edison as president of the company 265.00
Edison, Thomas A., Inc. (I), **1920s**, Signature of Thomas A. Edison as president of the company 750.00
Elgin National Watch Company (I), **1920s**, Father Time, eagle with watch vignettes 12.00
Elizabeth Brewing Corporation (I), **1930s, New Jersey** 12.00
Elkhart Bridge Company (I), **1900s**, Portraits of Washington and Lincoln, flying eagle vignette 14.00
Elkhart Opera House Company (I), **1900s, Indiana**, Scene of running bull, gold seal 54.00
Emhart Corporation—,Specimen Certificate, two figures with building vignette 20.00
Empire Tire and Rubber Corporation (I), **1910s, Virginia**, Plantation worker at rubber tree vignette 20.00
Equity Corporation (I), **1960s**, Seated lady with books and city skyline vignette 1.00
Erdman-Guilder Company (U), **1920s, Michigan**, Eagle vignette 2.00
Erie Forge and Steel Corporation (U), Specimen, eagle vignette 5.00
Erleme Corporation (I), **1930s**, Large eagle, two globes, and bolts and lightning vignette 3.00
Esquire, Inc. (I), **1970s**, Scholar vignette 8.00
Eureka Smelting Company (I-N), **1920s, Nevada** 10.00
Everett, C. F., Inc. (U), **1900s**, No vignette .60
Everett Knitting Works (I), **1910s, New Hampshire**, Red seal 25.00
Eversharp, Inc. (I), **1960s, Delaware**, Lady with book vignette 2.00
Eversharp (I), **1970s, Delaware**, Seated chemist with equipment vignette 1.00
Executone Company 1.00

F. and M. Schaefer Corporation (I), **1970s, New York**, Seminude man holding globe in front of mountains and city skyline vignette 4.00
F and W Grand Stores (I), **1910s**, Seated lady with lion vignette 6.00
Fallon Amusement Corporation (U), **1920s, Nevada**, Goddess vignette 4.00
Fame Mutual Insurance Company (I), **1850s, Pennsylvania**, Angel, eagle, and seal vignette 115.00

◀ ***Passaic, County of, Board of Education in the Township of Wayne (I), 1950s and 1960s, New Jersey,*** *Bonds* ***2.00***

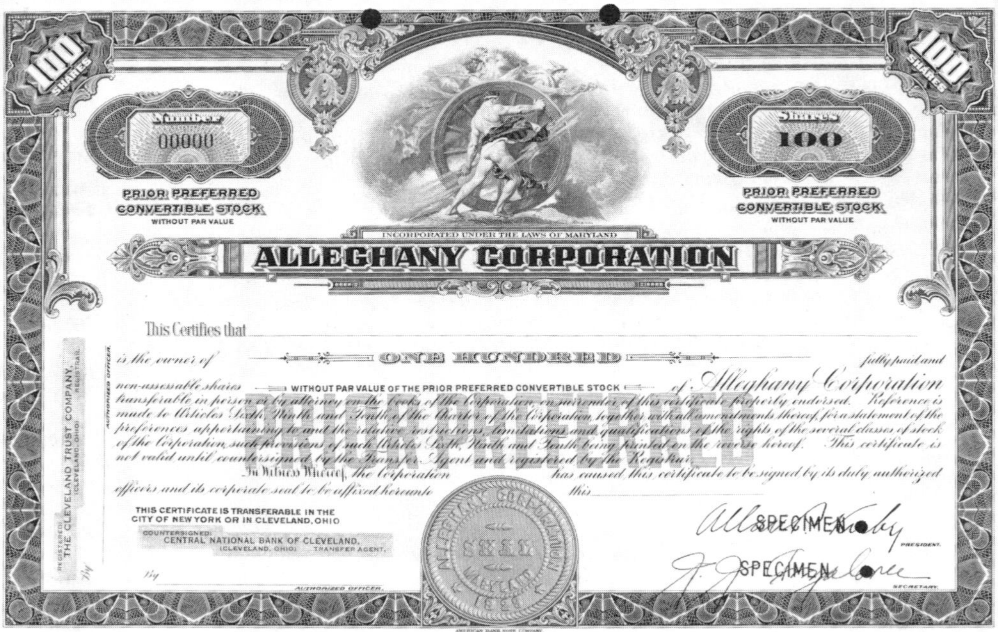

100 SHARES

Number 00000

Shares 100

PRIOR PREFERRED CONVERTIBLE STOCK WITHOUT PAR VALUE

INCORPORATED UNDER THE LAWS OF MARYLAND

ALLEGHANY CORPORATION

This Certifies that ______

is the owner of ONE HUNDRED fully paid and non-assessable shares WITHOUT PAR VALUE OF THE PRIOR PREFERRED CONVERTIBLE STOCK of Alleghany Corporation transferable in person or by attorney on the books of the Corporation, on surrender of this certificate properly endorsed. Reference is made to Articles Sixth, Ninth and Tenth of the Charter of the Corporation, together with all amendments thereof, for a statement of the preferences appertaining to and the relative restrictions, limitations and qualifications of the rights of the several classes of stock of the Corporation, such provisions of such Articles Sixth, Ninth and Tenth being printed on the reverse hereof. This certificate is not valid until countersigned by the Transfer Agent and registered by the Registrar.

In Witness Whereof, the Corporation has caused this certificate to be signed by its duly authorized officers and its corporate seal to be affixed hereunto this ______

PRIOR PREFERRED

THIS CERTIFICATE IS TRANSFERABLE IN THE CITY OF NEW YORK OR IN CLEVELAND, OHIO

COUNTERSIGNED: CENTRAL NATIONAL BANK OF CLEVELAND, (CLEVELAND, OHIO) TRANSFER AGENT.

By ______ AUTHORIZED OFFICER.

REGISTERED: THE CLEVELAND TRUST COMPANY, (CLEVELAND, OHIO) REGISTRAR.

By ______ AUTHORIZED OFFICER.

ALLEGHANY CORPORATION SEAL MARYLAND 1929

SPECIMEN PRESIDENT.

SPECIMEN SECRETARY.

AMERICAN BANK NOTE COMPANY

No. 49654

UNITED STATES OF AMERICA
State of Maine

25 Shares

American & Foreign Power Company Inc.

OPTION WARRANT

FOR VALUE RECEIVED AMERICAN & FOREIGN POWER COMPANY INC. promises to deliver to Abbott Hoppin & Co.

a certificate for TWENTY FIVE shares of its full-paid **Common Stock** (or at its option voting trust certificates therefor) at its office or agency in the Borough of Manhattan, City of New York, upon the surrender hereof at any time hereafter (without limit) and payment in cash for such stock at the rate of $25 per share; provided that the Company agrees that it will in lieu of cash accept one share of its Second Preferred Stock, Series A, in payment for each four shares of its said Common Stock deliverable under the terms hereof or of this and other similar option warrants so surrendered.

The rights represented hereby are transferable only on the books of American & Foreign Power Company Inc. at its office or agency in the Borough of Manhattan, City of New York, by the holder hereof in person or by attorney upon surrender of this warrant properly endorsed.

This warrant is not valid until countersigned by the Transfer Agent and registered by the Registrar.

WITNESS the seal of the Company and the signatures of its duly authorized officers this MAY 27 1931 of ______, 19___

AMERICAN & FOREIGN POWER COMPANY INC.

Attest: By

Assistant Secretary. Vice-President.

REGISTERED: CENTRAL HANOVER BANK AND TRUST COMPANY, Registrar. MAY 28 1931 By ______ Authorized Officer.

COUNTERSIGNED: BANKERS TRUST COMPANY, Transfer Agent. By ______ Assistant Secretary.

AMERICAN BANK NOTE COMPANY

Fame Mutual Insurance Company (I), 1860s, Pennsylvania, Angel, eagle, and seal vignette	110.00
Farmers Co-op Butter and Cheese (I-N), Minnesota, Eagle, gold seal vignette	2.00
Farmers' Mercantile (U), 1900s	2.00
Fat Man's Shop, Inc. (I), 1930s, Eagle vignette	10.00
Federal-Brandes, Inc.(I), 1920s, Delaware, Eagle vignette	3.00
Fellow's Company of New York (I), 1900s, Eagles with flag and shield vignette, Indian chief and buffalo in border	43.00
Fiberglass Homes of America (I), 1970s, Eagle vignette	.75
Fidelity Fund, Inc. (I), 1960s, Massachusetts, Statue vignette	3.00
Fidelity Investments Associates (U), Eagle vignette	2.00
Fiduciary Mutual Investing, Inc. (U), Maryland, Specimen, company logo vignette	3.00
Fieldcrest Mills (I), 1960s, Seated lady with winged wheel vignette	.75
Finck's Bridge Bond (I), 1860s, New York, Seven percent bond	50.00
Finnish Export Credit Ltd. (I), 1970s, Note guaranteed by representative of Finland	2.00
First Charter Financial Corporation (I), California, Large, bare-breasted lady, covered wagon and houses vignettes	5.00
First York Company (I), 1940s, Two men with company logo vignette	2.00
Florida Fruit Exchange (I), 1890s, Florida, Three vignettes of Indian, ship, and woman with bird	95.00
Florida, State of, Mortgage Company (I), 1920s, Six percent gold bond, shield vignette	3.00
FMC Corporation (I), 1970s, Four and one-quarter percent bond, vignette of science, industry, and farming	10.00
Food Dividend Corporation of America (I-N), 1960s, Large eagle vignette	.85
Food Fair Stores (I), Girl with horn of plenty, tractor, farm, and factory vignette	2.00
Fort Bragg Electric Company (I), 1900s, California, Woman holding light vignette, gold seal	20.00
Fort Bragg Electric Company (I), 1910s, Woman holding light vignette, gold seal	15.00
Fort Wayne Electric Company (I), 1890s, Indiana, Liberty with lightning vignette	20.00
Four Seasons Nursing Homes (I), 1960s and 1970s	10.00
Frank Fehr Brewing Company (I), 1940s, Woman vignette	8.00
Franklin Canal Company (I), 1850s, Pennsylvania, Bond, embossed seal	225.00
Franklin Fire Insurance of Philadelphia (I), 1930s, Portrait of Benjamin Franklin	10.00
Freeport Gas Works (I-N), 1870s, Pennsylvania, State seal	40.00
Fruit of the Loom, Inc. (I), 1930s, Multifruit vignette	5.00
Fun City, USA (U), Eagle vignette	2.00
G. E. Overseas Capital Corporation (I), 1960s, New York, Bond, man and woman vignette	20.00
Galeton Silk Mills (I), 1930s, Pennsylvania, Five percent bond	17.00
Gardner Denver Company (I), 1960s, Two seated figures with company logo vignette	1.00
Gardner Denver Company (I), 1970s, Man and woman with company logo vignette	.75
Gas and Electric Company of Bergen County (I), 1900s, Gold bond and state seal	14.00
General American Transportation (I), 1960s, Four and five-eighths percent bond, large eagle vignette	2.00
General Aniline and Film Corporation (I), 1960s and 1970s, Man and woman with company logo vignette	2.00
General Builders Corporation 1950s, Six percent bond, eagle vignette	1.00
General Electric Company (I), 1950s, Three and one-half percent bond, lady with light and man with dynamo vignette	3.00
General Foods Corporation (I), 1940s and 1950s, Two females with company sign vignette	2.00
General Foods Corporation (I), 1960s, Two females with company sign vignette	1.00
General Investors Fund (I), 1950s and 1960s, Early rifleman vignette	1.00
General Investors Trust (I), Massachusetts, Minuteman vignette	1.00
General Mills, Inc. (I), 1960s, Seated couple with globe and horn of plenty vignette, seal	2.00

◀ ***Alleghany Corporation**, Specimen, nude man with wheel vignette*	*5.00*
◀ ***American and Foreign Power Company, Inc., 1930s**, Warrant*	*3.00*

CERTIFICATE FOR LESS THAN ONE HUNDRED SHARES
NUMBER
C06981
SHARES
2
(INCORPORATED UNDER THE LAWS OF THE STATE OF MARYLAND)
AMERICAN FOUNDERS CORPORATION
COMMON STOCK WITHOUT ANY NOMINAL OR PAR VALUE
2733
This Certifies that James H. Rawley is the owner of
Two
FULLY PAID AND NON-ASSESSABLE SHARES WITHOUT ANY NOMINAL OR PAR VALUE OF THE COMMON STOCK,
of American Founders Corporation transferable on the books of the Corporation in person or by duly authorized attorney upon surrender of this certificate properly endorsed.
A statement of the rights, privileges, preferences and voting powers and of the restrictions, limitations and qualifications of or pertaining to the preferred and common stock of the Corporation is printed on the back hereof and set forth in the amended Certificate of Incorporation. By acceptance of this certificate and the shares represented thereby the holder hereof hereby consents and agrees to be bound by the said statement and by all of the provisions of the said amended Certificate of Incorporation and amendments thereto a copy of which is on file with the Transfer Agent. This certificate is not valid until countersigned by the Transfer Agent and registered by the Registrar.
Witness the Seal of the Corporation and the signatures of its duly authorized officers.
Dated
DEC 28 1925
ASSISTANT SECRETARY
VICE-PRESIDENT
REGISTERED: THE CHEMICAL NATIONAL BANK OF NEW YORK, REGISTRAR.
JAN 4 1929
AUTHORIZED OFFICER
COUNTERSIGNED: THE SEABOARD NATIONAL BANK OF THE CITY OF NEW YORK, TRANSFER AGENT.
HAMILTON BANK NOTE NEW YORK

American Reclamation Company
INCORPORATED UNDER THE LAWS OF ARIZONA
No B26
50 SHARES
Common Stock, $15,000,000
First Preferred Stock, $4,000,000
Second Preferred Stock, $6,000,000
Shares, $25 Each
CAPITAL STOCK, $25,000,000
Full Paid and Non-Assessable
This Certificate is not valid unless registered by the Registrar of the Company.
This is to Certify that James Waters is the owner of FIFTY (50) Shares of the Second Preferred Capital Stock of AMERICAN RECLAMATION COMPANY, transferable only on the books of the Company by the holder hereof in person or by duly authorized Attorney upon surrender of this Certificate.
SECOND PREFERRED
Witness the Seal of the Company and the signatures of its duly authorized officers affixed this 14 day of APRIL 1911
D. Wayne
SECRETARY
PRESIDENT

General Motors Corporation (I), 1950s, Three and one-quarter bond 5.00
General Motors Fuel (I), 1920s, Six percent bond 3.00
General Precision Equipment (I), 1960s, Nude man with wheel vignette 3.00
General Tire and Rubber Company (I), 1970s, Three seated figures with chemistry vignette 3.00
General Water Works and Electric Corporation (I), 1920s, Six percent gold bond, dam and power lines vignette 23.00
Georgia Pacific Corporation (I), 1950s, Bond, man reading chart with harbor scene vignette 2.00
Georgia Power Company (I), 1960s, Allegorical figures with map of state vignette 4.00
Germania Fire Insurance Company (I), 1880s, New York, Woman with sword in front of king's chair vignette 35.00
Germania Fire Insurance Company (I), 1900s, New York, Woman with sword in front of king's chair vignette 25.00
Gibson Hotel Corporation (U), Hotel vignette 4.00
Gimbel Brothers (I), 1940s, New York, Facsimile and signature of Bernard Gimbel, the president of the company 4.00
Gitchrest Company (U), Massachusetts, Eagle vignette 1.00
Glass Casket Company (I), 1920s, Eagle vignette, gold seal 12.00
Glen Mills (I), 1880s, Pennsylvania, Six percent bond, seal 210.00
Globe Iron Works (I-N), 1910s, California, Gold bond, gold seal vignette 14.00
Globe Telephone Company (I), 1880s, New York, Seated woman with phone, globe, and babies playing vignettes 110.00
Goddard Groome Drayton Company (I-N), 1910s, Pennsylvania, State seal 5.00
Goebel Brewing Company (I), 1960s, Two men with company logo vignette 7.00
Goebel Brewing Company (U), Has signatures, but specimen only. Train and eagle with beer barrel vignette 35.00
Golden Gate Bridge—Highway District (I), 1930s, Gold bond, Golden Gate Bridge over San Francisco Bay vignette 15.00
Goodrich, B. F. (I), 1960s, New York, Two men and company logo vignette 2.00
Goodrich, B. F. (I), 1970s, New York, Two men and company logo vignette 1.00
Goodrich, B. F. (I), 1970s, Nine and three-quarters percent note, $1,000/5,000s 10.00
Goodrich, B. F. (I), 1970s, Nine and three-quarters percent note, $100,000 20.00
Grand River Dam Authority (U), 1930s, Specimen, four percent bond 75.00
Grand Union (I), 1950s 2.00
Grand Union (I), 1960s, Two female figures vignette 1.00
Granite City Steel (I), 1960s, Blacksmith with anvil and tools vignette 2.00
Granite State Electric Works (U), 1900s, Two vignettes of girls 4.00
Grant, W. T. (I), 1920s, Bankrupt company 2.00
Grant, W. T. (I), 1910s 3.00
Grant, W. T., Company (I), 1920s, Signed by W. T. Grant 12.00
Gray and Davis (I), Massachusetts, Lady with light and dynamo vignette 1.00
Great America Corporation (I), Proof specimen, baby on globe and two allegorical figures vignette 4.00
Great America Inc. (I), 1970s, Company logo .75
Great Atlantic and Pacific Tea Company (I), 1960s and 1970s, Two angels, horn of plenty, and company logo vignette .85
Great Western Sugar Company (I), 1910s, Eagle on shield vignette 5.00
Greenwich Development Company (U), 1910s, Eagle vignette 4.00
Greger Manufacturing (I), 1890s, New Jersey, Streetcar tracks and seal vignette 20.00
Griffiths Electronics (I), 1970s 2.00

Haines and Slocum Company (I), 1910s, Eagle vignette 8.00

◀***American Founders Corporation (I), 1920s, Maryland,*** *Vignette of Washington and Jefferson, eagle and Washington Monument* ***3.00***

◀***American Reclamation Company (I), 1910s, Arizona,*** *Colorful certificate, Indian, buffalo, eagle, flag, and shield vignette* ***6.00***

INCORPORATED UNDER THE LAWS OF THE STATE OF ILLINOIS
NUMBER
56
SHARES
500
Ashland Industries Corporation
CAPITAL STOCK $1,500,000.00
SHARES $10.00 PAR VALUE
This Certifies that
A. HARRIS
is the owner of
Five Hundred
Shares of the Capital Stock of
Ashland Industries Corporation, fully paid and non-assessable,
transferable only on the books of this Corporation in person or by Attorney upon surrender of this Certificate properly endorsed.
IN WITNESS WHEREOF the said Corporation has caused this Certificate to be signed by its duly authorized officers and its Corporate Seal to be hereunto affixed
at Chicago, Illinois, this third day of
SECRETARY
PRESIDENT
SHARES $10.00 EACH

$1000
THE
ATLANTIC FRUIT & SUGAR COMPANY
EIGHT PER CENT. INCOME GOLD DEBENTURE BOND
DUE JANUARY 1, 1949
No M3394
No M3394
The Atlantic Fruit & Sugar Company
One Thousand Dollars

Haines and Slocum Company (U), **1910s**, Eagle vignette 3.00
Hamilton Watch Company (U), Specimen, two seated ladies vignette 35.00
Hancock Town Company (I), **1880s**, State seal, eagle vignette 44.00
Harmonia Fire Insurance Company (I), **1910s, New York**, State seal, green seal, with many stamps 4.00
Harsco Corporation (I), **1960s**, Seated man, factory and company logo vignette 1.00
Hartford Electric Company (U), Specimen, two seated women, streetcars, boat, and train vignettes 17.00
Hartford Rayon Corporation (I), **1930s**, Eagle on rock vignette 3.00
Hat Corporation of America (I), **1930s**, Company logo with angels vignette 8.00
Havana-American Company (U), **New Jersey**, Woman at cane field vignette 4.00
Heidelberg Brewing Company (U), Kentucky Specimen, vignette of brewery 33.00
Heitman Mortgage Investments (I) 1.00
Henninger, A. A., Inc. (I), **1930s, New York**, Gold bond, eagle vignette 3.00
Hermetical Barrel Company (I), **1860s, New York**, Old train, sailor with flag, and anchor vignettes 135.00
Heuck's Opera House Company (I), **1880s**, Seal 35.00
Highland Valley Power Company (I), **1900s**, Bond, river and dam in mountains vignette 35.00
Higley Automatic Sulky (U), Gold seal, eagle vignette 5.00
Hill Top Ice Company, Allegorical vignette 8.00
Holland's Far East, Tea, Coffee and Cocoa Corporation (I), **1920s**, Vignette of Asian workers 7.00
Home Insurance Company (I), **1880s, New York**, Three vignettes of people and one of a pyramid, with stamp 40.00
Home Insurance Company (I), **1930s, New York**, Three engineering vignettes 10.00
Home Insurance Company (I), **1960s**, Fireman, family, and woman vignettes 2.00
Homestead Fire Insurance Company, The (I), **1930s**, House and old car vignette 7.00
Hotel Harvey (I), **1920s**, Gold bond, female figure, and hotel under construction vignette 7.00
Hot Springs Hotel (I), **1920s, Colorado**, No vignette 9.00
Houdini Picture Corporation (I), **1920s**, Eagle vignettes, signed by Harry Houdini 635.00
Howell Electric Motors (I), **1960s** 3.00
Hoyt's Tree Support Company (U), **1900s, California**, Goddess vignette 12.00
Hubbard Ice, Hub vignette 15.00
Huck Finn Company (I), **1970s**, Cartoon Huck fishing 10.00
Hughes and Hatcher, Inc. (I), **1970s, New York**, Gladiator vignette 1.00
Hunt, P. H. Chemical Corporation (I), **1970s**, Two chemists, company logo vignette 1.00
Hydraulic Press Brick Company (I), **1890s**, Coat of arms vignette 8.00
Hydraulic Press Brick Company (I), **1890s**, Train and surveyors vignette 18.00
Hydraulic Press Brick Company (I), **1910s**, With stamps and record 6.00
Hydraulic Press Brick Company (I), **1920s**, Gold bond, eagle with shield vignette 6.00
Hydraulic Press Brick Company (I), **1920s and 1940s**, Coat of arms vignette 4.00

Illinois-Kentucky Bridge (Paducah-Ohio) (I), **1940s**, 4.00
Imperial Paper Company (I), **1970s**, Eagle vignette 1.00
Inair Company (I), **1960s**, Large eagle vignette .65
Incorporated Investors' Equities (I), **1930s**, Scrip Certificate 1.00
Independence Trust Shares (I), **1940s, Pennsylvania**, Vignette of Independence Hall and Liberty Bell 4.00
Independent Packing Company (I), **1920s**, Six percent bond 3.00
Indiana Sanitary Potters (I), **1920s**, Gold bond, Indian vignette 28.00
Insull Utility Investments (I), **1930s**, Gold bond 10.00
Insull Utility Investments (I-N), **1930s**, Gold bond, man, buildings, and generator vignette 15.00

◀ ***Ashland Industries Corporation (I), 1920s,*** *Seated lady with tools, ship, and train vignette* ***4.00***
◀ ***Atlantic Fruit and Sugar Company (I), 1920s,*** *Eight percent bond, lady holding globe, winged wheel, anchor, and ship vignette* ***32.00***

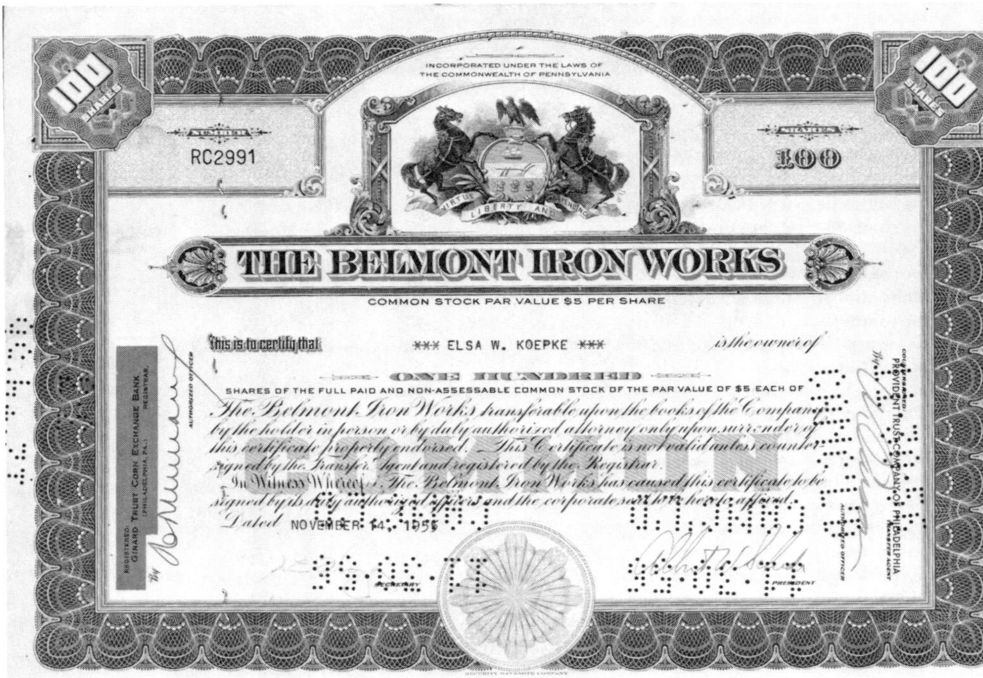
INCORPORATED UNDER THE LAWS OF THE COMMONWEALTH OF PENNSYLVANIA
100 SHARES
RC2991
100
VIRTUE LIBERTY AND INDEPENDENCE
THE BELMONT IRON WORKS
COMMON STOCK PAR VALUE $5 PER SHARE
This is to certify that
*** ELSA W. KOEPKE ***
is the owner of
ONE HUNDRED
SHARES OF THE FULL PAID AND NON-ASSESSABLE COMMON STOCK OF THE PAR VALUE OF $5 EACH OF
The Belmont Iron Works transferable upon the books of the Company by the holder in person or by duly authorized attorney only upon surrender of this certificate properly endorsed. This Certificate is not valid unless countersigned by the Transfer Agent and registered by the Registrar.
In Witness Whereof, The Belmont Iron Works has caused this certificate to be signed by its duly authorized officers and the corporate seal to be hereto affixed.
Dated NOVEMBER 14, 1955
SECRETARY
PRESIDENT
REGISTERED: GIRARD TRUST CORN EXCHANGE BANK (PHILADELPHIA, PA.) REGISTRAR,
AUTHORIZED OFFICER
COUNTERSIGNED: PROVIDENT TRUST COMPANY OF PHILADELPHIA TRANSFER AGENT
AUTHORIZED OFFICER

INCORPORATED UNDER THE LAWS OF THE STATE OF NEW YORK.
No. 132
Shares
Bronx Refrigerating Company
CAPITAL STOCK, $700,000.
PREFERRED STOCK, $300,000 COMMON STOCK, $400,000.
PAR VALUE OF SHARES $100. EACH.
This is to Certify, that C. R. Wood
is the owner of five fully paid and non-assessable shares of the par value of One Hundred Dollars ($100) each in the COMMON CAPITAL STOCK of the BRONX REFRIGERATING COMPANY, transferable only on the books of the Company by the holder hereof in person or by duly authorized attorney upon the surrender of this certificate.
COMMON
WITNESS the seal of the company and the signatures of its President and its Secretary this day of
191
SECRETARY
PRESIDENT

Interboro Lumber Company (U), 1920s, Lady portrait, gold seal vignette 2.00
International Bank Note Company (I), 1980s, New York, Globe vignette 15.00
International Business Machines (I), 1960s, Mercury with map of Northern Hemisphere 3.00
International Cellulose Company (I-N), 1910s, Nevada, Woman holding electric light with factory and dynamo vignette 6.00
International Investors, Inc. (I), 1960s, Large eagle vignette .65
International Match Corporation (I), 1930s, Bond, lady with lion vignette 24.00
International Money Machine Company (I), 1910s, Indiana 75.00
International Nickel Company (I), 1910s, Reclining woman with lion vignette 5.00
International Nickel Company, The (I), 1910s, Voting trust certificate, woman and lion vignette 4.00
International Nickel Company, The (I), 1920s, Reclining woman with lion vignette 4.00
International Nickel Company, The (I), 1930s, Three seminude workers vignette 3.00
International Nickel Company of Canada (I), 1930s, Three workers with anvil and pick vignette 4.00
International Paper Company (I), 1920s, Warrants 2.00
International Resistance Company (I), 1950s, Eagle vignette 1.00
International Resistance Company (I), 1960s, Delaware, Vignette of rocket and railroad radar equipment 4.00
International Safety Razor Corporation (I), 1920s, Large factory vignette plus six stamps 4.00
International Securities Corporation of America (I), 1920s, Ship, tugboat, trains, and plane vignettes 13.00
International Standard Electric (I), 1950s, Bond 8.00
International Telephone and Telegraph (I), 1930s, Woman and globe vignette 4.00
International Telephone and Telegraph (U), 1950s, Specimen, bond, man with telescope vignette 7.00
International Ticket Company (U), New Jersey, Allegorical figures with globe vignette 5.00
International Western Electric Company (U), 1910s, Eagle vignette 16.00
Investment Corporation of Florida (I), 1970s, Company logo 2.00
Investment Trust of Boston (I), 1960s, Capitol building vignette 1.00
Investors, Inc. (I), 1920s, Indiana, Green seal 3.00
Investors Underwriting Corporation (U), New York, Specimen, seated woman in front of harbor scene 20.00
Interstate Department Stores (I), 1960s and 1970s, Delaware, Lady with lyre vignette 2.00
Interstate Equities Corporation (I), 1920s and 1930s, Three allegorical figures with winged wheel 3.00
Iowa Power and Light (I), 1970s, Iowa, Seminude man with gears vignette 2.00
Ithaca and Geneva Turnpike Corporation (I), 1810s, No vignette 325.00
ITT Financial Corporation (I), Bond, seated woman with globe, skyline, and mountains vignette 3.00

Jack Eckerd Corporation (I), 1970s, Florida, Chemist and worker vignette 1.00
Jamaica Water and Utilities (I), 1960s, New York, Bond, eagle on mountaintop vignette 2.00
James Dunlap Carpet Company (I), 1900s, Pennsylvania, State seal 33.00
Jamestown Exposition (I), 1900s, Virginia, Large vignette of revelers 495.00
Japanese Tissue Mills (I), 1910s, Massachusetts, Lady with umbrella vignette 9.00
Jefferson Stores (I), 1960s, Large eagle vignette .75
Jersey Central Power and Light Company (I), 1940s, Bond, buildings and woman with light vignettes 12.00
Jersey Central Power and Light Company (I), 1960s, Bond, woman between generator and power line tower vignette 6.00
Johnstown Rendering Company (U), Pennsylvania, Eagle, streetcar, and tugboat vignette 5.00

◀ ***Belmont Iron Works, The (I), 1950s,*** *Horse and ship seal vignette, many stamps* ***2.00***

◀ ***Bronx Refrigerating (I), 1910s,*** *With many stamps, state seal* ***5.00***

100 SHARES

NUMBER 88 — SHARES 100

PREFERRED STOCK, SERIES A

BUSH SERVICE CORPORATION

INCORPORATED UNDER THE LAWS OF THE STATE OF DELAWARE

This Certifies that **F. J. LISMAN & COMPANY** is the owner of ONE HUNDRED fully paid and non-assessable shares of the PREFERRED STOCK, SERIES A, of the par value of $100 each of BUSH SERVICE CORPORATION (hereinafter called the Corporation) transferable in person or by duly authorized attorney upon surrender of this certificate properly endorsed. A statement of the respective rights privileges preferences and voting powers and of the limitations and restrictions of the several classes of stock of the Corporation as contained in the certificate of Incorporation of the Corporation as amended is printed upon the back hereof and this certificate and the shares represented hereby are issued and shall be held subject to all the provisions of the certificate of Incorporation of the Corporation as amended a copy of which certificate is on file at the office of the Transfer Agent to all of which the holder by acceptance hereof assents and is bound. This certificate is not valid unless countersigned by the Transfer Agent and registered by the Registrar.

Witness the signatures of its duly authorized officers.

Dated APR 3 1930

SECRETARY. PRESIDENT.

Registered APR 3 1930 The BANK of AMERICA NATIONAL ASSOCIATION, NEW YORK, REGISTRAR. By ASSISTANT CASHIER.

Countersigned APR 3 1930 BUSH SERVICE CORPORATION (NEW YORK) TRANSFER AGENT. By

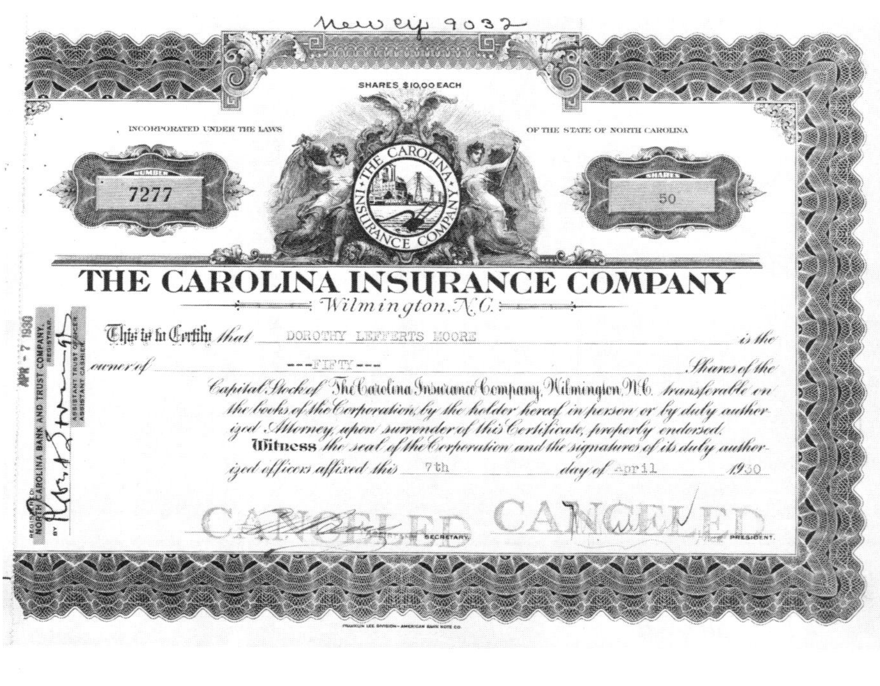
new cif 9032

SHARES $10.00 EACH

INCORPORATED UNDER THE LAWS OF THE STATE OF NORTH CAROLINA

NUMBER 7277 — SHARES 50

THE CAROLINA INSURANCE COMPANY

THE CAROLINA INSURANCE COMPANY

Wilmington, N.C.

This is to Certify that DOROTHY LEFFERTS MOORE is the owner of ---FIFTY--- Shares of the Capital Stock of The Carolina Insurance Company, Wilmington, N.C. transferable on the books of the Corporation, by the holder hereof in person or by duly authorized Attorney, upon surrender of this Certificate, properly endorsed.

Witness the seal of the Corporation and the signatures of its duly authorized officers affixed this 7th day of April 1930

CANCELED CANCELED

SECRETARY. PRESIDENT.

Registered APR - 7 1930 NORTH CAROLINA BANK AND TRUST COMPANY, REGISTRAR. By ASSISTANT TRUST OFFICER / ASSISTANT CASHIER.

FRANKLIN LEE DIVISION—AMERICAN BANK NOTE CO.

Kanes Falls Electric Company (U), 1900s, Gold bond, figure with light bulb vignette 12.00
Kanes Falls Electric Company (U), 1900s, Woman on winged wheel vignette 23.00
Kansas City Baseball Club, Inc. (I), 1930s, Transferred from Tris Speaker 400.00
Kansas Water Works and Irrigation (I), 1880s, Bond, farm scene with cattle and horses vignette 385.00
Kaufman and Broad (I), 1970s, Seated figures, lake, and woods vignette .75
Kentucky Brewing Company (U), Kentucky Specimen, Company logo between two seated ladies vignette 40.00
Kenwood Masonic Lodge, 1910s, Wisconsin, Gold bond, large gold seal with logo 5.00
Kern Incandescent Gas Light Company (I), 1900s, New Jersey, Portrait of young woman 38.00
Keystone Theatre Company (U), 1910s, Lady and theatrical masks vignette 7.00
Keystone Water Works and Electric Corporation (I), 1920s, Gold bond, seminude with torch vignette 25.00
Knickerbocker Fund (U), Specimen 8.00
Knollwood Cemetery (I), 1910s, Large mausoleum vignette 22.00
Kreuger and Toll Company (I), 1920s, Woman on winged wheel vignette 12.00

L. A. Pulp and Paper (U), Eagle vignette 2.00
L C O, Inc. (I), 1970s, Nevada, Eagle vignette, gold seal 3.00
Lake and Export Coal Sales Corporation of Illinois (I-N), 1920s, Eagle vignette, gold seal 4.00
Lake Geneva Lanes (I), 1950s, Wisconsin, Eagle vignette 4.00
Lancaster Caramel Company (U), 1800s, Pennsylvania, State seal 27.00
La Salle Wines and Champagne (I), Vineyard between two figures vignette 12.00
Law Association of Philadelphia (I), 1870s, Woman justice with sword and rearing horses vignette, seal 265.00
Lea Cattle Company (I), 1880s, New Mexico, Six percent bond, two cows vignettes 325.00
Lehigh Coal and Navigation (I), 1920s, Two portraits and horses vignettes 8.00
Lehigh Coal and Navigation (I), 1940s, Vignette of two founders portraits 3.00
Lehigh Coal and Navigation (I), 1950s, Vignette of two founders portraits 2.00
Lena Horne Beauty Products (I), 1960s 10.00
Leon B. Allen Fund (I), 1960s, Large eagle vignette 1.00
Lerner Stores Corporation (I), 1950s, Woman and two angels vignette 2.00
Lewis Publishing Company (I), 1900s, South Dakota, Many-sided building vignette 70.00
Lewiston Suspension Bridge Company (U), 1800s, Bridge over river in mountains vignette 38.00
Lexington Research Investing Corporation (I), 1960s, Minuteman with rifle vignette 2.00
Liebman Breweries (U), 1900s, No vignette 12.00
Lima Cord Sole and Heel Company 1930s, Seated woman by globe and lion vignette, stamp on reverse 3.00
Limestone Fertilizer (I), 1920s, Seven percent gold bond with stamps, eagle vignette 12.00
Lincoln Printing Company (I), 1960s, Lincoln portrait 4.00
Lincoln Stores, Inc. (I), 1930s, Massachusetts 2.00
Ling-Temco-Vought, Inc. (I), 1960s, Nude man with globe vignette 3.00
Ling-Temco-Vought, Inc. (I), 1960s, Seated man with telescope and books vignette 1.00
Lion Country Safari (I), 1980s, California, Car and lines in animal park vignette 15.00
Lion Country Safari (I-N), 1980s, California, Car and lines in animal park vignette 20.00
Lionel Corporation 1950s and 1960s, Boy with two trains vignette 8.00
Lit Brothers (I), 1920s, Pennsylvania, City seal, signed by Jacob and Samuel Lit 37.00
L N C Corporation (I), 1960s, Eagle vignette 1.00
Lockman, W. S., Construction (I), 1930s, Six percent bond, eagle with shield vignette 4.00
Lockwood, Green and Company (I), 1920s, Gold note 6.00

◀ ***Bush Service Corporation (I), 1930s,*** *Seated woman with winged wheel vignette, port city in background, railroad* ***3.00***
◀ ***Carolina Insurance Company, The (I), 1920s and 1930s, North Carolina,*** *Females and company logo vignette, with stamps* ***9.00***

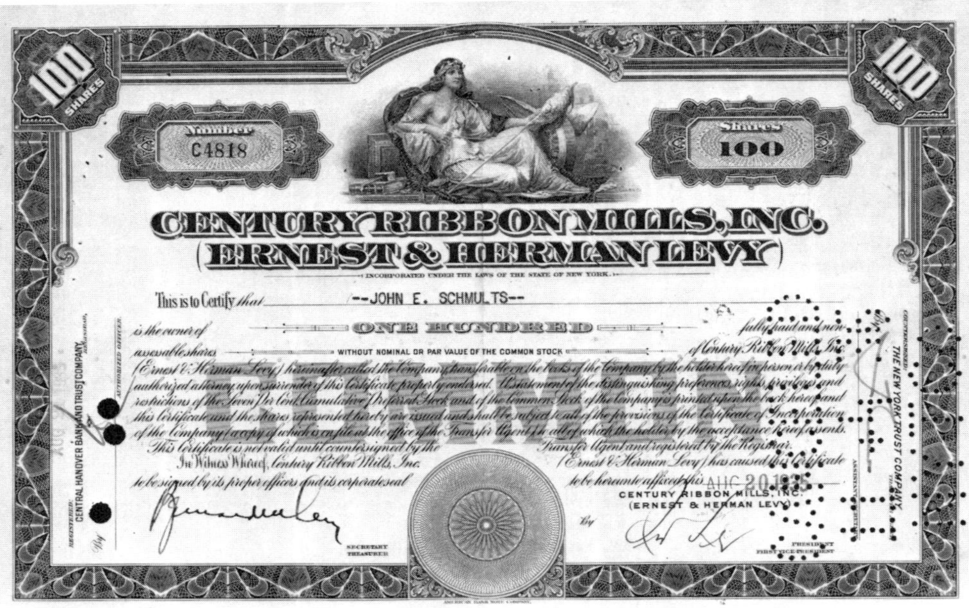

100 SHARES

Number C4818

Shares 100

CENTURY RIBBON MILLS, INC. (ERNEST & HERMAN LEVY)

INCORPORATED UNDER THE LAWS OF THE STATE OF NEW YORK.

This is to Certify that --JOHN E. SCHMULTS--

is the owner of ONE HUNDRED fully paid and non-assessable shares WITHOUT NOMINAL OR PAR VALUE OF THE COMMON STOCK of Century Ribbon Mills, Inc. (Ernest & Herman Levy) hereinafter called the Company, transferable on the books of the Company by the holder hereof in person or by duly authorized attorney upon surrender of this Certificate properly endorsed. A statement of the distinguishing preferences, rights, privileges and restrictions of the Seven Per Cent Cumulative Preferred Stock and of the Common Stock of the Company is printed upon the back hereof and this Certificate and the shares represented hereby are issued and shall be subject to all of the provisions of the Certificate of Incorporation of the Company (a copy of which is on file at the office of the Transfer Agent) to all of which the holder by the acceptance hereof assents.

This Certificate is not valid until countersigned by the Transfer Agent and registered by the Registrar.

In Witness Whereof, Century Ribbon Mills, Inc. (Ernest & Herman Levy) has caused this Certificate to be signed by its proper officers and its corporate seal to be hereunto affixed this AUG 20 1935

CENTURY RIBBON MILLS, INC. (ERNEST & HERMAN LEVY)

SECRETARY TREASURER

By PRESIDENT FIRST VICE PRESIDENT

COUNTERSIGNED: THE NEW YORK TRUST COMPANY

REGISTERED: CENTRAL HANOVER BANK AND TRUST COMPANY

AMERICAN BANK NOTE COMPANY.

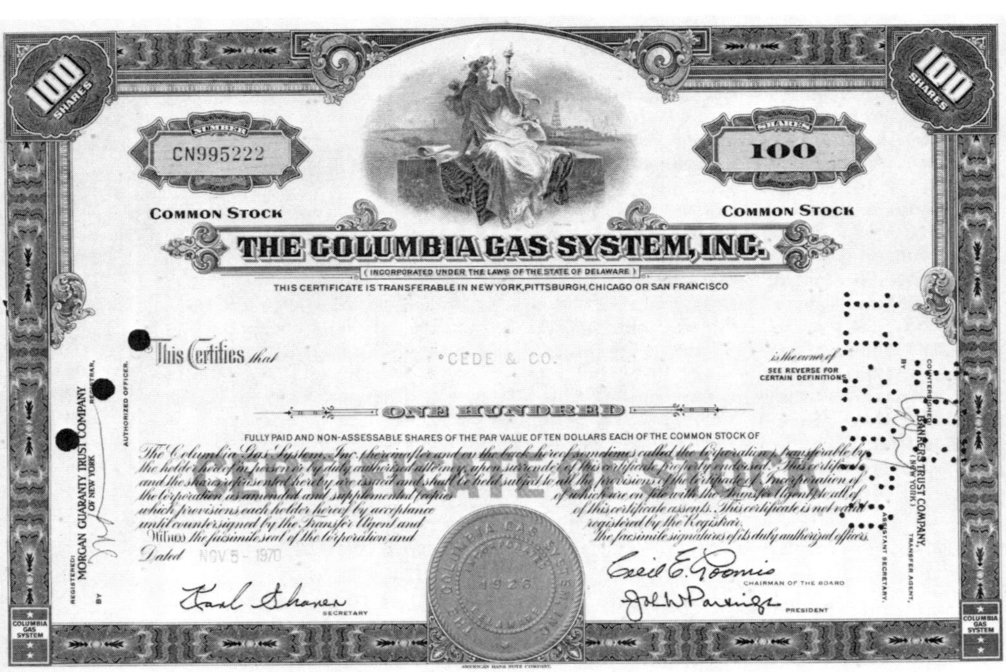

100 SHARES

NUMBER CN995222

SHARES 100

COMMON STOCK

COMMON STOCK

THE COLUMBIA GAS SYSTEM, INC.

(INCORPORATED UNDER THE LAWS OF THE STATE OF DELAWARE)

THIS CERTIFICATE IS TRANSFERABLE IN NEW YORK, PITTSBURGH, CHICAGO OR SAN FRANCISCO

This Certifies that CEDE & CO. is the owner of

SEE REVERSE FOR CERTAIN DEFINITIONS

ONE HUNDRED

FULLY PAID AND NON-ASSESSABLE SHARES OF THE PAR VALUE OF TEN DOLLARS EACH OF THE COMMON STOCK OF

The Columbia Gas System, Inc. (hereinafter and on the back hereof sometimes called the Corporation) transferable by the holder hereof in person or by duly authorized attorney, upon surrender of this certificate properly endorsed. This certificate and the shares represented hereby are issued and shall be held subject to all the provisions of the Certificate of Incorporation of the Corporation as amended and supplemented (copies of which are on file with the Transfer Agent) to all of which provisions each holder hereof by acceptance of this certificate assents. This certificate is not valid until countersigned by the Transfer Agent and registered by the Registrar.

Witness the facsimile seal of the Corporation and the facsimile signatures of its duly authorized officers.

Dated NOV 5 - 1970

SECRETARY

CHAIRMAN OF THE BOARD

PRESIDENT

COLUMBIA GAS SYSTEM

AMERICAN BANK NOTE COMPANY.

Loew's Boston Theaters (I), 1920s, Massachusetts, Two seated ladies vignette, many stamps on reverse **8.00**
Lomas and Nettleton Financial, Specimen, Two seated men with company logo vignette **24.00**
Long Island Lighting (I), 1950s, Bond, seated figure by electric motor with light vignette **7.00**
Loretta Lynn Western Stores (U), Eagle vignette **1.00**
Lorillard Corporation **1.00**
Louis Rosenbloom, Inc. (I), 1940s, Farm scene, plus stamp **2.00**
Lowell Electric Company (I), 1880s, Early electric stock certificate, embossed seal **20.00**
Lowell Electric Company (I), 1920s, Lady with lightning bolts vignette **8.00**
Lowell Electric Company (I), 1930s, Lady with lightning bolts vignette **7.00**
Lowell Electric Light Company (I), 1910s, Lightning bolt vignette **10.00**
Lukens Steel Company (I), 1930s, Eagle vignette **3.00**
Lundstrom Rim Corporation (I), 1920s, Portrait of Washington between two figures, eagle at bottom **14.00**
Luthy Storage Battery Company 1910s, Two people and generator vignette **17.00**
Luthy Storage Battery Company 1920s, Two people and generator vignette **13.00**
Lyman Cordage Company (U), Eagle vignette **1.00**

McDermott and Company, Inc. (I), 1970s, Four and three-fourths percent bond **2.00**
Mackay Company (I), 1920s, Lightning, transatlantic cable company, embossed seal vignettes **15.00**
Macy Credit Corporation (I), 1970s, Eight percent bond, seated lady vignette **1.00**
Magnolia Cemetery (U), **1800s, South Carolina**, Company logo **6.00**
Majestic Radio and Television (I-N), 1940s, Eagle vignette **15.00**
Mammoth Mart, Inc. (I), 1960s, Company logo of "Marty" (pig) **.75**
Mansell Heel Machine Company (I), 1880s, Machine vignette **43.00**
Manshel Ticket Machine Company (U), **Rhode Island**, Girl with light bulb, dynamo, and factory vignette **3.00**
Manufactured Rubber Company (I), 1920s, Three seminude seated figures vignette **18.00**
Marconi Wireless Telegraph Company (I), 1910, New Jersey, Woman with globes and transmission towers vignette **22.00**
Marconi Wireless Telegraph Company (I), 1920s, Transmission towers, woman between two globes vignette, with orange British stamp, dividend stamps on reverse **20.00**
Marion Ice and Cold Storage **10.00**
Martin Johnson African Expedition Company (U), **1920s** **20.00**
Mason Valley Telephone and Telegraph (U), **1910s Nevada**, River and falls, and telephone poles vignette **10.00**
Massachusetts Investor's Second Fund (I), 1940s, Old state building vignette **4.00**
Matawan and Keyport Gas Light Company (I), 1870s, New Jersey, Two seated ladies with horse head vignette, revenue stamp **55.00**
Matheson Alkali Works (I), 1930s, Virginia, Eagle vignette **5.00**
Mattel, Inc. (I), 1970s, Two children at play vignette, company logo **3.00**
Max Factor and Company (U), **1960s**, Two seated sexy ladies with world and company logo vignettes **1.00**
Maxim Soap Company (U), **1960s**, Two seated sexy ladies with world and company logo vignettes **1.00**
May Department Stores (I), 1950s, Bond ($1,000), eagle vignette **9.00**
Mayflower Investors, Inc. (I), 1970s, Vignette of Mayflower **1.00**
Med Com, Inc. (I), 1970s, Massachusetts, No vignette **1.00**

◀ ***Century Ribbon Mills, Inc. (I), 1930s,*** *Bare-breasted seated woman with winged wheel vignette* ***4.00***
◀ ***Columbia Gas System, Inc., The (I), 1970s,*** *Seminude lady with torch, oil derricks in rear* ***3.00***

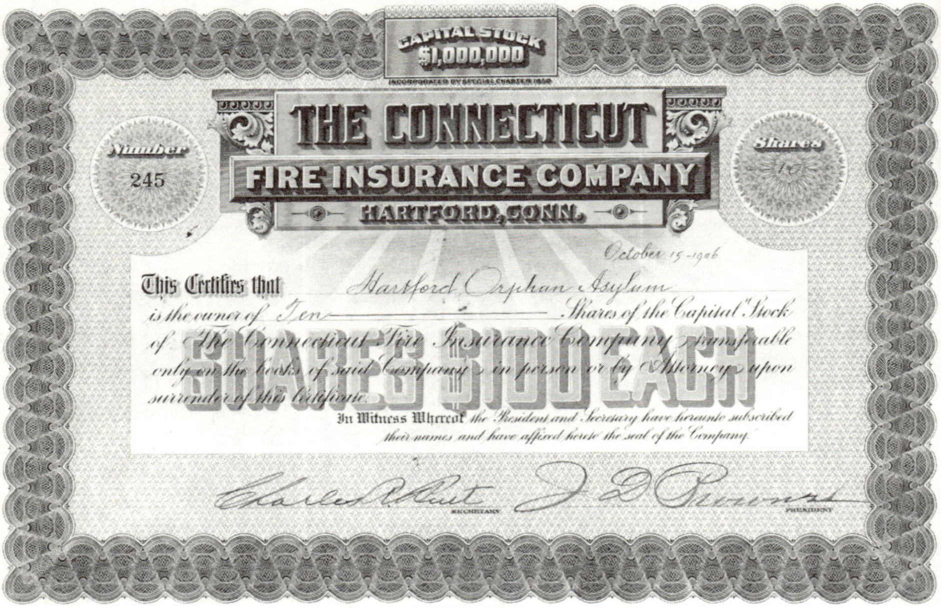

CAPITAL STOCK
$1,000,000
INCORPORATED BY SPECIAL CHARTER 1850
THE CONNECTICUT
FIRE INSURANCE COMPANY
HARTFORD, CONN.
Number 245
Shares 10
October 15 - 1906
This Certifies that Hartford Orphan Asylum
is the owner of Ten Shares of the Capital Stock
of The Connecticut Fire Insurance Company transferable
only on the books of said Company in person or by Attorney upon
surrender of this Certificate.
SHARES $100 EACH
In Witness Whereof the President and Secretary have hereunto subscribed
their names and have affixed hereto the seal of the Company.
SECRETARY
PRESIDENT

000-0147-66

CERTIFICATE FOR LESS THAN 100 SHARES
00000
COMMON
COMMON
CRESCENT CORPORATION
INCORPORATED UNDER THE LAWS OF THE STATE OF DELAWARE
THIS CERTIFICATE IS TRANSFERABLE IN NEW YORK CITY OR JERSEY CITY
This Certifies That
is the owner of
SEE REVERSE FOR CERTAIN DEFINITIONS
FULL-PAID AND NON-ASSESSABLE SHARES OF THE COMMON STOCK OF THE PAR VALUE OF $1 EACH OF
Crescent Corporation transferable on the books of the corporation in person or by duly
authorized attorney upon surrender of this certificate properly endorsed. This certificate is not
valid unless countersigned by the Transfer Agent and registered by the Registrar.
Witness the seal of the corporation and the signatures of its duly authorized officers.
Dated
CERTIFICATE OF STOCK
SPECIMEN
SECRETARY.
SPECIMEN
PRESIDENT.
REGISTERED: Empire Trust Company, REGISTRAR. BY AUTHORIZED OFFICER.
COUNTERSIGNED: FIRST NATIONAL CITY BANK, TRANSFER AGENT. BY AUTHORIZED OFFICER.
1 2 3 4 5 6 7 8 9 0
1 2 3 4 5 6 7 8 9 0

Merchant's and Miner's Transport Company (I), 1920s, Maryland, Two men with shield vignette 5.00
Merchants' Dispatch Transportation (U), 1880s, Freight dispatcher vignette 35.00
Merchants' Exchange of Saint Louis (I), 1880s, Horse and wagon in front of building, train, ships, and waterfront scene vignettes 55.00
Merchants' Exchange of Saint Louis (I), 1890s, Horse and wagon in front of building, train, ships, and waterfront scene vignettes 45.00
Merchant's Mutual Insurance Company (I), 1860s 75.00
Merchants' Transportation Company (I), 1850s, No vignette 60.00
Merchants' Union Express (I-N), 1860s, Galloping horses pulling wagon with railroad station in rear vignette 265.00
Mergenthaler Linotype Company (U), New York, Man at press logo, specimen with signatures 5.00
Merrimack Manufacturing Company (I), 1910s and 1920s, No vignette 4.00
Metropolitan Telephone and Telegraph (I), 1910s, Six percent gold bond 155.00
Metro-Urban Development (I), 1970s, Large eagle vignette 1.00
Mexican Banana Plantation (U), Eagle, shield, train, and ship vignettes 2.00
Mexican Telephone Company (I), 1880s, New York, Signed by Franklin Delano 20.00
Michigan-Wisconsin Pipe Line (I), 1960s, Four and seven-eighths percent bond, seated man and woman with company logo vignettes 2.00
Middlesex Electric (I), 1880s, No vignette 15.00
Middlesex Electric (U), 1880s 5.00
Middlesex Electric Light Company (I), 1880s, Embossed seal 12.00
Middletown Point and Keyport Gas Light Company (I), 1870s, New Jersey, Allegorical figures 75.00
Middlewest Utilities Company (I), 1930s, Night city scene 20.00
Midwest Asbestos Company (I), 1910s, Arizona, Young lady vignette, plus seal 5.00
Midwest Saints, Inc. (I), 1970s, Minnesota, Cartoon of winged angel, hockey player 25.00
Military Naval Corporation (I), 1910s, Gold bond 17.00
Milk Row Bleachery (U), 1800s 12.00
Millerstown Iron Company (U), 1800s, State seal 6.50
Millvale Hall Company (I), 1880s, Pennsylvania, State building vignette, red seal 55.00
Milton Bradley Company, Specimen, figures with world globe vignette 25.00
Minden Flour Milling Company (I), 1900s, Nevada, Indian on rock and sailing ships vignette 20.00
Minden Flour Milling Company (U), 1900s, Indian on rock and sailing ships vignette 5.00
Minnesota Mining and Manufacturing (I), 1960s, Woman seated in front of city vignette 3.00
Mission Development (I), 1950s, J. Paul Getty facsimile 5.00
Mission Equities Corporation (I), 1970s, Seated lady with globe vignette .65
Modern Data Techniques (I), 1960s, Company logo 1.00
Modern Mexico Cattle and Investment Company (U), 1900s, New Mexico territory, man and lion 10.00
Monarch Life Insurance Company (I), 1960s, Massachusetts, Lions and company logo vignette 4.00
Monarch Molybdenum 1.00
Monarch Timber Company (U), Idaho, State seal 8.00
Monroe Marsh Company (U), 1900s, Flying goose vignette 39.00
Montana Phonograph Company (U), 1800s, Montana Territory, Vignette of old phonographs 55.00
Montrose and Harford Plant Company (I), 1850s, No vignette 220.00
Morris Canal and Banking (I), 1860s, Figures with urns along canal scene 65.00
Morris Canal and Banking (I), 1870s, Figures with urns along canal scene 55.00
Morris Canal and Banking (I), 1880s 20.00
Mortgage Finance Company (I), 1920s, Florida, Six percent bond, eagle with shield vignette 3.00
Multi-Bestos Company (I), 1920s, Massachusetts, Old factory building vignette 5.00

◀ ***Connecticut Fire Insurance Company, The (I-N), 1900s,*** *Company logo* ***7.00***
◀ ***Crescent Corporation (U),*** *Specimen, winged Mercury, ship, plane, train and cars vignettes* ***5.00***

100 SHARES

Number DD16745

Shares 100

COMMON STOCK

COMMON STOCK

INCORPORATED UNDER THE LAWS OF THE STATE OF DELAWARE

Dayco Corporation

THIS CERTIFICATE IS TRANSFERABLE IN THE CITY OF NEW YORK OR DAYTON, OHIO

This Certifies that - - SHELDON & CO - - is the owner of

SEE REVERSE FOR CERTAIN DEFINITIONS

CUSIP 239577 10 9

ONE HUNDRED

FULLY PAID AND NON-ASSESSABLE SHARES OF THE COMMON STOCK OF

Dayco Corporation transferable on the books of the Corporation by the holder in person or by duly authorized attorney upon surrender of this Certificate properly endorsed. This Certificate and the shares represented hereby are issued and shall be held subject to all the provisions of the Certificate of Incorporation of the Corporation and all amendments thereto, copies of which are on file in the office of the Corporation and the office of each Transfer Agent, to all of which the holder by acceptance hereof assents. This Certificate is not valid unless countersigned by a Transfer Agent and registered by a Registrar.

Witness the facsimile seal of the Corporation and the facsimile signatures of its duly authorized officers.

Dated AUG 17 1971

SECRETARY

CHAIRMAN OF THE BOARD

PRESIDENT

DAYCO CORPORATION CORPORATE SEAL DELAWARE

REGISTERED: THE THIRD NATIONAL BANK AND TRUST COMPANY OF DAYTON, OHIO, REGISTRAR — By AUTHORIZED OFFICER

OR

REGISTERED: THE CHASE MANHATTAN BANK (NATIONAL ASSOCIATION), REGISTRAR — By AUTHORIZED SIGNATURE

COUNTERSIGNED: THE WINTERS NATIONAL BANK AND TRUST COMPANY OF DAYTON, OHIO, TRANSFER AGENT — By AUTHORIZED OFFICER

OR

COUNTERSIGNED: BANKERS TRUST COMPANY, (NEW YORK) TRANSFER AGENT — By ASSISTANT SECRETARY

Dayco

AMERICAN BANK NOTE COMPANY

Number -2-

Shares 60

Detroit Autoclave Mfg. Co

This Certifies that Jeanette F. Mangan is the owner of Sixty Shares of the Capital Stock of Detroit Autoclave Mfg. Co. transferable only on the books of the Corporation by the holder hereof in person or by Attorney upon surrender of this Certificate properly endorsed.

In Witness Whereof, the said Corporation has caused this Certificate to be signed by its duly authorized officers and to be sealed with the Seal of the Corporation this 22nd day of March A.D. 1928

Secretary

President

DETROIT AUTOCLAVE MFG. CO. SEAL DETROIT, MICH.

SHARES $10 EACH

© GOES

Murray Hill Allied Corporation (I), 1920s, Eagle vignette	2.00
Mutual Benefit Life Insurance (I), 1860s, Pelican with little ones in nest vignette	75.00
Mutual Benefit Life Insurance (I-N), 1860s, Pelican with little ones in nest vignette	85.00
Mutual Investment Union (U), 1890s	3.00
Narragansett Electric Lighting (I), 1880s, Viking ship, red seal vignette	55.00
Narragansett Racing Association (U), Rhode Island, Indian chief at racetrack and horses vignettes	6.00
Nash-Kelvinator (I), 1950s	4.00
Nashua Corporation (I), 1970s, Two men with chemistry equipment vignette	.65
Natco Iron	.75
National Alfalfa (I), 1960s, Eagle vignette	2.00
National Alfalfa Dehydrating and Milling (I), 1960s, Large eagle vignette	.75
National Color Printing Company (I), 1880s, Allegorical figures, red seal	12.00
National Consolidated Power (I-N), 1900s	15.00
National Distributors and Chemical Corporation (I), 1950s, Bond, chemistry vignette	15.00
National Electric Power Company (I), 1920s, Two seminude ladies holding company banner vignette	12.00
National Glass Company (I), 1900s, Pennsylvania, Gold bond, figure with goblet vignette	12.00
National Lace Paper and Specialty (U), 1900s, Eagle, capitol building vignette	.60
National Liberty Insurance Company (I), 1930s, Company logo	6.00
National Liberty Insurance Company (I), 1940s, Company logo	2.00
National Security Trading Corporation (U), New York, Eagle vignette	1.00
National Steel Corporation (I), 1950s, Three and one-half percent bond, large eagle vignette	2.00
National Steel Corporation 1970s, Bond, large eagle vignette	.75
National Stockyard Company (U), 1800s, Cowboys and cows scene	60.00
National Storage Company (U), 1860s, State seal, female with eagle vignette	15.00
National Sweepstakes,	1.00
National Tea Company (I), 1920s, Reclining lady vignette	4.00
National Tea Company (I), 1930s, Reclining lady vignette	3.00
National Tea Company (I), 1950s, Factory vignette	2.00
National Telephone Manufacturing Company (I), 1880s, New Hampshire, Seated lady with eagle vignette	125.00
National Toll Bridge Company (I), 1930s, Maryland, Suspension bridge vignette	22.00
National Tool Company (I), 1950s, Ohio, Eagle vignette	5.00
Nedick's Corporation (I), 1930, Six percent bond	25.00
Nes Silicon Steel Company (I), 1870s, New York, Indian and Pilgrim vignette	20.00
Nevada Irrigation District (I), 1930s, California, Bond	4.00
Nevada Power Company (I), 1970s, Lady with light and city scene vignette	2.00
New Albany Woolens Mills (I), 1890s, Indiana, Six percent gold bond, eagle vignette	40.00
Newark Gas Company (I), 1890s, Storage tanks, factories, stokers, and Miss Liberty vignettes	42.00
Newark Ohio Waterworks Company (I), 1880s, Certificate, water towers vignette	37.00
Newark Ohio Waterworks (I), 1880s, New York, Gold bond, waterworks beside lake vignette	130.00
Newark Ohio Waterworks Company (I), 1880s, New York, Six percent bond, water tower, and prehistoric creatures vignettes	50.00
Newburyport Gas and Electric Company, The (I), 1920s	3.00
New England Alloy Casting Corporation (I), 1950s, State seal	3.00
New England Cotton Yarn Company (I), 1910s, Eagle with shield vignette	10.00
New England Excelsior Manufacturing (U), 1800s	3.00
New England Gas and Electric Association (I), 1940s, Woman, gas tanks, and power lines vignette	3.00

◀***Dayco Corporation,*** *Orbiting electrons and girl vignette*	***1.00***
◀***Detroit Autocleno Mfg. Co. (I-N),*** *Train vignette, gold seal, stamps*	***15.00***

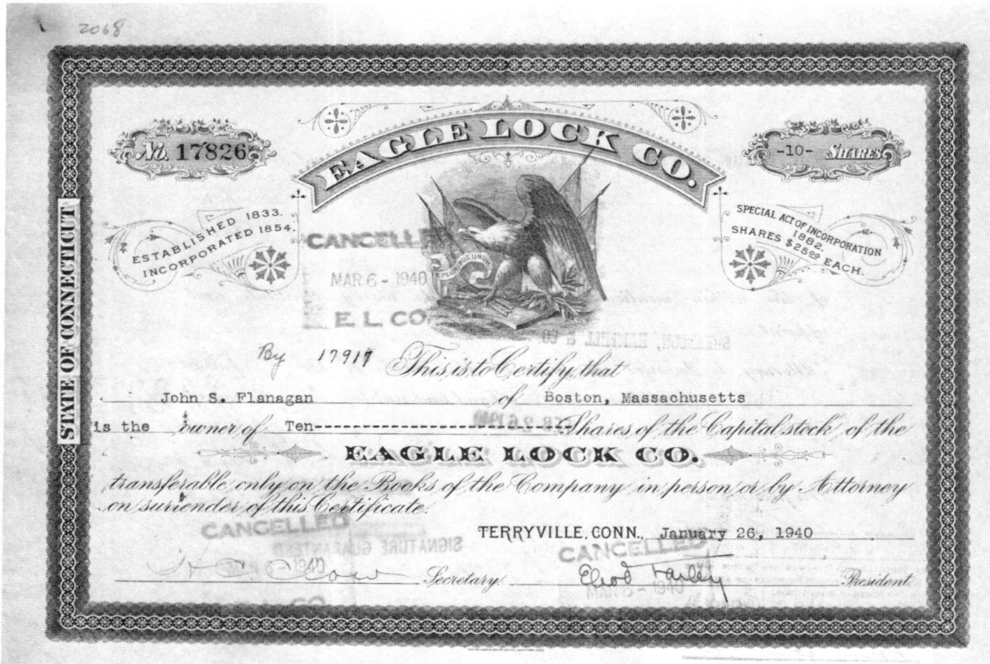

2068
No. 17826
EAGLE LOCK CO.
-10- SHARES
ESTABLISHED 1833.
INCORPORATED 1854.
SPECIAL ACT OF INCORPORATION 1882.
SHARES $25.00 EACH.
STATE OF CONNECTICUT
CANCELLED
MAR 6 - 1940
E. L. CO.
By 17917
This is to Certify that
John S. Flanagan of Boston, Massachusetts
is the owner of Ten Shares of the Capital stock of the
EAGLE LOCK CO.
transferable only on the Books of the Company in person or by Attorney on surrender of this Certificate.
CANCELLED
SIGNATURE GUARANTEED
TERRYVILLE, CONN., January 26, 1940
CANCELLED
Secretary
President

INCORPORATED UNDER LAWS OF
THE STATE OF NEW JERSEY
NUMBER 5
SHARES
Full Paid and Non-Assessable
The Corporation is Authorized to Issue 20,000 Shares of Stock without Par Value
Erleme Corporation
This is to Certify that Pauline Barron is the owner of One Shares of Stock without Par Value of
Erleme Corporation
transferable on the books of the Corporation by the holder hereof in person or by duly authorized Attorney upon surrender of this Certificate properly endorsed.
Witness the seal of the Corporation and the signatures of its duly authorized officers affixed this day of
Secretary
President

New England Manufacturing Works (I), 1870s, Connecticut, Two vignettes of blacksmiths **80.00**
New England Motive Power (I), 1880s, Maine, Trains and power plant vignette with seal **30.00**
New England Mutual Marine Insurance Company (I), 1870s, Scrip, two vignettes of old sailing ships, sailors on dock vignettes **160.00**
New England Telephone and Telegraph (I), 1960s, New York, Coat of arms vignette **3.00**
New Jersey Bell Telephone (I), 1950s, New Jersey, Bond, George Washington with generals vignette **20.00**
New Jersey Bell Telephone (I), 1950s, Two and three-quarters percent bond, framed house with two seated figures vignette **20.00**
New Jersey Patent Company (I), 1900s, Eagle vignette, signed by Thomas A. Edison on reverse as witness **575.00**
New Jersey Zinc Company, The, Specimen, state seal signatures **8.00**
New Orleans and Ohio Telegraph Company (I), 1850s, Kentucky, Bond **165.00**
New Orleans and Ohio Telegraph Lesses (I), 1850s, Train and three ladies vignette **100.00**
New Orleans Concordia Lodge (I), 1830s **350.00**
New Orleans Lighting and Wrecking (I-N), 1860s, Ship vignette **60.00**
New Paltz Water Works (U), 1890s, New York, Vignette of waterworks and tower **8.00**
New York, City of, Insurance Company (I), 1920s, New York, Skyline vignette **7.00**
New York Grape Sugar Company (I), 1880s, New York, Two ladies with eagle and shield vignette **40.00**
New York Manufacturing Society (I), 1780s, Stock share note **630.00**
New York Siphon (U), Eagle vignette **2.00**
New Yorker Zeitung Publishing Company (I), 1900s **6.00**
New Yorker Zeitung Publishing Company (U) **2.00**
Newport and Cincinnati Bridge Company (I), 1890s, Sailboats and steamboats on river under bridge vignettes **90.00**
Nickel Holdings Corporation (I), 1920s and 1930s, New Jersey, No vignette **45.00**
North American Gas and Electric (I), 1930s, Indian chief vignette **30.00**
North American Lumber Company (I), 1830s, New York, Bare-breasted woman, sailing ship, two portraits, and cherub vignettes **195.00**
North American Lumber Company (U), 1800s, Sailing ship vignette **30.00**
North American Phonograph (I), 1890s, Bond, vignette of phonograph, signed by Samuel Insull **750.00**
North American Rockwell Overseas Corporation (I), 1970s, Eight and one-half percent sinking fund debenture, seated seminude woman vignette **5.00**
North Eastern Insurance Company of Hartford (I), 1950s, Eagle on rock vignette **2.00**
Northwestern Guaranty Loan Company (I), 1890s, New York, Gold bond, large office building vignette **130.00**
Northwestern Mutual Life Mortgage and Realty Investors (I), 1970s, Girl in front of city vignette **2.00**
Northwestern Portland Cement Company (I), 1900s, Bond, factory vignette **10.00**
Northwestern Portland Cement Company (I), 1900s, Factory vignette **10.00**
Norton Company (I), 1920s, Male and female with company logo vignette **4.00**
Norwich Water and Power (U), 1850s, Connecticut **15.00**
Norwood Heights Company (I), 1900s, Ohio, Embossed seal **6.00**

Oak Park Shop (I-N), 1910s, Eagle, shield, train, and ship vignette **7.00**
Oakite Products (I), 1970s, New York, Chemist vignette **2.00**
Odd Fellows Association of Sacramento (U), 1860s, No vignette **38.00**
Ohio Cold Storage (U), Factory vignette **9.00**
Ohio Union Loan (I), 1860s, Vignettes of Ben Franklin, dog, and safe **260.00**

◀ ***Eagle Lock Co. (I), 1930s and 1940s,*** *Eagle with flag vignette* ***4.00***
◀ ***Erleme Corporation (I), 1930,*** *Large eagle, two globes, and bolts of lightning vignette* ***3.00***

LESS THAN 100 SHARES

NUMBER NYO 94941

SHARES —10—

INCORPORATED UNDER THE LAWS OF THE STATE OF DELAWARE

EVERSHARP, INC.

SEE REVERSE FOR CERTAIN DEFINITIONS

This Certifies that DeCOPPET & DOREMUS is the owner of

TEN

FULL-PAID AND NON-ASSESSABLE SHARES OF THE COMMON STOCK OF THE PAR VALUE OF $1.00 EACH

of Eversharp, Inc. (hereinafter called the Company) transferable on the books of the Company by the holder hereof in person or by duly authorized attorney upon surrender of this certificate properly endorsed. This certificate and the shares represented hereby are issued and shall be held subject to all the provisions of the Certificate of Incorporation and the By-Laws of the Company as from time to time amended (copies of which are on file with the Transfer Agent) to all of which the holder by acceptance hereof assents. This certificate is not valid unless countersigned by the Transfer Agent and registered by the Registrar. Witness the facsimile seal of the Company and the facsimile signatures of its duly authorized officers.

Dated DEC 15 1965

SECRETARY

PRESIDENT

EVERSHARP, INC. CORPORATE SEAL DELAWARE

REGISTERED: MANUFACTURERS HANOVER TRUST COMPANY (NEW YORK) REGISTRAR. BY AUTHORIZED OFFICER

COUNTERSIGNED: THE MARINE MIDLAND TRUST COMPANY OF NEW YORK TRANSFER AGENT. BY AUTHORIZED OFFICER

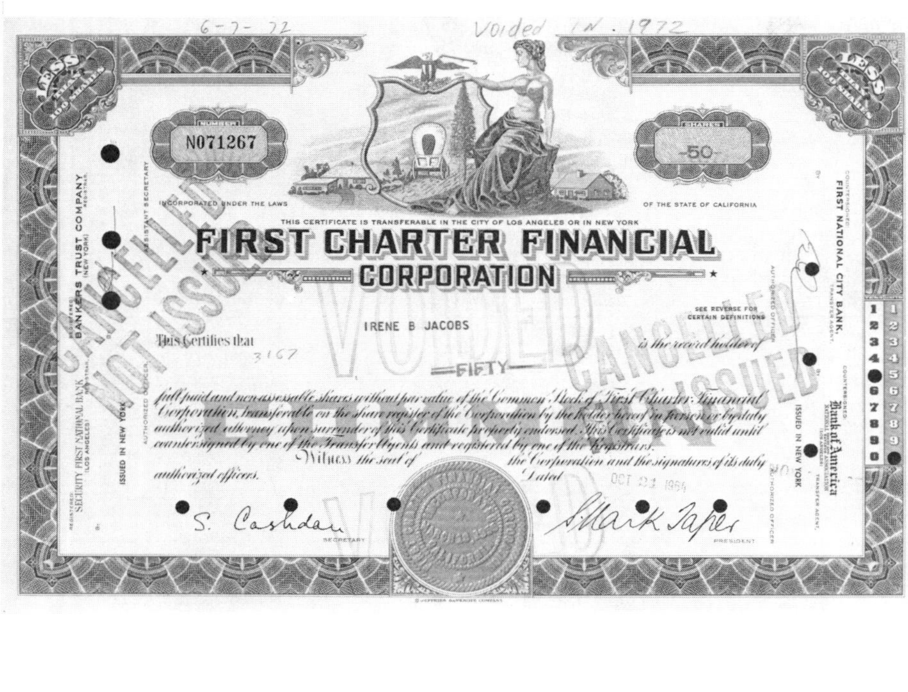
6-7-72 Voided IN. 1972

LESS THAN 100 SHARES

NUMBER N071267

SHARES -50-

INCORPORATED UNDER THE LAWS OF THE STATE OF CALIFORNIA

THIS CERTIFICATE IS TRANSFERABLE IN THE CITY OF LOS ANGELES OR IN NEW YORK

FIRST CHARTER FINANCIAL CORPORATION

SEE REVERSE FOR CERTAIN DEFINITIONS

This Certifies that IRENE B JACOBS is the record holder of

3167

FIFTY

full paid and non-assessable shares without par value of the Common Stock of First Charter Financial Corporation, transferable on the share register of the Corporation by the holder hereof in person or by duly authorized attorney upon surrender of this Certificate properly endorsed. This Certificate is not valid until countersigned by one of the Transfer Agents and registered by one of the Registrars. Witness the seal of the Corporation and the signatures of its duly authorized officers.

Dated OCT 23 1964

S. Cashdan SECRETARY

S. Mark Taper PRESIDENT

CANCELLED NOT ISSUED

VOIDED

CANCELLED NOT ISSUED

REGISTERED: BANKERS TRUST COMPANY (NEW YORK) REGISTRAR. BY ASSISTANT SECRETARY

REGISTERED: SECURITY FIRST NATIONAL BANK (LOS ANGELES) REGISTRAR. BY AUTHORIZED OFFICER. ISSUED IN NEW YORK

COUNTERSIGNED: FIRST NATIONAL CITY BANK, TRANSFER AGENT. BY AUTHORIZED OFFICER. ISSUED IN NEW YORK

COUNTERSIGNED: Bank of America NATIONAL TRUST AND SAVINGS ASSOCIATION (LOS ANGELES) TRANSFER AGENT. BY AUTHORIZED OFFICER

Old Tyme Distillers Corporation (I), 1930s, Two seated men and distillery vignette 4.00
Old Welch Company Inc. (I), 1950s, Eagle vignette 2.00
One Hundred Percent Special Oil Trust (I-N), 1920s, Washington 5.00
Oriental Fire and Marine Insurance (U), 1800s, California, Seated woman vignette 17.00
Orpheum Circuit, Inc. (I), 1920s, Female with lion vignette 14.00
Orpheum Circuits (I), 1920s, Temporary certificate 3.00
Orr Paper Company (I), 1900s, Five percent gold bond, waterfall and seal vignette 37.00
Ortero Gas Company (I), 1910s, Gold bond 5.00
Owensboro Water Works (I), 1880s, Six percent sinking fund bond, large eagle, gold seal vignette 90.00

Pabst Brewing Company (I), 1900s, Large company brewery vignette, Pabst's signature 70.00
Pabst Brewing Company (U), 1900s, Large company brewery vignette, Pabst's signature 14.00
Pacific Coast Redwood Company (I), 1900s, California, Eagle vignette, gold seal 12.00
Pacific Coast Redwood Company (I), 1910s, California, Eagle vignette, gold seal 9.00
Pacific Gas and Electric (I), 1940s, Ladies and generator vignette 6.00
Pacific Gas and Electric (I), 1940s, Two and seven-eighths percent bond, generator and ladies vignette 8.00
Pacific Gas and Electric (I), 1950s, Gold bond, generator, and power station, and seated lady vignette 7.00
Pacific Guano Company (U), 1850s, California, Eagle vignette 35.00
Pacific-Ohio Electric (I), 1920s, Woman with lamp, dynamo, and streetcar vignette 15.00
Pacific-Ohio Electric (U), 1920s, Woman with lamp, dynamo, and streetcar vignette 6.00
Pacific Press Syndicate (U), 1920s, California, Two women and man vignette 4.00
Pacific Sugar Construction Company (I), 1900s, Los Angeles, California, Eagle and seal vignette 6.00
Pacific Wireless Telephone and Telegraph (I), 1900s, Embossed seal 24.00
Palmer Mountain Tunnel and Power Company (I), 1900s, Seminude between rushing river and tunnel vignette 50.00
Pamida, Inc. (I), 1970s, Nebraska .75
Pan-American Exposition Company (I), 1900s, Vignette of Western Hemisphere, gold seal, revenue stamp 685.00
Pan-American Fisheries (I), 1930s and 1940s, California, Ship in harbor 8.00
Panhandle Eastern Pipeline (I), One hundred-thousand dollar bond, oil derricks, valves tanks, city skyline vignette 3.00
Parke Davis Company (I), 1960s, Two bare-breasted seated ladies with company logo, transfer tax on reverse 4.00
Parkersburg Aetna Corporation (I), 1960s, West Virginia, Oil well and ship vignette 5.00
Patapsco Female Institute (I), 1830s, No vignette 210.00
Pathe Film Corporation (I-N), Bare-breasted women on both sides of framed Pathe rooster 40.00
Pavelle Corporation (I), 1970s, New York, Large eagle and seal vignette, signed by president of the company .65
Peer-Elder (I), 1960s, Winged Mercury near globe vignette 2.00
Pemberton and Pennsylvania (I), 1920s, Virginia 5.00
Pennsylvania Canal Company (I), 1870s, Bond, train on bridge vignette 185.00
Pennsylvania Canal Company (I), 1870s, Six percent bond, canal scene 165.00
Pennsylvania Power Company (I), 1940s, Bond, chariot scene 12.00
Pennsylvania Seaboard Steel Corporation (I), 1920s, New York 6.00
Pensalt Chemicals Corporation (I), 1960s, Pennsylvania, Two chemists and company logo vignettes 2.00

◀ ***Eversharp, Inc. (I), 1960s, Delaware,*** *Lady with book vignette* ***2.00***
◀ ***First Charter Financial Corporation (I), California,*** *Large, bare-breasted lady, covered wagon, and houses vignettes* ***5.00***

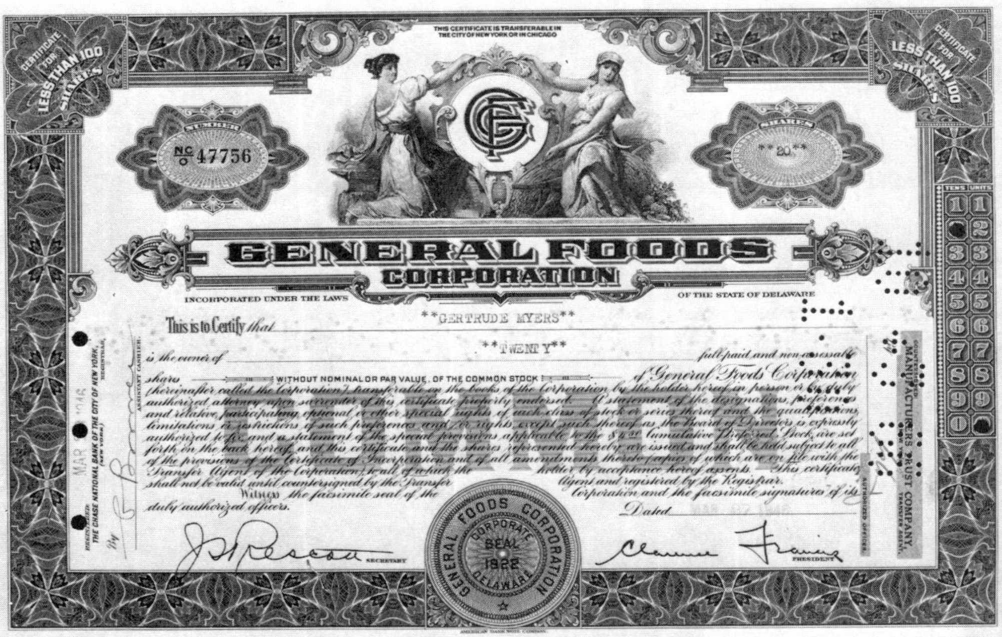
THIS CERTIFICATE IS TRANSFERABLE IN THE CITY OF NEW YORK OR IN CHICAGO

CERTIFICATE FOR LESS THAN 100 SHARES

NUMBER NC O 47756

SHARES **20**

GENERAL FOODS CORPORATION

INCORPORATED UNDER THE LAWS OF THE STATE OF DELAWARE

This is to Certify that **GERTRUDE MYERS**

is the owner of **TWENTY** full paid and non-assessable shares WITHOUT NOMINAL OR PAR VALUE, OF THE COMMON STOCK of General Foods Corporation (hereinafter called the Corporation) transferable on the books of the Corporation by the holder hereof in person or by duly authorized attorney upon surrender of this certificate properly endorsed. A statement of the designations, preferences and relative, participating, optional, or other special rights of each class of stock or series thereof and the qualifications, limitations or restrictions of such preferences and/or rights except such thereof as the Board of Directors is expressly authorized to fix, and a statement of the special provisions applicable to the $4.50 Cumulative Preferred Stock, are set forth on the back hereof, and this certificate and the shares represented hereby are issued and shall be held subject to all of the provisions of the Certificate of Incorporation and of all amendments thereto (copies of which are on file with the Transfer Agent of the Corporation), to all of which the holder by acceptance hereof assents. This certificate shall not be valid until countersigned by the Transfer Agent and registered by the Registrar.

Witness the facsimile seal of the Corporation and the facsimile signatures of its duly authorized officers.

Dated MAR 27 1946

SECRETARY PRESIDENT

GENERAL FOODS CORPORATION CORPORATE SEAL 1922 DELAWARE

REGISTERED: THE CHASE NATIONAL BANK OF THE CITY OF NEW YORK, REGISTRAR. By ASSISTANT CASHIER. MAR 1946

COUNTERSIGNED: MANUFACTURERS TRUST COMPANY, TRANSFER AGENT. AUTHORIZED OFFICER.

TENS UNITS

AMERICAN BANK NOTE COMPANY

INCORPORATED UNDER THE LAWS OF THE STATE OF PENNSYLVANIA

NUMBER 19

SHARES -4-

VIRTUE LIBERTY AND INDEPENDENCE

Goddard Groome Drayton Company

CAPITAL STOCK, $100,000.

FULL PAID AND NON-ASSESSABLE

This Certifies that John C. Groome, is the owner of Four (4) Shares of the Capital Stock of GODDARD GROOME DRAYTON COMPANY

Transferable only on the Books of the Company by the holder hereof in person or by Attorney upon surrender of this Certificate properly endorsed.

In Witness Whereof, the said Company has caused this Certificate to be signed by its duly authorized officers and to be sealed with the Seal of the Company this 29th day of November A.D. 1919

TREASURER PRESIDENT

Shares $100 Each.

People's Mutual Telephone Company (I), 1890s, California, Six percent gold bond, eagle and woman embossed seal vignette	130.00
Pepsi-Cola United Bottlers (I), Seminude woman holding world globe, also framed Pepsi vignette	10.00
Pere Marquette Light and Power (U), 1900s, Michigan, Gold bond, company logo	8.00
Perkin-Elmer Corporation (I), 1970s, Engineer holding blueprints with carpenter and rockets in rear vignette	1.00
Permeator Corporation (I), 1970s, Reduction unit and towers vignette	1.00
Petron Corporation (I), 1960s, Standing woman between two men vignette	1.00
Philadelphia and Lancaster Turnpike (I), 1790s, Covered wagon at tollbooth vignette	550.00
Philadelphia College of Pharmacy (I), 1860s, Six percent bond	200.00
Philadelphia Company, Registered note, eagle vignette	1.00
Philadelphia Company, Specimen, Bond	5.00
Philadelphia Electric Company (I), 1960s, Woman with dynamo vignette	3.00
Philadelphia Electric Company (I), 1970s, Woman with atomic symbol vignette	2.00
Philadelphia Lodge Number Two B.P.O.E. (I), 1920s, Six percent bond, elk vignette	30.00
Philadelphia-Warwick Company (I), 1940s, Voting trust certificate, no vignette	2.00
Phillip Hunt Chemical (I), 1970s, Two chemists with company logo vignette	.75
Phillip Morris (I), 1950s, Bond, reclining woman with lamp vignette	5.00
Phillips and Phillips (U), 1900s, Large eagle and harbor scene vignette	4.00
Phoenix Insurance Company (I), 1850s, Phoenix rising from fire vignette	45.00
Phoenix Insurance Company (I), 1860s, Phoenix rising from fire vignette	40.00
Phoenix Insurance Company (I), 1930s, Eagle vignette	3.00
Phoenix Insurance Company (I), 1950s and 1960s, Connecticut, No vignette	1.00
Phoenix Whaling and Manufacturing (I), 1900s, No vignette	16.00
Phonograph Corporation of Indiana (I), 1920s, Signed by Thomas Edison	525.00
Pike Corporation of America (I), 1960s, Woman with globe vignette	3.00
Pike's Peak Cottage City Corporation (U), 1920s, Colorado, Gold bond	5.00
Pillsbury Company, The (I), 1960s and 1970s, Man and woman vignette	2.00
Pittsburgh American China Company (I), 1920s, Eagle vignette	4.00
Pittsburgh Ice Company, 1910s, State seal, vignette of polar bear	15.00
Pittsburgh Screw and Bolt (I), 1940s, Screw and bolt piercing the world vignette	8.00
Planter's Cotton Seed Company (U), 1800s, Delaware, Cotton pickers and bales vignette	15.00
Playboy Enterprises, Reclining nude vignette	45.00
Playboy Enterprises, Specimen, reclining nude vignette	75.00
Playtime Distillers (I), 1930s	4.00
P. Lorillard Company (U), New Jersey, Specimen, Two seated ladies in tobacco field vignette	25.00
Pneumatic Scale Corporation (I), 1920s, Justice with hemispheres and seal vignette	20.00
Pneumatic Scale Corporation (I), 1930s and 1940s, Justice with hemispheres and seal vignette	15.00
Pneumatic Scale Corporation (I), 1960s, Woman holding scale and sword with two globes vignette	3.00
Polyplane Packaging Company (I), 1960s, Eagle vignette	1.00
Portage Fish and Game Company (I-N), 1920s, Ohio, Indian standing at shore of lake vignette	20.00
Poulsen Wireless Corporation (U), 1910s, California	7.00
Precision Polymers, Inc. (I), 1970s, Woman between two globes and train vignette	.75
Presidio Motion Pictures (U), 1900s, No vignette	10.00
Presidio Motion Pictures Corporation (U), 1920s, Nevada	4.00
Prestan-Moss Fund (I), 1960s, Large eagle vignette	.75
Princeton and Kingston Branch Turnpike (I), 1850s, No vignette, embossed seal	165.00
Providence Bowling Club (I), 1840s, Rhode Island, No vignette	155.00

◀ ***General Foods Corporation (I), 1940s and 1950s***, *Two females with company sign vignette* ***2.00***

◀ ***Goddard Groome Drayton Company (I-N), 1910s, Pennsylvania***, *State seal* ***5.00***

INCORPORATED UNDER THE LAWS OF NEW YORK.

NUMBER 212

SHARES Six,

EXCELSIOR

Harmonia Fire Insurance Company.

Capital Stock $200,000.

This Certifies that John M Meyer, is the owner of Six, Shares of the Capital Stock of Harmonia Fire Insurance Company. transferable only on the books of the Corporation in person or by Attorney upon surrender of this Certificate properly endorsed.

IN WITNESS WHEREOF, the said Corporation has caused this Certificate to be signed by its duly authorized officers and its Corporate Seal to be hereunto affixed at Buffalo, N. Y. this 19th day of October A.D. 1915.

President

Treasurer

SHARES $50.00 EACH

David F. Williamson Co., 202 Main St. (below W. Seneca St.) Buffalo, N. Y.

INCORPORATED UNDER THE LAWS OF THE STATE OF MARYLAND

FULL PAID AND NON-ASSESSABLE

NUMBER 14366

SHARES -10-

The Homestead Fire Insurance Company

PAR VALUE $10.00 EACH

This Certifies that **Laird, Bissell & Meeds** is the owner of ---------ten---------- Shares of the Capital Stock of THE HOMESTEAD FIRE INSURANCE COMPANY transferable only on the books of the Corporation in person or by Attorney on surrender of this Certificate properly endorsed.

IN WITNESS WHEREOF, the Corporation has caused this Certificate to be signed by its duly authorized officers and its Corporate Seal to be hereunto affixed this 7th day of January 1939

SECRETARY-TREASURER

VICE-PRESIDENT

Registered JAN 10 1939 The Fidelity Trust Company (Balto., Md.) Registrar By Assistant Secretary

Providence Securities Company (I), **1900s, Connecticut**, Four percent bond, three seated seminude figures vignette 40.00
Providence Securities Company (U), **1900s**, Gold bond, lady and two men vignette 13.00
Providence Washington Insurance Company (I), **1890s**, Portrait of George Washington 75.00
Public Service Electric and Gas (I), **1960s**, Gold bond, two men and woman vignette 3.00
Public Service Gas and Electric (I), **1970s**, Three figures with winged wheel vignette 2.00
Publiker Industries (I), **1960s**, Four allegorical figures and large winged wheel vignette 1.00
Puget Sound Commercial Company (U), **1870s, Washington**, Vignette of Port Gamble 95.00

Quaker Alloy Casting (I), **1960s**, Eagle vignette 2.00
Quil Extract Company (I), **1930s**, Eagle vignette 3.00

Ralston-Purina Corporation (I), **1950s**, Bond 3.00
Ransome's Patent Stone Company of New Jersey (I), **1860s, New Jersey** , Stoneworker vignette, state seal, eagle vignette, with revenue stamp 135.00
Reading Water Company (I), **1850s**, No logo 65.00
Real Silk Hosiery, Inc., Specimen, Woman with lion vignette 7.00
Red Hook Building Company (I), **1830s**, Blacksmith vignette 135.00
Red Wing Carriers, Inc. (U), **Florida, Specimen**, Red bird vignette 15.00
Reliance International Corporation (I), **1920s and 1930s**, Seated woman with globe, two topless seated women, and bare-chested man vignette 4.00
Remington Rand, Inc. (I), **1920s**, Warrant 4.00
Replogle Steel Company (I), **1910s**, Temporary certificate 3.00
Republic Life Insurance Company (I), **1870s, Illinois**, Large community building vignette 62.00
R. E. Rodda Candy Company (I), **1910s**, Eagle with shield vignette 6.00
Research Investing Corporation (I), **1960s**, Eagle with company logo vignette 2.00
Revere Racing Association, Inc. (I), **1960s, Massachusetts**, Nude runner with sash vignette 10.00
Rexall Drug (I), **1940s**, Drug jar between bare-breasted figures vignette 5.00
Rexall Drug (I), **1950s**, Drug jar between bare-breasted figures vignette 4.00
Rexall Drug and Chemical (I), **1960s**, Two men and chemical vignette 2.00
Richie Mineral Resin and Oil Company (I), **1860s, West Virginia**, Bond, state seal, and state products vignette 85.00
Ringling Bros., Barnum and Bailey (I), Circus parade vignette 365.00
Ringling Bros., Barnum and Bailey Combined Shows (I), Beautiful full page of circus acts vignette 365.00
R. J. Reynolds Tobacco Company (U), **Specimen**, Eagle vignette 25.00
Rock Manufacturing Company (I), **1830s** 85.00
Rodgers-Brown Company (I), **1920s**, Gold bond 7.00
Rome Turnpike Company (U), **1800s**, No vignette 38.00
Rossia Insurance Company (I), **1920s, Connecticut**, Eagle on rock vignette 3.00
Rossia Insurance Company (I), **1930s, Connecticut**, Eagle on rock vignette 2.00
Royal Axminster Carpet Company (I-N), **1890s**, Factory by river vignette 25.00
Russian-American Trade and Industry Development Corporation (U), **1910s**, Eagle, shield, and anchor vignette 7.00
Rutherford Drug Company (I), **1920s**, State seal 6.00

Salmon Falls Manufacturing Company (I), **1920s, Massachusetts** 4.00
Sandgate Corporation (I), **1970s**, Seated woman, two globes, train, and city skyline vignette .75
Sandra Post, Inc. (I), **1950s, New York**, Eagle vignette 1.00

◀ ***Harmonia Fire Insurance Company (I), 1910s, New York,*** *State seal, green seal, with many stamps* ***4.00***
◀ ***Homestead Fire Insurance Company, The (I), 1930s,*** *House and old car vignette* ***7.00***

D1578
25 SHARES
Number MB6408
Shares 25
INCORPORATED UNDER THE LAWS OF THE STATE OF NEW JERSEY.
THE INTERNATIONAL NICKEL COMPANY
THIS CERTIFICATE IS TRANSFERABLE IN THE CITY OF NEW YORK, IN THE CITY OF TORONTO, OR IN THE CITY OF MONTREAL.
PAR VALUE $ 25 EACH
This is to Certify that GEOFFRION & CO.
is the owner of TWENTY FIVE fully paid and non-assessable
shares OF THE PAR VALUE OF TWENTY-FIVE DOLLARS EACH, IN THE COMMON CAPITAL STOCK of The International Nickel Company, transferable in person or by attorney upon the books of said Company upon surrender of this certificate.
This certificate is not valid until countersigned by the Transfer Agent and registered by the Registrar.
Witness the signature of the president, or of a vice president, and the treasurer, or of an assistant treasurer, of said corporation
this day of JAN 31 1928 19
ASSISTANT TREASURER. VICE PRESIDENT.
AUTHORIZED CAPITAL STOCK $ 62,000,000.
PREFERRED STOCK $12,000,000. COMMON STOCK $50,000,000.
AMERICAN BANK NOTE COMPANY.

Jersey City 1 Exchange Place
CERTIFICATE FOR LESS THAN 100 SHARES
COMMON STOCK
Number NY CO 4748
Shares -10-
INCORPORATED UNDER THE LAWS OF THE STATE OF DELAWARE
INTERSTATE EQUITIES CORPORATION
This Certifies That -DRAKE JONES COMPANY-
is the owner of -TEN- full paid and non-assessable shares WITHOUT PAR VALUE, OF THE COMMON STOCK of Interstate Equities Corporation
This certificate is not valid until countersigned by the Transfer Clerk and registered by the Registrar.
In Witness Whereof, the Corporation has caused this certificate to be signed in its name by its proper officers, and its corporate seal to be hereunto affixed.
Dated NOV 2 3 1934
Interstate Equities Corporation,
By
ATTEST: SECRETARY. PRESIDENT.
NOV 26 1934
REGISTERED: The Chase National Bank of the City of New York, REGISTRAR.
INTERSTATE EQUITIES CORPORATION. TRANSFER CLERK.
AMERICAN BANK NOTE COMPANY.

Sandy Rock Investment (I-N), 1930s, Oregon, State seal	4.00
San Francisco Fire Protection Bond (I), 1900s, Gold bond, sailing ships in bay vignette	70.00
San Juan Portland Cement Company (I), 1900s, Mission and figures vignette	15.00
Santol Products Company (I), 1920s, Seven percent gold bond	6.00
Saugatuck Recreation Company (I-N), 1930s, Michigan, Eagle and gold seal vignette	6.00
Schaaf and Good Company (I), 1920s, Ohio, Allegorical figure and harbor scene	4.00
Schaeffer, F. M., Corporation (I), 1960s, Man with globe, mountains, and city view vignette	2.00
Schaeffer, F. M., Corporation (I), 1970s, New York, Man with globe in city vignette	1.00
Schering Corporation (I), 1960s, Man and woman with lab equipment and world globe vignette	2.00
Saint Joe Minerals (I), 1970s	3.00
Saint Louis Suburban Teachers' Association (I), 1960s, Ten-dollar debenture	4.00
Schuylkill River Bridge (U), 1810s, No vignette	100.00
Schuylkill Water Company (U), 1880s, Pennsylvania, Hunter with rifle, drinking from stream, and mountain waterfall vignettes	20.00
Science Resources, Inc. (I), 1960s, Lady with two globes vignette	.75
Scientific American Compiling Department (I), 1910s, New Jersey, Eagle vignette	38.00
Scudder, Stevens and Clark (I), 1950s, Sailor at wheel vignette	.75
Security-Columbian Banknote Company (U), Specimen, Seated woman with nude baby vignette	20.00
Seneca Falls Machine Company (I), 1940s, Massachusetts, Eagle vignette	3.00
Shannon Manufacturing Company (U), 1890s, Massachusetts, Girl vignette	5.00
Sharaf, R. M., Machine (I), Massachusetts, No vignette	1.00
Shering-Plough (I), 1960s and 1970s	.75
Shoshoni Power and Irrigation Company (I), 1910s, Wyoming, Dam with open floodgate vignette	18.00
Shrine of Our Lady of La Salette, 1960s, Five percent bond, eagle vignette	3.00
Shulton, Inc. (I), 1960s, Sailing ship and woman holding globe vignette	3.00
Shulton, Inc. (I), 1970s, Chemical equipment, sailing ship and sexy lady with globe vignette	1.00
Signode Steel Strapping Corporation (I), 1960s, Man at forge vignette	2.00
Silox Pure Water of Philadelphia (U), Shield and ship vignette	7.00
Simco Stores (I), 1970s, Lady between two globes vignette	1.00
Simpson, J., and Company (U), 1920s, New York, Commercial building vignette	4.00
Skouheagan Bridge (I), 1820s, No vignette	265.00
Smith, D. A. and Sons, Inc. (I-N), 1920s, Eagle on rock vignette	5.00
Smith, D. A. and Sons, Inc. (I-N), 1920s, No vignette	2.00
Social Insurance Company (U), 1800s, Massachusetts	40.00
Sohio, B. P. Trans Alaska Pipeline Finance, Inc. (I), 1970s, Bond	4.00
Somerset Lighting Company (I), 1890s, New Jersey, State seal with stamp	20.00
Somerset Lighting Company (I), 1900s, New Jersey, State seal with stamp	9.00
South Nevada Power Company (I), 1960s, Large eagle, river, and factory vignette	2.00
Southern Art Exhibition Company (I), 1880s, Embossed seal	110.00
Southern Art Exhibition Company (U), 1880s, Embossed seal	22.00
Southern Bell Telephone and Telegraph (I), 1930s, Three percent bond, two figures with telephone between vignette	5.00
Southern California Water Company (U), Filtration plant vignette	12.00
Southern Improvement Company (I), 1880s, Gold bond, beehive and portrait of lady vignette	15.00
Southern Telegraph Company (I), 1880s, Six percent bond, boys with torch and angels with electricity vignette	60.00
Sparky's Virgin Islands, Inc. (I), 1970s, Seal	1.00

◀ ***International Nickel Company, The (I), 1920s,*** *Reclining woman with lion vignette* ***4.00***

◀ ***Interstate Equities Corporation (I), 1920s and 1930s,*** *Three allegorical figures with winged wheel* ***3.00***

REGISTERED
REGISTERED
25,000
NUMBER
RB 1430
-25000-
ITT Financial Corporation
9.70% SENIOR NOTE DUE OCTOBER 15, 1983
I.T.T. Financial Corporation, a Delaware corporation (herein called the "Company") for value received, hereby promises to pay to
SEE REVERSE FOR CERTAIN DEFINITIONS
9.70%
DUE 1983
SALOMON BROTHERS
CUSIP 450680 AB 9
-TWENTY-FIVE THOUSAND-
or registered assigns the principal sum of
DOLLARS
In Witness Whereof, I.T.T. Financial Corporation has caused this instrument to be signed manually or by facsimile by its duly authorized officers and a facsimile of its corporate seal to be affixed hereunto or imprinted hereon.
Dated OCT 29 1975
I.T.T. Financial Corporation
By
TRUSTEE'S CERTIFICATE OF AUTHENTICATION
This is one of the Notes described in the within-mentioned Indenture.
FIRST NATIONAL CITY BANK, as Trustee
OR BY THE FIRST NATIONAL BANK OF CHICAGO, as Authenticating Agent of the Trustee
Authorized Officer
Authorized Officer
CORPORATE SEAL
Treasurer
President
AMERICAN BANK NOTE COMPANY

INCORPORATED UNDER THE LAWS OF
No 13
THE STATE OF ILLINOIS
Shares 996
Lake & Export Coal Sales Corporation of Illinois
CAPITAL STOCK $200,000.00
THIS CERTIFIES THAT ORCHARD COAL COMPANY is the owner of
NINE HUNDRED NINETY-SIX Shares of One Hundred Dollars each of the Capital Stock of
Lake & Export Coal Sales Corporation of Illinois, FULLY PAID AND NON-ASSESSABLE,
transferable only on the books of the Corporation by the holder hereof in person or by Attorney upon surrender of this Certificate properly endorsed.
THE AMOUNT ACTUALLY RECEIVED BY THE CORPORATION FOR THIS STOCK IS $99600.00 PAID FOR IN Property
In Witness Whereof, the said Corporation has caused this Certificate to be signed by its duly authorized officers and to be sealed with the Seal of the Corporation
at Chicago, Illinois, this 7th day of August A.D. 1922
SECRETARY
PRESIDENT
SHARES $100.00 EACH

Spencer Arms Company (I), 1880s, New York, Three hunters with dog under two long rifles vignette 310.00
Spencer Shoe Corporation (I), 1950s, Eagle vignette .75
Sperry Corporation (I), 1950s, Three vignettes of old plane and old ship 8.00
Sperry-Rand Corporation (U), 1950s, Specimen, Bond, chemist with machinery vignette 8.00
Sperry-Rand Corporation (I), 1960s and 1970s, Seated chemist with machinery vignette 3.00
Spinks, Wm. A. (I), 1920s, Illinois, Eight percent bond 4.00
Splitdorf-Bethlehem Electric Company (I), 1920s, New Jersey, Woman holding electricity, facsimile of Chas. Edison signature vignette 60.00
Splitdorf-Bethlehem Electric Company (I), 1930s, New Jersey, Woman holding electricity, facsimile of Chas. Edison signature vignette 55.00
Stafford Meadow Coal and Iron (I), 1850s, Bond, navy vignettes 70.00
Stafford Meadow Coal, Iron City Improvement Company (I), 1850s 60.00
Stafford Meadow Coal, Iron City Improvement Company (I-N), 1850s, Bond with seven vignettes 75.00
Standard Cattle Company (I), 1880s, Illinois, Cowboy on horse vignette 180.00
Standard Rope and Twine Company (I), 1890s, New Jersey, Waterfront vignette 70.00
Standard Rope and Twine Company (I), 1900s, Vignette of ships 37.00
Stauffer Chemical Company (I), 1970s, Seated lady chemist vignette .60
Stellum International (I-N) .85
Sterling Precision Corporation (I), 1960s, Large eagle and seal vignette .75
Stetson, John B., Company (I), 1920s, Portrait of John B. Stetson 14.00
Stoll Werck Chocolate Company (I), 1920s 4.00
Stratfield Amusement Company (I-N), 1920s, New York, Waterfront, Indians, and teepees vignette 25.00
Suetepec Electric Light and Power Company (I), 1910s, New York, Embossed seal 9.00
Suetepec Electric Light and Power Company (I), 1920s, New York, Embossed seal 7.00
Suetepec Electric Light and Power Company (I), 1920s, Seven percent bond 7.00
Sullivan Machinery Company (I), 1910s, Eagle with mountains and ship vignettes 7.00
Supervised Shares, Inc., Two men with world and dollar sign vignette 3.00
Sutro Mortage Investment Trust (I), 1970s, Company logo .85
Swanee Paper Corporation (U), Specimen, Two globes, lady, city, and train vignettes 5.00
Swedish Ball Bearing (U), Specimen, Two seated men with company logo vignette 5.00
Syntavco, Inc. (I), 1960s, Large eagle and gold seal vignette 1.00

Tacoma Ice Corporation (U), Washington, D. C., No vignette 2.00
Telepost Company (I-N), 1900s, Woman holding lightning vignette 15.00
Telstar, Inc. (I), Woman between two globes and train vignette 5.00
Tennessee Electric Power Company (U), Specimen, Woman on winged wheel and flying eagle vignette 20.00
Terminal Ice and Fuel Company (U), Government building 4.00
Terminal Ice Company (I), 1920s, Horse and buggies in front of buildings 6.50
Terminal Refrigerating and Warehousing (U), 1930s, Bond 3.00
Texas First Mortgage Reit (I-N), 1970s, Warrant 2.00
Texas Salt Company (U) 1.00
Thayer West Point Hotel Corporation (I), 1920s 20.00
Thermatomic Corporation (I), 1920s, Virginia, Large vignette of machinery 20.00
Thiokal Chemical (I), 1960s, Allegorical figures with gear vignette 2.00
Thiokol Chemical (I), 1970s, Man with chemical equipment vignette 2.00
Third Moravian Church School (U), 1850s, Pennsylvania, Old church building vignette 78.00

◀ ***ITT Financial Corporation (I)**, Bond, Seated woman with globe, skyline, and mountains vignette* ***3.00***
◀ ***Lake and Export Coal Sales Corporation of Illinois (I-N), 1920s**, Eagle vignette, gold seal* ***4.00***

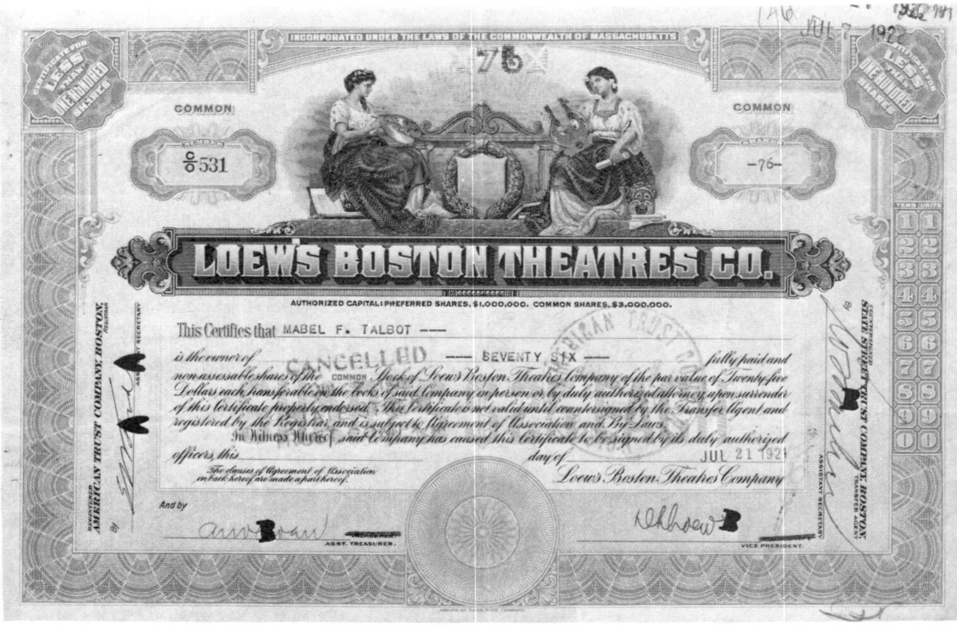
INCORPORATED UNDER THE LAWS OF THE COMMONWEALTH OF MASSACHUSETTS
CERTIFICATE FOR LESS THAN ONE HUNDRED SHARES
COMMON
C 531
COMMON
-76-
LOEW'S BOSTON THEATRES CO.
AUTHORIZED CAPITAL: PREFERRED SHARES, $1,000,000. COMMON SHARES, $3,000,000.
This Certifies that MABEL F. TALBOT ----
is the owner of CANCELLED ---- SEVENTY SIX ---- fully paid and non assessable shares of the COMMON Stock of Loew's Boston Theatres Company of the par value of Twenty five Dollars each transferable on the books of said Company in person or by duly authorized attorney upon surrender of this Certificate properly endorsed. This Certificate is not valid until countersigned by the Transfer Agent and registered by the Registrar, and is subject to Agreement of Association and By-Laws.
In Witness Whereof said Company has caused this Certificate to be signed by its duly authorized officers this day of JUL 21 1921
The clauses of Agreement of Association on back hereof are made a part hereof.
Loew's Boston Theatres Company
And by
ASST. TREASURER.
VICE PRESIDENT.
AMERICAN TRUST COMPANY, BOSTON, REGISTRAR
ASSISTANT SECRETARY
STATE STREET TRUST COMPANY, BOSTON, TRANSFER AGENT
ASSISTANT SECRETARY
JUL 7 1922

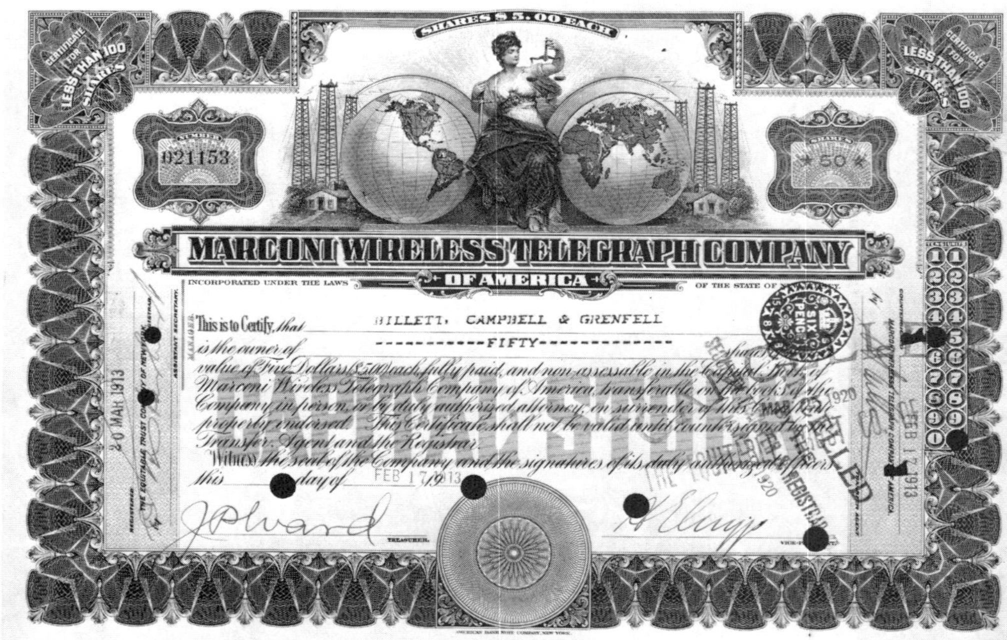
SHARES $5.00 EACH
CERTIFICATE FOR LESS THAN 100 SHARES
021153
50
MARCONI WIRELESS TELEGRAPH COMPANY
OF AMERICA
INCORPORATED UNDER THE LAWS OF THE STATE OF
This is to Certify, that GILLETT, CAMPBELL & GRENFELL
is the owner of ------------FIFTY------------ shares of the par value of Five Dollars ($5.00) each, fully paid, and non-assessable in the Capital Stock of Marconi Wireless Telegraph Company of America, transferable on the books of the Company in person, or by duly authorized attorney, on surrender of this Certificate properly endorsed. This Certificate shall not be valid until countersigned by the Transfer Agent and the Registrar.
Witness the seal of the Company, and the signatures of its duly authorized officers this day of FEB 17 1913
TREASURER.
VICE-PRESIDENT.
CAPITAL STOCK
CANCELLED
20 MAR 1913
THE EQUITABLE TRUST COMPANY OF NEW YORK, REGISTRAR
ASSISTANT SECRETARY
FEB 17 1913
SIX PENCE

Third National Corporation (**I**), Eagle vignette 1.00
Three Flags (**I-N**) .75
Tobacco Products Corporation (**I**), **1920s**, **Virginia**, Workers in tobacco field vignette 4.00
Tabacco Products Corporation (**I**), **1930s**, Five and one-half percent bond, two seated ladies with company logo 75.00
Tom Moore Distillery Company (**U**), **Michigan**, **Specimen**, two seated ladies with company logo 28.00
Topper Corporation, **New York**, City vignette 6.00
Trans Ocean Gulf Oil (**I**), **1970s**, Bond 5.00
Transit Warehouse Company (**I**), Seven percent bond, eagle vignette 2.00
Transportation Corporation of America (**U**), **1960s**, Bond, eagle vignette 1.00
Trenton Institute (**I**), **1860s**, **New Jersey**, State seal 55.00
Triangle Industry, Inc. (**I**), **1970s**, Man holding triangle vignette 1.00
Tri-Plex Safety Razor Company (**U**), **1900s**, Eagle vignette 4.00
Trow City Directory Company, **1870s**, **New York**, Cherub with directory vignette 70.00
Trow City Directory Company, **1880s and 1890s**, **New York**, Cherub with directory vignette 55.00
Tru-Tone Phonograph, Inc. (**U**), **New York**, State seal 7.00
Try-Utilities Corporation (**I**), **1920s**, Bond 7.00
Tube City Brewing (**I-N**), **1950s**, Eagle, brewery and farm scene 14.00
Twentieth Century Market (**I**), **1920s**, Eagle vignette 5.00

Union Bag–Camp Paper Company (**I**), **1950s**, Winged goddess with sword and horn and company logo vignette 1.00
Union Cattle Company (**I**), **1880s**, **Wyoming**, Seven percent gold bond, bust of horned cow vignette 310.00
Union Cement Company (**U**), **1860s**, **El Dorado County, California**, Portrait vignette 80.00
Union Ice Company (**I**), **1920s**, Company logo 12.00
Union Molasses Company (**I**), **1900s**, **New York**, Woman vignette, gold seal 12.00
Union Mutual Insurance Company (**I**), **1870s**, **New York**, Eagle, ship, and sailor vignette 52.00
Unique Theatre Company of Boston (**U**), **1900s**, Eagle with train vignette 5.00
United Cigar Store (**I**), Dividend certificate 2.00
United Corporation, The (**I**), **1930s**, Boy with light vignette 4.00
United Corporation (**I**), **1930s**, Nude man with wheel 4.00
United Corporation, The (**I**), **1950s** 1.00
United Drug (**I**), **1930s**, Two seminude winged figures and mixing bowl vignette, orange British imprinted stamp 4.00
United Founders Corporation (**I**), **1930s**, **Maryland**, Eagle and eagle on globe vignette 2.00
United Motor Clubs, Inc. (**U**), **1920s** 3.00
United Nuclear Corporation (**I**), **1960s**, Man with whirling atoms vignette 1.00
United Printers and Publishers (**I**), **1930s**, Whip and woman with books vignettes 3.00
United Printers and Publishers (**I**), **1940s and 1950s**, Ship and woman with books vignettes 2.00
United Refractories Company (**I**), **1910s**, Six percent bond, vignette of Miss America 25.00
United Retail Stores (**I**), **1920s**, Seated women with company logo vignette 5.00
United Shoe Machinery (**I**), **New Jersey**, Eagle vignette 3.00
United States and British International Company (**I**), **1920s**, **Maryland**, Ship, plane, and map vignettes 10.00
United States and Overseas Corporation (**I**), **1930s**, Harbor, ships, and seated seminude lady vignettes 10.00
United States Banknote Corporation (**I**), **1960s and 1970s**, Woman with printing press vignette 6.00
United States Bond-Union Reality and Investments (**I**), **1910s** 2.00
United States Gold Corporation (**U**), **1900s**, Winged eagle vignette 3.00

◀ ***Loew's Boston Theaters Co.*** ***(I), 1920s, Massachusetts,*** *Two seated ladies vignette, many stamps on reverse* ***8.00***
◀ ***Marconi Wireless Telegraph Company*** ***(I), 1910s, New Jersey,*** *Woman with globes and transmission towers vignette* ***22.00***

MORE THAN ONE HUNDRED SHARES

MATTEL, INC.

INCORPORATED UNDER THE LAWS OF THE STATE OF DELAWARE

NUMBER NCB10911

THIS CERTIFICATE IS TRANSFERABLE IN THE CITY OF NEW YORK OR IN LOS ANGELES

SHARES —200—

This certifies that CEDE & CO.

COMMON

SEE REVERSE FOR CERTAIN DEFINITIONS

CUSIP 577081 10 2

is the record holder of

TWO HUNDRED

FULL PAID AND NON-ASSESSABLE SHARES OF THE PAR VALUE OF $1.00 EACH OF THE COMMON STOCK OF *Mattel, Inc. transferable on the share register of the corporation by the holder hereof in person or by duly authorized attorney upon surrender of this certificate properly endorsed. This certificate is not valid until countersigned by one of the Transfer Agents and registered by one of the Registrars.*

Witness the seal of the corporation and the signatures of its duly authorized officers.

Dated SEP 8 - 1971

T. M. Horwitz, SECRETARY — Ruth Handler, PRESIDENT

MATTEL, INC. CORPORATE SEAL MARCH 1968 DELAWARE

COMMON

REGISTERED: Chemical Bank (NEW YORK) REGISTRAR, BY [illegible] AUTHORIZED SIGNATURE

COUNTERSIGNED: BANKERS TRUST COMPANY (NEW YORK) TRANSFER AGENT, BY [illegible] ASSISTANT SECRETARY

© JEFFRIES BANKNOTE COMPANY

100 SHARES

NUMBER NYC 226566

SHARES 100

INCORPORATED UNDER THE LAWS OF THE STATE OF DELAWARE

MINNESOTA MINING AND MANUFACTURING COMPANY

THIS CERTIFICATE IS TRANSFERABLE IN NEW YORK, N.Y. OR IN ST. PAUL, MINNESOTA

This Certifies that ESTELLE H WALLACH

is the owner of ONE HUNDRED

FULL PAID AND NON-ASSESSABLE SHARES OF THE COMMON STOCK WITHOUT PAR VALUE OF MINNESOTA MINING AND MANUFACTURING COMPANY

transferable on the books of the Corporation in person or by duly authorized attorney upon the surrender of this certificate properly endorsed. This Certificate is not valid until countersigned by the Transfer Agent and registered by the Registrar. This Certificate is subject to all terms, conditions and limitations of the Corporation's Certificate of Incorporation, to which reference is hereby made with the same effect as if they were herein set forth in full.

Witness, the corporate seal and the signatures of the duly authorized officers of the Corporation.

Dated [illegible] 1963

Minnesota Mining and Manufacturing Company

Robert A. Tucker, SECRETARY — H P Buetow, PRESIDENT

CORPORATE SEAL

REGISTERED: THE FIRST NATIONAL BANK OF SAINT PAUL, REGISTRAR, BY AUTHORIZED OFFICER. ISSUED IN NEW YORK OR REGISTERED: THE FIRST NATIONAL CITY BANK OF NEW YORK, REGISTRAR, BY AUTHORIZED OFFICER.

COUNTERSIGNED: FIRST TRUST COMPANY OF SAINT PAUL, TRANSFER AGENT, BY AUTHORIZED OFFICER. ISSUED IN NEW YORK OR COUNTERSIGNED: MORGAN GUARANTY TRUST COMPANY OF NEW YORK, TRANSFER AGENT, BY AUTHORIZED OFFICER.

3M

United States Plywood Corporation (I), 1960s, New York, Man with wheel vignette 3.00
United States Steel Corporation (I), 1940s, New Jersey, Steelworkers in mill vignette 5.00
United States Steel Corporation (I), 1950s, Four percent bond, steel foundry and figures vignette 5.00
United States Steel Corporation (U), 1930s, Specimen, Bond, workers in steel foundry furnace vignette 10.00
United States Steel Corporation (U), 1940s, Specimen, Bond, workers in steel foundry furnace vignette 8.00
United States Steel Corporation (U), 1950s, Specimen, Bond 6.00
United States Worsted Company (I), 1910s, Sheep vignette 17.00
United Stores Corporation (I), 1930s, Voting trust certificate 4.00
United Stores Corporation (I), 1940s and 1950s, Two angels and company logo vignette 2.00
United Traction (I), 1900s, New York, Allegorical figures with shield vignette 5.00
United Utilities Corporation (I), 1960s, Bond, sexy couple with globes and logo vignettes 2.00
United Water Improvement Company (I), 1900s, Gold bond, state seal 6.00
Universal Rockwell Corporation (I), 1970s, Eagle vignette .75
Upland Corporation (I), 1960s, Lady between two globes, train, and skyline vignette 1.00
Utica General Jobbing Foundry (I), 1920s, Eagle vignette 4.00
Utilities Associates, Inc. (I), 1920s 3.00
Utilities Associates, Inc. (I), 1930s, Massachusetts 2.00
Utilities Equities Corporation (I), 1930s, Three allegorical figures and winged wheel vignettes 3.00

Valentine Oil Warehousing and Transportation Company (I), 1860s, New Jersey, Old train and two seated ladies vignettes, revenue stamp 110.00
Veeder Industries (I), 1960s, Sexy couple with globe, blacksmith, anvil, and chemistry equipment vignettes 2.00
Vermont College Corporation (U), 1960s, Bond, voided 2.00
Victoria Bondholders Corporation (I), 1930s, New York 2.00
Vines Company of Pennsylvania (I), 1810s, One share certificate 165.00
Virginia Ice and Fuel Corporation (U), State seal 2.00
Vogue Instrument Corporation (I), 1960s, New York, Company logo 1.00
Vornado, Inc. (I), 1960s and 1970s, Girl and factory building vignette 3.00

Waldorf System, Inc. (I), 1920s, Massachusetts, Two seated ladies with company logo vignette 6.00
Waldorf System, Inc. (I), 1930s, Massachusetts, Two figures with apple and logo vignette 4.00
Wall-Nichols and Company (I), 1890s, Hawaii, eagle vignette 80.00
Waltham Watch Company (I), 1920s, Eagle with watch vignette 11.00
Waltham Watch Company (I), 1930s and 1940s, Eagle with watch vignette 7.00
Waltham Watch Company (U), Eagle with watch vignette 4.00
Warren County Warehouse Company (I), 1910s, Signed by Thomas Edison 495.00
Warren, S. D., Company (I), 1940s, Massachusetts, Lumberjacks at work vignette, with many revenue stamps 5.00
Warren, S. D., Company (I), 1950s, Massachusetts, Lumberjacks at work vignette 4.00
Warren, S. E., Company (I), 1920s, Factory building vignette 7.00
Warshow and Sons, Inc. (I), 1960s, Eagle vignette .85
Washington Fire Company Stock Association (U), 1860s, Old fire wagon vignette 78.00
Washington Market Company (I), 1920s, Horsecarts, old buildings and trolley vignette 6.00
Washington Water Power Company (U), Washington, Large dam vignette 2.00
Washita Lumber Company (I), 1910s 11.00
Waterbury and Marshall Company (I-N), 1890s, Sailor and workers vignettes 42.00
Waterford Manufacturing Company (I), 1810s, No vignette 360.00
Waterford Manufacturing Company (I), 1810s, Two attached certificates 625.00

◀***Mattel, Inc. (I), 1970s,*** *Two children at play vignette, company logo* *3.00*
◀***Minnesota Mining and Manufacturing Company (I), 1960s,*** *Woman seated in front of city vignette* *3.00*

INCORPORATED UNDER THE LAWS OF MONTANA MAY 1ST 1889.

NUMBER SHARES

MONTANA PHONOGRAPH COMPANY.

OF HELENA, MONTANA

This is to Certify that ______ is the owner of and is entitled to ______ Shares of One Hundred Dollars each, of the full paid non assessable Capital Stock of the MONTANA PHONOGRAPH COMPANY. of Helena, Montana transferable only on the books of the Company in person or by Attorney on the surrender of this Certificate

In Testimony Whereof said Company hath caused this certificate to be signed by its President, countersigned by its Secretary and attested by its Corporate Seal hereto affixed and all done at the Company's office in Helena, Montana this ____ day of ____ 18__

______ Secretary. ______ President

CAPITAL STOCK $250.000.

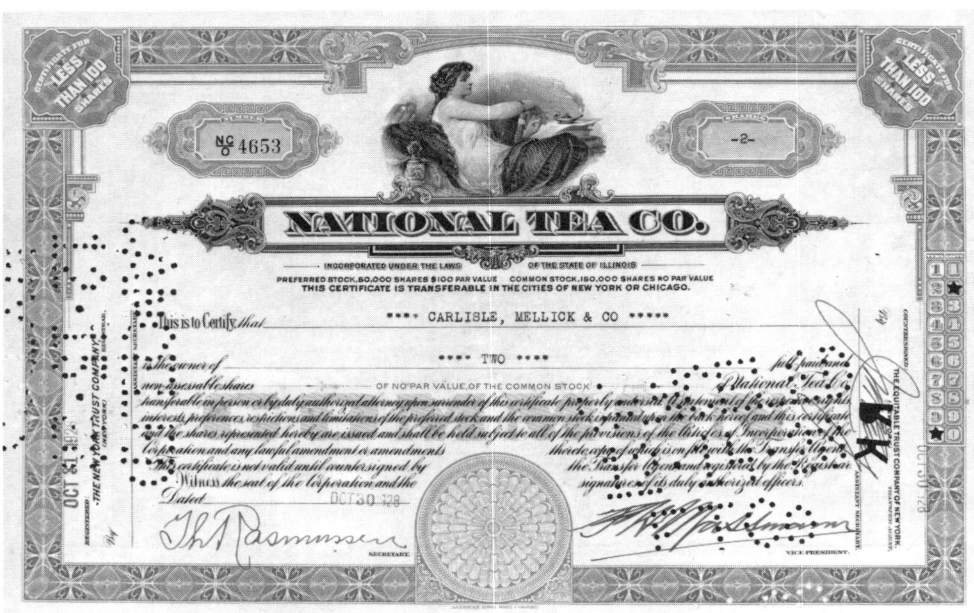

CERTIFICATE FOR LESS THAN 100 SHARES

NUMBER NO 4653 SHARES -2-

NATIONAL TEA CO.

INCORPORATED UNDER THE LAWS OF THE STATE OF ILLINOIS

PREFERRED STOCK, 50,000 SHARES $100 PAR VALUE COMMON STOCK, 150,000 SHARES NO PAR VALUE

THIS CERTIFICATE IS TRANSFERABLE IN THE CITIES OF NEW YORK OR CHICAGO.

This is to Certify that **** CARLISLE, MELLICK & CO *****

is the owner of **** TWO **** full paid and non-assessable shares OF NO PAR VALUE, OF THE COMMON STOCK of National Tea Co. transferable in person or by duly authorized attorney upon surrender of this certificate properly endorsed. A statement of the ... interests, preferences, restrictions and limitations of the preferred stock and the common stock is printed upon the back hereof and this certificate and the shares represented hereby are issued and shall be held subject to all of the provisions of the Articles of Incorporation of the Corporation and any lawful amendment or amendments thereto, copy of which is on file with the Transfer Agent. This certificate is not valid until countersigned by the Transfer Agent and registered by the Registrar.

Witness the seal of the Corporation and the signatures of its duly authorized officers.

Dated OCT 30 '28

SECRETARY. VICE PRESIDENT.

REGISTERED THE NEW YORK TRUST COMPANY (NEW YORK) REGISTRAR. OCT 31 1928

COUNTERSIGNED THE EQUITABLE TRUST COMPANY OF NEW YORK TRANSFER AGENT. ASSISTANT SECRETARY. OCT 30 1928

Watertown Water, Light, and Power (U), **1800s**, Waterworks, horse, and buggies 7.50
Watrous Varnish Company (U), **1910s**, State seal 3.00
Wayne Cotton Mills (I), **1920s, Mississippi**, Six percent gold bond, two seated women with portrait of George Washington vignette 35.00
Wayside Knitting Company (I), **1880s, New York**, Seal, one woman vignette 15.00
Welch Grape Juice (I), **1940s**, Large eagle vignette 3.00
Wells Fargo and Company (I), **1860s**, Certificate of deposit 135.00
West Coast Transmission Company (I), **1960s**, Man with pipeline, tractors, tanks, shoreline, mountains, and city skyline vignettes 3.00
West India Sugar Finance, Vignette of cane fields 15.00
Western Investment Company (I), **1890s**, Two old battleship stamps 12.00
Western Investment Company (U), **1890s, California** 6.00
Western Lock Company (I), **1870s, Ohio**, Embossed seal 15.00
Western Union Computer Utilities (I), **1960s**, Eagle vignette 2.00
Western Union Telegraph (I), **1950s**, Seminude woman with clock vignette 8.00
Western Union Telegraph (I), **1960s and 1970s**, Seated girl and city skyline vignette 2.00
White Stores, Inc. (I), **1960s**, Seated lady with globe and state buildings vignette 1.00
Whitman, Wm. Company (I), **1920s, Massachusetts**, Two ladies vignette 3.00
Wilkensburg Ice Company (I), **1920s**, Arctic hunter vignette 12.00
Williams Brothers Company (I), **1970s**, Bond, seminude man with oil rigs, tanks and pipeline vignettes, seal issued to and with Pendergast signature 5.00
Wilson and Company (I), **1920s**, Certificate of deposit .60
Wisconsin Investment Company (I), **1930s**, Seated lady with scales and globes vignettes 6.00
Wise, Smith and Company (I-N), **1920s, Connecticut**, Issued to and signed by company president, revenue stamps, eagle vignette 5.00
Wiswell Electric Mining Machinery Company (I), **1880s, Maine**, State seal 50.00
Woodland Cemetery (I), **1900s, Maryland** 20.00
Woodward Iron Company (U), **1900s**, Company logo 1.00
World Exploration (I), **1920s** 3.00
Wrigley Pharmaceutical (I), **1920s**, Vignette of toothpaste tube, signed by W. W. Wrigley (president of the company) and seal 100.00

Yardley Electric Company (I), **1920s, New York**, Man with two globes and company logo vignette 1.00
Yuba Construction Company (I), **1910s, California**, Gold dredge vignette 25.00
Yuba Manufacturing Company (U), **1900s**, Workers in machine shop vignette 9.00

Zackey Talking Machine Company (U), **1900s**, No vignette 12.00
Zion Food Corporation (I-N), **1960s**, Large eagle with arrows vignette 2.00

◀ ***Montana Phonograph Company (U), 1800s, Montana Territory,*** *Vignette of old phonographs* ***55.00***
◀ ***National Tea Co. (I), 1920s,*** *Reclining lady vignette* ***4.00***

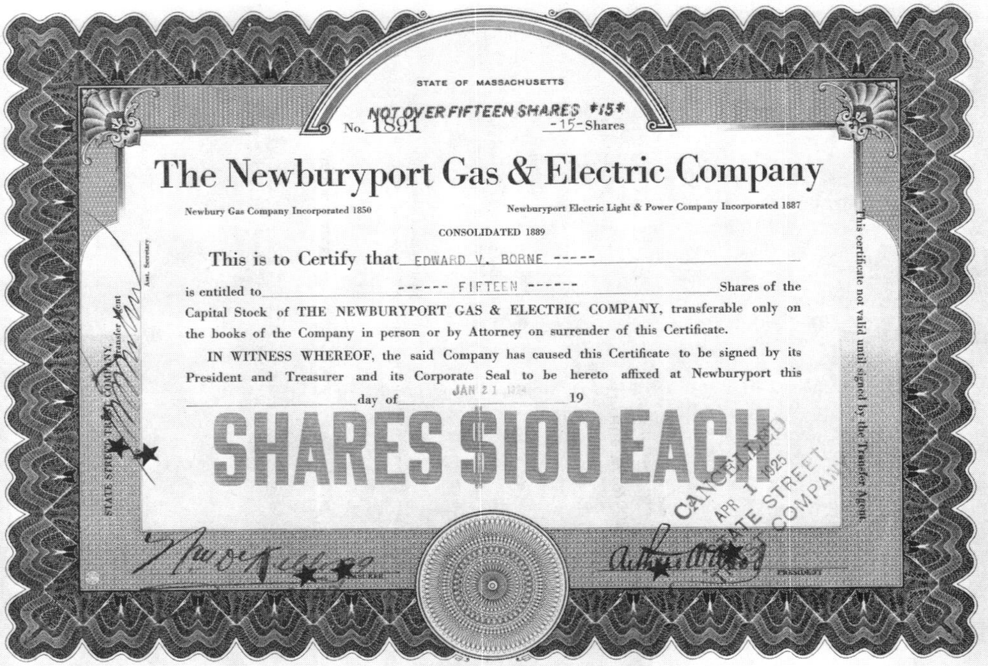

Newburyport Gas and Electric Company, The (I), 1920s **3.00**

New Jersey Zinc Company, The, *Specimen, state seal, signatures* **8.00**

Oak Park Shop (I-N), 1910s, *Eagle, shield, train, and ship vignette* ***7.00***

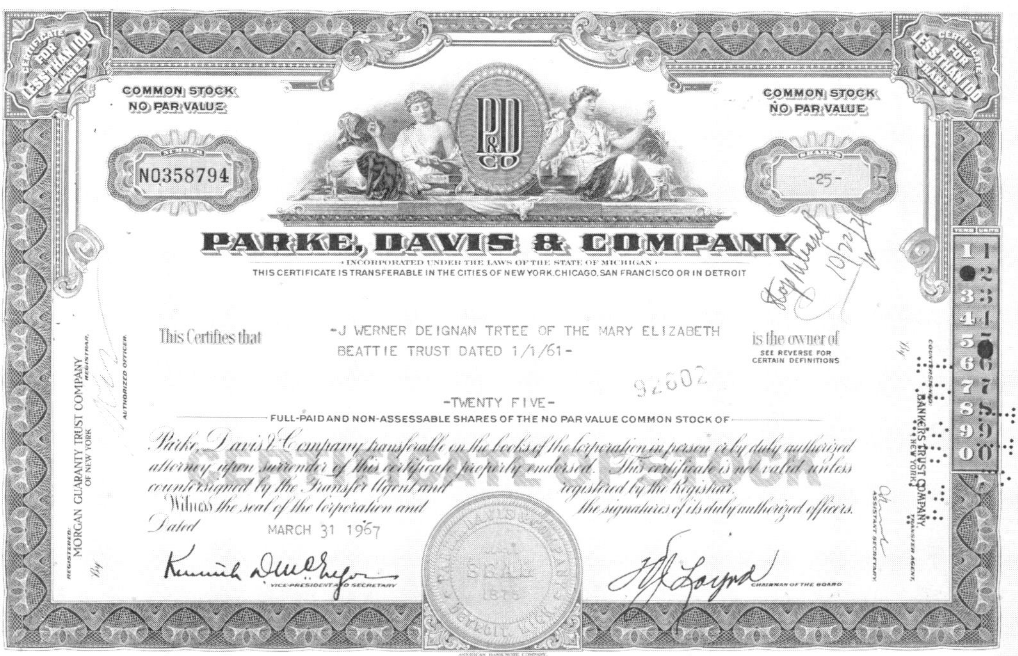

Parke-Davis and Company (I), 1960s, *Two bare-breasted seated ladies with company logo, transfer tax on reverse* ***4.00***

Pere Marquette Light and Power (U), 1906s, Michigan, *Gold bond, company logo* **8.00**

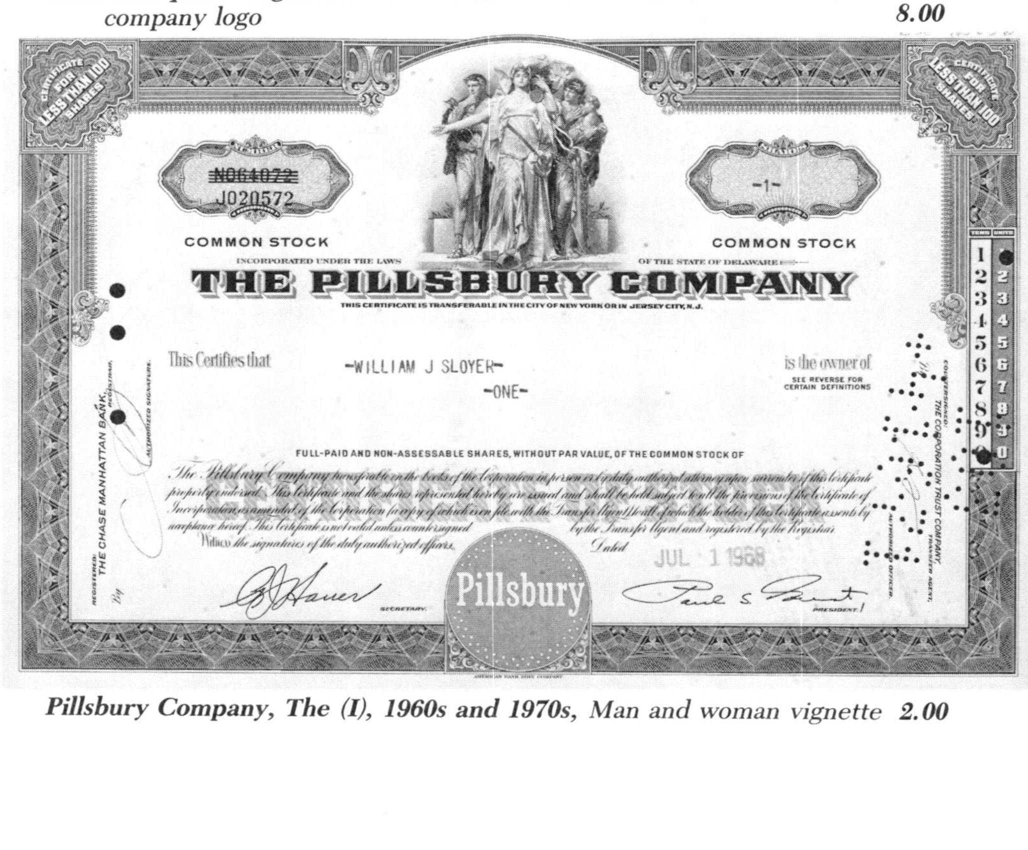

Pillsbury Company, The (I), 1960s and 1970s, *Man and woman vignette* **2.00**

Pneumatic Scale Corporation (I), 1960s, *Woman holding scale and sword with two globes vignette* ***3.00***

Revere Racing Association, Inc. (I), 1960s, Massachusetts, *Nude runner with sash vignette* ***10.00***

Saugatuck Recreation Company (I-N), 1930s, Michigan, *Eagle and gold seal vignette* ***6.00***

Seneca Falls Machine Company (I), 1940s, Massachusetts, *Eagle vignette* ***3.00***

Southern Improvement Company (I), 1880s, *Gold bond, beehive and portrait of lady vignette* ***15.00***

Telstar, Inc. (I), *Woman between two globes and train vignette* ***5.00***

Tobacco Products Corporation (I), 1920s, Virginia, *Workers in tobacco field vignette* **4.00**

United Corporation, The (I), *Boy with light vignette* **4.00**

United States Steel Corporation (U), 1930s, *Specimen, bond, workers in steel foundry furnace vignette* ***10.00***

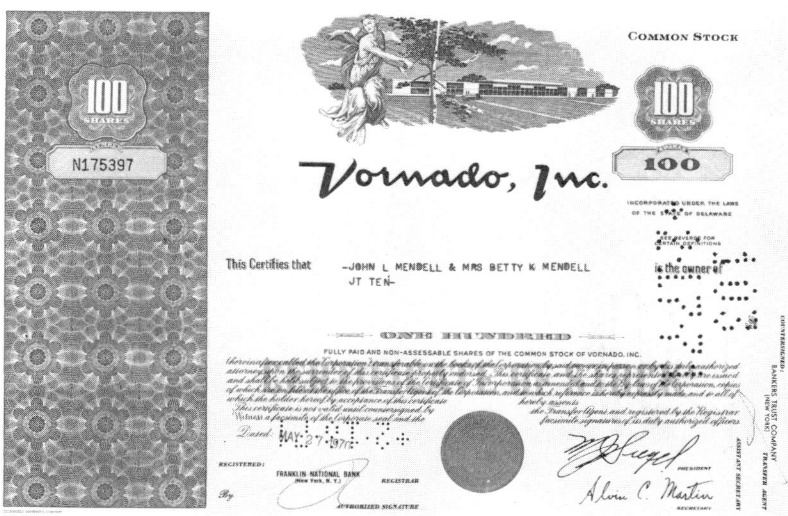

Vornado, Inc. (I), 1960s and 1970s, *Girl and factory building vignette* ***3.00***

Wayne Cotton Mills (I), 1920s, Mississippi, *Six percent gold bond, two seated women with portrait of George Washington vignette* **35.00**

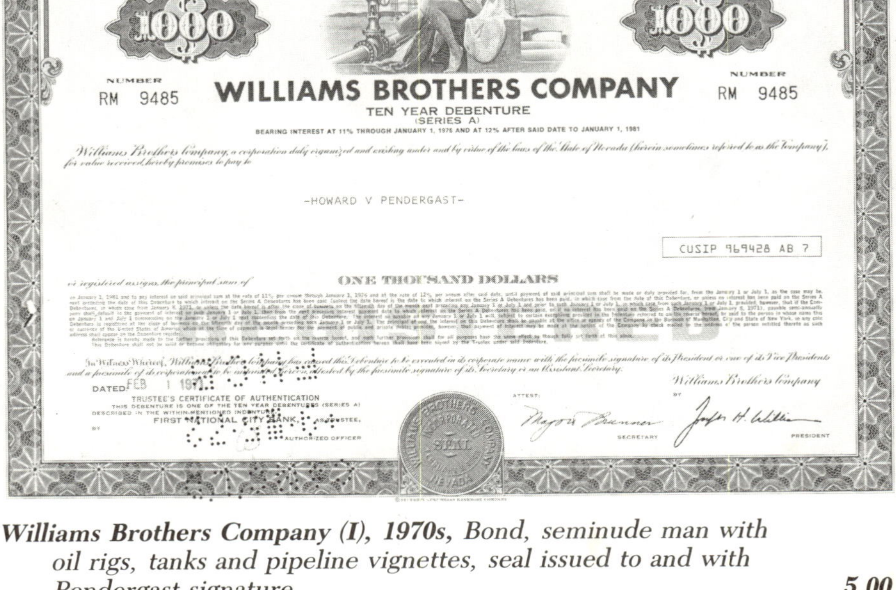

Williams Brothers Company (I), 1970s, *Bond, seminude man with oil rigs, tanks and pipeline vignettes, seal issued to and with Pendergast signature* **5.00**